FIFTH EDITION 2004-05

Understanding the Problems of Indian Economy

Uma Kapila, author/editor of several other books, has taught Indian Economy to undergraduate students for forty two years. She recently retired as Reader from the Department of Economics, Miranda House, University of Delhi. Presently she is Senior Editor, Academic Foundation.

An Honours Graduate from Miranda House, University of Delhi and M.A. and Ph.D. from Delhi School of Economics, Dr. Uma Kapila has also served on the Planning Commission Study Group on "Agricultural Strategies in the Eastern Region of India for the Seventh Five Year Plan" (Perspective Planning Division).

Dr. (Mrs.) Uma Kapila is the author of the book *Oilseeds Economy of India* (1982) published by the Institute of Economic Growth. She is also the author of two other textbooks on Indian Economy, one meant for B.A. Eco.(H), and the other for B.A.(Pass)/B.Com.(Pass)/Eco.(Subsidiary). She has also co-edited along with Mr. Raj Kapila, a number of books on India's economy, banking and finance. Detailed information on these publications is readily available at the publisher's website : **www.academicfoundation.com**

New, Revised & Enlarged **SIXTEENTH EDITION : 2004-2005**

Indian Economy Since Independence

Edited by **Uma Kapila**

1040 Pages • 38 Chapters • 5 Sections

CONTENTS...

About This Book...

Revised every year, and now into its 16th edition, this unique book is widely accepted as the **core text** for graduate / post-graduate courses in Indian economy, in various universities across India.

The book is essentially, a collection of select articles by some of India's topmost economists and experts. These highly recommended original readings are well-supported by editorial notes and excerpts from plan documents, that together present a comprehensive and critical analysis of Indian economy since independence : 1947-2004.

Academic Foundation
4772-73/23 Bharat Ram Road,
(23 Ansari Road), Darya Ganj,
New Delhi - 110002.
Phones : 23245001 / 02 / 03 / 04.
Fax : 23245005.
e-mail : academic@vsnl.com
www.academicfoundation.com

Paperback............Rs.350
Hard-back............Rs.995

FIFTH EDITION 2004-05

Understanding the Problems of Indian Economy

Uma Kapila

★ New, revised & updated, 5th Edition : 2004-2005
★ Based on latest recommended readings
★ Designed to serve as a textbook for B.Com (H)

Published by
Academic Foundation NEW DELHI
http://www.academicfoundation.com

5th Revised Edition: 2004

Published by
ACADEMIC FOUNDATION
4772-73 / 23 Bharat Ram Road,
(23 Ansari Road), Darya Ganj,
New Delhi - 110 002. INDIA.

Phones : 23245001, 02, 03, 04.
Fax : 011-23245005
e-mail : academic@vsnl.com
www : academicfoundation.com

Understanding the Problems of Indian Economy (5th Edition)
by Uma Kapila

ISBN 81-7188-405-9

Designed and typeset by Italics India, New Delhi.
Printed at Print Perfect, New Delhi.

Syllabus & Readings

As per the readings recommended by the Deptt. of Commerce, University of Delhi for B. Com. (Hons) Paper XIII for the Academic Years 2003-04 and 2004-05

B.Com. (Hons.) Paper - XIII

Problems of the Indian Economy

(UNIVERSITY OF DELHI)

Duration: 2 hours *Max. Marks: 50*

1. ISSUES IN DEVELOPMENT PLANNING

(i) Economic growth and economic development

Meier, G. Leading Issues in Economic Development 6th Edn. Ch. I-A, pp 7-9, Todaro, M., Economic Development 6th Edn. pp 13-18

Thirwall, A.P., Growth and Development, 5th Edn. pp 9

Hayami Yujiro (1998), Development Economics: From the Poverty to the Wealth of Nations, Ch. 7, pp 183-195, Oxford

UNDP, Human Development Report, OUP.

Pant, K.C. (2003) India's Development Scenario: Next Decade and Beyond, Ch. 20, *Core Indicators of Human Development*, pp 181-187 and Ch. 21, *National Human Development Report*, pp 188-193

Planning Commission, National Human Development Report-2001, OUP.

Balanced & Unbalanced Growth Strategies
Thirwall, A.P., op.cit. pp 181-7

(ii) Nature of the Indian economy

(As a developing economy; as a mixed economy)
For mixed economy also S.D. Tendulkar, IESI - 2000-01 (edition) Ch.5

World Development Report used in consonance with the characteristics outlined in Todaro, M., op.cit. pp 38-56;
Recent trends, Economic Survey latest

(iii) National income trends (data will be provided)

Stress on sectoral contribution, particularly industrial origin, private & public sectors, external sector, financial & industrial sectors,

Kapila, Uma, Understanding Problems of Indian Economy, Ch.4, Academic Foundation, 2003

RBI Report on Currency and Finance, 2001-02, Ch.3, Part-3, pp 41-45

(iv) Strategy for development and sustainable growth

Kapila, Uma, Indian Economy Since Independence, Ch. 2, (2003 edition).
Tendulkar, S.D., Indian Development Strategy: Compulsions and Constraints in Kapila, U, Indian Economy Since Independence (2000-01 edition).
Planning Commission, Tenth Five Year Plan, Vol.1, Ch.1, Perspective, Objective and Strategy, (Also in Kapila, U., Indian Economy Since Independence, 2003 edition)

(v) Self-reliance, modernisation and structural adjustment

Vaidyanathan, A, (2003), India's Economic Reforms and Development, Ch.2, *Structural Adjustment in Indian Economy,* Academic Foundation
———, Ch.1, *A Decade of Economic Reforms*

Rangarajan, C., *New Economic Policy and Role of State* in Kapila, U. op. cit. Ch.5.

Planning Commission, 9th Five Year Plan (1997-2002), Ch.1, Section on Self-reliance *(vi)* ***Issues in development – population, poverty, & unemployment***

Visaria Parveen M - *Demographic Aspects of Development: The Indian Experience* in Kapila, U., op. cit. (2003 edition), Ch. 10

Pant, K.C., (2003), op. cit. Vol.1, Ch.11, *Population Dynamics Choices and Challenges*, pp 117-123.

Vaidyanathan, A, (2003), op. cit. Ch.10, Poverty and Development Policy, Part I, II & V. (Also in Kapila, U., Indian Economy Since Independence, 2003 edition)

Planning Commission: Tenth Five Year Plan, Ch.5, *Employment Perspective* (Also in Kapila, U., op. cit)

(vii) ***Resource mobilisation and fiscal policies***

Kapila, U., op. cit. (2003) edition, Chs. 6, 7, 8

Mohan Rakesh, *Fiscal Corrections for Economic Growth* (Ch.7)

RBI Report on Currency and Finance 2001-02, Ch.4, *Fiscal Policy* (Also available in Kapila, U. 2003 edition) Economic Survey latest

(viii) ***Inflation and price control***

C. Rangarajan - Development, Inflation, and Monetary Policy, Kapila, U. (2003 edition) Economic Survey latest Chapter on Inflation
RBI Report on Currency and Finance 2001-02, Ch. V, pp. V-10 to V-14.

2. **SECTORAL ANALYSIS OF THE INDIAN ECONOMY**

(A) Domestic Sector:

(i) ***Agriculture*** - An overview of the growth and composition of output and commercialization and mechanization of agriculture, institutional factors - ownership, credit, factor inputs and technology- and agricultural price policy

Kapila, U., op. cit. (2003 edition) Ch.14. C.H.H. Rao, Reform Agenda for Agriculture, EPW, Feb. 15, 2003

Jeromi, P.D., *Is Indian Agriculture Reaching Limits to Growth?* in Economic Developments in India, Vol. 62, 2003, Academic Foundation

Vyas, V.S., *Changing Contours of Indian Agriculture* (NCAER Golden Jubilee Lecture, May 2000) in Facets of the Indian Economy, ed. Rakesh Mohan, Oxford, 2002

(ii) ***Industry*** - growth and policy, liberalization of the '90s, public sector's role and disinvestment, role of the small scale sector

Kapila, U., op. cit., Chs. 16, 17, article by K.L. Krishna - Industrial Growth and Diversification, (2003 edition).

Baijal, Pradip - Privatisation: Compulsion and Constraints, EPW, Oct. 12, 2002.

Mohan, Rakesh - Small Industry (Kapila, U. Ch. 17)
Rangarajan, C. (2000) - Essays on Money and Finance, Ch.26, *Disinvestment Stategies and Issues*, UBSPD. (Also in Kapila, U., Ch.20, 2003 edition)

(B) External Sector

(i) ***Trends in India's exports and imports*** - Composition and direction - constraints on growth arising from foreign trade and import-substitution based policies - balance of payments - foreign capital flows, *MNCs*,
Kapila, U., (2003 edition) Chs. 23 - articles by
T.N. Srinivasan - Foreign Trade Policies (Ch.24)
C. Rangarajan - India's Balance of Payments (Ch.26)

Jeromi, P.D., - *FDI in India: Policy, Trends and Impact* in Economic Developments in India, Vol.62.

(ii) ***India, and the Globalization process (WTO)***

Planning Commission: Tenth Five Year Plan, Vol.I, Ch.4, *External Sector Dimensions* Kapila, U. op.cit, Ch.28, article by C. Rangarajan - *Globalisation and Its Impact* in Economic Developments in India, Vol.58

Contents

Part - I

Issues in Development Planning

...Contd....

...Contd....

...Contd....

...Contd....

...Contd....

...Contd....

...Contd....

...Contd....

PART - II

Sectoral Analysis of Indian Economy

A. DOMESTIC SECTOR

...Contd....

...Contd....

...Contd....

...Contd....

...Contd....

...Contd....

...Contd....

...Contd....

...Contd....

■.■.■.■.■

Preface

THE first edition of the book *Understanding the Problems of Indian Economy* was published in the year 2000 covering the syllabus of B.Com (Hons.) of University of Delhi. The book has been very well received by teachers as well as students and is being used virtually as a text book in Delhi University colleges for B.Com (Hons.) and also in some other universities.

Encouraged by the response from the students and teachers of Delhi University, the second (2001-02) edition was thoroughly revised and new chapters added, keeping particularly in view, the revised syllabus.

In view of the further revision in the recommended reading list in 2003, the fourth edition (2003-04) had been accordingly revised. The discussion and analysis in various chapters is based on the new recommended readings. Full length articles recommended are available in my edited book *Indian Economy Since Independence* (running in its 16th edition) which is used as a reference text by B.A. (Hons) Economics of University of Delhi and some other universities also. A large number of chapters from *Indian Economy Since Independence* have been recommended in the revised reading list of B.Com (Hons) of Delhi University.

The present fifth edition (2004-05) has been updated and revised where required.

In writing this book, I have drawn from the relevant articles/papers written by renowned economists in their special fields. The analysis has been updated in the light of latest reports available such as RBI Report on Currency and Finance 2002-03, Economic Survey 2003-04, Tenth Five Year Plan 2002-07, Planning Commission Report on FDI (2002), Exim Policy 2003-04, Planning Commission reports and papers relating to the 10th Plan.

I owe my deep sense of gratitude to C.H. Hanumantha Rao, C. Rangarajan, T.N. Srinivasan, S.D. Tendulkar, V.S. Vyas, K.L. Krishna, Rakesh Mohan, Montek S. Ahluwalia, Jagdish Bhagwati, Pravin Visaria (late), Amaresh Bagchi, A. Vaidyanathan, J.C. Sandesara, Nagesh Kumar, S.K. Ray, Abid Hussain, Ashok Gulati, R. Nagraj, Rajesh Chadha and P.D. Jeromi, from whose writings I have been able to draw to benefit the students.

I am equally grateful to my colleagues teaching in different colleges who inspired me to write this book and have been making suggestions from time to time to make this book more relevant and easy to understand by the students..

I hope the students and teachers will find this revised edition more useful. Comments from teachers are most welcome as there is always scope for improvement.

August 2004 — *Uma Kapila*

PART - I

Issues in Development Planning

Chapters :

1

Economic Growth and Economic Development

What does Development Mean

THE term *development* may mean different things to different people. In strictly economic terms, development has traditionally meant a sustained annual increase in GNP (or GDP) at rates varying from 5 per cent to 7 per cent or more.[1]

A common alternative economic index of development has been the rates of growth of per capita GNP i.e., the ability of a nation to expand its output at a rate faster than the growth of population. Levels and rates of growth of "real" per capita GNP i.e., monetary growth of GNP per capita minus the rate of inflation, are normally used to measure the overall economic well being of a population.

ECONOMIC GROWTH AND ECONOMIC DEVELOPMENT

Till the 1960's, the term economic development was often used as a synonym of economic growth, the measure for the latter being the rise in per capita GNP in real terms. According to C.P. Kindleberger, "whereas economic growth merely refers to a rise in output, economic development implies changes in technological and institutional organisation of production as well as distributive pattern of income."[2] *Thus economic development is a broader concept than economic growth.* Compared to the objective of development, economic growth may be easy to realise. By larger mobilisation of resources and raising their productivity, output levels can be raised. The process of development is far more extensive. *Apart from the rise in output, it*

1. Todaro, Michael, *Economic Development in the Third World* (6th edition).
2. Kindleberger, C.P., *Economic Development* (2nd ed.) Chap. 1.

involves changes in the composition of output as well as a shift in the allocation of productive resources to ensure social justice.

In some of the underdeveloped countries, the process of economic growth has been accompanied by economic development. But this may not be the case always. *While there can be growth without development, development without growth is unconceivable.* A substantial rise in a country's GNP is required before it can hope to expand its industries and the services sectors. Nowhere in the world has the occupational distribution of population changed in the absence of growth.

Prior to the 1970's, development was seen as an economic phenomenon in which rapid gains in overall and per capita GNP growth would either "trickle down" to the masses in the form of jobs and other economic opportunities or create the necessary conditions for the wider distribution of the economic and social benefits of growth. Problems of poverty, unemployment and income distribution were of secondary importance to "getting the growth job done."

The New View of Economic Development

During the 1950s and 1960s while many of the Third World Nations did realise the economic growth targets, the respective levels of living of the masses remained unchanged. This resulted in the rejection of the narrow definition of economic development by an increasing number of economists who now clamoured for the "dethronement of GNP" and advocated direct attack on widespread absolute poverty, increasingly inequitable income distribution and rising unemployment. Thus, in the 1970s economic development came to be redefined within the context of a growing economy. "Redistribution from growth" became a common slogan. In this context Kindleberger argued that *"economic development is generally defined to include improvements in material welfare, especially for persons with the lowest incomes, the eradication of mass poverty with its corelates of illiteracy, diseases and early death, changes in the composition of inputs and outputs that generally include shifts in the underlying structure of production away from agricultural growth towards industrial activities, the organisation of the economy in such a way that productive employment is general among the working age population rather than the situation of a privileged minority and the correspondingly greater participation of broadly based groups in making decisions about the directions, economic and otherwise, in which they should move to improve their welfare".*[3]

3. Kindleberger, op.cit.

Dudley Seers posed three basic questions about the meaning of development :

What has been happening to poverty,

What has been happening to unemployment,

What has been happening to inequality?

If all three of these have declined from high levels then beyond doubt this has been a period of development for the country concerned. If one or two of these central problems have been growing worse, especially if all three have, it would be strange to call the result 'development' even if per capita income doubled.[4]

This assertion was a hard reality for a number of developing countries which experienced relatively high rates of growth of per capita income during the 1960s and 1970s but showed little or no improvement or even an actual decline in employment, equality and the real income of the bottom 40 per cent of their population. By the earlier definition of 'growth', these countries were developing, but by the new criteria of poverty, equality and employment, they were not. The situation in the 1980s worsened further as GNP growth rates turned negative for many less developed countries and the governments, faced with mounting foreign debt problems, were forced to cut back on their already limited social and economic programmes.

While during the 1980s, the World Bank championed "economic growth" as the goal of development, its *World Development Report of 1991* asserted that "the challenge of development ... is to improve the quality of life. For the world's poor countries, a better quality of life generally calls for higher income ... and it involves much more. It encompasses, as ends in themselves, better education, higher standards of health and nutrition, less poverty, a cleaner environment, more equality of opportunity, greater individual freedom, and a richer cultural life."

Development as a multi-dimensional process

According to Todaro, Development must, therefore, be conceived of as a multi-dimensional process involving major changes in social structures, popular attitudes and national institutions, as well as the acceleration of economic growth, the reduction of inequality and the

4. Todaro, Michael, op. cit.

eradication of absolute poverty. Development, in its essence, must represent the whole gamut of change by which an entire social system, tuned to the diverse basic needs and desires of individuals and social groups within that system, moves away from a condition of life widely perceived as unsatisfactory, toward a situation or condition of life as materially and spiritually "better". According to Prof. Goulet[5], at least three basic components as core values should serve as a conceptual basis and practical guidelines for understanding the "inner" meaning of development. These core values – sustenance, self-esteem, and freedom – represent common goals sought by all individuals and societies? They relate to fundamental human needs that find their expression in almost all societies and cultures at all times.

Three Core Values of Development

Sustenance: The life-sustaining basic human needs include food, shelter, health and protection. When any one of these is absent or in critically short supply, a condition of absolute "underdevelopment" exists.

Self-esteem: A second universal component of good life is self-esteem – a sense of worth and self-respect – of not being used as a tool by others for their own ends. Due to the significance attached to material values in developed nations, worthiness and esteem are now-a-days increasingly conferred only on countries that possess economic wealth and technological power – those that have developed.

Now-a-days the Third World seeks development in order to gain the esteem which is denied to societies living in a state of disgraceful "underdevelopment." ... Development is legitimized as a goal because it is an important, perhaps even an indispensable, way of gaining esteem.[6]

Freedom from Servitude: Arthur Lewis[7] stressed the relationship between economic growth and freedom from servitude when he concluded that "the advantage of economic growth is not that wealth increases happiness, but that it increases the range of human choice." Wealth can enable a person to gain greater control over nature and his physical environment than they would have if they remained poor. It

---

5. Denis Goulet, *The Cruel Choice: A New Concept in the Theory of Development* (New York, 1971) pp. 87-94.
6. Goulet, op. cit.
7. W. Arthur Lewis, "Is Economic Growth Desirable?" in the *Theory of Economic Growth.* (1963), p. 420, Allen & Unwin, London.

also gives them the freedom to choose greater leisure. The concept of human freedom should encompass various components of political freedom, freedom of expression, political participation and equality of opportunity. It is interesting to note that some of the most notable economic success stories of the 1970s and 1980s (Saudi Arabia, South Korea, Singapore, Malaysia, Thailand, Indonesia, Turkey and China among others) did not score highly on the 1991 Human Freedom Index compiled by the United Nations Development Programme (UNDP).[8]

Sustainable Human Development

The UNDP Human Development Report (1994) focusses on a new paradigm of development that puts people at the centre of development, regards economic growth as a means and not an end, protects the life opportunities of future generations as well as the present generations and respects the natural systems on which all life depends.

Such a paradigm of development enables all individuals to enlarge their human capabilities to the full and to put these capabilities to their best use in all fields – economic, social, cultural and political. It also protects the options of the unborn generations. It does not run-down the natural resource base needed for sustaining development in the future.

Sustainable human development addresses both inter-generational and intra-generational equity – enabling all generations, present and future to make the best use of their potential capabilities. In the final analysis, sustainable human development is pro-people, pro-jobs and pro-nature. It gives the highest priority to poverty reduction, productive employment, social integration and environmental regeneration. It accelerates economic growth and translates it into improvements in human lives, without destroying the natural capital needed to protect the opportunities of future generations.

The strongest argument for protecting the environment is the ethical need to guarantee the future generations opportunities similar to the ones previous generations have enjoyed. This guarantee is the foundation of "Sustainable Development."

The World Development Report 1999-2000 emphasises a comprehensive approach to development. The principal goal of development policy is to create sustainable improvements in the quality

---

8. Human Development Report, 1992, New York: Oxford University Press, 1992.

of life for all people. Sustainable development has many objectives. In so far as raising per capita income improves people's living standards, it is one among many development objectives. The aim of lifting living standards encompasses a number of more specific goals, bettering people's health and educational opportunities, giving every one the chance to participate in public life, helping to ensure a clean environment, promoting inter-generational equity and much more.[9]

The Environmental Problems in Developing Economies[10]

The environmental problem may be defined as the problem of natural resource exhaustion resulting from exploitation at speeds beyond their natural recovery rates, which endangers sustenance of life. This problem has existed almost from the beginning of human history. Primitive economies, based on hunting and gathering, could not have been sustained if people had killed wild animals and collected plants beyond their reproductive capacities to feed the multiplying mouths. This resource exhaustion crisis was overcome by development of agricultural technology and social institutions such as property rights.

If property rights on certain resources are given to particular individuals or groups, they will utilize their resources efficiently with due consideration for future living, thereby avoiding resource exhaustion — such as one would not kill the goose yielding the golden eggs. However, the stipulation and protection of property rights entails large costs. Compared with arable land near villages, which is fairly easy for villagers to monitor, protection of property rights on remote forests and grazing lands is far more difficult and costly. Further, it is nearly impossible to establish property rights on air and running water. With no property-right assignment, people can use resources without paying costs. Then they will be likely to abuse these resources to the point of zero marginal private utility, even if this endangers everyone's living because of eventual resource exhaustion. This human propensity to be 'free-riders' is responsible for deforestation and air and water pollution.

The reason that environmental problems are especially acute in developing economies is because changes in technology and institutions lag behind changes in resource endowments. Until the relatively recent past, many developing economies were characterized by sparse population and abundant natural resources. With the population

---

9. World Development Report, 1999-2000, p. 13.
10. Yujiro Hayami (1998), Development Economics from the Poverty to the Wealth of Nations, p. 183-185, Oxford.

explosion beginning during the 1920s and 1930s, scarcity of resources rose rapidly. Relative to this development, institutions for conserving scarce natural resources have been slow to develop.

This lag in institutional adjustment tends to become large in developing economies because of poverty and the high rates of discount for future consumption and income among people. Even if scarcity of natural resources increases, natural resources and environments can be adequately preserved by investment in conservation and anti-pollution activities such as reforestation, soil erosion prevention (such as terracing), and purification of gas emission. In order to promote these activities, institutional innovations are required, such as setting property rights where applicable, regulating and taxing natural resource utilization, and organizing governmental and non-governmental bodies for environmental monitoring.

Human Development Index

HDI is a quality of life index prepared by UNDP and published in Human Development Reports since 1990. It takes into account the three most basic human capabilities.

(i) longevity measured by life expectancy at birth

(ii) Educational attainment as measured by adult literacy rate and gross enrolment ratio GER (primary, secondary and tertiary level combined)

(iii) Adjusted real GDP per capita – PPP stands for purchasing power parity. PPP GDP is calculated after eliminating price differences among countries.

The HDI value indicates how far a country has gone to attain certain defined goals: an average life span of 85 years, access to education for all and a decent standard of living. The maximum and minimum values for each variable, which are fixed, are reduced to scale between 0 and 1.

Countries are classified into three groups:

(1) High human development countries - Countries with HDI values of 0.800 and above.

(2) Medium human development countries - Countries with HDI values of 0.500 to 0.799.

(3) Low human development countries - Countries with HDI values below 0.500.

India has moved from group of low human development countries to medium human development countries during the last decade or so. HDI value for 1992 being 0.439 and for 2001 as 0.590 and for 2002 it is 0.595. India's ranks is 127 out of 177 countries, lower to us Botswana with HDI value of 0.589 and above us is Namibia with HDI value of 0.607.[11]

Each index measures the degree of achievement of the country in a particular area. The value of an index varies from - 0 to 1. For example, the life expectancy index of India for the year 2001 is 63.3. It means that India's achievement rate of life expectancy is 63.3 per cent.

Higher the value of HDI of a country, higher is the level of welfare of the people of that country. HDI is thus a measure of the quality of life of the people.

However, HDI cannot be treated as a comprehensive index because it is based on only three variables. There are many other variables which affect welfare.

National Human Development Report - 2001

Releasing the National Human Development Report - 2001 (April 23, 2002) the Deputy Chairman, Planning Commission, Shri K.C. Pant remarked, "for any approach or development framework to be meaningful and effective in directing public policies and programmes, it has to be anchored in a specific social context. More importantly, it should reflect the values and development priorities of the society where it is applied. It is this concern that has led us to work on developing a contextually relevant approach to human development and identify and devise appropriate indicators to help formulate and monitor public policy for India. Such a policy must, of course, keep in view the many unique concerns and development priorities of the country, as well as her social and economic diversity. I am very happy to point out that the National Human Development Report has addressed these concerns."[12]

The Report has broken fresh ground in quite a few areas in presenting the status of human development at the State level in India.

---

11. UNDP, Human Development Report, 2003, 2004 Oxford University Press. Planning Commission (2002), National Human Development Report.
12. Pant, K.C. (2003), India's Development Scenario: Next Decade and Beyond, Academic Foundation, New Delhi.

It has, for the first time, put together an extensive database for at least two, and in some cases three points of time covering the period from 1980 to 2001.

Indicators

In India there is a considerable difference in the level of attainments of people depending on their place of residence, whether it is in rural or urban areas, and on the sex of the person. The Report highlights these inequalities by estimating the 'Gender Gap' and the 'Rural-Urban Gap' in all indicators where the data are available.

A number of carefully selected indicators have been combined to develop three composite indices. It may be noted that the indices developed in this Report are not identical to the UNDP indices, which are designed for inter-country comparisons. Our focus is not the same and, therefore, though the names may be similar, the substance is different. While the Human Development Index presents a quantitative estimate of attainments of the society as a whole, the Human Poverty Index measures the extent of deprivation in the society. In addition, for the first time, a Gender Equality Index has also been constructed to capture the relative attainments of women as against men. For each of these indices, critical indicators of well-being — capturing the ability to live a long and healthy life; the ability to read, write and acquire knowledge; and command over resources — have been identified keeping in view the context, societal values and development priorities of the country.

One of the factors kept in mind while conceptualising this Report was the need to evolve indices that could adequately reflect inter-temporal changes and policy sensitivity in various dimensions of human well-being.

The compilation of indicators in this Report extend beyond the economic, educational, health and demographic concerns of society. It also includes indicators on various aspects of the social environment, like the state of the elderly, the working children, the disabled, and violence and crime against women. Besides, aspects of the physical environment having a direct bearing on the well-being of people have also been highlighted.

In a sense, the Report marks a beginning and is a first step towards monitoring the process of development in a manner that directly captures the level of well-being and the quality of life of our people.

Also, a beginning has been made in the Tenth Plan by explicitly specifying monitorable targets covering economic, social and environmental dimensions of human development.

State of Human Development in India

Overall, human development as reflected in the HDI has improved significantly between 1980 and 2001. At the national level, during the eighties the index has improved by nearly 26 per cent and by another 24 per cent during the nineties. There has been an improvement both in rural, as well as in urban areas. Though the rural-urban gap in the level of human development continues to be significant, it has declined during the period. Inequalities across States on the HDI are less than the income inequality as reflected in the per capita State Domestic Product.

State Level

At the State level, there are wide disparities in the level of human development. In the early eighties, States like Bihar, Uttar Pradesh, Madhya Pradesh, Rajasthan and Orissa had HDI close to just half that of Kerala's. The situation has improved since then. Besides Kerala, among the major States, Punjab, Tamil Nadu, Maharashtra and Haryana have done well on the HDI. In general, HDI is better in smaller States and Union Territories. In terms of the pace of development, Tamil Nadu, Rajasthan, Madhya Pradesh, West Bengal and Bihar improved their HDI significantly in the eighties. However, in the nineties the momentum was maintained, from among these States, only in case of Rajasthan, Madhya Pradesh and Uttar Pradesh.

It turns out that the economically less developed States are also the States with low HDI. Similarly, the economically better off States are also the ones with relatively better performance on HDI. However, the relation between the HDI and the level of development does not show any correspondence among the middle-income States in the country. In this category of States, some States like Kerala have high attainments on HDI, at the same time; there are States like Andhra Pradesh or even West Bengal where HDI values are not as high. Allocation of adequate public resources for furthering human development alone is not enough. It is equally important to use them efficiently and effectively. Human attainments appear to be better and more sustained in those parts of the country where there is social mobilisation for human development, and where female literacy and empowerment encourages women to have a say in the decision making process at the household level.

2

Balanced and Unbalanced Growth Strategies

ECONOMIC development implies a process of securing higher levels of productivity in all the sectors of the economy which in turn is a function of the level of investment and the level of technology. For raising the level of technology, the economy has to have more and more of capital formation.

Without adequate availability of capital, neither technical progress nor the development of human resources can possibly be achieved. Capital formation is possible when the society is channelising a part of its resources to the production of capital goods, viz., tools, implements, machines, transport equipment and such other items as would enlarge the productive potential of a country. The size of a country's capital stock also governs the level of technology. Latest technology and automatic devices of production require huge capital investment. A capital-poor country cannot afford such technology and, therefore, techniques of production in such an economy are going to remain primitive.

Underdeveloped countries find it extremely difficult to step up the rate of capital formation. Their savings are very low – practically non-existent and the capital market is hardly developed. The consequent lower supply of capital results in low productivity which further reduces income and thereby impairs the capacity to save. Further, with low income and lower purchasing power in the hands of the people, the size of the market shrinks which reduces the inducement to invest. Lower savings combined with smaller investment results in perpetual backwardness of the underdeveloped economies.

The Vicious Circle of Poverty

Ragner Nurkse explains the problem of capital formation in underdeveloped countries through the vicious circle of poverty. To quote Nurkse : "Vicious circle of poverty implies a circular constellation of forces tending to act and react upon each other in such a way as to keep a poor country in a state of poverty." To clarify this Nurkse takes a poor man as his example. Owing to inadequate diet, a poor man remains weak which reduces his efficiency or capacity to work and thus lowers his earnings. As a consequence of lower income, the poor man continues to grow weaker and inefficient thereby perpetuating his poverty. This example of a poor individual can be generalised to enfold a country as a whole because a country's income depends on the efficiency of the individuals in the country. Therefore, Nurkse concludes that "a country is poor because it is poor."[1]

The vicious circle of poverty operates both on the supply as well as demand side of capital formation in the underdeveloped countries.

Theory of Balanced Growth

The theory of 'Balanced Growth' has been put forward as a solution to the problem of vicious circle of poverty that afflicts the demand side of capital formation. To break this vicious circle, the theory of balanced growth advocates a simultaneous setting up of a large number of mutually complementary industries that would generate demand for each other's products and thus expand the size of the market and increase inducement to invest.

Rosenstein Rodan gave the earliest version of the balanced growth theory. He observed that in underdeveloped countries, no new industry has a chance to survive due to limited size of market demand. Thus, if for example, a shoe factory is set up employing a hundred workers, the chances are that it would soon close down due to lack of demand for shoes. But if in place of one factory, we simultaneously set up, say, one hundred factories employing thousands of workers, the chances are that all these factories would survive. This is because the additional income in the hands of these workers arising from their employment, will create additional demand in the market as they spend money on various products produced by these industries. Thus demand for shoes, as well as for goods produced by other industries increases that enables all of them to survive and grow. Nurkse agreed with Rosenstein Rodan and

1. Ragnar Nurkse, *Problems of Capital Formation in the Underdeveloped Countries*, p. 2.

put forward the balanced growth theory on similar lines but enlarged the scope of the balanced growth programme to include many more industrial sectors.

According to Nurkse, the only way to remove the obstacles arising out of the small size of the market is "more or less synchronised application of capital to a wide range of different industries. Here is an escape from the dead lock, here the result is an overall enlargement of the market ... most industries catering for mass consumption are complementary in the sense that they provide a market for and thus support each other." The people working in these industries will be buyers of each others produce. Accordingly, each individual industry shall create a demand for the goods of the others. The essence of Nurkse's theory is that if large investment is undertaken in the mutually dependent industries, the vicious circle of poverty can be broken and the country can look forward to the economic advancement.

The Big Push Theory

The balanced growth theory has another version called the Big Push Theory. This theory, apart from suggesting the balanced development of the consumer goods industries and the social overhead capital, underlines the importance of simultaneously undertaking investment in the capital goods industries as well. The necessity for maintaining a balance between consumer goods industries and capital goods industries arises because of their technical complementarity. Generally, this complementarity is more pronounced in the capital goods industries which are dependent on consumer goods industries for the supply of their finished and semi-finished products, machinery and other types of capital equipment.

The "Big Push Theory" presents a comprehensive programme of economic development in which the following balances have to be maintained :

(i) A horizontal balance among the consumer goods industries according to expected emerging patterns of demand so that with the expansion in demand, the supply is increased accordingly.

(ii) A balance between the social overhead capital and productive activities so that one may not suffer in the absence of the others, and

(iii) A vertical balance between the consumer goods industries and the capital goods industries according to their degree of technical complementarity so that external economies can be fully reaped.

According to this theory, to take full advantage of external economies, all investments in all the interdependent industries should be made in accordance with a well chalked out plan of economic development.

This 'balanced growth' or simultaneous development of many industries would require mobilization of large amounts of resources at one time. According to Rosenstein Rodan and Nurkse, poor developing economies were characterized by a large surplus of labour employed at zero marginal cost in the traditional sector. Under this assumption of disguised unemployment, the labour supply would create no major bottleneck to a 'great leap forward' in industrialization.

The key to the success of the balanced growth strategy would, of course, be to mobilize sufficient funds for simultaneous development of many industries.

Weaknesses of the Theory of Balanced Growth

The Theory of Balanced Growth suffers from inherent weaknesses. Singer[2] has expressed his doubts about the practicability of balanced growth doctrine. According to him, if underdeveloped countries are to launch a large investment package in industries without paying much attention to agriculture, they are bound to run into difficulties. To avoid food and raw material shortage, the big push in industry will have to be accompanied by a big push in agriculture as well. But when we think of such a large and varied package of industrial investment and investment in agriculture at the same time, it creates serious doubts about the capacity of the underdeveloped countries to follow the path of balanced growth. As he says, "The resources required for carrying out the policy of balanced growth are of such order of magnitude that a country disposing of such resources would infact not be underdeveloped."

In underdeveloped countries there is an acute shortage of capital and other resources. To suggest that they can move on the path of economic progress by massive investment simultaneously in all sectors appears totally impractical. Infact, the balanced growth doctrine requires huge amounts of precisely these resources whose limited availability is the basic characteristic of the underdeveloped economies.

---

2. Singer, *Concept of Balanced Growth and Economic Development.*

A major weakness of the balanced growth theory is that it completely ignores the fundamental problems of scarcity of capital resources facing the underdeveloped countries. The theory seems to believe that all the required resources are available in sufficient quantities and the only problem before the backward countries is how to use them in accordance with a calculated programme of economic development. In fact scarcity of resources is the basic problem of underdeveloped countries. Thus underdeveloped countries can not afford balanced growth programmes. They will have to fall back upon a strategy involving unbalanced growth.

Theory of Unbalanced Growth

Prof. Hirschman, the leading exponent of the theory of unbalanced growth argues that a deliberate unbalancing of the economy in accordance with predesigned strategy is the best way to achieve economic growth. "An ideal situation obtains when one disequilibrium calls forth a development move which in turn leads to a similar disequilibrium and soon ad-infinitum". He observes that development has proceeded in this way with "growth being communicated from the leading sectors of the economy to the followers, from one industry to another, from one firm to another." Development process is a chain of disequilibrium that must be kept alive and the task of development policy is to maintain tension, disproportions and disequilibria.

Hirschman's theory of unbalanced growth is based on the following propositions :

(a) That technical complementarity is found among the various industries but in the case of some of them the degree of complementarity is more than the other. Therefore, the programme for economic development should aim at the establishment of those industries where these complementarities happen to be the greatest.

(b) That a simultaneous investment in a number of complementary industries according to the programme of balanced growth may achieve a once for all increase in national income. But after this, the economy will become stabilised at a higher level without any movement forward. The objective of development is not only to achieve a once for all increase in national income, rather this process of income propogation must continue year after year. In order to see that the development process moves on continuously, it is necessary to create and maintain deliberate imbalances in the economy. To create these imbalances Hirschman suggests investment either in Social Overhead Capital (SOC) or in Directly Productive Activities (DPA).

Social Overhead Capital is defined as "comprising all those basic services without which primary, secondary and tertiary productive activities can not function". This includes investment in education, public health, transport and communications, irrigation, drainage etc. Large investment in SOC will encourage investment in DPA by providing cheap inputs to agriculture and industry e.g., cheap electricity and power supply may encourage the development of industries both large and small and may stimulate activity in other sectors as well. To quote Hirschman "Investment in SOC is advocated not because of its direct effect on final output, but because it permits and infact invites DPA to come in some SOC investment as a prerequisite of DPA investment."

Imbalances in the economy can also be created by investment in directly productive activities such as investment in manufacturing industries and constructional activities. Expansion in investment in DPA without the corresponding expansion in SOC will lead to increase in cost of production in view of inadequate availability of overhead facilities. In such a situation, pressures are likely to be exerted and the government may step in and undertake investment in SOC for creating the necessary infrastructure which would lead to an all-round development of the economy.

The sequence of development from SOC to DPA is known as development via excess capacity. The second sequence viz from DPA to SOC is called development via shortages. Development via excess capacity of SOC is more continuous and smooth than development via shortages of SOC. According to Hirschman, "development via shortages is an instance of disorderly compulsive sequence while that with excess SOC capacity is essentially permissive."

Every investment project has both forward linkages (it may encourage investment in subsequent stage of production) and backward linkages (it may encourage investment in earlier stages of production) and the task of development policy is to find out projects with the maximum total linkage. Hirschman has worked out the forward and the backward linkage in case of number of industries and on the basis of that, the maximum linkage exists in the case of intermediate manufacturing industries. Therefore, if investment is made in such industries, it is bound to affect the demand and supply positions in other sectors of the economy and thus leading to their expansion as well.

Balanced Growth or Unbalanced Growth ?

After having discussed both the theories of Balanced Growth and Unbalanced Growth, the natural question to ask is which of these is more appropriate or largely feasible for bringing about a rapid development in the underdeveloped countries. Prof. Hirschman observes the balanced growth theory makes an impossible demand on the limited resources of the underdeveloped countries by asking them to simultaneously start investing in a number of complimentary industries which require a huge amount of capital, technical knowhow, and efficient organisational ability. If these countries were in a position to do so, they would surely not have remained underdeveloped till now. He feels that supply of these factors can be increased only over a long period of time and hence the minimum objectives of development policy should be to create the right type of imbalances which exert pressure on the different sectors of the economy, thus, automatically moving the country on the path of development. The case of unbalanced growth is based primarily on the impracticability of the balanced growth because of the non-availability of adequate resources, particularly of capital, in these countries.

The case for balanced growth on the other hand gets strengthened when one realises that stagnation in underdeveloped economies is deep rooted due to structural disequilibrium in its economy. Sustained growth requires a harmonious development of various complementary sectors but again the question arises – Do these economies have enough of resources to invest simultaneously in all the sectors? Thus, the case of unbalanced growth is based primarily on the impracticability of the balanced growth because of the non-availability of adequate resources of capital in these countries.

3

Nature of the Indian Economy

THE World Bank in its World Development Report[1] (2002) classified the various countries on the basis of per capita Gross National Product.

Developing countries are classified into :

(i) Low income countries with GNP per capita of $755 or less.

(ii) Lower-middle income with per capita GNP of $756 to $2995, upper middle income countries with GNP per capita ranging from $2996 to $9265 and,

(iii) High income countries with per capita GNP of $9266 or more.

According to data given in the World Development Report 2002, in 2000, *Low Income Countries* accounted for 40.6 per cent of the world population but contributed only 10.9 per cent to total World GNP. The *Middle Income Countries* constituted 44.4 per cent of world population but accounted for 34.2 per cent of World GNP. These two groups, popularly described as developing economies or underdeveloped economies, comprise about 85 per cent of the world population but account for only 45 per cent of world GNP. Most countries of Asia, Africa, Latin America and some countries of Europe are included in them.

The *High Income Economies,* which comprise only 15 per cent of World population, contribute 55.6 per cent to World GNP.

---

1. World Bank, World Development Report, 2002, Table I, p. 232.

TABLE – 1

DISTRIBUTION OF WORLD POPULATION AND WORLD GNP AMONG VARIOUS GROUPS OF COUNTRIES

	Population 2000 (Million)	*GNP 2000 (Billion $) PPP 2000*	*GNP 2000 (per capita) $*	*Average Growth of Annual Population (1990-00)*
World	6054	44506	7350	1.4
Low Income Countries	2459	4892	520	2.0
Middle Income Countries	2693	15229	2950	1.2
High Income Countries	903	24781	25510	0.7
India	1016	2432	2390	1.8

Source: World Development Report, 2002.

Common Characteristics of Underdeveloped Countries

The underdeveloped or the developing countries, as these are popularly known, inspite of their diverse structure, have some common characteristics. Todaro classifies these common characteristics into six broad categories:[2]

Indian economy possesses all the characteristics common to underdeveloped or developing countries.

1. Low levels of living
2. Low levels of productivity
3. High rates of population growth and dependency burden
4. High and rising level of unemployment and underemployment
5. Significant dependence on agricultural production and primary products exports
6. Dominance, dependence and vulnerability in international relations

2. Michael P. Todaro, *op. cit.*

1. Low Levels of Living

In developing nations general levels of living tend to be low for the vast majority of people. These low levels of living are manifested in the form of low incomes (poverty), inadequate housing, poor health, limited or low education, high infant mortality and low life expectancy.

The GNP per capita is often used as a summary index of the relative economic well being of people in different nations.

On account of low per capita income, population suffers from poor health, low education, high infant mortality and low life expectancy. In India, the life expectancy at birth was 32 in 1947 and the literacy was only 17 per cent. According to Planning Commission estimates, India's poverty ratio was 49 per cent in 1973-74. Although the percentage came down to 32.4 in 1993-94 which further declined to 23.6 in 1999-2000 the absolute number of poor remained as high as 260 million.[3]

2. Low Levels of Productivity

Throughout the developing world, levels of labour productivity are extremely low compared with those in developed countries. Low level of living and low productivity are self reinforcing social and economic phenomenon in Third World countries and as such, are the principal manifestation of, and contributors to, their development. Myrdal's well known theory of "circular and cumulative causation" in underdeveloped countries is based on the interaction between low living levels and low productivity.

Low productivity is due to low level of technology. The sharp differences in productivity between developed and underdeveloped nations can be traced to the level of technology in these countries. Productivity level in Indian economy has been low on account of backward or poor technology and this applies to all sectors of the economy – whether it is agriculture, industry or the tertiary sector.

3. High Rate of Population Growth and Dependency Burden

Fast growing population in the Third World is both a cause and effect of underdevelopment. These countries have effectively brought down the mortality rates but birth rates continue to be high due to wide spread poverty, ignorance and social and religious factors. Due to high birth rate, the dependency burden is about half of the population as

3. Planning Commission, January 2001, *Indian Planning Experience: A Statistical Profile*, P.19, Table 2.1 and P.23, Table 2.5.

against one fourth in developed countries. The active labour force has to support almost twice as many children as it does in richer countries. Population has been growing in Third World countries in the range of 2 to 3.5 per cent per annum as compared to less than 1 per cent in developed countries. In India, for instance, the rate of growth of population increased from 1.25 per cent per annum in 1951 to 2.5 per cent in 1981. It started declining only thereafter and 1991 census recorded a growth rate of 2 per cent with children under the age 15 forming 38 per cent of the total population.

4. High and Rising Levels of Unemployment and Underemployment

One of the principal manifestations of and factors contributing to the low level of living in developing nations is their relatively inadequate and inefficient utilisation of labour in comparison with the developed nations. Current rates of open unemployment in Third World average from 10 to 15 per cent and when the underemployed are added to the openly unemployed, almost 30 per cent of the combined urban and rural labour force in Third World nations is under-utilised.[4]

With *Low Developed Countries'* population growing rapidly, their labour force will also be accelerating for some time to come. This means that jobs will have to be created at equivalent rates simply to keep pace with the growth of labour supply. In India, for example, because of the high growth of population in the last decade, the growth rate in labour force will be 2.48 per cent as against 1.57 per cent growth rate in population in the year 2002.[5]

Thus, the need for providing work opportunities for the growing labour force and also to reduce the base level of unemployment significantly, assumes great importance so as to avoid the social tensions that arise from growing unemployment and underemployment.

5. Substantial Dependence on Agricultural Production and Primary Product Exports

The vast majority of people in Third World Nations live and work in rural area. Almost 80 per cent are ruraly based compared with less than 35 per cent in economically developed countries. The proportion of labour force engaged in agriculture in less developed countries is 66 per cent compared with 21 per cent for developed nations. Moreover,

4. Todaro, op. cit, p 40.
5. Planning Commission, *Ninth Five Year Plan 1997-2002*, (1999) Vol.I, P. 20.

agriculture contributes about 32 per cent to the GNP of the former while it accounts for only 8 per cent of GNP of the latter.

The basic reason for the concentration of people and production in agricultural and other primary production activities in developing countries is the simple fact that for the low income levels, the first priority is for food, clothing and shelter. Agricultural productivity is low not only because of the large number of people in relation to available land but also because in *Lower Development Countries* agriculture is often characterised by primitive technologies, poor organisation and limited physical and human capital inputs.

In India the predominance of the primary sector is reflected in the contribution of this sector to GDP and employment in the economy. In 1965, the contribution of primary sector to India's GDP was 47 per cent and to employment 73 per cent. Even today, primary sector provides employment to about 65 per cent of the workforce and its contribution to GDP is 25 per cent as compared with 3 per cent of workforce engaged in primary sector in UK and 4 per cent in USA contributing about 2 per cent to their GDP. Indian economy is in transition from underdevelopment to a developing economy.

6. Dominance, Dependence and Vulnerability in International Relations

For many less developed countries, a significant factor contributing to the persistence of low levels of living, rising unemployment, and growing income inequality is the highly unequal distribution of economic and political power between poor and rich nations. These unequal strengths are manifested not only in the dominant power of rich nations to control the pattern of international trade but also in their ability often to dictate the terms in which technology, foreign aid, and private capital are transferred to developing countries.

Examples include the transfer of often inappropriate educational structures, curricular, and school systems; the formation of Western-style trade unions; the organization and orientation of health services also following the Western model; and finally, the structure and operation of public, bureaucratic and administrative system that also may be inconsistent with the priority needs and the available manpower supplies in developing nations. Of even greater potential significance may be the influence of rich-country's social and economic standards on developing-country salary scales, elite life styles, and general attitudes towards the private accumulation of wealth. Such attitudes can often breed corruption and economic plunder by a privileged minority.

The net effect of all these factors is to create a situation of "vulnerability" among Third World nations in which forces largely outside their control can have decisive and dominating influences on their overall economic and social well-being.

Conclusion

According to Michael Todaro, the phenomenon of underdevelopment needs to be viewed in a national and an international context. Economic and social forces, both internal and external, are responsible for the poverty, inequality, and low productivity that commonly characterise most Third World nations. The successful pursuit of economic and social development will require not only the formulation of appropriate strategies within the Third World but also a modification of the present international economic order to make it more responsive to the development needs of poor nations.

Indian Economy in Transition

Indian economy is in transition from underdeveloped to a developing economy since 1951 when India embarked on a programme of planned economic development of the country.

In terms of HDI(UNDP), India has moved from group of low human development countries to medium human development during the last decade or so. In terms of World Development Report clarification, India comes in the category of lower middle income countries.[6]

Indian Economy as Mixed Economy

The declared social objective of the Indian development strategy since Independence has been growth with equitable distribution. This was sought to be achieved within the democratic political framework. The problem was of reconciling growth with equity in a democratic framework. This necessitated the adoption of mixed economy as an institutional form to reconcile the objectives of growth with equitable distribution in a democratic framework.

The second five year stated categorically, "The task before an underdeveloped country is not merely to get better results within the existing framework of economic and social institutions but to mould and refashion these so that they contribute effectively to the realisation of wider and deeper social values".

---

6. For more details see ch.1, p. 29-32.

These values or basic objectives have been summed up in the phrase "socialist pattern of society" (Second Plan). Essentially, this means that the basic criterion for determining the lines of advance must not be private profit but social gain, and that the pattern of development and the structure of socio-economic relations should be so planned that they result not only in appreciable increases in national income and employment but also in greater equality in incomes and wealth. Major decisions regarding production, distribution, consumption and investment – and in fact all significant socio-economic relationships – must be made by agencies informed by social purpose. The benefits of economic development must accrue more and more to the relatively less privileged classes of society, and there should be a progressive reduction of the concentration of incomes, wealth and economic power.

For creating the appropriate conditions, the State has to take on heavy responsibilities as the principal agency speaking for and acting on behalf of the community as a whole. The public sector has to expand rapidly. It has not only to initiate developments which the private sector is either unwilling or unable to undertake; it has to play the dominant role in shaping the entire pattern of investments in the economy, whether it makes the investments directly or whether these are made by the private sector. The private sector has to play its part within the framework of the comprehensive plan accepted by the community.

Public ownership, partial or complete, and public control or participation in management are specially required in those fields in which technological considerations tend towards a concentration of economic power and of wealth. In several fields, private enterprise can make little headway without assistance and support from Government. *In a growing economy which gets increasingly diversified there is scope for both the public and the private sectors to expand simultaneously, but it is inevitable, if development is to proceed at the pace envisaged and to contribute effectively to the attainment of the larger social ends in view, that the public sector must grow not only absolutely but also relatively to the private sector. (Second Plan)*

Features of the Mixed Economy

According to Tendulkar[7], two essential features of the mixed economy institutional form are relevant in the present context:

First, there is a predominance of the private ownership of property

---

7. Tendulkar, S.D., "Public Sector in the Context of an Overall Development Strategy", *Indian Economy Since Independence*, in Uma Kapila, (ed) op.cit. 2000-01.

and means of production and freedom to utilize them in economic activity within the legal and constitutional framework and with private profit as a motive force.

Secondly, while the state is not expected to be identified with the interest of any particular class and the operation of the countervailing forces of various interest groups is permitted within the system, the role of the State is recognized to be positive. In other words, the active state intervention in the free play of market mechanism is not only tolerated but considered warranted in the interest of promoting equity. The "active" state intervention in this sense is expected to go beyond the minimal functions of the State such as the provision of social and economic infrastructure, and to operate through the three classes of instruments, namely,

(i) aggressive fiscal and monetary policies;

(ii) market intervention without undertaking direct production;

(iii) undertaking directly productive economic activity through the public sector – essentially an extension of the public ownership of means of production.

The basic idea is that through these instruments, the government would be able to control the pace as well as the composition of private economic activity in the interest of equity. Since this control happens to be direct in the case of public sector, that provides the basic justification for the public sector as the most effective instrument with which the State in a mixed economy operating under the democratic framework would be able to pursue the social objective of growth with equitable distribution. It should be emphasized, however, that like any other instrument, effectiveness in serving a given social objective would be determined by the ability as well as the willingness of the state to enforce it in that direction.

In India, the rationale for the public sector indicated above has been explicit or implicit in almost all the plan documents as well as policy statements although the emphasis has changed in degrees depending upon the constraints faced and the emerging major issues of the time. As Tendulkar has rightly remarked "The growth promoting leading sector role assumed by the public sector in the context of the Mahalanobis strategy has undergone a significant change in the contemporary context – relatively more emphasis on procurement and distribution activities, much more on providing public services under minimum needs programme and comparatively less on directly productive growth-oriented lines of production.

4

National Income

Trends & Structural Transformation

Long-Term Trends in Real GDP 1950-51 – 2000-01

THE structural transformation that occurred in the Indian economy over the decades is a consequence of the development process witnessed since the beginning of planning in 1951. This is reflected in the growth rate and in the changing sectoral composition of the Gross Domestic Product (GDP). In the 'eighties (1980-81 through 1990-91), GDP has recorded a trend growth rate of 5.5 per cent; the average rate of growth at 5.8 per cent being slightly higher than the trend rate of growth. However, there was considerable volatility in the annual growth rate, and for a number of years during this period, GDP grew by less than 5 per cent. The volatility in real growth rate is most reflected in case of GDP originating in agriculture. However, the high growth phenomenon of the 'eighties could not be sustained, as the experience of the crisis year of 1991-92 revealed, when the annual GDP growth rate declined to a low of 0.8 per cent.

A comparison of the more recent period of the 'nineties (1992-93 to 1997-98) with the 'eighties (i.e., 1980-81 through 1990-91) reveals some notable features. The trend rate of growth of GDP at 6.9 per cent during the 'nineties was distinctly higher than 5.5 per cent recorded in the 'eighties. In terms of average rate of growth, the performance in the 'nineties (6.5 per cent) was better than that recorded in the 'eighties (5.8 per cent). While both the industrial and the services sectors experienced *high* growth rates during the recent period, agriculture and allied activities, registered a relatively *low* order of growth as compared with the 'eighties.

TABLE – 1

AVERAGE ANNUAL GROWTH RATE IN GDP

(Per cent)

Period		*Growth rate*
First Plan	: 1951-56	3.6
Second Plan	: 1956-61	4.1
Third Plan	: 1961-66	2.5
Annual Plans	: 1966-69	3.8
Fourth Plan	: 1969-74	3.3
Fifth Plan	: 1974-78	5.0
Annual Plans	: 1978-80	-6.0
Sixth Plan	: 1980-85	5.4
Seventh Plan	: 1985-90	5.8
Annual Plans	: 1990-92	3.3
Eighth Plan	: 1992-97	6.8
Ninth Plan	: 1997-02	5.6
Annual Average	: 1997-98	4.6
Annual Average	: 1998-99	6.5
Annual Average	: 1999-00	6.2
Annual Average	: 2000-01	4.4
Annual Average	: 2001-02	6.1
Annual Average	**: 2002-03 (Q)**	**3.7**
Annual Average	**: 2003-04 (Adv)**	**8.1**

Source: Planning Commission, *Indian Planning Experience: A Statistical Profile*, January, 2001 and CSO Estimates (Revised and Quarterly Estimates, June 28, 2002).
Economic Survey 2003-04.

The contrast between the 'eighties and the 'nineties is also sharp if the trend growth rates are considered at 1993-94 prices (i.e., during 1993-94 through 1998-99). This underlines a major structural shift in the Indian economy during the recent period, with economic growth becoming less vulnerable to agricultural performance and to vagaries of the monsoon. While the improvement in growth has emerged from both the industrial and services sectors, there is a marked difference in the sectoral composition of growth as between these two major sectors. Within the industrial sector, the major impetus to growth has come from manufacturing, while both 'mining and quarrying', and 'electricity, gas and water supply' registered lower rates of growth. The services sector, on the other hand, experienced higher growth in a more uniform and consistent manner with sectors like 'trade, hotels, restaurants, storage and communication', and 'financing, insurance, real estate, and business services', experiencing high trend growth rates. A possible interpretation of this phenomenon could be an upsurge of industry-related services sector in recent years.

Growth Rates in the 90's — Problem of Comparability

It needs to be mentioned at the outset that there is some problem of comparability of growth rates during the 'nineties. The real GDP numbers are available only up to 1996-97 with 1980-81 as the base year, while the GDP figures for the period 1993-94 to 1998-99 are available with 1993-94 as the base (consequent to the adoption of 1993-94 as the new base year by the Central Statistical Organisation (CSO) since February 1999). However, such changes in the base year emanating from the necessity of adapting the statistical system to the changing structure of the economy (Box-1), for the purpose of compiling the estimates of real GDP had been a regular feature in the past. Keeping those methodological changes in view and with a view to developing a more meaningful analytical framework for analysing the developments in the 'nineties, growth rates of real GDP and its components have been taken with 1980-81 as the base year for the period 1991-92 through 1993-94, and with the base year 1993-94 for the period 1994-95 through 1998-99.

For a meaningful comparison, the period of reforms can be sub-divided into two phases viz., Phase I (1992-93 to 1996-97) and Phase II (1997-98 to 2002-03). The entire period of Phase I can be further divided into two sub-periods based on the growth performance of the economy. The first sub-period (1992-93 to 1993-94) was the period of recovery from the crisis while the second sub-period (1994-95 to 1996-97) was marked by high growth of the economy. During the crisis year of 1991-92, the rate of growth of real GDP had dipped to 1.3 per cent. Both, agriculture and industrial sectors recorded negative rates of growth, the former primarily emanating from the occurrence of drought. However, the speed of recovery of the economy during the first sub-period of Phase I was quite impressive with the real GDP growth improving to an average of 5.5 per cent per annum spread over all the sectors (Table 2).

TABLE – 2

SECTORAL GROWTH RATES OF REAL GROSS DOMESTIC PRODUCT: REFORM PERIOD

(Per cent)

Sector	*Phase I*		*Phase II*
	Sub-period I: 1992-93 to 1993-94	*Sub-period II: 1994-95 to 1996-97*	*1997-98 to 2002-03*
	1	*2*	*3*
1. Agriculture and Allied Activities	**5.0**	**4.6**	**1.0**
Agriculture	5.2	4.7	*
2. Industry	**5.3**	**10.8**	**4.3**
Mining and Quarrying	1.3	5.2	4.0
Manufacturing	6.3	12.2	4.2
Electricity, Gas and Water Supply	3.1	7.2	5.7
3. Services	**6.0**	**7.9**	**7.9**
Construction	2.0	4.6	7.0
Trade, Hotels and Communication	6.3	10.5	7.9
Financing, Insurance, Real Estate and Business Services	9.6	6.9	7.3
Community, Social and Personal Services	4.0	5.8	8.6
4. GDP at Factor Cost	**5.5**	**7.5**	**5.3**

* Not available separately

Source : Computed on the basis of data from the Central Statistical Organisation.

With the economic recovery gathering momentum in the first sub-period of Phase I, the economy was placed on a higher growth trajectory in the subsequent period. During the second sub-period of the first phase, the growth rate of GDP averaged as much as 7.5 per cent per annum. This was the only period in India's economic history during which real GDP growth exceeded 7.0 per cent consecutively over a period of three years. The sharp acceleration in the rate of growth of overall GDP was largely the result of the phenomenal growth of 10.8 per cent per annum in the industrial sector. The upswing in industrial growth during this sub-period can be regarded as an outcome of removal of various constraints in the form of licensing and other restrictions as a part of the liberalisation initiatives. The growth of GDP, however, moderated in 1997-98, which marks the beginning of phase II.

The Growth Deceleration

The phase from 1997-98 to 2002-03 was marked by a deceleration in growth with the average rate of growth during this period turning out to be 5.3 per cent, which was much lower than the average growth of 7.5 per cent per annum recorded during the period of high growth from 1994-95 to 1996-97. The most disturbing feature of this phase was the steep decline in industrial growth, led by a severe slowdown in the manufacturing sector. The average rate of growth of manufacturing decelerated by as much as eight percentage points during this phase as compared with the second sub-period of the first phase.

Within the second phase, real GDP growth, after dipping to 4.8 per cent in 1997-98, recovered during the years 1998-99 and 1999-2000 to over 6.0 per cent. One of the factors contributing to this recovery was the high growth emanating from services sector, and within the services sector, the growth of 'community, social and personal services', particularly 'public administration and defence'. The Fifth Pay Commission Award led to an increase in GDP originating from the sub-sector of 'public administration and defence' in 1997-98, with its lagged effect persisting till 1999-2000. These years witnessed a striking increase in the weighted contribution of 'community, social and personal services' to the growth of GDP originating from the services sector. The period from 1997-98 to 1999-2000 also witnessed steady growth in other components of the services sector. In the more recent period, growth of overall GDP dipped to 4.4 per cent in 2000-01. This was a result of poor performance of agriculture, coupled with a significant deceleration in the growth rate of GDP from the services sector, particularly 'financing, insurance, real estate and business services'. The same rate of growth of 4.4 per cent has also been registered in 2002-03, as per the latest Advance Estimates, which has been an outcome of a sharp fall in agricultural growth to a negative of 3.1 per cent owing to the drought conditions.

Sectoral Composition of Real GDP

In developed and mature economies, the industrial and services sectors contribute a major share in GDP, with agriculture accounting for a relatively lower share. During the process of growth over the years, the Indian economy too experienced an improvement in the shares of industry and services sectors in overall GDP. The sectoral composition of real GDP at 1980-81 prices shows that the share of the agricultural sector in GDP gradually declined from 36.4 per cent in the 'eighties to

28.6 per cent in the 'nineties (1990-91 to 2000-01) (Table–3). In contrast, the shares of industry and services increased from 25.0 per cent to 27.1 per cent and from 38.6 per cent to 44.3 per cent, respectively during the same period.

TABLE – 3

SECTOR-WISE AVERAGE SHARES, GROWTH RATES AND CONTRIBUTION TO GDP GROWTH

(Per cent)

Period	*Services*			*Industry#*			*Agriculture*		
	Share in GDP	*Growth Rate*	*Contri-bution to GDP Growth*	*Share in GDP*	*Growth Rate*	*Contri-bution to GDP Growth*	*Share in GDP*	*Growth Rate*	*Contri-bution to GDP Growth*
1	*2*	*3*	*4*	*5*	*6*	*7*	*8*	*9*	*10*
1950-51 to 1959-60*	28.2	4.1	32.2	16.0	5.7	25.3	56.0	2.3	42.5
1960-61 to 1969-70	31.4	4.9	38.1	21.1	6.5	32.9	47.8	2.5	29.2
1970-71 to 1979-80	34.4	4.5	52.7	22.8	3.7	28.7	42.8	1.3	18.6
1980-81 to 1989-90	38.6	6.6	43.6	25.0	6.8	28.9	36.4	4.4	27.5
1990-91 to 2000-01	44.3	7.6	57.6	27.1	5.9	27.6	28.6	2.9	14.8
1999-00	53.2	9.4	79.2	21.6	4.2	15.1	25.2	1.3	5.7
2000-01	53.7	5.0	67.4	22.1	6.2	34.1	24.2	-0.2	-1.4
2001-02	54.1	6.2	61.1	21.6	3.3	13.6	24.3	5.7	25.4

\# Inclusive of construction

* 9 year data for growth and weighted contribution since data for 1949-50 are not available. Due to rounding off, sectoral data may not add up to 100.

Source : National Accounts Statistics, CSO.

Thus, there was a surge in the growth of the services sector since the early 'eighties, with the trend rate of growth being more pronounced in recent years. The recent years' experience shows that the growth of the services sector has imparted much of the resilience to the economy, particularly in times of adverse agricultural shocks.

Compositional Shift in Favour of Services

The RBI report on Currency and Finance (2000-01) states, the compositional shift in favour of services has been brought about by accelerated expansion in the services sector output at a rate of 7.6 per cent in the period 1990-91 to 2000-01 compared with 6.6 per cent during 1980-81 to 1989-90. While the growing contribution of the services sector to GDP is in line with the development experiences of a number of countries of the world, it is, however, not yet clear whether it is the comparative advantage that is driving up the share of the services sector in GDP or whether the sector also derives strength from the policies that are being pursued since the early 'nineties.

There has been a relative deceleration in the performance of agriculture during the 'nineties despite favourable monsoons, increase in net irrigated area and positive terms of trade. The decline in public investment and the limited infusion of new technologies may have contributed to the poor performance of agriculture.

However, Indian economy attained and maintained a high GDP growth in the 'nineties despite substantial deceleration in agricultural growth. For example in 1995-96 when the economy achieved a record 8.6 per cent growth in GDP, the agricultural sector witnessed a negligible 0.2 per cent growth over the previous year. In fact, as the RBI report on Currency and Finance states, *"the recent years' experience shows that the growth of services sector has imparted much of resilience to the economy particularly in times of adverse agricultural shocks."*

Thus, economic growth is becoming less vulnerable to agricultural performance and to vagaries of the monsoon. While the improvement in growth has emerged from both the industrial and services sectors, there is a marked difference in the sectoral composition of growth as between these two major sectors. Within the industrial sector, the major impetus to growth has come from manufacturing, while both 'mining and quarrying', and 'electricity, gas and water supply' registered lower rates of growth. The services sector, on the other hand, experienced higher growth in a more uniform and consistent manner with sectors like 'trade, hotels, restaurants, storage and communication', whereas 'financing, insurance, real estate, and business services' are experiencing high trend growth rates. A possible interpretation of this phenomenon could be an upsurge of industry-related services sector in recent years.

The phenomenal expansion of services world-wide led to services being regarded as an engine of the growth and even as a necessary concomitant of economic growth. Development economics suggest that development is a three-stage process. The dominance of the services sector in the growth process is usually associated with the third stage of growth. During the 1980s and 1990s, services accounted for a share of close to or above 70 per cent of GDP in industrialised countries and about 50 per cent in developing countries. In India, services accounted for 38.6 per cent of the GDP in the 1980s and 44.3 per cent in the 1990s and 54.1 per cent in 2001-02. In 2000-01 it was 53.7 and in 1999-2000 it was 53.2 per cent.

Sustainability of Services Growth

Since the 1980s, growth process in India has been marked by a robust performance of services sector. While this is partially in line with the experience of developed countries, the Indian experience is somewhat unique in the sense that the sectoral shift in favour of services sector accompanied almost stagnant share of industry and reduced share of agriculture. The momentum continued during the 1990s; in fact, it was the growth performance of the services sector that provided a resilience to the overall growth of the economy, particularly in times of adverse agricultural shocks and industrial slowdown.

The set of economic reform measures initiated since 1991 also impacted on the performance of the services sector.

First, reforms in the domestic industrial environment which resulted in rising manufacturing growth provided synergies to the services sector in the form of increased demand for producer services.

Second, the liberalisation of the financial sector provided an environment for faster growth of the financial services.

Third, reforms in certain segments of infrastructure services also contributed to the growth of services. Consequently, the services sector posted a much higher growth during the reform period as compared with the pre-reform period with its share touching nearly the 50 per cent mark.

Finally, the rapid growth in services sector appears to have benefited from external demand; the typical example of which is the software industry and call centres. Interestingly, the decelerating trend in manufacturing and overall GDP seems to have been much less pronounced in case of services. Nevertheless, there are apprehensions about its sustainability in view of the contribution of "public administration and defence" to growth in services.

Against the above backdrop, the present section* broadly looks into the following two issues: First, the performance of the services sector and second, the sustainability of services growth. After analysing the relative performance of the services sector in the reform period, the supply-side sources of services growth are examined followed by a discussion on the decomposition of services into three segments, viz., Producer services, Consumer services and Government services.

Performance of the Services Sector

Since the 1980s, services sector has come to occupy a position of dominance in the composition of GDP. The average share of services sector increased to 45.4 per cent during the reform period as against 38.9 per cent in the pre-reform period. In terms of growth, services sector posted a higher growth of 7.8 per cent during the reform period as against 6.7 per cent during the preceding period. However, services sector is actually vogue and unorganised entity; on the one hand, it includes sectors like 'public administration and defence', largely independent of the level of economic activity, and on the other, it has sectors like 'trade, hotels and restaurants'. At the sub-sector level, 'trade, hotels and restaurants' continued to be the major segment in terms of its share in services. The growth performance improved for all segments during the reform period barring 'financing, insurance, real estate and business services'. However, the 'financing, insurance, real estate and business services' improved its share during the reform period when all other segments witnessed shrinkage in their respective shares, which seems to be the result of the financial sector reforms that led to emergence of new participants, instruments and markets. The poor performance of the non-banking sector, among others, has been the cause for the deceleration in growth of this sector. Nevertheless, the relative contribution of this sub-sector to the services growth has been maintained across the periods (Table 4).

Factors underlying the Services Growth

Growth of services stemming from capital productivity/total factor productivity could be seen as an encouraging development in a capital scarce economy like India. The gross value added from services registered a higher growth in the reform period even though the trend growth of Gross Capital Formation (GCF) in services decelerated to 5.7 per cent from 5.9 per cent in the pre-reform period. This could imply an improvement in capital productivity and/ or total factor productivity in services. There is a broad consensus that the recent surge in services

* RBI Report on Currency and Finance, 2001-02, Ch.3, Part-3, pp 41-45.

has been contributed, among others, by the skill-intensive and high productivity activities such as Information Technology (IT) services, which have emerged as one of the fastest growing segments in the 1990s. The labour productivity in software services is estimated to be twice that of the manufacturing sector (Arora and Athreye, 2001). The rise of services can also be seen as an outcome of the economic liberalisation and encouragement of private investment in industry and infrastructure. Besides, increased expenditure on public administration and defence, social services and rural extension services has had a positive impact on the services growth in the 1990s.

TABLE – 4

SHARE AND GROWTH OF SUB-SECTORS OF SERVICES

(Per cent)

Sector	*1981-82 to 1990-91*		*1992-93 to 2001-02*		*Growth during the three phases of 1992-93 to 2001-02*		
					1992-93 to 1993-94	*1994-95 to 1996-97*	*1997-98 to 2001-02*
1	*2*	*3*	*4*	*5*	*6*	*7*	
	Share	Growth	Share	Growth	Growth	Growth	Growth
Trade, hotels and restaurants	32.2	5.9	30.7	8.1	6.6	10.9	7.1
Transport and communication	16.1	5.6	15.8	8.9	5.9	9.7	9.6
Financing, insurance, real estate and business services	21.0	9.9	26.1	7.8	9.6	6.9	8.1
Community, social and personal services	30.7	6.1	27.3	7.1	4.0	5.8	9.1
Services	100.0 (38.9)	6.7	100.0 (45.4)	7.8	6.5	8.2	8.1

Note : Figures in brackets are share of services in GDP.
Source : Central Statistical Organisation.

Composition of Growth in the Services Sector

(i) Intermediate versus Final Consumption of Services

For a meaningful analysis, the issue of absorption of services as intermediate vis-a-vis final consumption is examined by classifying them into Producer, Consumer and Government services. Their relative roles can provide insights as regards the sustainability of services growth. Activities like 'trade', 'transport, storage and communication', 'financing, insurance, real estate and business services', which are more of intermediate nature, are taken as producer services. Activities like 'hotels and restaurants' and 'other services', having the nature of final consumption, are classified as consumer services whereas 'public administration and defence' (PAD) are treated as Government services.

While producer and consumer services have recorded a higher growth in the reform period, the Government services have witnessed a marginal decline. This has implications for growth dynamics, not only for services sector but also for the overall growth process.

(ii) Producer Services

The increased share of producer services in total services in the reform period can be explained by the phenomenon of increasing relevance of outsourcing by the Indian industry. In an increasingly competitive environment in the reform period peripheral service-oriented activities, which were carried out earlier in-house, are being contracted out to the outside agencies. Furthermore, the increasing share of producer services reflects the growing complementarity between services and manufacturing (RBI, 2002). The expansionary potential of services can be viewed from the fact that 50 per cent of the industries are directly or indirectly services-intensive (Bhowmik, 2000). The major demand for producer services emanates from the manufacturing sector as well as exports.

Consumer Services and Private Final Consumption Expenditure

An upward trend was observed in consumer services, which recorded a growth of 8.0 per cent in the reform period as compared with 5.8 per cent in the preceding period. The increased growth in consumer services in the reform period has been accompanied by a similar growth pattern in private final consumption expenditure (PFCE) on services. The share of services in PFCE has moved up to 24.9 per cent in the reform period from 18.0 per cent in the preceding period. A disaggregated analysis of PFCE on services shows that medical care and hotels have recorded significant increases in growth during the reform period while growth in transport and communication has slowed down over the same period.

(iii) Government Services

Government services, comprising PAD is often singled out for the high growth in services since increased expenditure of the Government in the form of wage bill gets directly reflected in its value added even without any addition to services. An examination of the issue of faster growth of this sub sector in the 1980s showed that the tertiary sector growth was not solely due to increase in the growth of GDP originating from PAD (Nagaraj, 1990; Kumar, 1992). The steep wage hike in 1990s in line with the Fifth Pay Commission's recommendations brought back the issue into focus once again (Acharya, 2003). According to Shankar Acharya, a part of the services growth in the last four years is "spurious" in the sense that it simply reflects the revaluation of the sub-sector 'Public Administration and Defence' because of higher pay scales resulting from decisions on the Fifth Pay Commission. It is a peculiarity of national income accounting procedures that value added in this sub-sector of non-marketed services is estimated on the basis of cost. Thus higher salaries lead to faster growth here even when consumers of government services may not vouch for any increase in value added! These Pay Commission effects were spread mainly over three years, 1997/98 to 1999/2000 for the Centre and States. Allowing for trend growth, the "spurious" component of growth from this sub-sector to account for about half a per cent of GDP growth in each of these three years.

It is also observed that one percentage point of growth of 5.0 per cent in GDP for 1997-98 is attributed to the 20 per cent increase in real value added in the PAD sub-sector arising chiefly from pay increases to Government servants (Government of India, 1999).

The growth in PAD, during the period 1997-98 through 1999-2000, has been far higher than growth in services excluding PAD and therefore PAD undoubtedly contributed to the overall growth of services. During the reform period as a whole, an assessment of services excluding PAD, however, contradicts the perception that PAD alone is responsible for higher services growth. Although the Fifth Pay Commission related pay increases might have distorted estimates of GDP originating from services for a few years, they do not affect the trend growth which remains at 8.2 per cent during the reform-period even if Government administration is excluded altogether (Table 5). On the whole, the services sector growth appears to have accelerated in the reform period, with the impetus coming from sources other than PAD.

External Demand for Services

The growing role of tradable services in international trade and exchange has come to be recognised with the General Agreement on Trade in Services (GATS). India's share in world exports of commercial services has doubled from 0.6 per cent in 1990 to 1.2 per cent in 2000, while the share in world merchandise exports has gone up marginally from 0.5 per cent to 0.7 per cent during the same period. Interestingly, there has been a consistent surplus on account of trade in services. The compositional shifts in foreign trade in favour of services in the reform period has helped in the emergence of new sources of earnings in India's balance of payments. Earnings from software exports have increased from negligible levels in early 1990s to a level of US $ 7.5 billion in 2001-02. These are likely to surge by 30 per cent during 2002-03 as per the NASSCOM estimates. Thus, while the 1980s was dominated by tourism earnings, the second half of 1990s witnessed an unprecedented jump in India's earnings from new economy activities like software services exports and other information technology related skill intensive exports. The services exports thus, provided some element of stability to the external balance of the country and also positively impacted on the overall demand in the services sector.

TABLE – 5

GROWTH IN PUBLIC ADMINISTRATION AND DEFENCE (PAD)

Year	*PAD*	*Services Sector without PAD*	*Services Sector*
	1	*2*	*3*
1992-93	4.9	5.4	5.1
1993-94	2.6	8.5	7.1
1994-95	1.3	8.0	6.6
1995-96	6.8	11.0	9.5
1996-97	4.1	7.6	6.7
1997-98	14.5	9.1	8.9
1998-99	10.3	7.9	7.6
1999-00	12.2	9.3	8.8
2000-01	2.5	6.9	6.5
2001-02	2.9	7.3	6.8
1992-93 to 2001-02*	7.2	8.2	8.0
1981-82 to 1990-91*	7.4	6.7	6.8

* Log-linear trend rate of growth.
Source : Central Statistical Organisation.

Summing Up

The services sector has exhibited a strong trend component that has provided an element of stability to the growth process. The sector seems to have grown in the reform period, sustained by an increasing demand for producer and consumer services coupled with the external demand. The role of public administration and defence appears to have been limited in the growth process. The emergence of producer services as an important source of services growth reflects strong inter-linkage with commodity producing sectors of the economy. Apart from providing inputs, services contribute to the outward shift of the industrial sector's production frontier by enhancing productivity growth. Conversely, services growth could be sustained provided adequate demand impulses are generated in industry or agriculture. Given India's comparative advantage in information technology, services growth momentum can be sustained by exploiting new opportunities in international trade in services, particularly, in the area of communication and information services, technology transfer and software.

Trends in the Share of the Public Sector

The share of government sector in gross domestic product was 7.6 per cent in 1950-51, which rose to 14.9 per cent in 1970-71, 19.7 per cent in 1980-81 and 26.2 per cent in 1995-96. The increase in the share of the government sector has been due to the expansion of the economic activities of the State — enlarging administrative services as well as increasing productive activities in public enterprises. The factors contributing to the increase in the share of non-departmental enterprises are — setting up of new enterprises existing over, nationalisation of coal mining, banks and insurance and the like.

TABLE – 6

SHARE OF PUBLIC SECTOR IN GROSS DOMESTIC PRODUCT AT CURRENT PRICES

		1970-71	*1980-81*	*1995-96*
	Gross domestic product of public sector	14.9	19.7	26.2
(i)	Government administration	6.5	7.3	8.4
(ii)	Departmental enterprises	4.1	3.2	3.8
(iii)	Non-departmental enterprises	4.4	9.2	14.0

Source : CSO, National Accounts Statistics, 1986 and 1998.

Share of Organised and Unorganised Sector in NDP

There has been a shift in the composition of NDP from the unorganised to the organised sector which is due to the process of development. The share of organised sector has risen from 30 per cent in 1980-81 to 40.3 per cent in 1995-96, thus resulting in a fall in the share of unorganised sector from 70 per cent in 1980-81 to 60 per cent. The change in the share of organised sector has mainly been brought about in the mining, manufacturing and services sector. On the other hand, in agriculture, forestry and fishing, the contribution of the unorganised sector instead of declining increased marginally from 95.2 per cent in 1980-81 to 95.9 per cent in 1995-96.

TABLE – 7

PERCENTAGE SHARE IN NET DOMESTIC PRODUCT BY ORGANISED AND UNORGANISED SECTORS

	1980-81		*1995-96*	
	Organised	*Unorganised*	*Organised*	*Unorganised*
1. Agriculture, Forestry and fishing	4.8	95.2	4.1	95.9
2. Mining, manufacturing, etc.	56.8	43.2	62.5	37.5
3. Services	39.9	60.1	48.7	51.3
4. Total	30.0	70.0	40.3	59.7

Source : CSO, National Accounts Statistics (1998)

Inter-regional Variations of National Income

A study by Montek Ahluwalia[1] on Economic Performance of the States in the post reform period brings out that there is considerable variation in the performance of individual states, with some states growing faster than the average and others slower. What is important is that the degree of dispersion in growth rates of SDP (State domestic product) across states increased significantly in the 1990s. The range

1. Montek Ahluwalia, *The Economic Performance of the States in the Post Reforms Period*. 12th NCAER Golden Jubilee Lecture, in Economic Developments in India, Vol.30, 2000, Academic Foundation.

of variation in the growth rate of SDP in the 1980s was from a low of 3.6 per cent per year in Kerala to a high of 6.6 per cent in Rajasthan. In the 1990s the variation was much larger, from a low of 2.7 per cent per year for Bihar to a high of 9.6 per cent for Gujarat.

The differences in performance across states become even more marked when we allow for the differences in the rates of growth of population and evaluate the performance in terms of growth rates of per capita SDP (Table 8). The variation in growth rates in the 1980s ranged from a low of 2.1 per cent for Madhya Pradesh to a high of 4.0 per cent for Rajasthan, a factor of 1:2. In the 1990s it ranged from a low of 1.1 per cent per year in Bihar and 1.2 per cent in U.P., to a high of 7.6 per cent per year in Gujarat, with Maharashtra coming next at 6.1 per cent. The ratio between the lowest (Bihar) and the highest (Gujarat) is as much as 1:7.

TABLE – 8

ANNUAL RATES OF GROWTH OF GROSS STATE DOMESTIC PRODUCT (SDP)

		1980-81 *1990-91* *% p.a.*	*1991-92* *1997-98* *% p.a.*
1.	Bihar	4.66	2.69
2.	Rajasthan	6.60	6.54
3.	Uttar Pradesh	4.95	3.58
4.	Orissa	4.29	3.25
5.	Madhya Pradesh	4.56	6.17
6.	Andhra Pradesh	5.65	5.03
7.	Tamil Nadu	5.38	6.22
8.	Kerala	3.57	5.81
9.	Karnataka	5.29	5.29
10.	West Bengal	4.71	6.91
11.	Gujarat	5.08	9.57
12.	Haryana	6.43	5.02
13.	Maharashtra	6.02	8.01
14.	Punjab	5.32	4.71
	Combined SDP of 14 States	**5.24**	**5.94**
	GDP (National Accounts)	**5.55**	**6.89**

Notes : States are ranked in ascending order of per capita SDP in 1980-81. The growth rates have been estimated by fitting log linear trends to the State SDP data in constant 1980-81 prices obtained from the CSO and the GDP data from the national accounts.

The increased variation in growth performance across states in the 1990s reflects the fact that whereas growth accelerated for the economy as a whole, it actually decelerated sharply in Bihar, Uttar Pradesh and Orissa, all of which had relatively low rates of growth to begin with and were also the poorest states. There was also a deceleration in Haryana and Punjab, but the deceleration was from relatively higher levels of growth in the 1980s, and these states were also the richest.

Six states showed acceleration in growth of SDP in the 1990s. The acceleration was particularly marked in Maharashtra and Gujarat, both of which were among the richer states, but there was also acceleration in West Bengal, Kerala, Tamil Nadu and Madhya Pradesh all belonging to the middle group of States in terms of per capita SDP.

It is important to note that the high growth performers in the 1990s were not concentrated in one part of the country. The six states with growth rates of SDP in the 1990s above 6.0 per cent per year are fairly well distributed regionally i.e. Gujarat (9.6 per cent) and Maharashtra (8.0 per cent) in the West, West Bengal (6.9 per cent) in the East, Tamil Nadu (6.2 per cent) in the South and Madhya Pradesh (6.2 per cent) and Rajasthan (6.5 per cent) in the North.

The performance of Kerala deserves special attention. Kerala has justly celebrated for its achievements in human development but it has also been criticised for under performance in economic growth. It is important to note that its performance in the 1990s showed a marked improvement compared with the 1980s. From an SDP growth rate much below the 14 States average in the 1980s it accelerated to a growth rate only marginally below the average in the 1990s. However, because of the low population growth, its performance in per capita SDP growth in the 1990s was actually much better then the average (Table 8).

The fact that Gujarat and Maharashtra grew at rates normally associated with "miracle growth" economies also deserves special mention. It should be emphasised that if these States have benefited the most in the post reforms period, their superior performance was not the result of any conscious policy of limiting the benefits of liberalisation to these States, as was the case for example in China, where liberalisation was deliberately limited to designated coastal zones. The superior performance of Gujarat and Maharashtra must therefore be attributed to the fact that the States were able to provide an environment most conducive to benefiting from the new policies.

Implications of Inter-State Inequality

The differences in per capita income and other indicators of social development across States have long attracted attention and for good reasons. Punjab, the richest State has a per capita SDP which is 5 times that of Bihar at the other end of the spectrum and although our Plans have never explicitly fixed targets for reducing these differences, there has always been an unstated assumption that inter-State differences would narrow with development. This can only happen if the poorer States actually grow faster than the richest States but the pattern of growth witnessed in the 1990s has been quite different, generating concern that we may be witnessing an increase in regional inequality, with the poorer States being left further behind.

According to Montek Ahluwalia, while inter-State inequality as measured by the gini-coefficient has clearly increased, the common perception that the rich States got richer and the poor States got poorer is not entirely accurate. A closer look at Table 8 shows a slightly more complex pattern of behaviour.

i. It is not true that all the richest States got richer relative to poorer States. Punjab and Haryana were the two richest of the 14 States in 1990-91. The growth rates of per capita SDP of these two States in the 1990s were not only lower than in the 1980s, but in both cases actually fell below the national average. Except for Bihar, UP and Orissa, all the other States therefore narrowed the per capita income gap with the two richest States.

ii. Maharashtra and Gujarat, which were just below Punjab and Haryana in terms of per capita income levels and therefore in the richer group, accelerated very significantly in the 1990s and grew at rates much higher than the national average.

iii. It is important to note that not all the poorer States lagged behind. Rajasthan, which was also one of the poorer States, experienced much stronger growth in per capita SDP, more than double that of the other poor States. Rajasthan's performance in terms of SDP growth is actually better than the average of the 14 States (see Table 8) but it slips below the average in per capita SDP growth because of higher rates of population growth.

iv. Performance of six middle income States (Tamil Nadu, Kerala, West Bengal, Madhya Pradesh, Andhra Pradesh and

Karnataka) was clustered around the average rate. All six of these States grew faster in terms of per capita GDP than they did in the 1980s, though in some cases the difference was very marginal.

Implications for Policy

What are the policy implications that follow from the pattern of growth observed in the 1990s? First, it is important to emphasise that the mere fact that States grow at different rates should not be viewed as a failure of policy. Given our size and diversity, it is unrealistic to expect that all States will grow at the same rate. Some may grow faster than others at certain times because they may be particularly well placed to exploit some new opportunity that arises. For example, the green revolution technology was peculiarly well suited to conditions in Punjab and Haryana and led to a spurt of growth in these States in the 1970s. Coastal States may have a locational advantage in a globalising world because they suffer less from the disadvantage imposed on hinter land States by our poor transport infrastructure. Finally, differences in growth may arise because some States are better managed and therefore able to create an environment which generates higher growth. Since the "pay off" from superior management has also increased because of liberalisation it is very likely that variations in the quality of economic management will lead to greater inter-State variation in management performance than was the case earlier.

It needs to be clearly understood that the objective of balanced regional development should not be pursued by following policies which seek to achieve equality through a process of "leveling down" by preventing States from reaching their full growth potential. On the contrary, well managed States must be encouraged to reach their full growth potential, if only to show what is possible in Indian conditions. The lessons learnt from their superior performance could then serve as a model for others to emulate. This process is bound to generate some differences in growth performance across States, but such differences can have a healthy demonstration effect with best practice being spread through emulation.

Accepting differences in growth performance across States does not however mean that we should passively accept the pathologically low growth rates witnessed in Bihar, UP and Orissa. Continuation of such low growth rates into the future for a group of States representing almost a third of the total population, while the rest of the country enjoys robust growth has alarming implications. It means that inter-State inequality would continue to increase and poverty would become even more regionally concentrated than it is today, an outcome which would be socially and politically explosive. It would not only affect the politics of these parts of the country but, because of their size, it would undoubtedly have a debilitating impact on the politics of the country as a whole.

It is therefore necessary to increase the rate of growth of per capita SDP in these States from around 1.5 per cent experienced in the 1990s to somewhere between 3.5 and 4 per cent. This requires the rate of growth of SDP to increase from a little over 3 per cent per annum observed in the 1990s to at least 6 per cent per annum. This doubling in the growth rate of SDP is clearly necessary to deal with regional inequality since, by definition, inequality will increase if the poorer States do not grow at least as fast as the national average. However the acceleration in growth is also needed to tackle the problem of poverty in these States. Because they account for a large proportion of national poverty there is a tendency to think that the solution to the poverty problem in these States lies in intensifying anti-poverty programmes. This approach misses the point that a sufficiently broad based expansion in income earning opportunities, of the kind needed to achieve a sustainable reduction in poverty can only come from a substantially higher rate of growth, including especially faster growth in the agricultural sector. It is true that high growth by itself may not be enough. It needs to be broad based and it also needs to be supplemented by targeted poverty alleviation schemes to take care of groups which are left out of the growth process. However, these schemes can only be a supplement to a high growth strategy and not a substitute for it.

The Role of the Central Government

Given the severe resources problem of the poorer States, it is natural to ask whether the Centre can provide additional financial help to the weaker States? The Centre's own fiscal position is also far from comfortable and this makes it difficult to envisage any significant expansion in these flows.

While the scope for providing additional resources from the Centre to help the poorer States is very limited, an issue which has not received the attention it deserves is whether the Centre should introduce mechanisms which might improve the effectiveness of the resources it provides to the States. At present, Central assistance in support of State Plans is transferred by the Planning Commission as a "block transfer" without any significant linkage to actual performance. This system of unconditional transfer could be replaced by a system in which a substantial part of the Central assistance to the States is made available with a more explicit linkage to performance conditions.

Conclusion

The process of development of the economy gained momentum during the 'nineties with the initiation of major economic reforms in 1991.

The economy has since then been successfully launched on to a higher growth trajectory and has registered an improvement in a number of macro-economic indicators in a short span of less than a decade.

The sectoral composition of GDP has undergone a change in the 'nineties. The services sector has come to occupy a place of prominence in terms of relative contribution to GDP.

The higher contribution of the services sector to GDP has a number of implications for the economy, the most important being the increased resilience of the economy, particularly, in times of adverse agricultural shocks.

BOX 1

EVOLUTION OF OFFICIAL NATIONAL ACCOUNTS STATISTICS IN INDIA

In August, 1949, the Government of India set up a High Powered Expert Committee popularly known as the 'National Income Committee' under the chairmanship of Professor P.C. Mahalanobis. Based on the methodology and the pattern of presentation recommended by this Committee, the first official estimates of national income with 1948-49 as the base year were prepared by the Central Statistical Organisation (CSO) and published in the *Estimates of National Income* in 1956. Ever since, the CSO has regularly continued to undertake a review of the methodology and the database used in the estimation of various aggregates. In the past, national accounts were revised decennially, changing the base to a year coinciding with the decennial population census. This was primarily because in the base year estimates, the information on work force played an important role and the work force estimates were obtained from the population census conducted decennially. Accordingly, the base years of the National Accounts Statistics series have been shifted from 1948-49 to 1960-61 in August 1967, from 1960-61 to 1970-71 in January 1978 and from 1970-71 to 1980-81 in February 1988.

The national income series with 1948-49 as the base commonly known as the 'conventional series' continued till 1966. The special feature of the revised series of national income with 1960-61 as base was the estimate of 'capital formation' and 'saving'. Accordingly, in 1969, two special Brochures viz., *National Income Statistics-Estimates of Capital Formation in India-1960-61 to 1965-66* were published. Subsequently, the aggregates of capital formation and saving formed an integral part of the national income series published annually by the CSO. In course of time, the coverage was further extended to include private consumption expenditure, factor incomes, and consolidated accounts of the nation and detailed accounts of the public sector. Accordingly, with effect from January 1975, the title of the publication on national income was changed to *National Accounts Statistics (NAS)* to depict the expanded scope of the publication. The revised series with 1970-71 as the base was published in *NAS 1978*. These estimates had the same scope, coverage and methodology as in the earlier estimates included in NAS. In 1988, CSO released a new series of national accounts with 1980-81 as the base year. This series, besides making use of the latest available data, undertook, *inter alia*, revision of estimates of consumption of fixed capital stock using the Perpetual Inventory Method. The coverage of the series was enlarged to include the state of Sikkim.

In February 1999, the CSO released a *New Series of National Accounts Statistics* with 1993-94 as the base year replacing the earlier series with 1980-81 as the base year. The CSO has used for the first time work force estimates based on National Sample Survey Organisation (NSSO)'s quinquennial survey on employment and unemployment (1993-94) instead of the work force estimates based on population census. This deviation was necessitated because in the population census, the work force (especially female work force in the rural areas) was not adequately captured.

Source : Report on Currency & Finance, 1998-99.

5

Planning in India

Development Strategy and Sustainable Growth

JUST after the attainment of independence, the Government of India set up the Planning Commission in 1950 to make an assessment of the material, capital and human resources of the country and to formulate a plan for its most effective and balanced utilization of the country's resources.

The First Five Year Plan was launched in 1951 and with this India embarked upon the programme of planned economic development of the country. The First Five Year Plan covered the period 1951-56 followed by the Second Plan (1956-61) and the Third Plan (1961-66). After a Plan Holiday following the severe impact of exogenous shocks such as hostilities with Pakistan and unprecedented drought for two successive years 1965-66 and 1966-67, the country resumed the Fourth Plan in 1969 covering the period 1969-74. Then came the Fifth Five Year Plan (1974-79) which did not complete its five years because of the change of party in power. With the coming into power of the Janta Party Government, the Sixth Five Year Plan was launched in 1978 covering the period 1978-83. Again, with the change in Government in 1980, the new Sixth Five Year Plan was started, covering the period 1980-85 and followed by the Seventh Plan (1985-90) which was completed by March-end, 1990. The Eighth Five Year Plan, to begin from April, 1990 covering the period 1990-95 could not be finalised and, again, we had two years of annual plans. After a gap of two years, the Eighth Plan was launched in April 1992, covering the period 1992-97 followed by the Ninth Plan in April 1997 covering the period 1997-2002 and the Tenth Five Year Plan (2002-07) launched in April 2002.

Objectives of Planning

The First Five Year Plan contains one of the clearest early formulations of the need for planning and of the State's role in it. Planning, it pointed out, involves "acceptance of a clearly defined set of objectives in terms of which to frame overall policies..., formulation of a strategy for promoting the realization of the ends defined..., and working out a rational solution to problems – an attempt to coordinate means and ends".

The launching of the First Five Year Plan in April 1951 initiated a process of development aimed not merely at raising the standards of living of the people but also opening out to them new opportunities for a richer and more varied life. This was sought to be achieved by planning for growth, and social justice.

The guiding principles of Indian Planning are infact provided by these objectives. Within this framework, each Five Year Plan involves such directional changes to take into account new constraints and new possibilities.

Growth

Rapid economic growth has been one of the basic objectives of planning. The basic measure of economic growth is the continuous increase in real national income and per capita income. Each plan set for itself a target for raising national income and per capita income. The target ranged from 2.2 per cent per annum in the First Five Year Plan to 6.5 per cent in the Ninth Five Year Plan. The 10th Five Year Plan proposes a target of 8 per cent GDP growth for the period 2002-07. The actual achievement during the plans has been anywhere between 2.7 per cent and 6.8 per cent (Table-1).

The growth of national income depends on a complex interaction of large number of variables, not all of which are amenable to government control. However, it is well known that the quantum of investment and the productivity of this investment, as measured in a simplified model by the capital output ratio, exercise an important influence on the overall growth rate. The deficiency in investment and the higher capital-output ratios are only the immediate arithmetical explanations for the shortfalls in the growth targets. A further analysis is necessary to identify the factors which would account for the departures from forecasts and targets for these two key magnitudes. Some part of the difference is attributable to a degree of unrealism in the forecasts; but in the case of investment and capital productivity, the explanation lies to a considerable extent in deficiencies in effective implementation of plans.

TABLE – 1

GROWTH PERFORMANCE IN THE FIVE YEAR PLANS
(PER CENT PER ANNUM)

		Target	*Actual*
1.	First Plan (1951-56)	2.1	3.61
2.	Second Plan (1956-61)	4.5	4.27
3.	Third Plan (1961-66)	5.6	2.84
4.	Three Annual Plans (1966-69)	–	3.9
5.	Fourth Plan (1969-74)	5.7	3.30
6.	Fifth Plan (1974-79)	4.4	4.80
7.	Sixth Plan (1980-85)	5.2	5.66
8.	Seventh Plan (1985-90)	5.0	6.01
9.	Two Annual Plans (1990-92)	–	3.3
10.	Eighth Plan (1992-97)	5.6	6.78
11.	Ninth Plan (1997-02)	6.5	5.6
12.	Tenth Plan (2002-07)	8.0	–

Source : Tenth Five Year Plan vol.1 (2002) P.24 (Table 2.1)
Economic Survey 2003-04.

The Ninth Plan emphasised the integral link between rapid economic growth and the quality of life of the masses and the need to continue high growth policies with the pursuit of the ultimate objective of improving policies which are pro-poor and are aimed at correction of historical inequalities. Thus as the Ninth Plan document puts it, "The focus of Ninth Plan can be described as Growth with Social Justice and Equity".[1]

Sustainable Growth

The Indian planning process has always laid emphasis on measures to ensure sustainability of the development process not only in economic terms, but also in terms of social and environmental factors. Much of the measures adopted in the Agenda 21 of the United Nations Conference on Environment and Development already find reflection

1. Planning Commission, *Ninth Five Year Plan, 1997-2002,* Vol-I, (1999) P.2.

in the Indian plans. The Ninth Plan was to carry this tradition further and consolidate on the creation of conditions for sustainable development. Rapidly growing population, urbanisation, changing agricultural, industrial and water resource management, increasing use of pesticides and fossil fuels have all resulted in perceptible deterioration in the quality and sustainability of the environment. It is recognised that environment protection does not only involve a prevention of pollution and of natural resource degradation, but has to be integrated with the overall development process and the well-being of people.

Tenth Plan: Growth, Equity and Sustainability

It is important to emphasise that the equity-related objectives of the Plan which are extremely important are intimately linked to the growth objective and attainment of one may not be possible without the attainment of the other. For example, high rates of growth are essential if we want to provide a sufficient expansion of sustainable high quality employment opportunities to our expanding labour force and ensure a sufficient increase in incomes of the poor and the disadvantaged. However, the relationship is not just a one way relationship. It is also true that sustained high growth rates may not be sustainable if they are not accompanied by a dispersion of purchasing power which can provide the demand needed to support the increase in output without having to rely excessively on external markets. External markets are an extremely important source of demand and these need to be tapped much more aggressively for many sectors. However, given the size of the economy and the present relative size of exports, much of the demand needed to support high growth will have to come from the domestic economy itself.

Although growth has strong direct poverty reducing effects, the frictions and rigidities in parts of the Indian economy can make these processes less effective, and the Tenth Plan must therefore be formulated in a manner which explicitly addresses the need to ensure equity and social justice. There are several ways in which this can be achieved.

(i) First, agricultural development must be viewed as a core element of the Plan since growth in this sector is likely to lead to the widest spread of benefits especially to the rural poor including agricultural labour. Also, since the majority of women workers are engaged in agriculture, investments in this sector have enormous implications for gender equality and must be designed to have maximal impact on this dimension.

The first generation of reforms concentrated on reforms in the industrial economy and reforms in the agricultural sector were neglected. This must change in the Tenth Plan.

(ii) Second, the growth strategy of the Tenth Plan must ensure rapid growth of those sectors which are most likely to create high quality employment opportunities and deal with the policy constraints which discourage growth of employment. Particular attention must be paid to the policy environment influencing a wide range of economic activities which have a large employment potential. These include sectors, such as construction, real estate & housing, transport, SSI, modern retailing, entertainment, IT enabled services and a range of other new services, which need to be promoted through supportive policies. An activity, which has potential to stimulate most of these sectors through backward and forward linkages, is tourism. Development of this activity requires coordination across a wide range of agencies. The Tenth Plan must ensure realisation of the full potential of this activity.

(iii) Third, there will be a continuing need to supplement the impact of growth with special programmes aimed at special target groups which may not benefit sufficiently from the normal growth process. Such programmes have long been part of our development strategy and they will have to continue in the Tenth Plan. However, it is important to ensure that they are effective in achieving their objectives. Women being the most vulnerable group within every category, there is an urgent need to review the outcomes and impacts of on-going programmes of "social safety nets" for women, and redesign them as necessary to ensure that they advance gender equality goals.

To summarise, the broad objectives and targets of the Tenth Plan can be described as achieving an average rate of growth of GDP of 8 per cent, along with specific focus on a few key measures of human development. The aggregate growth target should ensure a broad based development which meets the objectives of equity and sustainability. The Plan should also specify state specific growth and development targets which take into account the constraints operating in individual states.

Development and growth are long term processes, and a five year plan represents only the characterisation of the economy and social processes over a period in which a fair degree of reliance can be placed on estimates and projections. The viability and sustainability of the development strategy embodied in a five year plan needs to be seen in the longer perspective in order to ensure that continuity of directions and the balance between interests of the present and the future generations is maintained.

BOX 1

Monitorable Targets for the Tenth Plan and Beyond

- Reduction of poverty ratio by 5 percentage points by 2007 and by 15 percentage points by 2012;
- Providing gainful and high-quality employment at least to addition to the labour force over the Tenth Plan period;
- All children in school by 2003; all children to complete 5 years of schooling by 2007;
- Reduction in gender gaps in literacy and wage rates by at least 50 per cent by 2007;
- Reduction in the decadal rate of population growth between 2001 and 2011 to 16.2 per cent;
- Increase in Literacy rates to 75 per cent within the Plan period;
- Reduction of Infant mortality rate (IMR) to 45 per 1000 live births by 2007 and to 28 by 2012;
- Reduction of Maternal mortality ratio (MMR) to 2 per 1000 live births by 2007 and to 1 by 2012;
- Increase in forest and tree cover to 25 per cent by 2007 and 33 per cent by 2012;
- All villages to have sustained access to potable drinking water within the Plan period;
- Cleaning of all major polluted rivers by 2007 and other notified stretches by 2012.

Modernisation

The objective of modernisation was explicitly mentioned as one of the objectives of Planning in the Sixth Plan Document. It states, "the term 'modernisation' connotes a variety of structural and institutional changes in the framework of economic activity. A shift in the sectoral composition of production, diversification of activities, an advancement of technology and institutional innovations have all been part of the drive to change a feudal and colonial economy into a modern and independent entity."

Progress towards Modernisation

The composition of national income has changed steadily over the planning period. The share of agriculture in GDP has declined from 50 per cent in 1951 to 25 per cent in 2001 increasing the share of mining, manufacturing, construction, productive infrastructure and other services from 18.8 per cent in 1950-51 to 75 per cent in 2001-02.[2]

Industry

The main component in the drive for structural diversification has been the effort to promote industrial growth and diversification. This effort commenced effectively with the Second Plan which, along with the Industrial Policy Resolution of 1956, articulated explicitly the objective of rapid industrialisation. Apart from rapid growth, this strategy involved certain other key components viz. a shift in the industrial structure towards industries producing basic materials and capital goods and the growth of the public sector in industry.

At Independence we inherited an industrial structure that was restricted to a few industries like textiles and sugar. The first steel plant had been set up and there was some limited development of engineering in railway workshops and assembly plants. The drive to diversify this structure, a drive linked to the search for self-reliance, has been the keynote of the industrial strategy of our plans. The relative share in industrial production of the traditional manufacturing sectors like food and textiles has declined and that of new sectors like chemicals and engineering has increased very substantially. In terms of sophistication of technology and the range of goods manufactured an extensive degree of industrial diversification has been achieved.

The organisation of industry has also undergone a major change with the development of the public sector. Between 1960-61 and 1977-78, the share of the public sector in the value added in mining and organised manufacturing grew from 8.1 per cent to 28.9 per cent. The development of the public sector has been the principal element in our drive for industrial diversification and in industries like steel, non-ferrous metals, petroleum, fertilisers, petrochemicals and heavy

---

2. for details see Ch. 4.

engineering, public sector units play a dominant role.

The industrial policy of the Government accepted the important role of the private sector and an elaborate network of institution has been established to support it and to regulate its activities. A major component of the support system is the network of development banking institutions which have been established to finance private investment in industry. This aspect has been well emphasised in the tenth plan.

Agriculture

The tasks of modernisation and structural change in agriculture were even more difficult and discouraging at the start of the planning era. The outmoded land tenure system, the primitive technology of cultivation and lack of an infrastructure for raising productivity proved formidable barriers to agricultural advance. The fact that these barriers have been overcome to an extent is one of the major successes of our planning effort. Zamindari and other intermediary tenures have been almost eliminated. The technology of cultivation has changed substantially with the spread of high-yielding varieties and the extension of irrigation, a change which was facilitated by the elaborate network of agricultural research and extension set up during the planning era. One further change of consequence is the establishment of a system of support prices, procurement and public distribution. Significant progress has been made not only in the production of major foodgrains but also in horticultural crops like apples and animal products like eggs, milk and fish.

Some data on the indicators of modernisation in agriculture are presented in (table 8 ch. 13). The growth in irrigation is a common feature which runs through the plans though the pace of expansion in recent years is far higher than before. The use of the new technology based on high yielding varieties and fertilisers spread rapidly only after 1965.[3] This difference is reflected in the larger contribution of productivity gain to production growth in the period after 1964-65.

Several changes have taken place in agricultural credit and marketing. The system of cooperative credit has spread, lessening the dependence of the cultivator on exploitative money-lending and trading practices. Institutional term finance for agriculture has growth with the reorientation of the banking system and the establishment of Land Development Banks, Regional Rural Banks and apex institutions like the Agriculture Refinance and Development Corporation. In agricultural

3. For more details see Ch. 13.

marketing, the dominant role of the Food Corporation of India in foodgrain trade and the growth of marketing and processing cooperatives have helped both farmers and consumers. In the case of milk, cooperatives and urban milk supply schemes have captured, a substantial part of the market. These and other changes in the field of credit and marketing have altered the very unequal relationship between the farmer and the trader and, by doing so, have stimulated agricultural progress. (for details, see ch. 17)

TABLE – 2

GROWTH RATE OF AREA, PRODUCTION AND YIELD

		Foodgrains		*Non-foodgrains*	
Sl. No.	*Item*	*1949-50 to 1964-65*	*1964-65 to 1978-79*	*1949-50 to 1964-65*	*1964-65 to 1978-79*
(0)	*(1)*	*(2)*	*(3)*	*(4)*	*(5)*
1	Area	1.4	0.6	2.5	0.8
2	Production	3.0	3.4	3.5	2.6
3	Yield	1.4	2.3	1.0	1.3

Financial Sector

The mobilisation of savings and their use in preferred directions is a crucial element in any development effort. Thus, primitive processes of accumulation in which households and small enterprises invest their savings directly in their own activities or in currency hoards have given way to more complex forms in which, through financial intermediaries and capital markets, households savings can be channelled into a much wider variety of activities.

The pattern of utilisation of savings has been influenced by several innovations like the development banks for industry and agriculture and the system of cooperative credit.

Planning implies state intervention in economic matters which involves not just a few big projects but also a large number of small works and programmes directed at individuals. At Independence we inherited a patchy administrative structure oriented towards maintenance of law and order and revenue administration. Over the planning period an elaborate development administration has been built up from the village, through the block and district to the secretariat level. Though there are deficiencies in this structure in terms of motivation, probity and efficiency, it atleast provides a point of contact between the government and the household or the enterprise. A further change has been introduced by the establishment of panchayati raj which, in many states, plays an important role in development administration.

Over fifty years of planning, the structure of the Indian economy, the technology of production in agriculture and industry and the institution framework within which economic activities are conducted have changed substantially. The bedrock on which these changes are based lies in the tremendous growth in human skills and, because of this firm base, the forces of modernisation and technological advance are firmly entrenched in all sectors of the economy even though the pace of diffusion varies from one sector to another and from one region to another. The major problems at present lie not in any lack of institutions or persons for the tasks at hand but in their effectiveness and in some parts of the institutional framework there is a mismatch between form and function which needs to be corrected.

Self-Reliance

Self-reliance is very often confused with self-sufficiency. Self-sufficiency implies that a country produces all goods and services it requires within the country without having to import them. Self-reliance on the other hand, implies that a country has sufficient foreign exchange reserves to pay for its imports. Thus, while self-sufficiency rules out imports, self-reliance allows a country to import provided it has the capacity to pay for it. In the days of globalisation, no country can be self-sufficient but a country can be self-reliant by paying for everything it imports.

Self-reliance did not receive high priority in the first two plans and was not listed as one of the objectives of planning. The emphasis was on self-sufficiency in food grains in the First Plan and the Second Plan adopted import substitution based industrialisation so that India became self-sufficient in capital goods and basic and heavy industries.

The concept of self-reliance adopted in the Third Plan was to do away with the need for external assistance. It stated that the balance of payment difficulties that the country is facing are not short term or temporary; they will continue for several years to come. External assistance is essential for this period but the aim must be to make the economy more and more self-reliant so that it is able to support within a period of 10 to 12 years an adequate scale of investment from its own production and savings. Normal inflow of foreign capital may continue but reliance on special forms of external assistance has to be reduced progressively and eliminated.[4]

Although the Third Plan was considered an important landmark in the country's advance towards self-reliance, in practice the country could neither reduce its balance of payment deficit nor its dependence on external assistance. Infact, external assistance accounted for 26 per cent of the total plan outlay during the Third Plan as compared to 22.5 per cent during the Second Plan. During the period of Annual Plans 1966-69, external assistance provided 36.4 per cent of the total plan outlay.

The Fourth Plan concretised the goal of self-reliance and laid down the time phasing for its realisation. It stated, "dependence on foreign aid will be greatly reduced in the course of the Fourth Plan. It is planned to do away with concessional imports of food grains under P L 480 by 1971. Foreign aid net of debt charges and interest payments will be reduced to about half by the end of the Fourth Plan compared to the current level." It further added, national self-reliance and growth with stability can be attained only if additional effort is put forward at every level; Planned increase in the production of food grains, raw materials and manufactured goods are calculated to make it possible to limit the growth of other inputs to manageable proportion. A sustained increase of exports by about seven per cent a year is another essential element of strategy in the Fourth Plan to secure balance on foreign account and approach speedily towards the goal of self-reliance.

Under the *Fifth Plan*, a high priority was accorded to export promotion and a number of new measures were adopted to boost up exports. Import control also received particular attention. The Planning Commission once again hopefully stated that "by 1985-86 we would be in a position to meet the maximum of our foreign exchange requirements, including debt service charges, from our own resources, thus obviating the need for any significant inflow of concessional aid."

The external assistance as a percentage of plan outlay was 12.2 per cent in the Fifth plan which was more or less at the same level as in the Fourth Plan.

The *Sixth Plan* considered removal of poverty and achievement of self-reliance as its two main objectives. The strategy of the Sixth Plan assumed a considerable degree of import substitution in a number of

4. Planning Commission, *Third Five Year Plan, (1956-1961)* P.115.

industries, namely, steel, cement, fertilisers, crude oil and capital equipment of all brands including electronics. The Plan was against indiscriminate import substitution as such a policy was bound to be counter productive. *The Plan emphasised efficient import substitution so as to improve India's balance of payment as well as national income.*

Elaborating on the successes achieved in the area of self-reliance, the *Seventh Plan* states "The pursuit of self-reliance with growth now requires a faster growth of export earnings." Throughout Seventh Plan period the balance of payment situation remained grim. The ratio of current account deficit to GDP was 2.4 per cent, much higher than the projected figure of 1.6 per cent in the plan document. In 1990-91, the difficult balance of payments situation acquired a crisis proportion when in June 1991, India's foreign exchange reserves declined to a level sufficient only to meet 13 days import requirements. Thus, during the Eighth Plan period Government of India undertook various stabilisation measures and structural reforms. These have certainly reduced the strain on balance of payments.

Self-Reliance in the Ninth Plan

The Ninth Plan (1997-2002) stated, self-reliance as one of the four important dimension of state policy. "India has embarked on a process of gradual and phased opening of its economy to take advantage of new opportunities in trade and investment. While this process needs to be continued and taken forward, it should be from a position of strength and not through either external compulsions or a lack of alternatives. In this sense, 'Self-reliance' must remain an important component of development policy and strategy."

Detailing the concept of economic self-reliance, the draft of Ninth Plan stated: "The first, and perhaps most important, component of self-reliance is to ensure balance of payments sustainability and avoidance of excessive external debt. This end can be best served by a focus on expanding the export base of the nation. In a market-based system, micro-level decision making by private economic agents can collectively lead to excessive draft on the foreign exchange resources of the nation and growing external debt. It is the responsibility of the government to create the conditions by which such tendencies can be corrected by the agents themselves. A framework of prudent macro-management and greater reliance on non-debt creating external flows for financing balance of payments needs are aspects of such conditions."[5]

---

5. Ninth Five Year Plan 1997-2002 (1998) Vol.1, p.10.

Elucidating further the recourse to external assistance to finance development, the Ninth Plan categorically states, "Accelerating the growth of the economy will require a significant step up in the availability of investible resources. Self-reliance demands that most of these resources should be generated domestically and recourse to external sources be resorted to the extent dictated by a sustainable proportion of external liabilities." Again, it mentions: "Self-reliance in food is a basic element in any strategy of self-reliance."

On the question of technological self-reliance, the Ninth Plan stated in a very forthright manner: "A critical element of self-reliance is self-reliance in technology. While it is desirable to access the best and most appropriate technologies from wherever they are available, in the long-run it is necessary that domestic capacity is developed in respect of all critical technologies needed by the country."

Social Justice

The objective of social justice as articulated in the plans has two major dimensions. The first dimension is an improvement in the living standards of the poorest groups in society and second is a reduction in inequalities in asset distribution. Poverty alleviation and raising average standard of living have been the central aims of economic planning in India.

THE DEVELOPMENT STRATEGY

According to I.G.Patel "Strategy implies essentially a deliberate choice – a choice of the point and timing and manner of attack on the problem at hand"? Resources in underdeveloped countries being scarce, it is essential to identify the leading sectors and deploy the scarce resources there rather than thinly diffusing the resources all over. An economy which has stagnated for a long time can not grow unless a 'big push' is given to it. The Indian economy needed this kind of push when the country got independence in 1947.

Structural Constraints and the Development Strategy

According to Chakravarti[6] "The underlying causes of structural backwardness were perceived as follows. First, the basic constraint on development was seen as being an acute deficiency of material capital,

6. S. Chakravarti, *Development Planning, The Indian Experience*, (1989) Ch.2, P.9.

which prevented the introduction of more productive technologies. Secondly, the limitation on the speed of capital accumulation was seen to lie in the low capacity to save. Thirdly, it was assumed that even if the domestic capacity to save could be raised by means of suitable fiscal and monetary policies, there were structural limitations preventing conversion of savings into productive investment. Fourthly, it was assumed that whereas agriculture was subject to secular diminishing returns, industrialization would allow surplus labour currently underemployed in agriculture to be more productively employed in industries which operated according to increasing returns to scale. A fifth assumption was that if the market mechanism were accorded primacy, this would result in excessive consumption by the upper-income groups, along with relative under-investment in sectors essential to the accelerated development of the economy. Sixthly, while unequal distribution of income was considered to be a 'bad thing', a precipitate transformation of the ownership of productive assets was held to be detrimental to the maximization of production and savings. In other words, there was a tolerance towards income inequality, provided it was not excessive and could be seen to result in a higher rate of growth than would be possible otherwise."

Given all these perceptions, it was felt that economic theory indicated that the basic questions relating to how much to save, where to invest, and in what forms to invest could be best handled with the help of a plan.

"It will be observed from the above that the Indian planners subscribed to a basically supply-side view of the planning problem. The argument that domestic demand can possibly be a constraint on the growth process was not even mentioned as a hypothesis that needed to be rejected. The reason, presumably, was the belief that with an active state policy on investment, all possible slack in the economic system would be utilized. Statistically considered, the argument was right. There was little Keynesian-type unemployment in India in the early fifties. There was consequently justification for concentrating on factors promoting savings or productive accumulation. Indian planners could at that stage maintain that what mattered most was growth in the aggregate level of investment. That led them to look into areas where public investment could be more fruitfully deployed, in the long term. There were three major possibilities which could be expected to balance supply with demand along a growing trend.

First, public investment would be concentrated in the area of infrastructure.

Secondly, public investment could be directed primarily towards agriculture.

Thirdly, public investment could be directed primarily towards industrial development.

Indian planners obviously did attempt all three, as any reasonable planner can be expected to do in such situations. The First Five-Year Plan (1950-55) focused on the first two types of investment. At the time of the Second Five-Year Plan (1955-60), however, a major change was brought about. Indian planners operated on the assumption of a low elasticity of export demand accompanied by a system of strict import allocation. Thus they were in reality operating on the assumption of a nearly closed economy. In such an economy, if savings were to be substantially raised from a low initial level of around 5 per cent in 1950 to 20 per cent in 1975, inter-sectoral consistency over time would demand that the productive capacity of the capital goods sector would have to rise at an accelerated rate to convert growing savings into additional real investment. *It was therefore the need to raise the real savings rate that led Indian planners to accord primacy to a faster rate of growth in the capital goods sector, although doubtless there could have been other considerations such as building up defence capability.*

"Indian planners ignored the trade option as a major source of growth? The issue was posed at the time when the Second Five-Year Plan was formulated. A projection of the balance of trade was attempted in the plan document, and the planners concluded that no significant increase in export earnings in the short run could be expected. However, they recognised that 'it is only after industrialization has proceeded some way that increased production will be reflected in larger export earnings...."

"The argument, briefly, was as follows. The development of a heavy capital goods base over a period of time would lead to the diversification of the export basket in the direction of manufactured goods, including machinery and equipment; while the increase in employment, leading to an expanded demand for consumer goods, would be met by pursuing 'capital-light' methods of production."[7]

The 1956 Industrial Policy Resolution emphasized that the state must play a progressive role in the development of Industries and as the Resolution puts it "the adoption of socialist pattern of society as the national objective, as well as the need for planned and rapid

---

7. S. Chakravarti (1989) op. cit., P.16.

development require that all industries of basic and strategic importance, or in the nature of public utility services, should be in the public sector. Other industries which are essential and require invesment on a scale which only the state, in present circumstances, could provide, have also to be in the public sector. The state has, therefore, to assume direct responsibility for the future development of industries over a wider area." The encouragement of labour-intensive forms of producing mass consumer goods was seen to be a potentially important way of reconciling the conflict between emphasis on heavy industry (which would generate faster growth of income and employment in the long run) and the need to generate adequate jobs for the currently unemployed and underemployed in the transitional period.

The dominant growth orientation was articulated in the Mahalanobis strategy of the Second Plan and continued into the Third Plan. Thus the economic growth was expected to take place through the modern industrialization. The industrialization in turn, was expected to be a replica of the same processes that had taken place in the historical past in the advanced countries. However, the relatively greater emphasis on the long-term growth in an import-substitution oriented strategy required a modification in the industrialization process. This consisted of a strong accent on the creation of domestic capacity in the direction of producing capital goods to produce more capital goods. In this strategy, the public sector was expected to play a dual role of (a) promoting the growth of infrastructural facilities and the creation of capacity in the basic and heavy industries and (b) reducing the concentration of economic power through the expansion of public ownership of means of production.

An attempt was made with a reasonable success in implementing the long-term growth maximizing Mahalanobis strategy during the second and the third Five Year Plans. There was, as a result, a considerable acceleration in public sector investment in infrastructure (roads, railways, major and medium irrigation) and indirect productive investments in universal intermediates like steel, coal, power and heavy electrical machinery. Although the encouragement to the cottage, village and small scale industries as a means of providing employment as well as expanding the supplies of consumer goods were conceived as part of this strategy, very little was achieved in this regard. Similar was the fate in regard to the policies towards the reduction of inequalities.

In terms of the aggregate performance, this phase recorded a fairly sustained 8 to 10 per cent compound growth rate of industrial output, 3 to 3.5 per cent compound growth rate in the foodgrains output and around 1.75 per cent growth rate in per capita income. All these growth rates represented a sharp acceleration over the pre-Independence past. A diversified industrial structure came to be established. This was taken to be a success of the planning efforts. Planning was regarded during this period as a "going."[8]

Thus the first phase spanning roughly over the first three Five Year Plan periods was characterized by fairly sustained growth in per capita incomes, distinct acceleration in public sector investment and in the growth of industrial output. This phase was dominated *by the growth oriented development strategy.*

Changing Perceptions

This atmosphere changed dramatically after the drought and the foreign exchange crisis of the mid-sixties. The sudden increase in defence expenditure consequent to the armed conflicts with China and Pakistan and the levelling-off of foreign aid, all in the short span of three years (1962-65), put the economy under severe strain. A crisis occurred when two consecutive droughts hit the country in 1966 and 1967 and real GDP declined in absolute terms.

The sharp deterioration of the economic situation and the security environment highlighted two main weaknesses of the existing strategy, namely, the relative neglect of agriculture and a critical dependence on foreign aid. Under the stress of circumstances some policy changes were made to encourage growth. These included a greater role for price incentives, the relaxation of some controls on the private sector to enable it to play a larger part in the economy, and greater emphasis on export promotion. The decision to devalue the rupee in 1966 was part of the same process of policy revision. Changes in policies were required not only to meet the domestic crisis but also to take advantage of opportunities provided by new agricultural technologies and the unprecedented increase in the volume of world trade.

The two-year period 1965 and 1966 witnessed the worst drought in recent memory and consequent famines in large parts of north India. At the same time, all aid was cut off to India by the donor countries on account of the Indo-Pakistan War of 1965, including food aid. The consequence was a virtual collapse of the economy, and recourse had to be taken to extraordinary financing from the International Monetary

8. S.D. Tendulkar, *Indian Development Strategy : Compulsions and Constraints*, in Uma Kapila (ed), op. cit.

Fund (IMF) and the World Bank, which were accompanied by stiff conditionalities.

This traumatic experience brought food security into the forefront of our policy imperatives, which was further buttressed by the observation that sustained industrialization was not possible without adequate provision of wage-goods. The Fourth Plan, conceived after three years of Plan Holiday, therefore, had to have food security as its centre-piece.

The Fifth Plan recognized that growth and industrialization would not necessarily improve the living conditions of the people, particularly the poor. The concepts of "minimum needs" and directed anti-poverty programmes were innovations of this Plan, whatever may have been the success achieved in implementing them effectively. The Fifth Plan also marks the beginning of a period of steady increase in the growth rate of the economy, which continued right through to the Eighth Plan.

The Sixth Plan for the first time recognized that the success of the Mahalanobis heavy industrialization strategy in raising the savings rate of the country had created a situation where excess capacities were becoming evident in certain industries. A shift in the pattern of industrialization, with lower emphasis on heavy industries and more on infrastructure, begins here. The Seventh Plan represents the culmination of this shift. In perspective, it may justifiably be termed as the infrastructure plan. *It was also during this period that a reappraisal of the import-substitution strategy begins, and a gradual liberalisation of the Indian economy is initiated.*

The Eighth Plan was overtaken by the crisis of 1991, and the economic reforms that came in its wake. The dramatic events and policy initiatives of the two-year plan holiday period between 1990 and 1992 demanded a full reappraisal of the planning methodology, and the Eighth Plan represents the first efforts at planning for a market-oriented economy.

The Planning Commission had by then also accepted the flaws of the 'big push-high growth' strategy and actively supported the political initiatives for expansion of anti-poverty programmes. But instead of ensuring that these programmes were properly targeted and efficiently implemented, it made them 'soft' by making them subsidy-intensive and failed to check the growing central control over these programmes. The role of the Planning Commission as a force in favour of greater mobilization and efficient use of resources was weakened in the process.

The Development Strategy : Ninth Five Year Plan

Referring to the development strategy, the Ninth Plan states "The gradual shift in development strategy that has occurred since the early 1980s in India is now at a stage where it needs to be articulated fully and unambiguously." Although India has always had a vibrant private sector and a functioning market economy, the role of the government has been dominant, not only as a significant investor and producer of goods and services in its own right, but also as an arbiter of the action of the private sector. The former role will have to continue in the foreseeable future, since the economy is still not at a stage where the most pressing needs of public goods and services have been met in adequate measure. Nor for that matter are the private sector and the peoples' organisations at a stage where they can shoulder the responsibilities of meeting these needs. In so far as the latter role is concerned, it too will have to continue, but its manner and content will need to change. In the development strategy of earlier years, government intervention was overly focused on guidance through prevention. As a consequence, there was insufficient room for market signals to determine the course of private behaviour. Greater reliance on market forces and people's initiatives implies that the focus of government action will have to shift towards evolving transparent and unambiguous policies with limited scope for discretionary action, greater decentralisation and improved monitoring and enforcement systems.

An important component of government intervention in markets is in the area of promoting the degree of competition. An important source of inadequate competition and inefficient markets is the lack of adequate and appropriate information being available to all concerned.

Greater reliance on the market is only one facet of the process of decentralisation which is at the heart of the development strategy. Equally important is the decentralisation within the government system itself. The Ninth Plan is based on the concept of cooperative federalism whereby much greater freedom would be given to states to determine not only their own priorities but also the modalities of public intervention and provisions of goods and services. This concept also embodies a higher degree of dialogue and coordination between the states. The central government's principal role in this regard would be to raise the issues which appear to be of national interest and to provide a forum for arriving at a consensus.

The development strategy also has to take cognisance of the changing role of the public sector in general in the allocation of responsibilities for harmonious development of the economy. In order to effectively discharge the altered responsibilities, the structure of not only public investment but also of public assets have to be changed in a significant way. Investments which have been made in areas which can be effectively discharged by peoples'organisations and the private sector, need to be gradually turned over to the appropriate organisations. The resources thus released can then be devoted to building up assets and facilities in such areas where private investments are likely to be either absent or inadequate. It is in this context that the portfolio of public sector undertakings at both the Centre and the States would need to be examined and decisions regarding divestment and reorientation would need to be taken.

The Development Strategy: Tenth Plan

The Tenth Plan provides an opportunity, at the start of the new millennium, to build upon the gains of the past and also to address the weaknesses that have emerged. There is growing impatience in the country at the fact that a large number of our people continue to live in abject poverty and there are alarming gaps in social attainments even after five decades of planning. To meet this challenge squarely, the Tenth Plan must learn from past experience. It must strengthen what has worked well, and at the same time also avoid repeating past mistakes. There must be willingness to modify policies and institutions based on past experience, keeping in mind the changes that have taken place in the Indian economy and in the rest of the world.

An important aspect of the redefinition of strategy that is needed relates to the role of government. This redefinition is necessary both at the Central Government level and also at State Government level. It is now generally recognised that government in the past tended to take on too many responsibilities, imposing severe strains on its limited financiai and administrative capabilities and also stifling individual initiative. An all-pervasive Government role may have been necessary at a stage where private sector capabilities were undeveloped, but the situation has changed dramatically in this respect. India now has a strong and vibrant private sector. The public sector is much less dominant than it used to be in many critical sectors and its relative position is likely to decline further as Government ownership in many existing public sector organisations is expected to decline substantially. *It is clear that industrial growth in future will depend largely upon the performance of the private sector and our policies must therefore provide an environment which is conducive to such growth.*

This is not to say that government has no role to play, or only a minimalist role, in promoting development. On the contrary, Government has a very important role indeed, but a different one from that envisaged in the past. There are many areas, e.g. the social sectors, where its role will clearly have to expand. There are other areas, e.g. infrastructure development, where gaps are large and the private sector cannot be expected to step in significantly. In these areas, the role of Government may have to be expanded and restructured. It will have to expand in some areas of infrastructure development which are unlikely to attract private investment, e.g. rural infrastructure and road development. In others, e.g. telecommunications, power, ports, etc., the private sector can play a much greater role, provided an appropriate policy framework is in place. Here, the role of the government needs to change to facilitate such investment as much as possible while still remaining a public sector service provider for quite some time. In all these areas, the role of the government as a regulator ensuring a fair deal for consumers, transparency and accountability, and a level playing field is also extremely important.

Agriculture as Centre-piece of Development Strategy

The Tenth Five Year Plan reflects a subtle shift in our development perspective, but a shift which can have far-reaching implications. The fundamental message conveyed by the Plan is that the agricultural sector can no longer be treated as being a residual or peripheral component of our growth path, but must take centre-stage of all our development efforts. This recognition stems from two important observations. First, our experience since the mid-1980s, and more particularly since the initiation of economic reforms in the early 1990s, strongly indicates that the Indian industrial sector has reached a stage of maturity whereby it no longer requires focussed attention of the Government, whether for promotion or protection. Our industrial and commercial entrepreneurs are perfectly capable of generating high growth rates in industry on their own, and the government needs only to play a facilitative role by creating a conducive policy environment. It has become increasingly clear that there is tremendous potential that remains untapped in our agricultural economy.

In the Tenth Plan, therefore, agriculture is projected to be the centre-piece of our development strategy. Its importance is highlighted in three distinct components of the broad objectives of the development strategy articulated in the Plan. First, it is viewed as being essential for the acceleration of the overall growth rate of our economy, not only by achieving a high rate of growth itself, but also through pulling up the growth rates of other sectors through a widespread distribution of purchasing-power and consequently of demand for industrial products and services. This represents a virtual inversion of the "trickle-down" theory, and embodies a belief that high agricultural growth can itself be an engine of growth.

Second, agricultural growth is recognized to be the surest way to bring about equity in income and wealth, so that an accelerating growth rate will be reflected in rapid reduction in the incidence of poverty. The evidence for this is overwhelming, both from our own and from international experiences.

Finally, it is central to all our efforts at self-reliance. No country can call itself secure unless it has food security, not only in the aggregate, but also at the level of every household and, indeed, every individual. Food security in a macro sense has influenced our development policy for over thirty years now, but its link with household incomes and intra-household distribution has received less than adequate recognition.

There is no alternative but to focus on raising the productivity of our land, water and, most importantly, human resources in a manner which is sustainable over the longer term.

Summing up

Summing up the development strategy, we may quote K.C. Pant, "the imperatives for development planning in India have changed from time to time, and the planning system has attempted to keep pace with the change. Indian planning is not quite as wooden and hide-bound as it is sometimes made out to be, and that it has been sensitive to the changes that have taken place in the objective conditions of the Indian economy."

"India's development strategy, like that of most other developing countries, has evolved over successive plan periods, reflecting the growing strength of our economy, structural transformations taking place in the domestic economy and also developments in the world economy. In the early stages of development planning, government was viewed as the principal actor in development exercising strict control over private investment, ensuring a dominant role for the public sector in all important industries. Trade policy tended to be inward oriented focusing on industrial development through import substitution which was encouraged through a tight control over imports and maintenance of high tariffs. The limitations of this strategy became evident by the end of the 1970s and early 1980s when it became clear that these policies reduced efficiency and competitiveness and growth was much lower than targeted. While government was over-active in industry, it was underactive in many areas, especially relating to social development and this was reflected in a very slow pace of improvement in critical social indicators."[9]

Some efforts were made to reform the system in the second half of the 1980s to address the shortcomings in our development strategy. However it was not until 1991 that a wide ranging programme of economic reforms aimed at decontrolling and debureaucratising the economy was initiated. These reforms have been pursued by successive governments since 1991 and enjoy a broad base of support. They have also yielded good results thus far. There is no doubt that the Indian economy has responded well to the change in policy direction and the growth rate increased from 5.8 per cent in the Seventh Plan (1985 to 1990) to about 6.5 per cent in the Eighth Plan and Ninth Plan making India one of the ten fastest growing developing countries. Encouraging progress has also been made in other dimensions. The percentage of the population in poverty has continued to decline, even if not as much as was targeted. Population growth has decelerated below 2 per cent for the first time in four decades. Literacy has increased from 52 per cent in 1991 to 65 per cent in 2001 and the improvement is evident in all States. Sectors such as software services and IT enabled services have emerged as new sources of strength creating confidence about India's potential to be competitive in the world economy.

These positive developments are, however, clouded by other features which give cause for concern. The economy is currently in a decelerating phase and urgent steps are needed to arrest the deceleration and restore momentum. This reversal is all the more difficult because it has to take place in an environment where the world economy is slowing down. There are several aspects of development where our progress is clearly disappointing. Although employment growth has almost kept pace with the labour force growth, the incidence of unemployment on Current Daily Status basis is relatively high at above 7 per cent. More than half of the children 1-5 years old in rural areas are undernourished, with girl children suffering even more severe malnutrition. The infant mortality rate has stagnated at 72 per 1000 for the last several years.

---

9. Planning Commission, *Ninth Five Year Plan 1997-2002* Vol-1 (1999) P.2, Para 1.7.

As many as 60 per cent of rural households and about 20 per cent of urban households do not have a power connection. Only 60 per cent of urban households have taps within their homes, and far fewer have latrines inside the house. Deterioration in urban environment, increase in slum population, and in air, river and water pollution has vastly affected the quality of life of the urban poor. Land and forest degradation in the rural areas, and over-exploitation of groundwater is seriously threatening sustainability of food production.[10]

The Tenth Plan according to the Planning Commission provides an opportunity, at the start of the new millennium, to build upon the gains of the past but also to address the weaknesses that have emerged. We must be willing to modify policies and institutions based on past experience, keeping in mind the changes that have taken place in the Indian economy and in the rest of the world.

10. Planning Commission, Approach Paper to the Tenth Five Year Plan (2002-07).

6

Structural Adjustment in the Indian Economy

The Background

AFTER pursuing an inward-looking development strategy with the state assuming an important role for more than four decades, India decided to take a historic step of changing tracks in 1991. It embarked on a comprehensive reform of the economy to widen and deepen its integration with the world economy as a part of structural adjustment. There seems to be a general consensus on the desirability of reforms to dismantle the bureaucratic regulatory apparatus evolved over the years that may have outlived its utility. However, there has been considerable debate on the contents of the reform package, their sequencing and the pace, their implementation and their impact.

After a period of relatively robust economic performance in the late 1980s, the Indian economy entered into a period of unprecedented liquidity crisis during 1990-91. This crisis was a combined effect of a number of events coinciding. These included collapse of the Soviet Union that had emerged as India's major trading partner. The Gulf War that erupted in January 1991 worsened the balance of payments crisis not only with rising oil prices but also by causing a virtual stoppage of remittances from Indian workers in the Gulf. These events coupled with political uncertainty prevailing in the country led international credit rating agencies to lower India's rating both for short and long-term borrowings. The erosion of international confidence in the Indian economy not only made borrowings in international markets difficult but also led to outflow of deposits of non-resident Indians with Indian banks. These developments together brought the country to the verge of default with respect to external payments liability which could be averted by resorting to borrowings from the IMF under the stand-by arrangements and CCF and by mortgaging gold to the Bank of England. This was complemented by emergency measures to restrict imports.

The Macroeconomic Crisis

The macroeconomic crisis was precipitated mainly by the growth of the public spending through the 1980s that increased the budget deficit as a proportion of our GNP, although external shocks played a contributory role.

The state of our public finances had indeed reached crisis proportions by the end of the 1980s. The public debt-to-GNP ratio increased through the 1980s, going up to almost 60 per cent at the end of the decade, implying a doubling of the ratio at the end of the previous decade. As is now well-known, the proximate reasons for this situation were the failure of the public sector to generate investible resources and the explosive growth of governmental current spending that saw the budget deficit as a proportion of GDP rising from 6.4 to 9 per cent during the 1980s.

According to Jagdish Bhagwati and T.N. Srinivasan, the question must be addressed: Did the microeconomic inefficiencies have anything to do with this, or was "profligacy" the true, final and sole cause of the macroeconomic crisis? Evidently, it was the former.

Of course, the failure of the public sector enterprises to generate profits (and hence their contribution to the macro crisis) is a micro-economic efficiency failure. But, in turn, because these enterprises have dominated the provision of infrastructure and critical intermediates, their inefficiency has led to downstream inefficiencies in a multiplier fashion. Then again, the restrictive trade and industrial licensing frame-work, for instance, led to serious loss of efficiency by reducing the scale of output, eliminating effective competition, creating bottlenecks. The result was to reduce the returns from our investments and our growth rate. In turn, surely the revenues raised from the economy, for any given tax rates, were adversely affected, the political ability to raise tax rates in a situation of slowly-growing incomes was impaired, and the necessity to undertake budgetary expenditures to support the creation of public sector jobs and for consumption were also increased — all factors contributing to the budget deficit crisis.

The rise in foreign borrowing was a major component of the fiscal crisis, reflecting in turn the excess of domestic expenditure over income. Thus, as evident from the external public-sector debt (and not just the domestic public sector debt) increased greatly as a proportion of GNP during the 1980s, rising to 21 per cent by 1987-88. This increase in external indebtedness meant that debt service as a proportion of exports increased more than threefold to 32 per cent in 1996-97 from 1980-81.

The macro imbalance, fuelled by the budget deficit and financed by the external borrowings and the decumulation of reserves, was accompanied by accelerated inflation to double-digit levels.

Given the magnitude of the fiscal and balance of payment problems, there can be no question about the need for structural adjustment. But there were questions about its context as well as viewing it primarily as a means of liberalisation and opening of the economy.

Rationale for the Reforms

As is now well-understood, India faced a macroeconomic crisis that required immediate attention when Prime Minister Rao took office. This crisis had to be attended to forthwith. But, as in many South American countries in the 1980s, the macroeconomic crisis became also the occasion for undertaking substantial microeconomic (or what are sometimes called "structural") reforms that had been long overdue.

In fact, these structural reforms were necessary because we had evidently failed to generate adequate rates of growth of income and of per capita income. Not merely did India's weak performance in this regard fall below her own expectations as defined in the earlier Plans, it also put India behind many other developing countries, and way behind the super performers in the Far East.

"Indeed, it is necessary to appreciate that we had become marginalised in the world economy. Not merely were our growth, and hence all else such as poverty alleviation, unsatisfactory, the multiplying success stories were to be found elsewhere. Increasingly, many of our economic policies were also seen as wittingly foolish, impossible to explain as sensible. Among these were our maze of senseless bureaucratic controls on production and investment. Perhaps the most compelling reason for reforms was then to clean the house and to restore India eventually to the position of respect in the world economy and polity that she enjoyed during the years of Prime Minister Nehru's stewardship."[1]

---

1 Jagdish Bhagwati and T.N. Srinivasan *"India's Economic Reforms"*. Paper submitted to Finance Ministry (1993).

Macroeconomic Reforms

By the time the crisis of 1991 occurred, there was considerable support among key figures in and out of government for the view that a thorough going reform was necessary to pull the economy out of the morass it had gotten into.

The reform package outlined by Manmohan Singh in 1991 had three distinct components:

(1) Fiscal stabilization to check the growing fiscal deficit and contain it at a much lower level in such a manner that public investments in basic social and economic infrastructure could be substantially stepped up without generating inflationary pressures;

(2) Internal liberalization to increase competitive pressures, leaving enterprises free to make their production and investment decisions in the light of market conditions and enlarging the scope and freedom for private enterprise;

(3) Integration with the global economy by removing controls on foreign trade and exchange rates, lowering tariffs and rationalizing their structure and substantially relaxing regulations regarding external capital flows and a proactive policy for attracting foreign direct investment. This package, it was claimed, would release powerful growth impulses and lift the economy to a high growth trajectory comparable to that of east Asia. This view prevailed and has come to be accepted by successive governments since.[2]

The policy changes brought into force since July 1991 fall broadly into two categories. The first set of measures is part of what is normally known as stabilisation policy. The second set of measures come under the category of structural reform policies. As Rangarajan[3] rightly points out, while the stabilisation policies were intended to correct the lapses and put the house in order in the short term, the structural reform policies were intended to accelerate economic growth over the medium term. Structural reform policies cannot succeed unless a degree of stabilisation has been brought about. But stabilisation by itself will not be adequate unless structural reforms are undertaken to avoid the

2. A. Vaidyanathan (2003), *India's Economic Reforms and Development*, pp 17-18, Academic Foundation, New Delhi.
3. C. Rangarajan, *The New Economic Policy and the Role of the State*, in Uma Kapila (ed.) Indian Economy Since Independence, op. cit.

recurrence of the problems faced in the recent period.

Structural Reforms

Structural reforms were broadly in the area of industrial licensing and regulation, foreign trade and investment and the financial sector. There is considerable unanimity among the economists about the need to reduce and, as far as possible, eliminate barriers to the entry and expansion of firms. The policy of licensing as has been practised in the past has had no particular merit and, in fact, the Approach Document of the Eighth Plan submitted in May 1990 had also said: "A return to the regime of direct, indiscriminate and detailed controls in industry is clearly out of question. Past experience has shown that such a control system is not effective in achieving the desired objective. Also the system is widely abused and leads to corruption, delays and inefficiency." In relation to foreign trade policy, the aim was to liberalise the regime with respect to imports and try to bring about a closer link between exports and imports.

As regards import duties the policy has been gradual even though it is accepted by all that the tariff rate in India is perhaps the highest even among the developing countries. A progressive reduction becomes essential in order to avoid a high-cost economy. As regards foreign investment, the new policy measures certainly make a break with the past. In an era in which capital is mobile and moving across borders in a big way and where technology transfer is through investment, we cannot afford to close our country to the flow of foreign investment. In fact, the flow of foreign investment into the country has been meagre. If retained earnings are excluded the flow is almost negligible. The relaxations that we have made in relation to foreign investment are yet very modest as compared with the concessions offered by many developing countries. Many of the fears expressed in this context are in the nature of putting the cart before the horse. We must take action when and if it becomes apparent that the flow of foreign investment is excessive and it is undermining the domestic economy.

Finally, in relation to the financial sector it has to be noted that while there has been a considerable widening and deepening of the Indian financial system, many inefficiencies have crept into the system during the past 15 years. An administered interest rate structure had put the whole system in a straight-jacket. The extent of cross-subsidisation in lending rates has undermined the profitability of the banking system. Equally, due to various pressures, the quality of loan assets has also deteriorated. With low profitability, the banking system in particular has not been in a position to provide adequately for loan losses. The capital of the Indian banking system is woefully inadequate. Thus a reform of the financial system to provide greater autonomy to the institutions both in terms of the interest rate structure and operational matters had become necessary.

Implementation of the Agenda

The implementation of the agenda of the reforms over the eight years has covered the following:

Trade policy reforms: A major reform of trade policy regime has been effected since 1991. The import licensing system has been dismantled. All non-tariff barriers (NTBs) have been phased out from all tradables except consumer goods. The peak tariff rates have been brought down to maximum 50 per cent from up to 355 per cent. Besides India has also undertaken a major commitment to liberalise its trade regime under WTO Agreement.

Removal of QRs

The process of removal of import restrictions, which began in 1991, has been completed in a phased manner with removal of restrictions on 715 items (Exim Policy 2001-02). Out of these 715, 342 are textile products, 147 are agricultural products including alcoholic beverages and 226 are other manufactured products including automobiles.

Industrial policy reforms: Although some liberalisation and streamlining of the industrial policy had been effected in the mid-1980s, the New Industrial Policy (NIP) announced on July 24, 1991 and subsequent amendments brought far-reaching changes in the policy regime governing industrial investments. The NIP dismantled the industrial licensing (or approval) system that regulated the industrial investments in the country by abolishing the requirement of obtaining an industrial licence from the government in all except 14 specified industries. These specified industries need to be regulated in view of environmental hazards, national security or social well-being considerations.

NIP has thrown open new industries and services to private including foreign private sector by pruning the list of 'Industries Reserved for the Public Sector'. Only six industries, which are now reserved for exclusive development by public sector, include those considered sensitive from national security point of view. Thus a large number of industries and services including infrastructure such as telecommunication, roads, ports, power generation, petroleum refining have become accessible to the private sector. NIP accords a much more liberal attitude to foreign direct investments (FDI) than ever in post-independence India. The policy allows automatic approval system for priority industries by the Reserve Bank of India within two weeks subject to their fulfilling specified equity norms. A more favourable treatment is also accorded to non-resident Indian (NRI) investors who are allowed up to 100 per cent ownership priority industries.

A Foreign Investment Promotion Board (FIPB) has been set up to consider all other proposals that do not qualify for automatic clearance. However, to bring transparency into the working of FIPB, elaborate guidelines and time frame of six weeks in normal cases are also specified. FIPB is authorised to negotiate with foreign investors in person to expedite the clearances. FIPB is empowered to approve up to 100 per cent foreign ownership in cases involving transfer of high technology, projects producing predominantly for exports, energy and infrastructural projects, consultancy or trading companies. The restrictions on investments by large industrial houses and foreign controlled companies under the MRTP Act were also abolished.

A phased programme of disinvestment of public ownership in public sector corporations has been launched. A Disinvestment Commission followed by Department of Disinvestment was set up to make recommendations on the phasing of the disinvestments.

The outward investments by Indian enterprises were also liberalised and proposals fulfilling certain norms could now be granted automatic approval.

Exchange rate reforms: The rupee was devalued twice in July 1991 leading to a 20 per cent depreciation in its value. The partial convertibility of rupee on the trade account was announced in the 1992-93 budget that was subsequently broadened to full convertibility on current account by August 1994.

Capital market: The Capital Issues Control Act was repealed and the Securities and Exchange Board of India (SEBI) was set up as a watchdog for regulating the functioning of the capital market. SEBI has focused on regulatory reform of the capital market as well as on market modernisation. Online trading and dematerialised trading have been introduced. Companies have been allowed to buy back their own shares subject to the regulations laid down by SEBI.

In September 1992, the government announced guidelines for investments by foreign institutional investors (FIIs) in the Indian capital market. FIIs were now welcome to invest in all types of securities traded on the primary and secondary market with full repatriation benefits and without restrictions on either volume of trading or lock-in-period.

Financial sector: In January 1993 a package of financial sector reforms was announced that included permission to new private sector banks including foreign joint ventures. The government has also established a policy regime for functioning of private non-banking finance companies (NBFCs) and agencies for rating their credit worthiness.

Thus the government since 1991 has undertaken a comprehensive reform of the economy. In addition to the above measures there has been an emphasis in the government budget-making to restricting budget deficits.

National Structural Adjustment Programme

All these reforms — and the list is far from exhaustive — calls for a high order of political management. In the first place, the sense of the crisis, the imperative need for systemic reform and the rationale for the main element of the reforms need to be effectively communicated to all levels of government and to the people at large. Second, the task of structural reform should not be viewed as the responsibility of the Centre alone. States spend nearly as much as the Centre. They are responsible for key segments of infrastructure (namely electricity, roads and water supply) as well as the social welfare and anti-poverty programmes; the implicit subsidies (unrecovered costs) passing through the State budgets are some 60 per cent more than in the Central budget; and the State governments taken as a whole also show a substantial and growing revenue deficit. Unless the States also show a high degree of fiscal discipline — which must necessarily consist of a mixture of measures designed to raise revenues, contain expenditure growth and improve the effectiveness of expenditure — it would be hardly possible to bring down the overall fiscal deficit without impinging adversely on the expansion and improvement of essential infrastructure (so crucial for the success of trade and industrial liberalisation) and on the employment and anti-poverty programmes (which provide a safety net for the vulnerable segments).

Given this, and the vast ramifications of structural adjustment, one would expect a serious and sustained effort by the Centre to take the

States fully into confidence about the nature and magnitude of the crisis facing the economy and the rationale for and implications of the "structural adjustment" programme, even while impressing on them the contribution they have to make and the responsibilities they have to share in order to make the programme a success. What we need is a national structural adjustment programme based on the maximum possible understanding and consent among the States and the Centre. Apart from informal meets, the NDC and the inter-State Council provide formal mechanisms for informing, counselling and discussing these issues with the States. Unfortunately these have not been used to any significant extent in shaping the adjustment reforms.

In the final analysis no structural adjustment programme can be effectively implemented without broadbased political support. This support will not be easy to muster merely on the basis of promises of faster growth of income and employment and of lower rate of inflation at the end of the adjustment process. It requires not only a great deal of public education about the need for and rationale of policy changes but also to generate a feeling that the costs of adjustment — by way of lower subsidies, higher price of utilities and services, higher taxes, insistence on productivity norms, the redeployment and even some retrenchment of workers, restraints on increase in wages and salaries, restricting the scope for using public institutions for political patronage at every level — are being shared equitably. As it is farmers are being asked to pay more for water, electricity and fertilizers; workers to accept wage restraints, retrenchment and closures; and the users of PDS to pay higher prices for foodgrains, sugar, kerosene and transport services. Necessary as all these are, they also provoke — and understandably so — a great deal of resistance. And the farm lobby and trade unions are forces to reckon with. Their opposition can, however, be to some extent mitigated by measures to contain the adverse effects on employment and incomes specially for the vulnerable segments of the population.

Safety Net

A "safety net" for workers in the organised sector who may lose their jobs in the process of adjustment is on the agenda. It is extremely important, at a minimum, to ensure that the employment and anti-poverty programmes and access of the poor to the PDS do not get whittled down in the name of fiscal crisis.

Above all it is essential to demonstrate that the better off segments, especially in urban areas, bear their due share of the costs of adjustment.

The Government must show greater willingness and ability to deal with this class, make them pay the taxes due from them, pay for the full cost of public services they use, and take measures to enforce greater austerity among them than is currently in evidence. As Vaidyanathan has rightly remarked, "regrettably, the tendency is to assume that nothing much can be done to make tax administration effectively enforce existing tax laws relating to income, wealth and property. Amnesties and incentives to flush out black money reflect this presumption and tantamount to sanctifying a culture of non-compliance with the law among the well-to-do. So is the plea for lowering of the tax rates on the ground that it will reduce incentives for evasion. There is also a vocal lobby for raising the exemption limit for income tax, removing restrictions on the level of executive compensation, and reducing excise duty on durables and other goods largely catering to the better-off segments in the face of recession. Should the government yield to these pressures, the effective tax burden on the well-to-do will be reduced — even as all other classes are being asked to bear hardships for the sake of the "larger good". Can we really expect a democratic polity to support, or is it even proper to expect it to support, such an inequitous sharing of the cost of adjustment?"[4]

Macroeconomic Impact of Reforms

The compound rate of growth for the second half of 1980s was 5.8 per cent per annum. Compared to that for the post-reform period excluding 1991-92 as year of exceptional crisis, the average for 1992-98 comes to 6.5 per cent per annum. The average rate for the 1993-94 to 1998-99 period (based on the new series of GDP) comes to 6.8 per cent. Similarly, the trend rate for the post-reform period estimated at 6.9 per cent is higher than 5.5 per cent applicable for the 1980s. The post-reform growth, therefore, has been at least 1.1 percentage points higher than the average rate achieved during the pre-reform period.[5]

The rate of growth in 1998-99 has been estimated at 6.0 per cent by CSO. To some extent the recent slow down could be on account of the contagion effect of the east Asian crisis on India indirectly and economic sanctions imposed on India in May 1998 following Pokhran II by major industrial countries. In large part the recent slow down reflects the effect of industrial recession that started in the year 1996-97.

---

4. A. Vaidyanathan (2003), op. cit., Ch.2, pp 84-87.
5. Nagesh Kumar, *Economic Reforms and their Macroeconomic Impact*, in Uma Kapila (ed.), 2001-02, Indian Economy Since Independence.

Signs of industrial revival: Recent trends and surveys do indicate that the industry may finally be coming out of the recession. Liberalisation is expected to bring efficiency and productivity gains in the industry.

FDI inflows: Liberalisation of FDI policy regime has been an important aspect of the reforms. Compared to approvals of FDI in 1991, the approvals of FDI inflows since the liberalisation of policy in 1991 reveal a dramatic jump.

While the magnitudes of inflows have recorded impressive growth, they are still at a small level compared to the country's potential. Furthermore, one of the objectives of the current reforms of policies is to remove impediments for export-oriented manufacture in general and to attract MNEs to locate efficiency-seeking FDI in the country. These investments could help India in expanding manufactured exports by using her as an export platform. The majority of the recent approvals of FDI, however, aim to exploit India's sizeable and expanding domestic market. The efficiency seeking or export-oriented FDI have yet to start flowing to the country in a considerable manner.

Fiscal Adjustment and Stabilisation

A key aspect of the structural adjustment programmes is to restrict the fiscal deficits of the governments. Table 1 summarises the trends in budget deficit of the central government in the late 1980s and 1990s. In the second half of 1980s, the fiscal imbalance worsened with average fiscal deficit rising to 8.2 per cent of GDP compared to 6.3 per cent in the early 1980s (*Economic Survey, 1992-93*). Compared to this, the average fiscal deficit in the post-reform period has been 5.7 per cent of GDP. This suggests that the government has succeeded in managing the fiscal situation quite well.

However the extent of fiscal deficits tends to mask the method adopted by the government to balance the budget and its implications.

Firstly, the revenue deficit which represents the gap between revenue receipts and revenue expenditure has increased in the post-reform period (at 2.9 per cent) on average compared to an average of 2.6 during the second half of 1980s. This implies that the government has been unable to contain its current expenditure. Therefore, fiscal deficit has been contained either by reducing capital investment or by raising capital receipts such as borrowings or disinvestment of public sector holdings of the government. A rising level of revenue deficit has

TABLE – 1

TRENDS IN CENTRAL GOVERNMENT DEFICIT
AS PERCENTAGE OF GDP

Year	*Revenue Deficit*	*Fiscal Deficit*
1985-86	2.2	8.3
1986-87	2.7	9.0
1987-88	2.7	8.1
1988-89	2.7	7.8
1989-90	2.6	7.8
1990-91	3.5	8.4
1991-92	2.6	5.9
1992-93	2.6	5.7
1993-94	3.7	6.9
1994-95	3.0	5.6
1995-96	2.4	4.9
1996-97	2.3	4.7
1997-98	3.0	5.7
1998-99(RE)	3.4	5.9
Averages		
1985-91	2.6	8.2
1992-99	2.9	5.7

Source: Economic Survey 1992-93 and RBI (1999).

thus been sustained with government borrowings of the scale of the revenue deficit to finance its consumption expenditure rather than producing a revenue surplus to finance capital expenditure in social sectors (and defence) which do not yield a future income flow to the exchequer. Deepak Nayyar[6] among other analysts, has argued that such a fiscal regime "is not sustainable in medium-term for it is bound to fuel inflationary pressures or strain the balance of payments, and thus disrupt the process of growth".

Secondly, Fiscal adjustment has been achieved by squeezing public investment rather than government consumption. Capital expenditure as a proportion of total government expenditure has declined steadily from

6. Deepak Nayyar (1996) *Economic Liberalisation in India: Analytics, Experience and Lessons*. in R.C. Dutt Lectures, Orient Longman, New Delhi.

30.18 per cent in 1990-91 to 21.8 per cent in 1998-99 (Table 2). As a proportion of GDP, capital expenditure has come down from 5.5 per cent to 3.6 per cent during the same period.

TABLE – 2

RECEIPTS AND EXPENDITURE OF CENTRAL GOVERNMENT

Years	*Capital Expenditure as Per cent of Total*	*Capital Expenditure as Per Cent of GDP*	*Total Expenditure as Per Cent of GDP*
1985-86	40.4	8.2	21.5
1990-91	30.2	5.5	18.1
1994-95	24.0	3.7	15.5
1995-96	21.5	3.2	14.6
1996-97	20.9	3.3	14.3
1997-98	22.3	3.3	14.8
1998-99 (RE)	21.8	3.6	16.0
1999-2000 (BE)	16.5	2.3	14.2

Source: Economic Survey 1998-99 and RBI (1999).

Finally, it has been shown that the burden of adjustment has been unequal in that it has led to declining expenditures on social sectors such as education, health and poverty alleviation. Panchamukhi and Mahendra Dev have observed a decline in social sector spending especially during the early post-reform period. Hence, concerns have been raised regarding the levels of human development.

Prices: An important focus of the stabilisation programme is to bring the rate of inflation under check. The rate of change in wholesale and consumer prices suggest that the overall trend in prices has been on decline since 1992. One striking trend noticeable from Table 3 is the growing divergence between the rate of inflation based on wholesale prices and that for consumer price index since 1993-94. Until 1993-94 the two rates generally converged. Since 1995-96, the consumer price index based rate of inflation has exceeded that one based on wholesale prices by a wide margin. The diverging trend in the wholesale and consumer prices has been explained in terms of the change in the weighting scheme for the two indices. The consumer price index has a 57.0 per cent weight of the food group compared to just 27.5 per cent in WPI. The divergence between the two indices therefore, reflects substantial increases in food prices in the 1990s. Besides, a spurt in prices of housing, medical care and personal care has also contributed to the rise in CPI. *The rise in food prices and other goods of mass consumption at a faster rate than prices of other goods also indicates that sharing of burden of adjustment by different sections of society has been uneven and weaker sections may have been affected more.*

TABLE – 3

INFLATION IN INDIA

Years	*Index No of WP*	*Annual Change*	*Index No of CP (General)*	*Annual Change*
1986-87	132.7	–	137	–
1987-88	143.6	8.21	149	8.76
1988-89	154.3	7.45	163	9.40
1989-90	165.7	7.39	173	6.13
1990-91	182.7	10.26	193	11.56
1991-92	207.8	13.74	219	13.47
1992-93	228.7	10.06	240	9.59
1993-94	247.8	8.35	258	7.50
1994-95	274.7	10.86	279	8.14
1995-96	295.8	7.68	313	12.19
1996-97	314.6	6.36	342	9.27
1997-98	329.8	4.83	366	7.02
1998-99	352.5	6.9	414	13.1
1999-2000 up to Oct	–	2.9	–	7.5

Notes: Base: 1981-82 =100.
WP = Wholesale prices, all commodities, average of weeks;
CP = Consumer prices for urban industrial workers general index (average of months).

Political Resistance to Reform

Political resistance to the reform measures was to be expected from diverse sources, for diverse reasons and with varying force. Industrialists and exporters had most reason to welcome the new economic policy. But their enthusiasm has waned over time and given place to demand for a variety of protective measures. (Vaidyanathan 2003)[7]

The 'middle class' with access to higher professional education constitute perhaps the most enthusiastic supporters of the new economic

7. A. Vaidyanathan (2003), *op.cit.*, Ch.1, pp 45-49.

policy. Most of the large and growing number of Non-Resident Indians (NRIs) and those employed in the burgeoning software industry belong to this group. Globalisation has vastly improved the opportunities and earning potential of this class both within and outside the country. One has only to see the veritable explosion in salaries of executives and professional personal in recent years. Some of the most ardent and passionate advocates of free markets, globalisation and capital account convertibility belong to this class.

The strongest opposition comes from farmers and from workers in the organised sector including, especially those employed in the public sector. Farmers have fiercely, and so far successfully, resisted any increase in the price of inputs in the name of reducing subsidies. Their argument is that farmers are unable to recover costs at current level of input and output prices and that farm prices are too low to enable them to have a 'decent' income. Subsidising inputs and pegging output prices higher than warranted by the balance between supply and demand is neither fiscally feasible nor a viable way of raising farmers' incomes to a higher level and even less so for ensuring their progressive improvement. Moreover, since there is much scope for increasing the productivity of water and fertilisers, higher prices do not necessarily mean an increase in unit costs. On the other hand, by encouraging excessive use of scarce resources, low input prices damage the environment and endanger long-term sustainability of agriculture.

Labour in the organised sector is the other locus of strong and organised resistance to the reform: Organised sector (registered factories, financial institutions, government agencies, public sector undertakings) constitute barely 10 per cent of the country's work force (and 20 per cent of the non-agricultural work force). Trade unions, though largely confined to this segment of the economy, have played, and continue to play a key role in protecting the interests of their members and in influencing state policy. They comprise an important section of the better-off segments of the population (most of them belong in the top quartile of the population in terms of per capita income) and get the lion's share of the benefits of subsidised or free facilities and services (higher education, healthcare, public transport, electricity, water) provided by the state.

Unions in the organised sector have had considerable success in securing better wages, working conditions and other benefits for workers in this sector and also legislative protection against lay-off and retrenchment. Several of the activities, especially in the public sector, being crucial to the orderly governance and smooth functioning of economy and society, those employed in them are strategically positioned to resist lay-offs, redeployment, restraint on salaries and benefits.

All this is threatened by proposals to permit flexibility in hiring and firing, retrenchment and redeployment of excess work force, privatisation of public undertakings, allowing market forces a greater role in determining wages; and measures to check leakages and corruption. As consumers, they also stand to lose by increased user charges for public services and possibly having to pay more taxes. The fierce resistance of trade unions to reforms — especially in the public sector — is hardly surprising.

Concerns regarding Social and Political Implications of Reform

Overarching the resistance from particular interest groups are wider concerns about the larger social and political implications of the reform. These include several apprehensions:

- that trade liberalisation and domestic regulation and disbanding protection for small industry would have huge and widespread adverse effects on employment and incomes;
- that in the name of fiscal consolidation, expenditures are being squeezed and the compression is at the expense of pro-poor programmes (like basic social services, social welfare, security and poverty alleviation);
- that in the name of providing incentive for enterprise and professional skills, inequalities are allowed to increase;
- that the policy of open door for foreign capital and agreeing to the jurisdiction of international organisations (like World Trade Organisation) created under unequal treaties in an unequal world dominated by the developed countries reduces the country's autonomy and makes, it vulnerable to external pressure and interference.
- an added dimension is the increasing concern about the consequences of pursuing current patterns of development for the environment and sustainability.

According to Vaidyanathan, criticism based on these concerns as paranoia or ideologically motivated, would be serious mistake.

Impact of the New Economic Policy on the Vulnerable Sections

Coming to the issue of the impact of the new economic policy on the vulnerable sections, Rangarajan argues, "analytically, we need to address two sets of issues. One is whether the new economic policy affects in any way the specific policy measures that we normally undertake in order to improve the conditions of the poor. Second, is there anything in the new economic policy which *per se* has an anti-poor bias? The new economic policy which may be a convenient expression to refer to the measures introduced since July 1991 is not the total economic policy of the Government. There are many other elements which continue to remain as an integral part of the overall economic policy. Among these are the measures which can be broadly termed as anti-poverty programmes. In the total economic policy there are four elements which can be identified as being meant specifically for poverty alleviation :

First, since agriculture is the mainstay of the majority of the population, growth in agriculture and, therefore, resources allocated for agriculture are an important part of the attack on poverty. This is not an acceptance of the trickle-down theory. It is common knowledge that in states in which agriculture has made spectacular progress poverty levels have come down. Therefore, allocation of resources for agriculture is an important indicator.

Second, we have evolved over time a reasonably satisfactory food security system. An integral part of this is the public distribution system. With all its shortcomings, the public distribution system has played a notable role in avoiding acute conditions of scarcity and met to a certain extent the minimum requirements.

Third, there has been a substantial expansion in programmes which are intended to provide additional employment. The various employment guarantee schemes as well as the credit-related integrated rural development programmes are examples of such programmes.

Fourth, expenditure on education and health also has an important bearing on reducing poverty levels."

"Is there anything in the new economic policy which is inherently anti-poor? The poor are affected most when growth is low and when prices rise. The slowdown in growth in 1991-92 and the sharp increases in prices in the same year are sometimes cited as consequences of implementing the new economic policy. This is not a correct assessment.

There was a decline in agricultural production in 1991-92 and it is well known that the performance of agriculture from year to year is mostly a function of the weather. The collapse of industrial production in 1991-92 can be traced in a large measure to the high degree of import compression that was brought about which would have been inevitable in any case whether or not we shifted to a new policy orientation. Has the attempt to contain fiscal deficit affected, anyway, the poor more? While there has been some attempt to reduce fertiliser subsidy as part of the efforts to moderate the fiscal deficit, the food subsidies have been maintained. There is a dilemma here which we have to resolve. Unless we make the public distribution system more focused and directed towards only the weaker sections and low-income groups, keeping the issue price unaltered or changed moderately despite an increase in procurement prices will not be sustainable over a long time."

One aspect of the new economic policy which has created certain misgivings among the organised labour relates to the several suggestions that have been made with respect to non-viable public sector units. While the approach should be to reorganise the loss-making public sector units in such a way as to improve their viability, quite clearly, there are cases in which their viability will depend on some reduction in the labour force. The Government is again going slow in this area because of the anxiety not to create a difficult situation for labour. That is why various alternative schemes have been thought of, such as the sale of the company to the labour if they are willing to accept it, setting up a national renewal fund to provide compensation for people who may be rendered jobless, etc. The public sector units being compelled to carry on with all the labour force, irrespective of whether or not the units are viable, is also a situation that is not sustainable over a long time. Hence a solution which is also reasonable and acceptable to labour will have to be found.[8]

As rightly pointed out by C. Rangarajan, "redundancies and closures occurring as a consequence of modernisation and technological upgradation are not a new phenomenon. This has occurred in a big way in centres like Ahmedabad and Kanpur where there has been a concentration of the textile industry. It must be recognised that restructuring of the workforce becomes necessary for efficient growth which alone can lead to sustainable employment growth in the medium and long term. At the same time, workers rendered unemployed in these

---

8. C. Rangarajan, *The New Economic Policy & the Role of the State* in Uma Kapila (ed.) op. cit.

processes cannot be left high and dry. Provision for fair and reasonable separation benefits is necessary, but more important is their redeployment, with training, if necessary, as a part of the overall strategy of expansion of employment opportunities. What, in fact, is being attempted in the new economic policy, with the instrumentality of the national renewal fund, is that the hardships of the workers affected in the unavoidable and inevitable loss of jobs are minimised by providing them a fair deal in terms of separation benefits and opportunities for their productive redeployment. The national renewal fund, constituted on a non-statutory basis, envisages the provision of resources solely for the rehabilitation of labour resulting from modernisation, technological upgradation, restructuring (including revival) or closure of industrial units. It will assist workers in this process for their retraining, redeployment and placement in new employment, besides contributing towards compensation payments, including legal dues and those under the Voluntary Retirement Scheme, under the fund called the National Renewal Grant Fund (NRGF).

Far from adversely affecting employment elasticity, the restructured growth during the 1990s is expected to be far less capital-intensive and far more employment-friendly. First, with the removal of distortions in the factor markets, the new economic policy regime can be expected to lead to greater use of labour in the production processes as has been the experience of several labour-surplus developing countries which have succeeded in increasing their exports and overall growth of manufacturing industries. Second, the processes of deregulation and liberalisation are likely to particularly benefit the employment-intensive small and decentralised sector which, it must be recognised, had to bear a heavy burden of bureaucratic hurdles in the past. In the restructured economy these sectors, particularly the rural non-farm sector, agro-processing and agri-business in general, urban small enterprises and the services sector, all of which have shown high potential for employment generation, are likely to grow faster. Third, the overall objective of the new economic policy is to improve productivity and efficiency. In a competitive environment, both public and private sector units are expected to show improved productivity and greater expansion in output.

7

Population

IN recent years, there has been an increasing focus on the relationship between population growth and economic development. The most difficult problem for such an analysis is to be able to separate cause from effect. Does economic development accelerate or retard population growth or does population growth contribute to or retard economic development? What are the linkages and how strong they are and in what direction do they operate?

Economic Development and Population Growth

The Theory of Demographic Transition

The Theory of Demographic Transition attempts to explain why all contemporary developed nations have more or less passed through the same three stages of population growth. Before their economic modernisation, these countries, for centuries, had stable or very slow growing population as a result of a combination of high birth rate and almost equally high death rate. With economic development resulting in higher incomes, improved public health facilities, there was marked decline in mortality that gradually raised life expectancy from under 40 years to over 60 years. However, the decline in death rate was not immediately accompanied by a decline in fertility. With declining death rate but birth rate not falling correspondingly, these countries passed through stage two, marking the beginning of Demographic Transition i.e. transition from stable or slow growing population to rapidly increasing number. Finally, stage three is reached when the forces and influences of modernisation and economic development cause fertility to decline so that eventually falling birth rate converge with lower death rate leaving little or no population growth.[1] Thus, how does economic

1. Michael Todaro, P.18, op. cit.

development affect population growth can be explained through the theory of demographic transition.

The Micro Economic Theory of Fertility

In recent years, economist have begun to look more closely at the micro economic determinants of family fertility. They have utilised the principles of economy and optimisation to explain family size decisions. In deciding whether or not to have additional children, parents are assumed to weigh economic benefits against costs. The principle of benefits are the expected income from child labour usually on the farm and their family support for elderly parents. Balance against these benefits are the two principle elements of costs. (1) The opportunity cost of mother's time, the income she could earn if she were not at home caring for her children. (2) The cost of educating children that is the trade off between having fewer "high quality" high cost, educated children with high income earning potentials versus more "low quality", low cost, uneducated children with much lower earning prospects.

Statistical studies have shown that birth rates among the poor are likely to fall where there is —

(i) An increase in the education of women and consequent change in their role and status.

(ii) An increase in female non-agricultural wage employment opportunities which raises the price or cost of their traditional child bearing activities.

(iii) A rise in family income through increase in direct employment and earning of husband and wife and or redistribution of income and assets from rich to poor.

(iv) A reduction in infant mortality through expanded public health programme and better nutritional status for both parent and child.

(v) The development of old age and social security systems to bridge the economic dependence of parents on their offsprings.

Thus efforts to make jobs, education and health more broadly available to poverty groups in Third World countries will not only contribute to their income and physical well being but it can also contribute substantially to their motivation for smaller families which is vital to reducing growth rates.

How Does Population Growth Affect Economic Development ?

So far we have tried to analyse the effect of economic development on population growth, now let us examine how does population growth affect economic development? We may begin by asking the question how does population growth affect the Net National Product?

Until recently, the literature of economic demography drew attention to two main relationships through which population growth affect the economy, what we may call (i) the 'saving effect' and (ii) 'composition of investment effect.'[2] The former of these argues that savings are reduced by population growth because of the so called burden of dependency. With high fertility and declining mortality in younger and older age groups, the population acquires an increasing proportion of people in the non-working age groups relative to those of working age. Since all must consume, in the absence of increasing output per worker, saving per head must fall. Even if productivity is increasing, savings are less than they would be with a smaller number of dependents per worker.

The investment argument is like this : with increasing population, a share of investible resources has to be devoted to reproducing for additional people unproductive facilities, duplication of social services which would be unnecessary if population were not growing. A number of studies starting with Coale and Hoover have shown through comparison of high and low fertility paths that there have been greater growth of GNP with the lesser rate of population growth. Robert Cassen has raised doubts on the validity of the above saving and investments effect. He argues, if bulk of savings in poor countries come from small wealthy class whose fertility is low and if cost of additional children are met out of consumption rather than saving, the saving cost of additional children would be quite inconsiderable.

In the macroeconomic picture, if population growth leads to slower growth of output, then one would expect slower growth of saving but to avoid circularity, the negative effect of population on GNP growth must be established independently of the saving effect. Similarly, regarding the composition of investment effect, Cassen observes that one important area which has not been incorporated in the existing demographic models is the question of changing composition of the resource costs of producing basic consumption goods, that is food. As

2. R.H. Cassen, *India, Population, Economy and Society*, Ch.4., p. 221.

long as a society can increase agricultural output by mainly labour using means, the chief resource to feed growing population is provided by the population itself, the capital required is circulating capital, wage good to support the labour force. But a point is reached where required increases in agricultural output necessitated yield improving inputs which are expensive in both capital and foreign exchange. Just as Coale and Hoover model argued that with slower population growth more capital would have been available for raising per worker productivity because of reduced welfare expenditure, similarly Cassen argues that more capital and foreign exchange would have been available from reduction in expenditure devoted to raising agricultural output.

The composition of investment argument according to Cassen is really quite general. Wherever population growth requires increase in production, which in turn require investment, a lesser rate of population growth would release investible funds for use elsewhere. One fails to understand why past models have concentrated on welfare investment. Food production is infact the least postponable of all forms of population related output needs and if agriculture enters a phase of fundamental alteration in production function or in other words changing resource requirements for additional output, this can be a major burden of population growth. India reached this stage since mid 1960's when increases in agricultural output had to be brought out by yield improving technology which is capital intensive instead of increasing acreage. The biggest problem for India if current trend continues is the increasing share of investible surplus that will be taken up by food needs of the growing population.

According to K. Sundaram the implications of growing demographic pressures in India for the process of development in general and the progress towards poverty eradication become clearer once we focus on the labour force consequences of population growth. The sheer magnitude of the addition to work force brings to the fore the capital constraints in raising the productivity of the labour force. The capital requirement of equipping the labour force would be astronomically large.[3]

It will be seen, that the growth rate of labour force is likely to be highest during the Ninth Plan period and only gradually decline thereafter. As a result, any planning over the perspective period will have to have employment generation as its central focus. If adequate work opportunities are not created, there would be growing incidence

3. K. Sundaram, *Demography and Development*, in Uma Kapila, op. cit.

of unemployment in the country and an increase in the social tensions that arise therefrom.

The labour force expansion also puts direct pressure on the single most important natural resource in a predominantly agrarian economy, namely, land. Admittedly, the effective supply of land can be augmented by the use of reproducible capital. Irrigation is the most obvious example making it possible to increase the gross cropped area. The inadequate expansion of gross cropped area and of the irrigated area reflects the fact that the irrigation system has not expanded even upto the limits of currently known irrigation potential. This again is a manifestation of the inadequacy of capital resources. Further, it may be emphasized that even if currently known irrigation potential is fully utilised, it will leave a good chunk of the net sown area dependent on rain which may or may not be adequate. Thus, the moisture availability may act as an independent constraint on raising agricultural productivity and hence on over-all economic development.

Population and Labour Force Projections

The changes in the age structure of population[4], given the present demographic transition of the Nation, are such as to lead to a much faster growth of population in the working age group than the entire population, and this, given the different participation rates in different age groups will lead to a faster growth of labour force as compared to the working age population (Table 1 and 2).

TABLE – 1

AGE STRUCTURE OF POPULATION

(age distribution in per cent; population in millions)

Age group	*2001*	*2006*	*2011*	*2016*
1-14	35.6	32.5	29.7	27.1
15-59	58.2	60.4	62.5	64.0
60+	6.3	7.0	7.9	8.9
All age groups	100.0	100.0	100.0	100.0
Population	1,027.0	1,113.7	1,194.4	1,267.5

Source: Planning Commission.

4. Planning Commission, Tenth Five Year Plan, Ch. 5, p. 143.

TABLE – 2

GROWTH IN POPULATION AND LABOUR FORCE

(per cent per annum)

	2002-2007	*2007-2012*	*2012-2017*
Population (All age groups)	1.63	1.41	1.20
Population (15-59 years)	2.41	2.08	1.70
Labour Force (1) (15-59 years)	2.42	2.15	1.78
Population (15+)	2.57	2.26	1.93
Labour Force (1) (15+)	2.51	2.25	1.92

Note :

(1) Labour force projections here are on the basis of labour force participation rate for each quinquennial age group remaining unchanged, i.e. the changes in labour force growth in relation to population are due to changes in the age composition of the population.

Source : Planning Commission.

The Ongoing Demographic Transition: Challenges and Opportunities

The ongoing demographic transition poses challenges and provides opportunities for improving the health indices of the population. There will be a reduction in the under-10-year child population from 243 million in 1996 to 219 million in 2006. The health care providers should take full advantage of the respite from ever-increasing numbers, to improve the quality and coverage of immunisation, & health and nutrition services. Special attention should also be paid to improving access to education and skill development.

The next decade will witness a massive increase in the number of adolescents in the 10-19 age group from 200 million to 239 million. This age group has in the past received very little attention. There is an urgent need to improve the access of this vulnerable age group to a wide range of services e.g. in the field of social development, counselling and health care.

The population in the 15-59 age group will increase from 519 million in 1996 to 800 million in 2016. This age group has the least morbidity and mortality rates. Appropriate inputs into health care would therefore result in substantial improvement in the health indices of the population in the next two decades. If all the needs for contraception are met it will be possible to achieve rapid population stabilisation.

It is obvious that the *current phase of demographic transition is both a challenge and an opportunity.* The opportunity is that the country has the right combination of factors, which if properly utilised will enable us to gain a higher socio-economic status in the next two decades. The challenge is to ensure that optimum use is made of the human resources to hasten completion of the demographic transition and achieve rapid improvement in the quality of life.[5]

Demographic Trends in India

India is the second largest populated country in the world to cross the one billion mark, in 2001-02, population being 103.7 crore, China being the first. It is now estimated that by 2050, India will most likely overtake China to become the most populous country on the earth with 17.2 per cent population living here (UN Population Division, World Population Prospects: The 1998 Revision). The United Nations has estimated that world population grew at an annual rate of 1.4 per cent during 1990-2000, China registering a much lower annual growth rate of population of 1 per cent as compared to that for India, at 1.93 per cent during 1991-2001.

Data pertaining to selected population statistics for India since 1901 including the estimated average annual growth rates, the level of urbanisation or the percentage of urban population and the sex ratio (males per 1000 females) of the total population are presented in table 3.

Period of Low Population Growth

Prior to 1921 population was either not growing or growing at a very low rate. The main factor underlying the slow growth and decline were the recurrence of epidemics of plague and cholera and of famines and also the influence of epidemics of 1918-19 and its after-effects.

Period of Rapid Growth and Population Explosion

Between 1921-51, the average annual growth rate of population was 1.2 per cent as against 0.2 per cent during the period 1900-21. After 1921, a progressive control of epidemics resulted in raising the rate of population growth between 1 percent and 1.03 percent.

---

5. Pant, K.C. (2003), *Population Dynamics: Choices and Challenges* in India's Development Scenario: Next Decade and Beyond, Vol.1, Ch.11, pp 117-123, Academic Foundation, New Delhi.

TABLE – 3

KEY POPULATION STATISTICS OF INDIA, 1901-1991[6]

Census Year	*Total population (million)*	*Average annual growth rate (per cent)*	*Density (persons per sq km)*	*Sex ratio (males per 1000 females)*	*Per cent of urban population*
1901	238.3	0.3	77	1029	10.8
1911	252.0	0.6	82	1038	10.3
1921	251.2	N	81	1047	11.2
1931	278.9	1.1	90	1053	12.0
1941	318.5	1.3	103	1058	13.9
1951	361.0	1.3	117	1057	17.3
1961	439.1	2.0	142	1063	18.0
1971	548.2	2.2[b]	178	1075	19.9
1981	683.3	2.2[b]	216	1071	23.3[a]
1991	846.3	2.1	267	1067	25.7
2001	1027	1.9	324	1072	27.8

Notes: a Includes only an estimate for Assam.

b Growth rate for 1961-71 and 1971-81 take account of the fact that the reference data of the 1971 Census was 1 April, whereas that of the 1981 Census (like the 1951 and 1961 Census) was 1 March.

N: Negligible.

Since 1951, India is passing through a period of population explosion. Between 1951 and 1981, the addition to numbers was 32.2 crores and the average annual rate of growth turned out to be 2.15. The economic development since 1951 brought about a sharp decline in death rate while birth rate has not shown a corresponding decline.

Period of Some Decline in rate of Growth 1981 Onwards

According to 1991 census, there has been some decline in the rate of growth of population between 1981 and 1991, the average annual growth rate declined from 2.2 per cent to 2.1 per cent and the census of 2001 showing a further decline to 1.9 per cent. But even this rate of growth is very high as compared to other developing countries and with a large population base of over 100 crores, additions every year at this rate of growth are simply alarming.

6. Pravin Visaria, *Demographic Aspects of Development : The Indian Experience*, in Uma Kapila (Ed) Indian Economy Since Independence.

Trends in Birth and Death Rates

The trends in birth and death rates since 1901 are presented in table 4.

TABLE – 4

VITAL RATES PER 1000 POPULATION, INDIA, 1901-1990

	Birth rate	*Death rate*	*Rate of natural increase*
1901-10	49.2	42.6	6.6
1911-20	48.1	47.2	0.9
1921-30	46.2	36.3	9.9
1931-40	45.2	31.2	14.0
1941-50	39.9	27.4	12.5
1951-60	40.9	22.8	18.1
1961-70	40.0	17.8	22.2
1971-80	37.8	15.4	22.4
1980-82	33.8	12.3	21.5
1988-90	30.6	10.3	20.3
2001	25.8	8.5	13.3

* Provisional

Sources: Davis (1951); India, Registrar General (1954); Jain (1982); Office of the Registrar General, Sample Registration Bulletin (various issues).
Economic Survey 2002-03.

In India while death rate has registered a remarkable decline, birth rate has not fallen to that extent resulting in high growth of population particularly since 1951. While death rate fell immediately with improvement in medical facilities, improved sanitation and better living standard, birth rate depends on a complex set of factors: social, religious, economic and political.

Causes of Declining Death Rate

1. Improved medical and health care facilities: Resulting in control of epidemics like plague, small pox, malaria etc. which earlier took a heavy toll of life. Infant mortality rate and maternity death rates have considerably declined on account of better health care facilities.

2. Impact of social reforms: With the spread of education and empowerment of women, female infanticide and sati pratha have considerably declined resulting in decline in death rate.

3. Control of famines: With the improvement in means of transport and communication and government intervention in supply of foodgrain, the spread of famines has been effectively checked. Of course occasionally, we do have famine condition on account of drought or floods, but timely supply of food and medicines prevent starvation deaths.

Causes of High Birth Rate

Social factors like universality of marriage and marriage at young age, joint family system, preference for a son result in high birth rate.

Economic factors such as widespread poverty, high infant mortality and children as an insurance have also contributed to high birth rate. Among poor families, additional children do not add to any burden, rather they provide helping hands for the family. Further low survival rate among infants also encourages high birth rate. Because of lack of savings due to poverty, a large number of children act like insurance for their parents. These children when grown-up provide security to their parents in old age.

Economic Development: Economic development of the country has been single most significant factor causing a sharp decline in death rate. With rising incomes and levels of living, nutritional levels have improved making people less prone to diseases. Improvement in personal hygiene and sanitary conditions which go with better standard of living have prevented the spread of communicable diseases. Education increases the awareness of preventive measures. Thus the impact of economic development has been to promote better health and longer life. The life expectancy at birth has gone up from 32 years in 1950-51 to 64 years (males) and 67 years (females) in 2001. Thus on an average people now live longer. Special programmes aimed at improving income and living standards of poorer section of society, provision of basic needs such as pure drinking water, health care facilities, houses for homeless etc. have all contributed to better life and lower death rate.

TABLE – 5

SELECTED HEALTH INDICATORS

	Parameter	*1951*	*1981*	*1991*	*Current Levels*
1	Crude Birth Rate (Per 1000 population)	40.8	33.9	29.5	25.0 (2002*)
2	Crude Death Rate (Per 1000 population)	25.1	12.5	9.8	8.1 (2002*)
3	Total Fertility Rate (Per woman on average)	6.0	4.5	3.6	3.2 (1999)
4	Maternal Mortality Rate (Per 100,000 live births)	N.A.	N.A	437 (1992-93)	407 (1998)
5	Infant Mortality Rate (Per 1000 live births)	146 (1951-1961)	110	80	64 (2002*)
6	Child Mortality Rate (0-4 years, per 1000 children)	57.3 (1972)	41.2	26.5	19.5 (2000)
7	Couple Protection Rate (%)	10.4 (1971)	22.8	44.1	48.2 (1998-99) NFHS
8	Life Expectancy at birth (in years)				
	Male	37.2	54.1	59.7 (1991-95)	63.9 (2001-06)
	Female	36.2	54.7	60.9 (1991-1995)	66.9 (2001-06)

Note : The dates in the brackets indicate years for which latest information is available.
NFHS: National Family Health Survey NA: Not Available
* Provisional

Source : Ministry of Health and Family Welfare.

Possible Pathways to a Faster Decline in Fertility

On the basis of the experience of several countries in Europe, North America and East Asia, the classical model of demographic transition postulates a link between a desire for fewer children and changes in macro-development variables such as urbanisation, industrialisation, literacy and education, and the status and roles of women (Coale, 1973; Freedman, 1982). A study by the United Nations (1965) has added means of communications to the list. These changes affect the aspirations relating to children, functions of the family and the perceptions of the costs and benefits of children.

There are lessons to be drawn from the experience of Kerala and

Tamil Nadu which have already attained the replacement level of fertility (or a net reproduction rate of one) by 1988. The term 'replacement level of fertility' or a net reproduction rate of one (or unity) implies that each woman would give birth, on an average, to only one daughter.[7]

The Technical Group on Population Projections has made population projections for the period 1996-2016. The population of India was 846 million in 1991 and is expected to grow to 1263 million by 2016. If the current trend of population growth continues India is expected to achieve replacement level of fertility only by 2026. Reduction in the population growth rate has been recognised as one of the priority objectives during the Ninth Plan period and also in the Tenth Plan. With effective implementation of special action programme and meeting all the felt needs for Reproductive and Child Health, it is expected that the Total Fertility Rate, can be brought to 2.6 by 2002 and replacement level of fertility can be achieved by 2011.[8]

Urbanisation

Economic development is generally associated with the growth of urbanisation. During the first half of the 20th century, India passed through a period of economic stagnation. Consequently, the extent of urbanisation was very limited. Urban population which accounted for 11 per cent of total population in 1901 reached the figure of 14 per cent in 1941. With a very liberal definition of the urban area adopted in 1951, urban population became 17.6 per cent of total population. Much of the increase, therefore, was statistical. This explains why the adoption of a little more strict definition of the urban area in 1961 census resulted in recording a very small increase in the urban population and it was estimated at 18.3 per cent of total population. The 1981 census has also continued with the definition adopted in 1971, both from the point of view of administrative convenience and maintenance of comparability.

An urban area has thus been defined as follows:

(a) all places with a municipality, corporation, cantonment board or notified town area committee,

(b) all other places which satisfy the following criteria:

  (i) a minimum population of 5,000;

---

7. Visaria, op. cit.
8. Pant, K.C. (2003), op.cit.

(ii) atleast 75 per cent of male working population engaged in non-agricultural pursuits; and

(iii) a density of population of atleast 400 persons per sq. km.

The definition of the "Urban Area" though very strict as compared to definitions adopted in earlier censuses is still not comparable with the definition of urban area provided in other countries. For instance, in Japan, a place having 30,000 or more inhabitants is classified as Urban area.

Degree of Urbanisation in India – A Comparison with Some Selected Countries

A comparison of the level of urbanisation in India with the developed countries of the world reveals that India is far behind the high income countries. The proportion of urban population to total population in 1992 was 74 per cent in Russia, 76 per cent in USA, 77 per cent in Japan, 85 per cent in Australia and 89 per cent in U.K. Compared to them, the Indian percentage of 25.7 in 1991 was too low. Obviously, employment strategies should be planned so that they attract population to urban areas. It is only the pull exercised by economic development that can bring about the much desired change towards urbanisation.

Table 6 reveals that the proportion of urban population in class I towns (with a population of over 1 lakh) has increased from 25.7 per cent in 1901 to 65.2 per cent in 1991. Obviously, there is a trend towards concentration of population in the bigger towns. The relative proportion of urban population in Class II and Class III towns taken together has remained practically constant i.e., around 26-28 per cent during 1901-91. But in contrast, the relative proportion of population in Class IV, Class V and Class VI towns has come down sharply from 47.2 per cent in 1901 to barely 10.7 per cent in 1991.

Class I towns have been the seats of administration and general economic activity. Industry, transport, trade and commerce, administrative and liberal services have been concentrated in class 1 towns. This explains the increasing concentration of urban population in this size-class.

In the context of the need to accelerate fertility decline, it does not seem a feasible option to adopt conscious policies to promote urbanisation. The economies of agglomeration need to be recognised and the state policy cannot effectively neutralise them without considerable cost to society. At the same time, the processes underlying urbanisation are not easily amenable to state intervention, particularly in view of the severe resource crunch.

TABLE – 6

TREND OF URBANISATION IN INDIA

	Towns with different population size-classes						
	Class I 1,00,000 & above	*Class II 50,000 to 99,999*	*Class III 20,000 to 49,999*	*Class IV 10,000 to 19,999*	*Class V 5,000 to 9,999*	*Class VI (Less than 5,000)*	*All Classes*
Number of Urban Agglomerations/Towns							
1951	76	91	327	608	1,124	569	2,795
1961	102	129	437	719	711	172	2,270
1971	148	173	558	827	623	147	2,476
1981	216	270	738	1,053	739	229	3,245
1991	296	341	927	1,135	725	185	3,609
Urban Population (Lakhs)							
1951	275	61	97	84	80	19	616
1961	399	87	132	99	53	6	776
1971	612	117	171	117	48	5	1,070
1981	945	182	224	149	56	8	1,564
1991	1,388	233	281	165	55	6	2,128
Percentage Distribution of Urban Population							
1901	25.7	11.3	15.8	20.9	20.1	6.2	100.0
1951	44.6	10.0	15.7	13.6	13.0	3.1	100.0
1961	51.4	11.2	16.9	12.8	6.9	0.8	100.0
1971	57.2	10.9	16.0	10.9	4.5	0.4	100.0
1981	60.4	11.6	14.3	9.5	3.6	0.5	100.0
1991	65.2	10.9	13.2	7.8	2.6	0.3	100.0

Note: Excludes Assam and Jammu & Kashmir
Source: Registrar General of India.

Literacy

At the time of independence, India had much lower literacy rates, particularly in the case of women than Sri Lanka or Thailand. Since independence, the availability of schooling facilities has expanded substantially.

Literacy as seen in the 2001 census

The progress of literacy rates in India since 1951 is listed in Table-7. While the rates for the years 1951, 1961 and 1971 Censuses relate to the population in the five years plus category, those for 1981, 1991 and 2001 relate to the population which is seven years and above. The literacy rates for the country as a whole increased from 18.33 per cent in 1951 to 65.38 per cent in 2001 (Table 7), with literacy rate for males at 75.85 per cent and that for females at 54.16 per cent. The literacy rate recorded an increase of 13.17 percentage points from 1991 to 2001, the highest increase in any one decade. An encouraging feature is that the growth rate of literacy has been higher in case of females at 14.87 per cent than for males at 11.72 per cent during this decade. The gap in male-female literacy rates has decreased from 24.84 percentage points in 1991 to 21.70 percentage points in 2001. The rate of growth of literacy in the decade ending 2001 has been higher in the rural areas, at 14.75 per cent as compared to the 7.2 per cent increase in urban areas. Despite these improvements literacy in urban areas was 80.3 per cent and that in rural areas 59.4 per cent.

Kerala, which has the highest literacy rate of 90.92 per cent, occupies the top slot in both male and female literacy, at 94.20 and 87.86 per cent respectively. Bihar has the lowest literacy rate of 47.53 per cent, along with the lowest literacy rate for males at 60.32 per cent and for females, at 33.57 per cent. The number of literates has more than doubled in Dadra and Nagar Haveli and Rajasthan during the decade 1991-2001. As per the 2001 Census, all States and Union Territories have now achieved a male literacy rate of over 60 per cent. States/UTs having less than 50 per cent female literacy rates are Rajasthan, Arunachal Pradesh, Dadra and Nagar Haveli, Uttar Pradesh, Jammu & Kashmir, Jharkhand and Bihar.

The National Literacy Mission (NLM) set up in 1988, seeks to achieve full literacy i.e. a sustainable threshold level of 75 per cent literacy by the end of the year 2005, by imparting functional literacy to the non-literates in the 15-35 age group. The NLM aims at ensuring that the Total Literacy Campaigns and their sequel, the Post Literacy Campaigns successfully move on to "Continuing Education". Under this scheme, greater emphasis is placed on development and acquisition of new learning. To prevent the non-literates from relapsing into illiteracy and also acquire skills, the NLM has been restructured to provide for an integrated approach combining the Total and Post Literacy Programme under one "Literacy Project" to achieve continuity, efficiency and convergence.

TABLE – 7

RURAL-URBAN LITERACY RATES 1951-2001

Year	*Male*	*Female*	*Persons*
1951			
Rural	19.02*	4.87*	12.10*
Urban	45.60*	22.33*	34.59*
Total	27.16	8.86	18.33
1961			
Rural	34.30	10.10	22.50
Urban	66.00	40.50	54.40
Total	40.40	15.35	28.30
1971			
Rural	48.60	15.50	27.90
Urban	69.80	48.80	60.20
Total	45.96	21.97	34.45
1981			
Rural	49.60	21.70	36.00
Urban	76.70	56.30	67.20
Total	56.38	29.76	43.57
1991			
Rural	57.90	30.60	44.70
Urban	81.10	64.00	73.10
Total	64.13	39.29	52.21
2001			
Rural	71.40	46.70	59.40
Urban	86.70	73.20	80.30
Total	75.85	54.16	65.38

Note :-

(*) For 1951, the population male, female and persons refers to effective literacy rates and the break up of Rural, Urban and male-female components are crude literacy rates.

(1) Literacy rates for 1951,1961 and 1971 Censuses relates to population aged five years and above. The rates for the 1981,1991 and 2001 Census relate to population aged seven years and above.

(2) The 1981 Literacy rates exclude Assam where census could not be conducted and the 1991 literacy rates exclude Jammu & Kashmir where Census could not be conducted due to disturbed conditions.

(3) The 2001 Census, literacy rates exclude entire Kutch district, Morvi, Maliya-Miyana and Wankaner talukas of Rajkot district, Jodiya taluka of Jamnagar district of Gujarat State and entire Kinnaur district of Himachal Pradesh where population enumeration of Census of India, 2001, could not be conducted due to natural calamities.

Source : Census of India 2001

The need for accelerating the rate of the levels of school attendance and literacy among children of school going age is widely recognised.

But, the situation is not likely to improve without substantial changes in the quality and content of instruction offered by many of the rural as well as urban schools. The inclusion of population education in the curriculum of schools would also help only if the teachers can hold the interest of their pupils.

The Status of Indian Women

Among the frequently used indicators of the status of women in a society are the sex differentials in life expectancy at birth and child mortality rates, school enrolment ratios, school retention rates and maternal mortality rates. The age at marriage and the worker-population ratios of women are likely to reflect their status as well as roles. A telling index, however, is the sex ratio or the number of males per 1000 females.

Most developed countries have a higher proportion of females in their population because women are biologically sturdier and live longer than men. In India, however, all the censuses have shown lower proportion of women; women enumerated in the 1991 Census number 31 million less than men. The data shown in table 3 indicate a stability of the sex ratio since 1971 around 93 females per 100 males. Also, Punjab and Haryana with the lowest proportion of women have continued to show an improvement during 1971-91.

Earlier analytical work has shown higher female mortality as the primary cause of the deficit of women in India (Visaria, 1971).

The situation with respect to some of the other indicators of the status of women has already been noted above. The level of literacy and education as well as the mean age at marriage have been rising and the proportion of widows has been falling since Independence. The pace of change is slower than we would like but its direction is certainly right. Some analysts have taken the employment of women or the female worker-population ratio as an indicator of their status. However, as noted earlier, contrary to the widespread belief based on the census data, the NSS surveys have confirmed a stability of the level of work participation by women.

Despite the improvements noted above, Indian women face many handicaps and discriminations with regard to nourishment and growth, access to medical care in the event of an illness, choice of spouse, rights of ownership and inheritance, and even freedom of movement and decision-making for routine matters. On all these matters, very large inter-group differences preclude any generalisation. The growing awareness about these problems also augurs well for their solution. An elimination of all discriminations must indeed be our national goal. But given the difficulty of enforcing new social norms through laws or constitutional provisions, the scope for state intervention to raise the status of women in order to accelerate the decline in fertility seems extremely limited.

The Experience of Kerala and Tamil Nadu

The two southern states of Kerala and Tamil Nadu with a population of about 94 million (9 per cent of the total) in 2001 illustrate the alternative ways of reaching a replacement level of fertility.

In Kerala, with its very low infant and child mortality rate, the adoption of a two-child norm has led to a total fertility rate of 2.0; allowing for mortality, its fertility is below (87.8) the replacement level.

An almost universal female literacy and a low level of infant and child mortality, and the high status of women, all intrinsically desirable goals, are considered crucial in the decline in fertility in Kerala. However, other important contributory factors include the very high pressure of population density on land and an associated low proportion of rural male workers engaged in agriculture (the lowest, 54 per cent, among the major states according to the 1987-88 survey of the NSS), a very low proportion of the self-employed, and relatively very high rates of open unemployment (the highest in the country). The persistent high level of unemployment has been accompanied by the demonstration by the emigrants to the Middle East of the feasibility of getting out of the vicious circle of poverty. Such a combination of forces favourable to fertility decline through both delayed marriage and control of marital fertility is not easy to find elsewhere in the country.

The decline in fertility in Tamil Nadu has been attributed to the political support for both an increase in the age at marriage and an imaginative programme of information, education and communication (IEC).

Policy Shift Essential to Check Population Growth

According to Pravin Visaria, the replication of the experiences of Kerala and Tamil Nadu elsewhere in the country, particularly in the four large states in north India is a formidable task. The experience so far reveals a few lessons that might be useful in achieving the long-term goals of the country. In brief, they must include:

1. A well designed programme of increasing the efficacy of the large body of health workers for the difficult task of persuading their clientele to modify their reproductive behaviour.
2. The adoption of a scheme of incentives and disincentives to delay marriage and to limit the number of children after marriage.

In a country with over 575,000 villages and 4,700 urban centres, the means of modifying traditional behaviour have to be adapted to the local conditions. For this purpose, health workers must focus their attention on the level of birth and death rates and strive to register all pregnancies, births, and infant, child and adult deaths. An identification of a pregnancy can be followed by a systematic sequence of ante-natal, intra-natal and postnatal care for both the mother and the child. The result would be a high degree of rapport between the health workers and their clientele. A carefully monitored experiment in some 15-20 target fixed districts for a period of 5 to 10 years in cooperation with some non-governmental voluntary agencies and researchers deserves a high priority.

System of Incentives and Disincentives

Finally, an effective system of 'incentives and disincentives' for lowering the rate of growth of population can make an invaluable contribution. Incentives and disincentives must be used to encourage youth to marry late and to delay and limit their child bearing age after marriage. Incentives seem to be difficult to administer without adding to the corruption except in the organised sector of employment; also, given the fiscal crisis faced by the Indian state, their scope is likely to be limited. Therefore, the focus must be on disincentives. Obviously, we cannot penalise childen born to what may be called 'improvident' parents; but an environment in which the seriousness of our population problem is fully recognised by everyone must be created. Visaria advocates "A law may be enacted disqualifying anyone from applying for a job in the government or the public sector if at the time of marriage, the bride was below 21 years of age. Given the large number of aspirants for government and public sector jobs, the proposed law would have the salutary effect of raising the age at marriage. (The organised private sector can also be persuaded to follow a similar policy.) We might also consider whether the right to contest an election and to hold public office can be denied to couples who decide to have more than two children. Such a restriction on the privileges enjoyed by our citizens would have a much wider impact than is usually realised."[9]

National Population Policy 2000

The National Population Policy (NPP) 2000 outlines the long-term objective as one "to achieve a stable population by 2045, at a level consistent with the requirements of sustainable economic growth, social development, and environment protection." The medium-term objective of NPP is to bring down the Total Fertility Rate (TFR) to the replacement level of 2.1 by 2010. Though in absolute terms, 180.6 million persons have been added to the population during 1991-2001, the net growth in population has witnessed a declining trend over the decades starting from 1961. The decadal growth of population at 21.34 per cent between 1991-2001, witnessed the sharpest decline since independence with the average growth rate for the corresponding period declining to 1.93 per cent per annum. This indicates that the country is entering a phase of rapidly declining fertility in the process of demographic transition. States registering low growth rates in population during 1991-2001 are Kerala, Tamil Nadu, Andhra Pradesh. States which have shown an upward swing in population growth rates during this period are Bihar, Haryana, Uttar Pradesh, Sikkim, Nagaland, Delhi, Chandigarh and Gujarat.

The demographic profile across States reveals that 9 States and Union Territories including Kerala, Tamil Nadu and Punjab are reported to have already reached the replacement level of fertility. These States account for about 15 per cent of total population. Another 10 States with about 41 per cent of the country's population are likely to achieve replacement rates by 2010. The remaining 11 States and UTs which account for about 44 per cent of the country's population and include the more populous States like Uttar Pradesh, Rajasthan, Bihar, Madhya Pradesh may not achieve replacement rates of fertility by 2010. (Source: Fertility Estimates of the National Commission on Population).

Along with the implementation of the National Population Policy involving all social sector programmes, the State Governments have an important role to play in improving the social, economic and demographic indicators specially in the high fertility regions. Formulation of State level Population Policies is already under way and effective implementation of population stabilisation efforts in concerned States would determine the year and size of the population at which the country achieves demographic stabilisation.

---

9. Visaria, op. cit.

8

Unemployment and Employment Perspective

Tenth Five Year Plan

TO understand the concept of unemployment it is necessary to understand the concept of labour force, for by definition, one who is not in the labour force can not be unemployed. By the internationally accepted definitions, all persons who are working (have a job) and though not working, are seeking and are available for work, are deemed to be in the labour force. Correspondingly, all those who are not working and are neither seeking nor available for work are considered outside the labour force and hence do not figure in employment or unemployment statistics.[1]

The growth rate of labour force is determined partly by the age structure of the population and the age and sex specific labour force participation rate that can be expected to obtain.

Population and Labour Force Projections

The changes in the age structure of population,[2] given the present demographic transition of the Nation, are such as to lead to a much faster growth of population in the working age group than the entire population, and this, given the different participation rates in different age groups will lead to a faster growth of labour force as compared to the working age population (Table 1).

---

1. M.L. Dantwala, *Understanding Poverty and Unemployment*, in Uma Kapila (Ed.) "Indian Economy Since Independence", 1999-2000, P. 865.
2. Planning Commission, Tenth Five Year Plan, Ch.5, p. 143.

TABLE – 1

GROWTH IN POPULATION AND LABOUR FORCE

(per cent per annum)

	2002-2007	*2007-2012*	*2012-2017*
Population (All age groups)	1.63	1.41	1.20
Population (15-59 years)	2.41	2.08	1.70
Labour Force (1) (15-59 years)	2.42	2.15	1.78
Population (15+)	2.57	2.26	1.93
Labour Force (1) (15+)	2.51	2.25	1.92

Note: (1) Labour force projections here are on the basis of labour force participation rate for each quinquennial age group remaining unchanged, i.e. the changes in labour force growth in relation to population are due to changes in the age composition of the population.

Source: Planning Commission.

There was a substantial gap in the growth rates of working age population and labour force in the period 1993/1994 – 1999/2000, leading to a sharp fall in the growth of labour force to 1.31 per cent per annum from 2.43 per cent during the preceding period 1983 – 1993/94. The Planning Commission Special Group on Creation of 10 million Employment Opportunities a Year in Tenth Plan noted that the causes underlying this sharp fall need to be investigated further. One view is that withdrawal from labour force is to invest one's time in acquiring education for better returns in future, while the Special Group observes that this factor can only partially explain withdrawal from labour force, and suggests that lack of work opportunities can also lead to complete withdrawal from labour force. The decline in the rate of growth of labour force, however, is not expected to continue unabated in future. Hence the special Group adopted the higher of the two alternative labour force growth scenarios suggested by the Task Force on Employment Opportunities. Accordingly, the Group has adopted a 1.8 per cent growth rate of labour force in the Tenth Plan period (2002-07), i.e. a much slower decline in the age-specific participation rates in the period beyond 2007-12. Therefore, the projections of labour force are made here on 1.8 per cent growth.

Concepts & Measurement

National Sample Survey Organisation have used three concepts of unemployment.

(i) Usual status unemployment

(ii) Current weekly status unemployment

(iii) Daily status unemployment

The usual status or chronic unemployment measured in number of persons i.e. persons who remain unemployed for major part of the year. Activity status is determined with reference to a longer period, say a year preceding to the time of survey.

The weekly status unemployment (measured in number of persons) i.e. persons who did not find even an hour of work during the survey week.

Daily status unemployment (measured in number of days or person years) i.e. persons who did not find work on a day or some days during the survey week.

The usual status unemployment is generally recorded as a measure of open unemployment during the reference year. The current weekly unemployment rate also measures chronic unemployment with reduced reference period of a week. The current daily status is considered to be a comprehensive measure of unemployment including both chronic unemployment as well as under employment on a weekly basis.

Measurement of Employment and Unemployment

In the Ninth Plan, the calculations of employment and unemployment were based on Usual Principal and Subsidiary Status basis (UPSS). The Report of the Special Group[3] has viewed that current daily status (CDS) is a better measure to capture unemployment and underemployment, than the usual status, and therefore recommended the use of CDS basis for estimation purpose.

The rationale for using CDS as measuring employment and unemployment is the following. The Approach Paper to the Tenth Plan recommends creation of gainful employment opportunities for the entire additions to labour force in the Tenth Plan and beyond. Therefore,

3. Planning Commission, Report of the Special Group on Targeting Ten million Employment opportunities per year over the 10th Plan period, Chairman: S.P. Gupta, (2002)

policies and programmes to fill the gap between requirement and availability of gainful employment opportunities are to be worked out. At any point of time, there is a large unemployed and under-employed workforce i.e., not having any gainful employment, although by using the measurement on UPSS basis, several of them are declared employed. This results in overestimation of the level of employment. To avoid this, largely, the Special Group suggested estimation of the extent of employment and unemployment on CDS basis.

According to the NSSO employment and unemployment survey report of 1999-2000 'The usual status approach adopted for classification of the population is unable to capture the changes in the activity pattern caused by seasonal fluctuations. But the estimate obtained by adopting the current weekly or current daily status approaches are expected to reflect the overall effect caused by the intermittent changes in the activity pattern during the year. The latter (CDS) reflects also the changes, which take place even during the week. *The estimate of the employed based on current daily status gives average daily picture of employment.' Therefore the Special Group regarded the CDS measurement as the most appropriate measure to have an estimate of the gap i.e., jobs to be created on gainful basis, in order to bring out recommendations as to how they can be filled up by changes in policies and programme.*

The NSSO Report also provides estimates of the likely under-employment that is hidden in the number of the employed category, calculated by the UPSS approach when they are compared with CDS. The activity pattern of the usual employment during the days within the reference week is indicated by the distribution of their activity by current daily status. The relevant results for rural and urban India are presented in Table 2. It is observed that the proportion of person days of the usually employed, utilised for work, is lower for females as compared to the males throughout the period 1987-88 to 1999-2000. During 1999-2000, this proportion was estimated at about 68 per cent and 79 per cent for females in the rural and urban India respectively, as against 90 per cent and 94 per cent for males in rural and urban India respectively. If the work is not available, large portion of the females withdraw from the labour force rather than report themselves as unemployed. The distribution obtained from the 1999-2000 survey is presented in Table 2.

TABLE – 2

PER 1000 DISTRIBUTION OF PERSON-DAYS OF USUALLY EMPLOYED (PRINCIPAL AND SUBSIDIARY STATUS WORKERS TAKEN TOGETHER) BY THEIR BROAD CURRENT DAILY STATUS

Current daily status	*Rural*						*Urban*					
	Male			*Female*			*Male*			*Female*		
	1999-00	*1993-94*	*1987-88*	*1999-00*	*1993-94*	*1987-88*	*1999-00*	*1993-94*	*1987-88*	*1999-00*	*1993-94*	*1987-88*
(1)	*(2)*	*(3)*	*(4)*	*(5)*	*(6)*	*(7)*	*(8)*	*(9)*	*(10)*	*(11)*	*(12)*	*(13)*
Employed	897	909	926	676	663	638	942	949	938	791	766	716
Unemployed	53	40	27	41	30	26	27	27	37	22	24	37
Not in Labour Force	51	51	47	283	306	336	31	25	25	187	210	247
All	1000	1000	1000	1000	1000	1000	1000	1000	1000	1000	1000	1000

Source: NSSO

Recent Trends in Employment and Unemployment Situation

There was a slight decline in population growth between the periods 1983-1993/94 and 1993/94-1999/2000 from 2.0 per cent per annum to 1.9 per cent. Though growth of output in the economy accelerated between these two periods – from 5.2 per cent gross domestic product (GDP) growth to 6.7 per cent, the pace of employment growth slowed down from 2.7 per cent to 1.07 per cent as per National Sample Survey Organisation (NSSO) employment surveys (Annexure 1). Slow-down in pace of employment growth, in the nineteen nineties, is also borne out by demographic census data - growth of main workers decreased from 2.34 per cent to 0.81 per cent. Similar trends in deceleration of employment growth are revealed for specific segments of employment– growth of workers in establishment covered by economic census came down from 2.84 per cent per annum in 1980-1990 to 1.71 per cent in 1990-1998; employment in establishments covered by Employment Market Information System of Ministry of Labour grew at 1.20 per cent per annum during 1983-1994 but decelerated to 0.53 per cent during the next five years 1994-1999. However, the latter decline was mainly due to a decrease in employment in public sector establishments, whereas the private sector showed acceleration in the pace of growth from 0.45 per cent to 1.87 per cent (Annexure 2). Thus, the employment intensity of the growth process of the Indian economy is coming down (Annexure 3).

The decrease in employment intensity of output growth can be explained by either an increase in capital intensity or increase in labour productivity, releasing labour. Both happened partly in this period. Incremental capital output ratio (ICOR) increased greatly and also capital substituted labour. Both suggest strategies to look for labour intensive areas and technologies.

Projections of Employment Opportunities

The employment generating capacity of output growth has been seen to be reduced in recent years (Annexure 3). The baseline scenario of growth of GDP is 6.5 per cent, as indicated in the Tenth Plan Approach Paper. This scenario shows that on the 'business as usual basis' (i.e., with the present employment elasticity) the percentage of unemployed will grow up to 11.0 at the end of the Tenth Plan, giving a total unemployed labour force of 45.56 million person years. This picture is not acceptable on any socio-economic or political ground. Therefore, a much higher growth rate (8 per cent) is needed for the future along with positive policies and programmes for changing the sectoral pattern and technology in favour of labour-intensive production, if unemployment is to be tackled.

The estimates of employment and unemployment of the Tenth Plan's base year (2001-02) are given in Annexure 4. The estimates of unemployed for the year 2001-02 have been given around 34.85 million person years (defined on CDS basis) when the unemployment rate went up around 9.21 per cent. It also provides the estimates of addition to labour force over the Tenth Plan period as 35.29 million person years. Thus, over the Tenth Plan, we have to deal with the problem of creating job opportunities against a potential job demand of more than 70.14 million person years (i.e., 34.85 million base period unemployment and 35.29 million new labour entry net of exits). The Approach Paper recommends providing gainful employment opportunities to all the additions in the labour force over the five year period, and reducing significantly the rate of unemployment over the Tenth Plan, so that by the end of the Eleventh Plan, the unemployment rate will be near zero.

The Tenth Plan visualises a substantially higher growth rate of 8 per cent per annum. Given this growth pattern and assuming the present sectoral employment elasticities, an estimate has been made of the level of employment and unemployment over the Tenth Plan. Increased employment opportunities of around 29.67 million person years (i.e., an increase from the base figure of 343.36 million to 373.03 million) will be created with the help of a 8 per cent per annum growth over the next five-year period. This 'business as usual' scenario means, an employment growth of 1.7 per cent per annum as against a labour force growth of 1.8 per cent per annum. The result: even with as high a growth as 8 per cent, the objective of providing employment opportunities to all additions to labour force will not be achieved; an additional 5.62 million employment opportunities will have to be created. This, added to the base period stock unemployment of 34.85 million, will give an unemployment rate of 9.79 per cent at the end of the Tenth Plan, an increase from 9.21 per cent at the base. This arises largely due to the near jobless growth character in many sectors of the economy especially in the organised sector, and a growing capital intensity in many of the organised sectors and even in some of the unorganised sectors including some small scale industries. The unemployment rate at the end of the Tenth Plan can even go up by a minimum one percentage point (adding four million more unemployment) if the labour force growth increases to 2.0 per cent per annum. The answer is, therefore, to look for a development strategy, which will revamp the activities in those sectors where the comparative advantage lies in a labour-intensive nature of production.

As the economy is now operating under the impact of globalisation, all care should be taken in the reallocation of activities between sectors and sub-sectors, so that every sector can meet the open market competition. To give a simple example, without the changes in the overall growth rate of agriculture, the sub-sector compositions can be changed by changing the cropping patterns and resources allocated between food and non-food, from less to more labour intensive sectors. Even this strategy may not always need additional investment resources. In fact, it is often said that a change in favour of labour intensive activities is accompanied by saving of capital by substitution of capital by labour and knowledge/technology. Specific programmes and projects are to be identified and launched, keeping this goal in view. As per the findings of the Special Group on Employment Generation, agriculture and allied sector activities have a very large employment generating potentiality. This is to be achieved not necessarily by heavy additional investment, but by reallocation of funds and choice of appropriate technologies. But to be sustainable under the present globalised system, this should be supported by appropriate policies to increase their productivity and competitiveness, which would make them viable.

The maximum addition to employment generated from special programmes will come from:

(i) agriculture and allied activities,

(ii) small and medium enterprises, broad-based rural non-farm activities and some of the social services sectors like education and health. Besides, appropriate policy changes have been identified for the fast development of sectors of high labour intensity like construction, tourism, communication and information technology and financial services. There are many potential areas in the informal sectors, and especially in the self-employment area, which can provide high employment, and therefore should also be developed.

The summary Annexure 5 shows that, with suitable programmes and policy changes, the 8 per cent growth rate can generate an additional 19.32 million person years of employment opportunities over the Tenth Plan period, giving a total of 50 million person years of employment opportunities over the Tenth Plan. This recommended scenario will not only absorb all additions to labour force generated over the Tenth Plan in gainful manner, but also reduce the level of unemployment by nearly half and will eliminate it completely by the end of the Eleventh Plan. The percentage unemployed will go down from 9.21 per cent to 5.11 per cent by the end of the Tenth Plan and unemployment will be eliminated by the end of the Eleventh Plan. To summarise, nearly 20 million person years of employment opportunities have to be created by selective innovative programmes and policies leading to a changed pattern of growth in favour of labour intensive sectors; the remaining 30 million will come from the normal buoyancy of growth as perceived over the recent past (1993-94 to 1999-2000), giving a total of 50 million person years over the Tenth Plan.

Strategies and Policies for Employment Generation

While a higher rate of economic growth is a necessary condition for increasing the demand for labour, the pursuit of growth objective in isolation may not be sufficient, at least in an immediate foreseeable future, to gainfully absorb the annual additions to labour force. Therefore, in the short-term perspective of a Five Year Plan, growth will have to be supplemented by increasing the employment content of growth in order to fulfill the employment objectives of Plan.

Sectoral Policy Initiatives for Opening up New Employment Opportunities

There are many labour intensive sectors, where employment-generating growth can be rejuvenated if right kind of sectoral policies can be put in place. An indicative list of such sectors is given in Box.

BOX

Some Labour Intensive Sectors which Require Policy Intervention

- Agriculture and Allied Activities
  - There is a need to step up public investment in agriculture. Simultaneously, bringing additional acreage under cultivation of oilseeds and pulses by switching from cereals holds substantial potential for employment generation. Horticulture, farm management programmes, agri-clinics and seed production are other potential areas for employment generation.
  - Re-generation of degraded forests, watershed development and highly labour intensive activities.
  - Wasteland Development.
  - Development of Medicinal Plants and Energy Plantation which have high growth and employment potential.
  - Minor irrigation
  - Cultivation of Bamboo and manufacturing of bamboo based products
- Food Processing
- Rural Non-Farm Activities/ Industries, including Khadi and Village Industries
- Small and Medium Enterprises
- Services Sectors
  - Health
  - Nutrition
  - Education
  - Information technology and communication

ANNEXURE – 1

PAST AND PRESENT MACRO SCENARIO ON EMPLOYMENT AND UNEMPLOYMENT ON CDS BASIS

(Person years)

	(Million)			*Growth per annum (%)*	
	1983	*1993-94*	*1999-2000*	*1983 to 1993-94*	*1993-94 to 1999-2000*
ALL INDIA					
Population	718.20	894.01	1003.97	2.00	1.95
Labour Force	261.33	335.97	363.33	2.43	1.31
Workforce	239.57	315.84	336.75	2.70	1.07
Unemployment Rate (%)	(8.3)	(5.99)	(7.32)		
No. of Unemployed	21.76	20.13	26.58	-0.08	4.74
RURAL					
Population	546.61	658.83	727.50	1.79	1.67
Labour Force	204.18	255.38	270.39	2.15	0.96
Workforce	187.92	241.04	250.89	2.40	0.67
Unemployment Rate (%)	(7.96)	(5.61)	(7.21)		
No. of unemployed	16.26	14.34	19.50	-1.19	5.26
URBAN					
Population	171.59	234.98	276.47	3.04	2.74
Labour Force	57.15	80.60	92.95	3.33	2.40
Workforce	51.64	74.80	85.84	3.59	2.32
Unemployment Rate (%)	(9.64)	(7.19)	(7.65)		
No. of Unemployed	5.51	5.80	7.11	0.49	3.45

Note : All estimates are on CDS (Current Daily Status basis)
Figures in brackets denote percentage

Source : NSSO & Population Census

ANNEXURE – 2

TOTAL EMPLOYMENT AND ORGANISED SECTOR EMPLOYMENT GROWTH RATE (PER CENT P.A.)

Heads	*1983 to 1993-94*	*1993-94 to 1999-2000*
Total Population	2.00	1.95
Total Labour Force	2.43	1.31
Total Employment	2.70	1.07
Organised Sector Employment*	1.20	0.53
Public Sector	1.52	(-)0.03
Private Sector	0.45	1.87

Note : * Organised Sector Employment growth rates correspond to the periods 31.3.1983 to 31.3.1994 and 31.3.1994 to 31.3.1999

Source : DGE&T, Ministry of labour

ANNEXURE – 3

SECTORAL EMPLOYMENT ELASTICITIES ON CDS BASIS

Sectors	*Employment Elasticity*		
	1983 to 1987-88	*1983 to 1993-94*	*1993-94 to 1999-2000*
Agriculture	0.87	0.70	0.01
Mining and Quarrying	1.25	0.59	-0.41
Manufacturing	0.59	0.38	0.33
Electricity, Gas and Water Supply	0.30	0.63	-0.52
Construction	2.81	0.86	0.82
Trade, Hotels and Restaurant	0.87	0.68	0.62
Transport, Storage and Communication	0.47	0.55	0.63
Financing, Insurance, Real Estate and Business Services	0.49	0.45	0.64
Community, Social and Personal Services	0.52	0.68	-0.25
ALL	0.68	0.52	0.16

Note : Elasticity may change after adjustment of workers of Repair services

Source : NSSO (For estimating employment growth rates) and NAS (for estimating GDP growth rates)

ANNEXURE – 4

EMPLOYMENT SCENARIO FROM 8% GROWTH PER ANNUM AND EXTRAPOLATED INDUSTRIAL STRUCTURE

(Based on Actual Elasticity (1994-2000) -CDS & 1.8% p.a. Growth in L.F.)

	Unit	*1999-2000$*	*2001$$*	*2002$$*	*2007*	*2012*	*Employment Growth over 10th plan per annum*
Labour Force (1.8% p.a. Growth)	million	363.33	371.52	378.21	413.50	451.53	1.8%
Employment** #	million	336.75	340.82	343.36	373.03	403.52	1.7%
(Unemployment Rate)	(%)	7.32	8.26	9.21	9.79	10.63	
No. of Unemployed	million	26.58	30.70	34.85	40.47	48.01	3.0%

Note : ** Based on 8% Growth in GDP during 2002-07
Current Daily status basis
$ 1999-2000 figures related to NSS 55th (July, 1999-June, 2000) Rd.
$$ Based on 5.2% GDP Growth during 2000-01 and 2001-02

Source : Planning Commission

ANNEXURE – 5

ESTIMATES OF GENERATION OF SECTORAL EMPLOYMENT OPPORTUNITIES OVER THE TENTH PLAN

Sectors	Sectoral GDP Growth (%) 10th Plan	Base Employment (CDS) (million) 2001-2002	Increased Employment Opportunities Over Tenth Plan (million)			
			on Estimated Employment Elasticities	Programme and Policy Based	Total Incremental	Total Employment 2007
Agriculture & Allied (Including Rural activity)*	4.20 4.20	191.01 (55.63)	0.41	9.06	9.47	200.48 (51.09)
Mining & Quarrying	4.70	2.21 (0.64)	-0.20		-0.20	2.01 (0.51)
Manufacturing & SSI Pradhan Mantri Rozgar Yojana (PMRY) and Rural Employment Generation Programme (REGP)	10.00	42.09 (12.26)	7.42	4.20	11.62	53.71 (13.70)
Electricity, Gas & Water Supply	8.30	1.09 (0.32)	-0.21		-0.21	0.88 (0.22)
Constructions	8.30	16.16 (4.71)	6.30		6.30	22.46 (5.72)

(contd...)

ANNEXURE – 5 *(...Contd...)*

ESTIMATES OF GENERATION OF SECTORAL EMPLOYMENT OPPORTUNITIES OVER THE TENTH PLAN

Trade, Hotel & Restaurant	8.00	40.99 (11.94)	11.23		11.23	52.22 (13.28)
Transport, Storage & Communications	10.30	14.92 (4.35)	5.51		5.51	20.43 (5.21)
Financial Institutions, Real Estate & Business Services	10.00	5.32 (1.55)	1.93		1.93	7.25 (1.84)
Community Services, Social & Personal Services	7.60	29.57 (8.61)	-2.71	3.20	0.49	30.06 (7.64)
Sampoorna Gramin Rozgar Yojana (SGRY)				1.29	2.09	2.09
Swaranjayanti Gram Swarojgar Yojana (SGSY)				0.80		
Pradhan Mantri Gram Sadak Yojana (PMGSY)				0.77	0.77	0.77
Aggregate	**8.00**	**343.36**	**29.67**	**19.32**	**48.99**	**392.35**

Note : Brackets denote percentage composition to total.
Source : Planning Commission

9

Poverty in India

THE problem of poverty and unemployment is considered as the biggest challenge to development planning in India. High poverty levels are synonymous with poor quality of life, deprivation, malnutrition, illiteracy and low human resource development. The slogan of poverty eradication has been adopted by all political parties in one form or another and there is a national agreement for the goal of poverty alleviation. The national consensus on poverty alleviation provided the necessary condition for launching various schemes and programmes aimed at achieving this objective. But the persistence of poverty during all these years suggests that the national consensus on objectives did not and could not provide sufficient conditions for poverty alleviation.

Magnitude and Determinants

There is no agreement among scholars on the extent of poverty in India. The question arises why should there be such differences in the extent of poverty when the basic source of data used by all scholars is the same i.e., the various rounds of the NSS?

The starting point for estimating the number of households below the poverty line is a normative nutritional requirement per person per day at some base point. There is a debate on the minimum calorie requirement, and whether it should be the same for all parts of the country. Most acceptable figures are 2,400 calories per person per day in rural areas, and 2,200 calories per person per day in urban areas. The next step is to translate the nutrient requirement into monetary terms. The expenditure level of households which are able to spend the requisite amount to obtain the desired calories serves as the cut-off point, or the poverty line. To adjust the poverty line over a period of time, price variations have to be considered and an appropriate price deflator has to be selected. The problem arises in deciding upon such a deflator.

Thus, the following elements mainly affect the magnitude of the poverty ratio:

(i) the nutrition norm (translated into monetary terms) in the base year;

(ii) price deflator used to update the poverty line; and

(iii) pro rata adjustment in the number of households in different expenditure classes to determine the number of households below and above the poverty line. Different assumptions and methods are used for these three purposes, which accounts for the different estimates provided by scholars.

The Planning Commission has been estimating the incidence of poverty at the national and state level using the methodology contained in the report of the Expert Group on Estimation of Proportion and Number of Poor (Lakdawala Committee) and applying it to consumption expenditure data from the large sample surveys on consumer expenditure conducted by the NSSO at an interval of approximately five years. On this basis, comparable estimates of poverty are available at national and state level from 1973-74 to 1999-2000.

According to the latest large sample survey data on consumer expenditure made available by the National Sample Survey Organisation (NSSO) from its 55th Round Survey (July 1999- June 2000), the poverty ratio on a 30 day recall basis, is estimated at 27.09 per cent in rural areas, 23.62 per cent in urban areas and 26.10 per cent for the country as a whole. The incidence of poverty expressed as a percentage of people living below the poverty line has witnessed a steady decline from 55 per cent in 1973-74 to 36 per cent in 1993-94 and 26 per cent in 1999-2000. (Table 1). Though the poverty ratio declined, the number of poor remained stable at around 320 million for a fairly long period of two decades, (1973-1993), due to a countervailing growth in population. The latest estimates for 1999-2000 reveal a significantly reduced number of poor, at about 260 million out of a total population of 997 million.

Results of two annual surveys of household consumer expenditure conducted by NSSO for 2000-2001 and 2001-2002 have also become available. As per the results of the 57th NSS round, at the all-India level the proportion of chronically hungry households (not getting enough to eat during any month of the year) has declined to 0.5 per cent in rural areas and 0.1 per cent in urban areas. As for seasonal hunger, 16 per thousand households in rural areas and 3 per thousand households in urban areas reported getting enough food only in some months of the year.

TABLE – 1

ESTIMATES OF POVERTY

Year	*All India Number (Million)*	*Poverty Ratio (per cent)*	*Rural Number (Million)*	*Poverty Ratio (per cent)*	*Urban Number (Million)*	*Poverty Ratio (per cent)*
1973-74	321	54.9	261	56.4	60	49.0
1977-78	329	51.3	264	53.1	65	45.2
1983	323	44.5	252	45.7	71	40.8
1987-88	307	38.9	232	39.1	75	38.2
1993-94	320	36.0	244	37.3	76	32.4
1999-2000	260	26.1	193	27.1	67	23.6
2007*	220	19.3	170	21.1	49	15.1

* Poverty projection for 2007.

Source : Tenth Five-Year Plan.

Poverty at the national level is estimated as the weighted average of state-wise poverty levels. The poverty ratio is estimated from the state-specific poverty lines and the distribution of persons by expenditure groups obtained from the NSS data on consumption expenditure. The state specific poverty ratios at the national and state levels are listed at Table 2.

State Level Poverty Ratios

State-wise poverty ratios have witnessed a secular decline from 1973-74 to 1999-2000. Though poverty has declined at the macro-level, rural-urban and inter-state disparities are visible. The rural poverty ratio is still relatively high in Orissa, Bihar and the North Eastern States. In Orissa, Madhya Pradesh, Bihar and Uttar Pradesh, the urban poverty ratios were in the range of 30.89 to 42.83 per cent in 1999-2000. The combined rural and urban poor make up 47.15 per cent of Orissa and 42.60 per cent of Bihar. For the states of Madhya Pradesh, Sikkim, Arunachal Pradesh and Assam the combined poverty ratios in 1999-2000 were in the range of 33.47 to 37.43 per cent. There has been a significant reduction in poverty during the period in Kerala, Jammu & Kashmir, Goa, Lakshadweep, Delhi, Andhra Pradesh, Gujarat, Tamil Nadu, Karnataka, West Bengal and Andaman and Nicobar Islands. Thus, while some states such as Punjab and Haryana have succeeded in reducing poverty by following the path of high agricultural growth, others have focussed on particular areas of development e.g. Kerala has focussed on human resource development, West Bengal on vigorous implementation of land reform measures and empowerment of Panchayats, and Andhra Pradesh on direct public intervention in the form of public distribution of foodgrains.

The results of the 55th Round Employment-Unemployment confirms that the poverty ratios have indeed declined over the 1990s. However, at the level of individual states, the results are more mixed. While in eight out of fifteen major States, poverty ratios have indeed declined over the 1990s, in seven others it has remained either unchanged or have even increased. In all cases, even at the all-India level, the order of decline (wherever that has materialised) in the poverty prevalence rates revealed by the Employment-Unemployment Survey has been significantly smaller than that revealed by the 55th Round Consumer Expenditure Survey.

Basic Minimum Services

It is well accepted that high growth of incomes is by itself not enough to improve the quality of life of the poor. Unless all the citizens of the country, and most particularly the poor, have certain basic minimum services, their living conditions cannot improve. These minimum services include among other things literacy, education, primary health care, safe drinking water and nutritional security. The Government had convened a meeting of Chief Ministers to identify such basic minimum services and a list of seven services had unanimously been agreed upon. *These seven services are safe drinking water, primary health facilities, universal primary education, nutrition to school and pre-school children, shelter for the poor, road connectivity for all villages and habitations, and the Public Distribution System (PDS) with a focus on the poor.*

Poverty can effectively be eradicated only when the poor start contributing to the growth by their active involvement in the growth process. Implementation of the programmes should be increasingly based on approaches and methods which involve the poor themselves in the process of poverty eradication and economic growth. This is possible through a process of social mobilisation, encouraging participatory approaches and institutions and empowerment of the poor.

TABLE – 2

POVERTY RATIO AT THE STATE LEVEL

(per cent)

S.No.	State	Rural			Urban			Combined		
		1973-74	*1993-94*	*1999-2000*	*1973-74*	*1993-94*	*1999-2000*	*1973-74*	*1993-94*	*1999-2000*
1	Andhra Pradesh	48.41	15.92	11.05	50.61	38.33	26.63	48.86	22.19	15.77
2.	Arunachal Pradesh	52.67	45.01	40.04	36.92	7.73	7.47	51.93	39.35	33.47
3.	Assam	52.67	45.01	40.04	36.92	7.73	7.47	51.21	40.86	36.09
4.	Bihar	62.99	58.21	44.30	52.96	34.50	32.91	61.91	54.96	42.60
5.	Goa	46.85	5.34	1.35	37.69	27.03	7.52	44.26	14.92	4.40
6.	Gujarat	46.35	22.18	13.17	52.57	27.89	15.59	48.15	24.21	14.07
7.	Haryana	34.23	28.02	8.27	40.18	16.38	9.99	35.36	25.05	8.74
8.	Himachal Pradesh	27.42	30.34	7.94	13.17	9.18	4.63	26.39	28.44	7.63
9.	Jammu & Kashmir	45.51	30.34	3.97	21.32	9.18	1.98	40.83	25.17	3.48
10.	Karnataka	55.14	29.88	17.38	52.53	40.14	25.25	54.47	33.16	20.04
11.	Kerala	59.19	25.76	9.38	62.74	24.55	20.27	59.79	25.43	12.72
12.	Madhya Pradesh	62.66	40.64	37.06	57.65	48.38	38.44	61.78	42.52	37.43
13.	Maharashtra	57.71	37.93	23.72	43.87	35.15	26.81	53.24	36.86	25.02
14.	Manipur	52.67	45.01	40.04	36.92	7.73	7.47	49.96	33.78	28.54
15.	Meghalaya	52.67	45.01	40.04	36.92	7.73	7.47	50.20	37.92	33.87
16.	Mizoram	52.67	45.01	40.04	36.92	7.73	7.47	50.32	25.66	19.47
17.	Nagaland	52.67	45.01	40.04	36.92	7.73	7.47	50.81	37.92	32.67
18.	Orissa	67.28	49.72	48.01	55.62	41.64	42.83	66.18	48.56	47.15
19.	Punjab	28.21	11.95	6.35	27.96	11.35	5.75	28.15	11.77	6.16
20.	Rajasthan	44.76	26.46	13.74	52.13	30.49	19.85	46.14	27.41	15.28
21.	Sikkim	52.67	45.01	40.04	36.92	7.73	7.47	50.86	41.43	36.55
22.	Tamil Nadu	57.43	32.48	20.55	49.40	39.77	22.11	54.94	35.03	21.12

(Contd...)

...Contd...

S.No.	State	Rural 1973-74	Rural 1993-94	Rural 1999-2000	Urban 1973-74	Urban 1993-94	Urban 1999-2000	Combined 1973-74	Combined 1993-94	Combined 1999-2000
23.	Tripura	52.67	45.01	40.04	36.92	7.73	7.47	51.00	39.01	34.44
24.	Uttar Pradesh	56.53	42.28	31.22	60.09	35.39	30.89	57.07	40.85	31.15
25.	West Bengal	73.16	40.80	31.85	34.67	22.41	14.86	63.43	35.66	27.02
26.	A & N Island	57.43	32.48	20.55	49.40	39.77	22.11	55.56	34.47	20.99
27.	Chandigarh	27.96	11.35	5.75	27.96	11.35	5.75	27.96	11.35	5.75
28.	Dadra & Nagar Hav.	46.85	51.95	17.57	37.69	39.93	13.52	46.55	50.84	17.14
29.	Daman & Diu	N.A.	5.34	1.35	N.A.	27.03	7.52	N.A	15.80	4.44
30.	Delhi	24.44	1.90	0.40	52.23	16.03	9.42	49.61	14.69	8.23
31.	Lakshadweep	59.19	25.76	9.38	62.74	24.55	20.27	59.68	25.04	15.60
32.	Pondicherry	57.43	32.48	20.55	49.40	39.77	22.11	53.82	37.40	21.67
	All India	**56.44**	**37.27**	**27.09**	**49.01**	**32.36**	**23.62**	**54.88**	**35.97**	**26.10**

N.A. Not Available

1. Poverty Ratio of Assam is used for Sikkim, Arunachal Pradesh, Meghalaya, Mizoram, Manipur, Nagaland and Tripura.
2. Poverty Line of Maharashtra and expenditure distribution of Goa is used to estimate poverty ratio of Goa.
3. Poverty Line of Himachal Pradesh and expenditure distribution of Jammu & Kashmir is used to estimate poverty ratio of Jammu & Kashmir.
4. Poverty Ratio of Tamil Nadu is used for Pondicherry and A & N Island
5. Urban Poverty Ratio of Punjab used for both rural and urban poverty of Chandigarh
6. Poverty Line of Maharashtra and expenditure distribution of Dadra & Nagar Haveli is used to estimate poverty ratio of Dadra & Nagar Haveli.
7. Poverty Ratio of Goa is used for Daman & Diu.
8. Poverty Ratio of Kerala is used for Lakshadweep.
9. Urban Poverty Ratio of Rajasthan may be treated as tentative.
10. Estimates on a 30 day recall basis for 1999-2000.

Source: Planning Commission.

POLICY

Some people – especially among those who see rapid overall economic growth as both a necessary and sufficient condition for eradicating poverty and who see excessive state intervention as the major impediment to growth – consider this obsession with poverty, and counting the number of poor, as distracting attention and resources from growth promoting policies. The government according to them should confine itself to ensuring law and order, enabling markets to function freely, facilitating free trade and capital movements and providing universal elementary education, health care, water supply, sanitation and essential infrastructure. On the other hand they question the efficacy of various poverty alleviation programmes and, by implication, the justification for spending huge amounts on social programmes. These arguments according to Vaidyanathan* are fundamentally flawed.

Growth – necessary as it is – does not 'benefit' automatically and in equal proportion to all regions and sections of the population. For a variety of reasons – historical factors, resource endowments, social and political conjunctures and, of course, government policy – growth happens to be very uneven across regions. This fact is beyond dispute. It also happens that regions which are poorly developed to begin with have also grown at a slower rate than average. This tendency cannot be dismissed as an inevitable but transitional phase which will get corrected over time. Nor can one accept the proposition that so long as there is no decline in level of development in any region, there is no need for intervention. Such a proposition, apart from being questionable on merits, is politically unacceptable in a democracy. Concern for equity and political necessity are compelling arguments for government intervention to correct the imbalance.

This argument acquires even greater force in relation to people: both as a proportion of the population and in absolute terms, those who do not have and cannot afford even the quite modest minimum living standard currently accepted as the norm in the Indian context are very large.

The evolution of policies and programmes meant to tackle this problem may be haphazard and in some respects even incoherent. Nevertheless one can see a clear pattern in the way they seek to recognise and address differing needs of backward areas with special problems, and of different segments of the poor and underprivileged.

---

* A. Vaidyanathan, *Poverty and Development Policy* in Uma Kapila (ed.) Indian Economy Since Independence, Ch. 33, pp. 910-922 (2003-04).

Broadly they can be divided into the following groups:

(1) Affirmative action by way of reservations for scheduled castes and tribes in elected bodies, public sector jobs and educational institutions supplemented by special programmes, with earmarked allocations, for their development and welfare.

(2) Programmes (notably IRDP, TRYSEM, DWACRA) designed to help poor segments to acquire or add to their productive assets and enable them to make more productive use of such assets.

(3) Various special programmes to provide additional employment to the poor.

(4) Schemes to ensure that all villages have access to a minimum standard of educational and health facilities, safe drinking water and roads.

(5) Various forms of direct transfers by pension and insurance schemes for aged, disabled and widows, school feeding and child nutrition programmes and subsidised distribution of foodgrains and other essential commodities to the poor.

(6) Special programmes for the development of production potential for hill tracts, deserts and drought prone areas.

For the most part these programmes are conceived and funded by the central government which determines the criteria for allocation between states (and in some cases within states). Actual implementation is left to the state government agencies subject to guidelines (sometimes quite detailed) regarding the scope and content of schemes, and their targeting and implementation procedures. Only a few (notable being the Maharashtra Employment Guarantee Scheme and Tamil Nadu's Midday Meals Programme for school children) have been taken up entirely at the initiative of states.

Over the years the functioning of these programmes and their impact on the poor has attracted a great deal of attention. Numerous studies – several under the auspices of the government, and many more based on independent surveys, micro studies and analyses of available macro data – have highlighted their achievements as well as weaknesses.

Flaws in Policies and Programmes

Official claims of the number of beneficiaries, projects carried out, additions to productive assets and employment generated are unreliable and exaggerated.

(1) Poor targeting is reflected in the high proportion of non-poor and other non-eligible persons among the beneficiaries.

(2) Leakages due to inappropriate works, inefficient implementation and corruption are high.

(3) Quality of assets provided/created under these programmes is poor and their impact on income level of beneficiaries dubious. Assets and schemes are frequently not appropriate to the needs and potentials of particular regions or groups.

(4) There is little consultation with, not to speak of involvement of local communities generally and target groups in particular, in deciding and implementing schemes.

(5) Lack of accountability remains a major problem. The structure, content and funding of these programmes remain mostly in the hands of the central government.

(6) There is considerable overlap among these schemes as well as between them and development schemes included under the normal state plans. Typically each programme is administered by a separate agency each with its own line hierarchy and operating independently.

These features, taken together with the rigidity of central guidelines, make for fragmentation and duplication of schemes. Coordination is difficult; so is monitoring of accomplishments in terms of efficacy of targeting, quality of works actually completed and impact on the beneficiaries.

(7) The programmes tend to emphasise loans and subsidies and provision of current wage employment rather than ensuring that they are used to augment productive capacity for achieving a higher level of employment and income on a sustained basis. The selection of beneficiaries, the distribution of loans and subsidies, and the recovery of loans offer much scope for patronage and corruption at the political and bureaucratic levels.

(8) The public distribution system (PDS) does not accomplish its aim of ensuring essential consumer goods to the poor at reasonable prices. Large parts of the country (especially states which have the largest concentration of poor) simply do not have a distribution network to reach the supplies where they

are most needed. In states (Kerala, West Bengal, Tamil Nadu) which have such networks, the coverage is not limited to the poor. And attempts to ensure better targeting have been thwarted by administrative difficulties and political opposition. The efficiency of PDS as a poverty alleviation measure and the desirability of continuing it in the present form is being questioned. Supporters of PDS, who see it as a major instrument for ensuring food security for the poor, strongly oppose this prescription even as they recognise the need for restructuring the programme.

These widely known and documented deficiencies have given poverty alleviation programmes a bad name. Critics argue – some explicitly and more by implication – that the effective contribution of these schemes to sustained poverty reduction is not commensurate with the resources spent on them. That given the high level of fiscal deficits and the severe shortage of resources for infrastructural investments needed for overall growth, the country can ill afford this luxury.

It is certainly true that outlays on targeted poverty alleviation programmes have increased rapidly both in absolute terms and relative to total public sector plan outlay. Prior to 1970, these were limited to special schemes for scheduled castes and tribes, social welfare, backward areas. Total outlay for these was Rs 6 billion, or less than 4 per cent of public sector plan during the 4th Plan. During the Eighth Plan (1992-1997), the outlay on a vastly larger and more varied poverty alleviation programme amounted to Rs 460 billion (about 11 per cent of the total public sector plan). Also, outlays on PA programmes have grown considerably faster than total plan outlay in a period marked by severe infrastructure shortage and bottlenecks. However large these figures might seem, the fact remains that they account for barely 1 per cent of the GDP.

This is not to deny the need and immense scope for improving the efficacy of poverty alleviation programmes by better targeting, reducing waste and corruption, making the programmes more meaningful in terms of relevance to local needs and priorities, and creating institutional conditions for greater accountability. The focus should be on rationalising the approach, organisation and priorities of the PA programmes rather than on cutting back the outlays. The number of PA programmes can, and should, be drastically reduced and streamlined to minimise duplication and fragmentation. We need distinguish only between 3 and 4 basic PA programme categories:

(1) Those which are meant to ensure that all communities in the country have a minimum standard of school, primary health care, water supply, sanitation and connectivity.

(2) Those which are meant to enable resource poor segments of the population to acquire productive assets and to use them effectively.

(3) Programmes to provide additional employment opportunities to those poor who do not have productive assets and depend on wage employment.

(4) Programmes to enable scheduled castes and tribes to take advantage of educational and health facilities so that they are better equipped to take advantage of growing opportunities.

IRDP in its present form deserves to be scrapped. Identification of poor, the kinds of assets to be provided, ensuring the back up needed for their programme cannot, as experience has shown, be managed efficiently by government. The difficulties are compounded when they involve heavy subsidies and are implemented by a bureaucracy to political interference. Instead, public investment ought to concentrate on providing infrastructure to facilitate overall development and in each region according to its resource potential thereby opening up greater and more diverse opportunities for employment and entreprenurial activity.

The poor of course, need special help by way of information, technical advice and training to take advantage of growing investment opportunities. The government has a key role in providing this help. But it is neither necessary nor desirable for the government to decide what assets are to be provided, to whom and on what terms. These tasks are better left to individual's choices. Those who want to invest in any enterprise can seek credit from financial institutions who must be left free to judge the viability of the loan and the borrowers. The government's role here would be essentially to lay down guidelines (such as priority sector lending) and providing interest subsidies or insurance of loans given to the poor.

There is also a strong case for including land among the assets eligible for institutional credit for the rural landless and land poor. Redistribution of land through conventional approach to land reforms has not worked and seems unlikely to make much headway. However, the spread of education among the bigger farmers is leading to increasing migration to urban areas; they are also seen to be investing their surplus in non-agricultural activities. The resulting weakening of their economic stake as well as their power in the village communities is creating a situation where they are willing to sell their land. This process has already occurred on a significant scale in several parts of the country and seems to be spreading. In such a situation, asset poor households wanting to acquire land – the most important productive resource in rural areas – deserves as much emphasis in poor-oriented credit programmes as for the acquisition of other assets or setting up other enterprises.

The rationale for special area programmes as a separate category is also questionable. Practically all the components of these programmes figure in the sectoral programmes. Scrapping the special area programme and merging them into sectoral and area development programmes will make for more effective use of public funds by eliminating dysfunctional and wasteful fragmentation of resources and effort. From the view point of poverty alleviation, agriculture and related activities are the most important. The scale and content of these programmes should however be tailored to the diverse resource potentials in different regions and constraints impeding their realisation. This is the rationale for watershed development and planning on the basis of agro-climatic regions. But these are at present no more than in name. If these are pursued seriously and the organisational arrangements for planning are recast on that basis, there is really no need for special area (or for that matter special crop specific) schemes.

In implementing integrated regional resource planning, it would be perfectly legitimate to earmark allocations, and even provide special extra funds, for use in regions which rank low in terms of per capita income and employment. The distribution of funds between regions must however be based not only on needs, but also potential for development of land, water and livestock resources as part of integrated area development plans.

Employment schemes can all be merged into one and allocations between and within states determined on the basis of the magnitude of poverty incidence, magnitude of unemployment and development potential.

Within the framework of the above broad approach, it is possible to provide earmarked allocations for schemes to ensure minimum standard of amenities and acquisition of assets for scheduled castes and tribes; and for assistance (by way of subsidies or loans) to enable them to finance higher education and skill acquisition. These would make better sense and be more effective when they are part of an overall regional plan.

Targeting

The other, and in many ways more important, issue is targeting. The search for ways to reduce chances of mistargeting has largely focused on more effective monitoring of beneficiary selection; creating credible checks against mistargeting; and creating incentives for 'self selection'. Incomes are notoriously difficult to ascertain. And once it is known to determine eligibility for benefits, there is a strong general incentive to understate incomes. It is better to rely on more easily verifiable attributes (family size, land holding, caste, etc) associated with poverty. Though this does not eliminate scope for falsification, it certainly reduces the scope for it compared to the income criterion.

Clearly, targeting errors can be reduced if conditions of eligibility and/or the scale of benefits are so defined as to reduce the incentives for those above the poverty line to get into the programme. Insisting on a certain portion of beneficiaries being drawn from poor/vulnerable groups (SC, ST, women) and providing wage employment in employment schemes at wages somewhat below the market/minimum wage rate and at locations away from the residence would be a more effective way of reaching target population than relying on discretionary authority.

Targeting has not only a class/individual dimension, but also a spatial aspect. The poor being unevenly distributed between regions, spatial targeting is an important, but relatively neglected, aspect.

There is thus a strong case for rationalising the criteria for spatial allocation along the following lines. Allocations for all employment and production oriented PA schemes should be pooled and distributed between states, and within states, in proportion to the absolute number of poor or preferably, income deficit and the number of unemployed. Funds for programmes to ensure a minimum standard of basic amenities (elementary education, health care, water supply and access to roads) can be similarly pooled and distributed in proportion to the magnitude of deficiency in relation to the accepted minimum levels of facility. This would greatly add to the transparency of the programme and its effectiveness.

Accountability

Public accountability for ensuring proper choice of beneficiaries and proper use of funds remains a serious problem. Efforts to publicise the scale and nature of PA programmes in a particular block or district, the criteria by which beneficiaries are selected, the specific benefits to which they are entitled under each programme, and the procedures for availing of them have not been effective. Even when the information is available, there are no institutional mechanisms for making complaints or seeking redressal of grievances. Involvement of MLAs, MPs and other local leaders – whether formally as members of advisory committees or because of their ability to exert informal pressure – has not helped. On the contrary, irrespective of their party affiliation, politicians tend to use the opportunity to influence choice of schemes, locations and beneficiaries under these programmes as a source of power, and as instruments for consolidating their political base and often for personal gain. Surprisingly, neither elected representatives nor local cadres of political parties (even when they belong to the opposition) have shown much interest in taking up these issues.

Role of NGO and Voluntary Organisations

NGOs also play a role in making people aware of the various PA programmes and benefits available under them; and intervening with concerned government agencies to secure benefits for eligible people. Some have taken the role of mobilising public opinion to assert people's entitlements under various PA programme or to press the government to allocate more resources and permit greater flexibility in programming to adapt scheme to local conditions. NGOs have played an active role in lobbying for freedom of information concerning details of public development schemes, entitlements to their benefits and the beneficiaries.

Non-governmental and voluntary organisations have a particularly key role in obtaining and disseminating information on the working of government (including local government), making people aware of their entitlements and obligations, and enabling them to vent their grievances and seek redress. Besides interceding with the concerned authorities to secure benefits for the eligible and minimise leakages, they have a role in motivating and organising local communities to take active interest in the working of specific programmes and persuading bureaucracy to work with the community for improving the effectiveness of programmes.

Anti-Poverty Programmes: Tenth Plan

The major anti-poverty programmes aimed at providing self-employment and supplementary wage employment to people living below a defined poverty line have been in existence for over two decades. However, these have been restructured periodically in order to improve their efficacy as instruments of poverty reduction. The Ninth Plan further recognized the need to redesign and rationalize these programmes. The erstwhile IRDP and its several sub-schemes have been merged into a single selfemployment programme called the Swarnajayanti Gram Swarozgar Yojana (SGSY). The approach is a holistic one, through formation of self-help groups with capacity building, selection of activity clusters, infrastructural support, technology, credit and market access as essential ingredients built into the programme. In the Tenth Plan, the SGSY will be a process oriented programme with a focus on social mobilization and group formation in the first phase, thrift and credit amongst the members of the group augmented by a revolving fund in the second phase, and access to credit from micro finance institutions in the third phase. Micro enterprises would only be taken up when groups acquire the entrepreneurial abilities, know-how and market access in the fourth stage. Local people would be trained as animators and facilitators through a systematic programme especially in areas where NGOs do not exist.

There would be single wage employment programme, namely, the Sampoorna Gramin Rozgar Yojana (SGRY), instead of the Jawahar Rozgar Yojana and Employment Assurance Scheme, wherein the benefits would accrue to the people by way of direct transfer benefits through wage payments with some indirect benefits accruing through the creation of rural infrastructure. Under the SGRY the payment of wages would be partly in foodgrains and partly in the form of cash, which would ensure a minimum level of food security for the poor. At the village level the works would be largely labour intensive for creation of rural infrastructure. Further in selective backward districts, it is envisaged that 100 mandays of employment would be generated per person with an element of guarantee.

ANNEXURE

MAJOR POVERTY ALLEVIATION AND EMPLOYMENT GENERATION PROGRAMMES

- ***Pradhan Mantri Gramodaya Yojana (PMGY)***

PMGY was launched in 2000-2001 in all States and Union Territories (UTs) in order to achieve the objective of sustainable human development at the village level. The PMGY envisages allocation of Additional Central Assistance (ACA) to the States and UTs for selected basic minimum services in order to focus on certain priority areas. PMGY initially had five components viz., primary health, primary education, rural shelter, rural drinking water and nutrition. Rural electrification was added as an additional component from 2001-02. For 2002-03 as well as 2003-04, the allocation of ACA for PMGY was Rs. 2,800 crore. Both financial and physical monitoring of the programme is being carried out by the Planning Commission.

- ***Swarnajayanti Gram Swarozgar Yojana (SGSY)***

After a review and restructuring of the erstwhile Integrated Rural Development Program and allied schemes, SGSY was launched in April, 1999 and is the only self employment Programme currently being implemented. The objective of the SGSY is to bring the assisted Swarozgaris above the poverty line by providing them income-generating assets through bank credit and Government subsidy. The Scheme is being implemented on a 75:25 cost sharing of between the Centre and the States. Since its inception, and up to April 2004, a total allocation of Rs. 6,734 crore was made available by the Centre and States. Rs. 4,980 crore, have been utilized up to April 2004, benefiting 45.67 lakh Swarozgaris.

- ***Sampoorna Grameen Rozgar Yojana (SGRY)***

The SGRY was launched in September 2001, by merging the ongoing Schemes of Jawahar Gram Samridhi Yojana (JGSY) and Employment Assurance Scheme (EAS). The objective of the programme is to provide additional wage employment in the rural areas as also food security, along with the creation of durable community, social and economic infrastructure in rural areas. The SGRY is open to all rural poor who are in need of wage employment and desire to do manual and unskilled work in and around the village/habitat. The Scheme is implemented through Panchayati Raj Institutions. The scheme envisages generation of 100 crore many-days of employment in a year. The cost of each component of the programme is shared by the Centre and States in the ratio of 75:25. During the year 2003-04 an amount of Rs. 4,121 crore as cash component and 49.97 lakh tones of food grain were released to the States/UTs and 76.45 crore man-days (Provisional) have been generated as reported by the States/UTs. Under the Special Component of the SGRY, 65.84 lakh tonnes of foodgrain have been released to 12 calamity affected States during 2003-04.

- ***Rural Housing Schemes***

Rural housing schemes such as *Indira Awaas Yojana (IAY)* aim at providing dwelling units, free of cost, to the poor families of the Scheduled Castes (SCs), Scheduled Tribes (STs), freed bonded laborers and also the non-SC/ST persons Below Poverty Line (BPL) in the rural areas. The Scheme is funded on a cost-sharing basis of 75:25 between the Center and States. Till the end of 2003-04, the ceiling on construction assistance under IAY was Rs. 20,000/- in plain areas and Rs. 22,000/- in hilly areas, which has been increased to Rs. 25,000/- per unit for plain areas and Rs. 27,500/- for hilly areas from April 1, 2004. Twenty per cent of the allocation is allowed for upgradation of unserviceable Kutcha houses for which ceiling of Rs. 12,500 per unit applies since April 2004. *Credit-cum-Subsidy Scheme* for rural housing targeting rural families having annual income up to Rs. 32,000 was launched on April 4, 1999. An amount of Rs. 10 crore as equity support was provided to Housing and Urban Development Corporation (HUDCO) during 2003-04 by Ministry of Rural Development. In addition, the innovative scheme of *Rural Housing and Habitat Development and Rural Building Centres* (RBCs) was introduced to encourage innovative, cost effective and environment friendly solutions in building/housing sectors in rural areas. A *National Mission for Rural Housing and Habitat* has also been set up to address the critical issues of 'housing gap' and induction of science and technology inputs into the housing/construction sector in rural areas. Since inception (up to June 1, 2004) 113.96 lakh houses have been constructed/ upgraded by incurring an expenditure of Rs. 19,869 crore. During 2003-04, against the target of 14.84 lakh, 12.54 lakh (provisional) houses have been constructed/upgraded.

- ***Pradhan Mantri Gram Sadak Yojana (PMGSY)***

The PMGSY, was launched in December, 2000, to provide road connectivity to 1.6 lakh unconnected habitations with population of 500 persons or more (250 in case of hilly, desert and tribal areas) in the rural areas by the end of the Tenth Plan period. It is being executed in all the States and six UTs. Although the initial estimates indicated a requirement of Rs. 60,000 crore for the program, the present indications are that about Rs. 1,30,000 crore will be needed for achieving the intended connectivity. As per the Budget announcements of 2003-04, the diesel cess which is the source for funding the programme, was increased from Rs. 1 per litre to Rs. 1.50 per litre, in order to provide additional funds for the programme. Since the inception of the program, project proposals for Rs. 14,417 crore have been cleared and 88,685 Kms. of rural roads have been taken up under this program 20,740 road works had been completed till March 2004, and an expenditure of over Rs. 6,547 crore has been incurred by the States/UTs. The National Rural Roads Development Agency (NRRDA), registered under the Societies Registration Act, provides Operations and Management support for the program.

The Asian Development Bank (ADB) has agreed to support the development of rural roads in Madhya Pradesh and Chhattisgarh, which have been identified as recipient States for the first tranche. The ADB Board has approved a loan of $400 million (in a project size of $571 million). The States of Assam, Orissa and West Bengal have been identified for the second tranche of ADB assistance, of the order of US $500 million. A first tranche of $400 million for funding projects in Himachal Pradesh, Jharkhand, Rajasthan and Uttar Pradesh is likely to be available from the World Bank by the end of 2004-05.

Drought Prone Areas Program (DPAP), Desert Development Program (DDP) and Integrated Wastelands Development Program (IWDP) are being implemented for the development of wastelands/degraded lands. DPAP was launched in 1973-74 to tackle the special problems faced by those areas constantly affected by drought conditions. DDP was launched in 1977-78 to mitigate the adverse effects of desertification. IWDP has been under implementation since 1989-90. These programs were implemented on a sectoral basis till 1994-95. Since April 1995, these programs are being implemented on watershed basis. For the project DPAP, total number of the projects sanctioned were 2,535, with funds released by the Centre at Rs. 295 crore. Under DDP, 1,562 projects have been sanctioned with funds of amount Rs. 215 crore; and under IWDP, 190 projects with funding of Rs. 306 crore, were sanctioned.

The cost norms for all the three schemes have been revised to Rs. 6,000 per hectare. Under DPAP and DDP, the cost is shared between the Centre and the States in the ratio of 75:25, while in the case of IWDP, Rs. 5,500 is borne by the Central Government and Rs. 500 is shared by the States.

- ***Antyodaya Anna Yojana (AAY)***

AAY was launched in December 2000. Under the scheme 1 crore of the poorest among the BPL families covered under the targeted public distribution system are identified. Twenty five kilograms (kg) of food grains were made available to each eligible family at a highly subsidized rate of Rs. 2 per kg for wheat and Rs. 3 per kg. for rice. This quantity has been enhanced from 25 to 35 kgs with effect from April, 2002. The scheme has been further expanded in June 2003 by adding another 50 lakh BPL families. Under the scheme, during 2002-03, against an allocation of 41.27 lakh tonnes of foodgrain, 35.39 lakh tonnes have been lifted by State Governments, and during 2003-04, 38.24 lakh tonnes of foodgrain have been lifted against an allocation of 45.56 lakh tonnes.

- ***Swarna Jayanti Shahari Rozgar Yojana (SJSRY)***

The Urban Self-Employment Program and the Urban Wage Employment Program are two special schemes of the SJSRY initiated in December 1997, which replaced various programs operated earlier for urban poverty alleviation. Between the Centre and the States, SJSRY is funded on a 75:25 basis. During 2002-03, the full allocation of Rs. 105 crore provided for various components of this program was released. For 2003-04, an allocation of Rs. 94.50 crore plus Rs. 10.5 crore for North East and Sikkim was provided for various components of this program. The expenditure during 2003-04 was Rs. 105 crore

- ***Valmiki Ambedkar Awas Yojana (VAMBAY)***

The VAMBAY was launched in December 2001 to ameliorate the conditions of the urban slum dwellers living below the poverty line without adequate shelter. The scheme has the primary objective of facilitating construction and upgradation of dwelling units for slum dwellers and providing a healthy and enabling urban environment through community toilets under Nirmal Bharat Abhiyan, a component of the scheme. The Central Government provides a subsidy of 50 per cent, the balance 50 per cent being arranged by the State Government. There are prescribed ceilings on costs both for dwelling units and community toilets. During 2003-04, Central subsidy to the extent of Rs. 239 crore has been released. Since inception up to May 2004, Rs. 522 crore have been released as Government of India subsidy for the construction/upgradation of 2,46,035 dwelling units and 29,263 toilet seats under the scheme.

Source: Economic Survey 2003-04.

10

Resource Mobilisation and Pattern of Plan Financing

Pattern of Plan Financing: First Plan to Ninth Plan

THE main sources of funds for financing development expenditures contemplated in the plans are grouped under the following heads :

1. Balance from current revenue of government;
2. Surpluses of public enterprises;
3. Borrowings;
4. Additional resource mobilization;
5. External assistance; and
6. Deficit financing.

The balance from current revenue (BCR), that is the excess of government's revenues over non-plan current expenditure (item 1 above) and resources raised additionally through new measures undertaken during a plan period (item 4) together with the surpluses of public sector enterprises (item 2) constitute public savings and were expected to be a major source of finance for the Plans, being the least inflationary instrument for raising resources for public investment expenditure. The other domestic source of finance is borrowings and deficit financing (item 3 and 6). The pattern of plan financing as originally contemplated and as it emerged in reality since the First Five Year Plan is set out in Table 1.

Looking at the pattern of financing, one finds that plan financing in India depended primarily on domestic sources. External assistance has constituted no more than 12 per cent of the total outlay in the recent plans (4th, 5th, 6th, 7th and 8th plan). While in the Fourth and the Fifth

TABLE – 1

FINANCING OF PLAN OUTLAY IN PUBLIC SECTOR DURING FIVE YEAR PLANS

Figs. in (000 Crores)
(In bracket percentage)

	First Plan (1951-1956)		*Second Plan (1956-1961)*		*Third Plan (1961-1966)*		*Fourth Plan (1969-1974)*	
	Original	*Actual estimates*	*Original*	*Actual estimates*	*Original*	*Actual estimates*	*Original*	*Actual estimates*
Balance from current revenues	5.7[2] (27.55)	6.8 (32.50)	3.5 (7.29)	-5 (-1.09)	5.5 (7.33)	-4.2 (-4.90)	16.7 (10.52)	-2.4 (-1.46)
Public enterprises CPSEs including Railways	1.7 (8.22)	1.2 (5.87)	1.5 (3.13)	1.6 (3.26)	5.5 (7.33)	4.4 (5.07)	22.3 (14.03)	14.3 (8.86)
Borrowings	5.2 (25.04)	6.9 (35.20)	14.5 (30.21)	14.4 (30.84)	19.4 (25.87)	21.1 (24.62)	55.4 (34.84)	68.3 (42.26)
Additional resource mobilisation	—	2.6 (13.27)	8.5 (17.71)	10.5 (22.48)	17.1 (22.80)	28.9 (33.72)	32.0 (20.11)	42.8 (26.49)
External assistance (net)	5.2 (25.18)	1.9 (9.69)	8.0 (16.67)	10.5 (22.48)	22.0 (29.33)	24.2 (28.23)	26.1 (16.42)	20.9 (12.93)
Deficit financing	2.9 (14.02)	3.3 (16.84)	12.0 (25.00)	9.5 (20.34)	5.5 (7.33)	11.3 (13.19)	8.5 (5.35)	20.6 (12.75)
Aggregate resources	20.0 (100.00)	19.7 (100.00)	48.0 (100.00)	46.0 (100.00)	75.0 (100.00)	85.7 (100.00)	159.0 (100.00)	161.6 (100.00)

(Contd...)

TABLE – 1 (Contd...)

	Fifth Plan (1974-1979)		Sixth Plan (1980-1985)		Seventh Plan (1985-90)		Eighth Plan (1992-97)		Ninth Plan (1997-02)
	Original	Actual estimates	Original	Actual estimates	Original	Latest estimates	Original	Latest estimates	
Domestic Budgetary resources									
Current revenues	49.0	66.4	144.8	18.9	-52.5	-12.5	35.0	-46.25	-14.06
	(12.47)	(16.30)	(14.85)	(1.71)	(-2.92)	(-7.00)	(8.06)	(12.01)	-
Public enterprises CPSEs including Railways	8.5	25.8	94.0	58.1	354.9	140.8	148.2	101.3	340.5
	(2.20)	(6.35)	(9.64)	(5.24)	(19.72)	(7.89)	(34.13)	(26.34)	-
Borrowings	110.7	124.2	363.9	459.4	730.6	101.2	202.3	223.7	460.2
	(28.61)	(30.52)	(37.32)	(41.45)	(40.59)	(56.68)	(46.59)	(58.19)	-
Additional resource mobilisation	146.9	103.0	213.0	329.7	447.0	313.1	-	-	-
	(37.97)	(25.30)	(21.85)	(29.75)	(24.83)	(17.58)	-	-	-
External assistance (net)	58.3	52.1	109.3	85.3	180.0	161.0	287.0	381.1	600.0
	(15.07)	(12.79)	(11.21)	(7.70)	(10.00)	(9.03)	(6.61)	(9.93)	-
Deficit financing	13.5	35.6	50.0	156.8	140.0	282.0	200.0	290.0	-
	(3.49)	(8.74)	(5.13)	(14.15)	(7.78)	(15.82)	(5.01)	(7.55)	-
Aggregate resources	386.9	407.1	975.0	1108.2	1800.0	178.6	399.0	384.6	859.2
	(100.00)	(100.00)	(100.00)	(100.00)	(100.00)	(100)	(100)	(100)	-

Source : Planning Commission, January 2001, *Indian Planning Experience: A Statistical Profile*, P.39, Table 4.1.

Plan, external assistance contributed about 12 per cent to plan finances, in Sixth Plan 7.7 per cent, in Seventh Plan 9 per cent and in the 8th plan the net inflow from abroad although projected at 6.6 per cent, turned out to be little less than 4 per cent.

The most important sources of financing are "Additional Resource Mobilisation" (ARM) and domestic borrowings. The term ARM represents the resources which the government and the public enterprises at the Centre and in the States (the federating units of the Indian Union) are expected to raise over and above the surplus which their budgets are likely to generate. This surplus is worked out after projecting the current revenues and non-Plan current expenditure in the five years of a given Plan period, assuming normal growth in both revenues and expenditures. The growth rates of revenues of government are derived on the basis of past trends and / or their elasticities with respect to major determinants (e.g., with respect to GDP in the case of income-tax). Similarly, in the case of public enterprises, the growth is worked out on the basis of the existing structure of prices and costs. The ARM figures are based on an assessment of what the governments at the Centre and in the States and the public enterprises run by them can raise through additional efforts such as by raising the tax rates or intensifying collection efforts and cutting down non-Plan expenditures. In the case of public enterprises ARM represents what they can raise by revising their prices upwards or by cutting costs and improving their operational efficiency.

Borrowings, currently the biggest single item of domestic resources for the Plans, are made up of market borrowings, small savings, state provident funds, term loans from financial institutions and miscellaneous capital receipts. Market borrowings come mainly from the subscription primarily by the commercial banks. The commercial banks are required compulsorily to keep a fraction of their deposits in government securities to maintain what is called the statutory liquidity ratio and this has been a major instrument for channelizing the flow of household savings into the public sector. The other sources of borrowings are the small savings schemes designed to garner the savings of the households in the form of deposits with post offices which are spread all over the country reaching the far corners of rural areas, state provident funds and deposits of other financial institutions like the Life Insurance Corporation of India, General Insurance Corporation of India and so on.

The biggest single item of domestic resources for the Plan comprises borrowings viz market borrowings, small savings, state provident funds, term loans from financial institutions and miscellaneous capital receipts. Borrowings constituted 40 per cent to 58 per cent of plan finances (42 per cent in the 4th plan, 30.5 per cent in the 5th plan, 41.5 per cent in the 6th plan, 58 per cent in the 7th plan and for the 8th plan against the projected figure of 46.5 per cent the actual turned out be 63.1 per cent of the total finances). Amaresh Baghchi points out that as a result of the large shortfalls in budgetary savings and inadequate surpluses of PSU's, the financing of public sector plan outlay had to depend heavily on borrowings. Total domestic borrowings contributed anything between 40 and 60 per cent to plan finances in recent years (6th, 7th and 8th plan) as compared to about one-fifth to one-fourth in most of the earlier Plans. Inadequacy of current revenues to meet even current expenditures has resulted in the use of borrowed funds to meet current expenditures, leading close to what is called an internal debt trap. The main factor responsible for the falling contribution of the Central budget to the financing of the plans is the mounting burden of non-plan expenditure in the form of interest payments and subsidies on food and fertilisers.

Table 2 indicates the projection and realisation of the Ninth Plan resources and its funding of the Centre.

TABLE – 2

NINTH PLAN RESOURCES OF THE CENTRE

(Rs. crore at 1996-97 prices)

Sources of Funding	*Projection*	*Realization*	*% Realisation*
1. Balance from current revenues	-2,778 (-0.7)	-1,56,790 (-49.6)	-5,544.0
2. Borrowings including net MCR	3,16,760 (84.7)	4,55,624 (144.1)	143.8
3. Net inflow from abroad	60,018 (16.0)	17,452 (5.5)	29.1
4. Gross budgetary support to plan (1 to 3)	**3,74,000 (100.0)**	**3,16,286 (100.0)**	**84.6**
5. Central assistance to States & UTs	-1,70,018 (45.5)	-1,38,394 (43.8)	81.4
6. GBS for Central plan (4+5)	**2,03,982**	**1,77,892**	**87.2**
7. Resources of public sector enterprises	2,85,379	2,28,795	80.2
8. Resources for Central Plan (6+7)	**4,89,361**	**4,06,687**	**83.1**

Note : Figures in parentheses are percentage of Gross Budgetary Support.

The realised pattern of funding the GBS reflects a significant deterioration of non-debt contribution vis-a-vis the Ninth Plan projections. The share of balance from current revenues (BCR) in GBS reduced to a negative 49.6 per cent as against a projected share of a negative 0.7 per cent only. The realised share of borrowings therefore had to increase to 144.1 per cent as against a projected share of 84.7 per cent, to bridge the BCR gap.

The 5,544 percent deterioration in BCR was caused by stagnant level of revenue receipts and substantial growth in non-plan revenue expenditure (NPRE) in relation to GDP. Net Central revenues declined by 0.43 percentage points of GDP from 9.23 per cent in 1996-97 to 8.80 in 2001-02. Tax revenue (net) decreased by more than 1 percentage point from 6.85 per cent in 1996-97 to 5.80 per cent in 2001-02. The fall in tax revenue (net) could not be compensated by a 0.69 percentage points increase in non-tax revenue from 2.38 per cent to 3.07 per cent during the same period. As against a 1.05 percentage points fall in tax revenue (net), the gross tax revenue of the Centre fell by 1.21 percentage points from 9.41 per cent in 1996-97 to 8.20 per cent in 2001-02. This implied that the impact of the fall in gross Central tax revenues on Central finances was somewhat shared with the States.

The deterioration of the gross Central tax revenues in relation to GDP has given rise to concern on the following issues.

- Shrinkage of the tax base, as implied by inadequate coverage of the service tax base.
- Growth in various types of tax concessions and exemptions.
- Increase in the coverage of Modified Value Added Tax (MODVAT) without upward adjustment of tax rates.
- General slackening of the tax administration leading to revenue leakage.

Fiscal and Budgetary Developments 1980-2000

In order to understand the current fiscal predicament of the central government it is necessary to examine the pattern of central government expenditure and revenues over at least the last 20 years.

The total expenditure of the central government increased from an average of 16.8 per cent of GDP in 1980-85 to about 20.5 per cent in 1985-90 and has then declined to between 16 to 17.5 per cent in the late 1990s. At the same time non-plan expenditure has increased substantially from about 10 per cent in the early 1980s to about 13 per cent of GDP now. What is most notable is the very significant increase in expenditure that occurred in the second half of the 1980s. These increases took place in almost all categories of non-plan expenditure such as interest payments, defence expenditure, subsidies, pensions, and loans to states. During this period other non-plan expenditures, which consist mostly of salary payments to government servants, remained roughly stationary at about 2.25 per cent of GDP. Plan expenditures were kept high at about 6.5 per cent to 7 per cent of GDP throughout the 1980s. Correspondingly capital expenditures of central government were sustained at levels of 6 per cent to 7 per cent of GDP. Both plan expenditures and capital expenditures of the central government have fallen to levels of about 4 per cent of GDP since 1990s.

Interest payments are now at least three times that of non-plan government expenditure excluding the military and the police. The key area for action in correcting this fiscal imbalance is related to rising debt servicing obligations of the central government.

As Rakesh Mohan has rightly emphasised[1] the debt service burden of the government would not rise as a proportion of total expenditure if the investments made by the government from borrowings yield it adequate returns either through the generation of non tax revenues or through tax revenues. As the government borrows resources from the public to invest in new assets, tax revenues should rise through additions to public good assets. Improvement in public infrastructure should lead to improvement in efficiency and in aiding new private investment, and hence to buoyancy in tax revenues. Similarly, non-tax revenues should rise through increasing dividends from public enterprise investment in infrastructure and other activities. If, however, resources are borrowed for investment in activities which do not yield adequate returns, debt service payments will rise continuously as a proportion of total revenues. This is what seems to have happened in India over the last 20 years. The return on net worth in central public sector enterprises, excluding the petroleum companies is not significantly different from zero. Thus investments made in infrastructure or other activities through public sector enterprises have not yielded pecuniary returns to the government. Such returns would occur as increasing dividend payments from the public enterprises to the central government. In the budget they would be shown as "non tax revenues". Wrong pricing policies, inefficient public enterprise operations and other difficulties have all

1. Rakesh Mohan, *Achieving Higher Economic Growth: The Fiscal Deterrent*, in Uma Kapila op.cit.

contributed to this situation of low returns. With the government running a revenue deficit since the early 1980s, all government and public sector investment has come from resources borrowed by the central government. In the presence of no returns from such investments, debt service payments are bound to become an increasing burden.

Revenue Pattern of the Central Government

We may now examine the revenue pattern of the central government over the last 20 years to understand how debt service payments have been increasing so continuously. Corresponding to the increase in expenditure in the late 1980s an attempt was clearly made to also increase revenues over that period. The main increase in revenues took place in collection from custom duties, rising from about 2.8 per cent of GDP in the early 1980s to about 3.9 per cent in the late 1980s. This happened both as a consequence of increased imports (which led to the balance of payments crisis) and increase in levels of custom duties. The latter of course led to greater inefficiency in resource allocation as well as decline in export competitiveness. By the end of the 1980s, at an average of almost 110 per cent, India probably had the highest level of customs duties in the world. Subsequent to the economic reforms in 1991 there has been a consistent increase in the share of direct taxes from about 2 per cent of GDP right through the 1980s to about 3 per cent now. This increase has taken place both in corporate income tax collection and in personal income tax collection despite reduction in rates. The loss in tax revenues has taken place in indirect taxes, both in customs and in excise duties. Whereas customs duties collection were expected to fall as a result of major cuts in customs duties levels the fall in excise duty collection is more difficult to understand. In principle, rising industrial production should give rise to buoyancy in excise duty collection levels as a proportion of GDP. However two factors seem to have inhibited such expected growth. First, apart from the period 1993-96, industrial growth has not been as high as had been expected from the economic reforms. Thus the share of industry in GDP has remained stagnant. It is the share of services that has risen continuously; and services largely remain untaxed at the central level. Second, the progressive extension of MODVAT to the whole industrial sector has also led to a fall in excise duty collection as a proportion of GDP. The share of non-tax revenues has remained stagnant between 2.6 per cent and 3 per cent since the mid 1980s higher investment has not provided higher returns.

Gross tax revenues have remained at a level of about 10 per cent over the last 20 years except for the second half of the 1980s. During this period total expenditure, however, was at much higher levels both for the late 1980s and in the early 1990s. The shortfall in revenues has been made up by the central government through consistently high capital receipts, of between 6 per cent to 7.5 per cent of GDP right through the last 20 years. The notable feature in the pattern of capital receipts over the last 20 years is the increasing share of both public borrowing (internal debt) and small savings: the most expensive sources of capital receipts for the government. Whereas these two sources amounted to about 2.7 per cent of GDP in 1980-85 and about 43 per cent of total capital receipts in 1980-85 they now account for about 6 per cent of GDP and about 75 per cent of total capital receipts. External assistance is no longer an important source of financing for the government. Small saving receipts are extremely expensive forms of borrowing for the government because of the associated tax benefits that are given to small savers. 75 per cent of small savings receipts are passed on to state governments to finance their fiscal deficits.

Two changes in the system have made the cost of borrowing much higher for the central government in the 1990s. Earlier, a substantial portion of the fiscal deficits was financed by monetisation. This is no longer resorted to and hence the explicit interest cost of a fiscal deficit has consequently increased. Second, interest rate deregulation has made the cost of government borrowings equivalent to market rates, which was not the case earlier, when banks had to lend to the government at lower than market interest rates.

The consequence of a sustained high fiscal deficit over 20 years can be seen in table 3. Debt service payments of the central government have risen inexorably from about 30 per cent of tax revenues in 1980-85 to about 70 per cent now. According to Rakesh Mohan the day is not far off when the tax revenues will equal debt service payments. As a proportion of total revenue receipts debt service has increased from about 24 per cent in 1980-85 to about 50 per cent now. As a proportion of GDP, debt service payments have increased from about 2.2 per cent in 1980-85 to about 5 per cent now. Another consequence of rising debt service is that the revenue deficit has increased from about 17 per cent as a proportion of fiscal deficit in 1980-85 to about 50 per cent now. In another words half of current borrowing goes to finance current expenditure. By definition current expenditure yields no economic returns in the future and hence debt service payments will continue to rise in the foreseeable future unless a significant correction is made in this situation.

TABLE – 3

BURDEN OF RISING DEBT SERVICE OF CENTRAL GOVERNMENT (1980-2000)

	1980-85	*1985-90*	*1990-95*	*1995-99*	*1997-98*	*1998-99 (RE)*	*1999-00 (BE)*
As:							
% of Tax Revenue	30.1	40.5	58.9	65.9	68.6	70.5	71.7
% of Revenue Receipts	23.5	30.4	43.7	47.6	49.0	49.0	50.8
% of Total Revenue	14.3	18.4	26.4	29.3	28.3	27.7	31.0
% of Total Expenditure	13.3	16.5	24.6	28.3	28.3	27.4	31.0
% of GDP	2.2	3.4	4.4	4.6	4.6·	4.8	4.9
Revenue Deficit/ Fiscal Deficit	17.0	32.0	48.0	50.0			

Source: Govt. of India, Budget documents various years.

The Approach Paper to the 10th Plan stated that the fiscal situation of Central Government has deteriorated continuously in 1990s and especially during the Ninth Plan. The combined balance of current revenues of the Centre and the States declined from a negative Rs. 13,324 crore in 1996-97 or 1 per cent of GDP to negative Rs. 92,969 crore or 4.8 per cent of GDP in 1999-2000. This has occurred because of a substantial increase in interest payments and the increased wages and salaries on account of the Fifth Pay Commission award and equally importantly because the revenue receipts of Centre as a proportion of GDP have declined from 11.3 per cent in 1989-90 to 9.3 per cent in 2000-01. The shortfall between the revenue receipts and expenditure (non-plan) has been increasing and is around 3.6 per cent of the GDP. The Central Government has bridged this gap through consistently high public borrowings including borrowing from small savings - the most expensive source of capital receipts for the Government.

As a result, debt service payments of the Central Government have risen in inexorably from about 30 per cent of tax revenue in 1980-85 to about 70 per cent at present. A rise in debt service burden has meant that revenue deficit, which was 17 per cent as a proportion of fiscal deficit in 1980-85, has now increased to about 50 per cent. In other words, nearly half of the current borrowings go to financing current expenditure.

In 1982-83, interest and subsidies added up to 34.2 per cent of revenue receipts. In 2002-03, this had doubled to 79.6 per cent. This has increasingly reduced the fiscal space available for the legitimate expenditures of government on the production of public goods. These numerical values understate the extent of this problem, to the extent that the full extent of subsidies is larger than portrayed by these statistics.

According to Kelkar Taskforce (July, 2004) in the case of subsidies, there are important problems of measurement. The elements of expenditure which are classified as a 'subsidy' in budget documents are only a subset of the overall subsidies. There are also many other expenditures which are actually subsidies, i.e. narrow transfers to a few households or firms, without any public goods characteristics. Hence, the size of subsidies as seen using the standard budget data substantially understates the actual extent to which the expenditures of government are being devoted to transfers/subsidies instead of being deployed on producing public goods.

Another area where subsidies exist but are not explicitly reported is the issue of 'tax expenditure'. One of the important reasons for the low Tax/GDP ratio is the erosion of the tax base through a large number of exemptions. Such exemptions are fiscally identical to subsidies. That is, *tax revenues foregone are no different from explicit subsidies paid out.*[1]

FRBM

While interest rates have fallen, and have generally been below nominal GDP growth, persistent revenue deficits have been financed by new debt. This has led to an escalation of the Debt/GDP ratio. In particular, the fiscal deterioration has been particularly marked in the eight-year period from 1996-97 to 2004-05, where the Liabilities/GDP ratio worsened by 12.2 percentage points.

The persistent fiscal deficits, and the steadily growing Debt/GDP ratio, constitute the most important challenges affecting India's growth prospects. In response to this challenge, Parliament passed the Fiscal Responsibility and Budget Management (FRBM) Act, which was notified on August 26, 2003. A central requirement of the FRBM concerns the revenue deficit in 2007-08: ıt requires that government undertake:

> "appropriate measures to reduce the fiscal deficit and revenue deficit so as to eliminate revenue deficit by 31st March 2008 and threafter build up adequate revenue surplus".

1. Kelkar Task Force, July 2004.

What is to be done? The key objective of fiscal reform has to be a reduction in debt service payments. This has to be achieved by a progressive reduction in public debt and through higher revenues. The possibility of achieving higher revenues through increased rates of taxes is both undesirable and infeasible. Higher tax revenues can be achieved only through buoyancy and expansion of the tax base. Thus the main instruments for achieving a sustained increase in overall revenues are (i) Expansion of the tax base; (ii) widespread and bold imposition of user charges on all non-merit goods and (iii) widespread and bold privatisation.

Projection of the Tenth Plan (2002-07): Resources of the Centre

In keeping with the requirement of stepping up public sector investments for attaining an 8 per cent GDP growth during the Tenth Plan, the GBS of the Centre has been projected to grow from 4.33 per cent of GDP in 2001-02 to 5.39 per cent in 2006-07. Thus, the Tenth Plan projected average GBS stands at 4.93 per cent of GDP as against the Ninth Plan realisation of 4.02 per cent.

Fiscal sustainability considerations demand a reduction in debt financing for funding of GBS for the Tenth Plan. Accordingly, the gross fiscal deficit, which stood at 5.90 per cent of GDP in 2001-02 has been projected to reduce to 4.32 per cent in 2006-07, obtaining a Tenth Plan average of 4.73 per cent. The Ninth Plan average realisation had stood at 5.82 per cent. The gross fiscal deficit is implicit in own borrowings, inclusive of net miscellaneous capital receipts (MCR). Own borrowings inclusive of MCR in the Tenth Plan are projected at 4.78 per cent of GDP, down from 5.78 per cent realised during the Ninth Plan. Net inflow from abroad, in the form of external assistance, is projected at 0.19 per cent of GDP, slightly diminished from 0.22 per cent realised during the Ninth Plan.

The BCR is arrived at as a small negative of 0.04 per cent of the GDP as against a negative 1.98 per cent realised in the Ninth Plan. To achieve a BCR of this order, Central revenues (net) must grow from 8.80 per cent of GDP in 2001-02 to 9.98 per cent in 2006-07, an increase of 1.18 percentage points. NPRE must come down from 10.60 per cent of GDP in 2001-02 to 9.06 per cent, a decrease of 1.54 percentage points. Thus, an improvement of 2.72 percentage points in BCR during the Tenth Plan is being sought mainly from a contraction of NPRE.

The GBS of the Centre is placed at Rs.7,06,000 crore at 2001-02 prices. Central assistance to State & UT plans works out to Rs.3,00,265 crore. After deducting Central assistance to States and UTs, the GBS available for the Central plan is Rs.4,05,735 crore at 2001-02 prices. With an IEBR of CPSUs indicated at Rs.5,15,556 crore at 2001-02 prices, total resources available for the Central Plan is projected at Rs.9,21,291 crore at 2001-02 prices. The Central Ministries have indicated an IEBR of Rs.4,87,448 crore, which falls short by Rs.28,108 crore vis-a-vis the required IEBR. The IEBR currently indicated by the Central Ministries, if taken in place of the projected IEBR, reduces the Central resources for the Tenth Plan to Rs. 8,93,183 crore.

A funding pattern as envisaged in Table 4 is a challenging task, the extent of which could be gauged by comparing the Tenth Plan projected levels to the Ninth Plan realisation.

TABLE – 4

PROJECTION OF TENTH PLAN RESOURCES OF THE CENTRE

(Rs. crore at 2001-02 prices)

	Sources of Funding	*Projection*
1.	Balance from Current Revenues	-6,385 (-0.9)
2.	Borrowings including net MCR	6,85,185 (97.0)
3.	Net inflow from abroad	27,200 (3.9)
4.	Gross Budgetary Support to Plan (1 to 3)	7,06,000 (100.0)
5.	Central Assistance to States & UTs	-3,00,265 (42.5)
6.	GBS for Central Plan (4+5)	4,05,735
7.	Resources of Public Sector Enterprises	5,15,556
	7.1. Internal Resources	4,09,000
	7.2. Extra Budgetary Resources	1,06,556
8.	Resources for Central Plan (6+7)	9,21,291

Note : Figures in parentheses are percentage of GBS.
Source : Tenth Five Year Plan (Dec. 2002).

For achieving these targets, following steps in Box 1 have been listed in the 10th Plan document.

BOX 1

- Comprehensive computerisation of the income tax system and universal usage of tax identification numbers in monetary transactions must be employed for facilitating improved enforcement of the income-tax administration.
- The policy direction for removing unnecessary exemptions under corporate tax must continue so that corporate income, liable to taxation, comes nearer to book profits as declared by the companies.
- The current policy of moving progressively to a truly single excise rate should continue to be pursued while tightening up much more on existing exemptions, particularly those under small enterprises, all for improving tax compliance.
- The coverage of the service tax must be extended continuously under the union excise system so that much greater tax buoyancy can be achieved through increased coverage of the economy as a whole.
- The extension of VAT at the State level must be taken up at the earliest for facilitating its integration with the Central VAT and bringing about harmonisation of tax rates levied by different tax jurisdictions.
- Peak customs tariff must be continuously lowered for enabling greater integration with the world economy and consequently raising customs revenue through larger volumes of imports as would arise from expansion of international trade.
- User charges must be raised to cost recovery levels and made acceptable by a communication campaign to convince members of the general public that such a system would be in their own overall interest.
- The recommendation of the Expenditure Reforms Commission, on the road map provided by it for progressive reduction in fertilizer subsidy, as also fully eliminating petroleum subsidy for reducing NPRE must be pursued.
- A change has to be made in the design of the food subsidy programme whereby a shift from the one based on minimum support price to Food for Work Programme is taken for reducing as well as effectively directing food subsidy.
- Curtailment in pay and allowances of the government must be pursued on a continuous basis as, in the wake of the implementation of the Fifth Pay Commission's recommen-dations, downsizing has become most critical to reducing NPRE.
- The operational efficiency of Indian Railways and the power sector CPSUs must be improved with a view to eventually eliminating all budgetary support and generating adequate internal resources for expanding the transport and power facilities in the country.

11

Fiscal Policy

Background to Fiscal Reforms

THE need for comprehensive fiscal reforms in India was apparent during the late 1980s, as there was rapid deterioration in Government finances. During this period, the expenditure of the Central Government rose much faster than its revenue leading to a steep rise in the Centre's fiscal deficit to GDP ratio. For the States, given the restrictions on their capacity to borrow, the increase in expenditure was relatively aligned to the corresponding rise in revenue. Consequently, the rise in the fiscal deficit of States was relatively less steep. The sharp increase in revenue deficit of the Central Government and the emergence of such deficits in State finances were the most worrisome developments in the fiscal scenario during the 1980s.

Reflecting these developments, there was a sharp increase in the outstanding liabilities of both Central and State Governments as ratio to GDP from 41.6 per cent and 16.7 per cent, respectively, in 1980-81 to 55.3 per cent and 19.4 per cent, respectively, in 1990-91. The growing size of liabilities eventually generated a considerable debt-service burden, with interest payments as ratio to GDP rising from 1.8 per cent to 3.8 per cent in case of the Centre and from 0.9 per cent to 1.5 per cent in case of States during the same period.

The underdeveloped nature of the Government securities market and the heavy dependence of Small Saving collections on the level of income resulted in an implicit upper ceiling on Government's access to the market resources.[1] This necessitated a large order of monetary accommodation from the Reserve Bank with its attendant monetary

---

* Excerpted from RBI Report on Currency and Finance 2001-02, Ch.4.

1. Govt. Securities India Captive Market of Banks and Financial Institutions.

implications. The outstanding net Reserve Bank credit to the Government as ratio to GDP rose from 11.4 per cent as at end-March 1981 to 15.6 per cent as at end-March 1991. In order to partially abate the inflationary pressure resulting from growing monetisation of fiscal deficit, discrete upward changes in Cash Reserve Ratio (CRR) were necessitated. With both CRR and Statutory Liquidity Ratio (SLR) approaching their statutory upper limits at the time of the onset of unprecedented macroeconomic crisis of 1991, and given the adverse macroeconomic consequences of high fiscal deficit, the only option available was to adopt a quick fiscal restructuring programme along with other macroeconomic and institutional reforms.

Fiscal Reforms in India: Policy Measures and Developments

While a move towards fiscal adjustment was visible in the pronouncements made as a part of long-term fiscal policy announced in the mid-1980s, a comprehensive fiscal reform programme at the Central Government level was initiated only at the beginning of the 1990s as part of the economic adjustment programme initiated in 1991-92. On the other hand, in the case of States, efforts towards fiscal adjustment began only in the late 1990s. Fiscal reforms in the States were necessitated by:

- growing fiscal imbalances;
- sluggishness in Central transfers resulting from falling tax to GDP ratio;
- introduction of reform-linked assistance as a part of Medium-Term Fiscal Reform Programme on the basis of the recommendation of the Eleventh Finance Commission; and
- adjustment programme undertaken in some of the States which are linked to borrowings from multilateral agencies.

Central Government

Fiscal reforms at the Centre covered tax reforms, expenditure pruning, restructuring of PSUs, and better coordination between monetary and fiscal policies.

(i) Tax Reforms

Restructuring of the tax system constituted a major component of fiscal reforms with the aim of augmenting revenues and removing anomalies in the tax structure. The main focus of the reforms was on simplification and rationalisation of both direct and indirect taxes drawing mainly from the recommendations of the Tax Reforms Committee, 1991 (Chairman: Raja J. Chelliah). Since the rates were very high and the structure of indirect taxes highly complex, it was considered undesirable to augment revenues merely by raising tax rates. The Committee had recommended adoption of a small number of simple broad-based taxes with moderate and limited number of rates, and with very few exemptions and deductions.

Accordingly, the tax rates were significantly rationalised and progressively brought down to the levels comparable to some of the developed economies.

The concern with tax rationalisation has been reflected in the appointment of a number of committees to review the tax system in the last few years. The Advisory Group on Tax Policy and Tax Administration for the Tenth Plan, 2001 (Chairman: Parthasarathi Shome) recommended deletion of a number of exemptions and deductions which have become redundant and are not in harmony with a modern tax regime (Government of India, 2001a). Similarly, the Expert Committee to Review the System of Administrative Interest Rates and Other Related Issues, 2001 (Chairman: Y.V. Reddy) recommended the withdrawal of tax concessions available on small savings (Government of India, 2001b). Furthermore, the Task Force on Direct Taxes and Indirect Taxes, 2002 (Chairman: Vijay Kelkar) has reiterated the need to withdraw exemptions and concessions to widen the tax base.

(ii) Expenditure Management

Successive Central Government budgets in the 1990s contemplated a host of measures to curb built-in growth in expenditure and to bring about structural changes in the composition of expenditure. These included subjecting all ongoing schemes to zero-based budgeting and assessment of manpower requirements of Government departments. This was sought to be achieved by reviewing norms for creation of posts and fresh recruitment and introduction of a Voluntary Retirement Scheme (VRS) for surplus staff. The process also involved review of all subsidies with a view to introducing cost-based user charges wherever feasible, review of budgetary support to autonomous institutions and encouragement to PSUs to maximise generation of internal resources. These measures, by and large, focused on downsizing Government and reducing its role and administrative structure. Further, as an institutional arrangement, the Government constituted an Expenditure Reforms

Commission (ERC) to look into areas of expenditure correction. Areas identified by the ERC include, inter alia, creation of a national food security buffer stock and minimisation of cost of buffer stock operations and rationalisation of fertiliser subsidies through dismantling of controls in a phased manner. It also included optimising Government staff strength by a ban on the creation of new posts for two years, introduction of VRS and redeployment of surplus staff in various Government departments and autonomous institutions, to which the Government provides budgetary support through grants.

(iii) Restructuring of the Public Sector

During the reform period, there has been a distinct change in the public perception in favour of reducing the size of public sector and improving private participation. With these underlying objectives, a two-pronged strategy was adopted by the Central Government – reduction in budgetary support to the PSUs and privatisation of existing PSUs.

(iv) Fiscal-Monetary Coordination

Another important objective of the reform process has been to improve fiscal-monetary coordination. This involved steps to ensure wider participation in the Government securities market so as to facilitate elimination of automatic monetisation and pre-emption of institutional resources by the Government. During the 1990s, the Reserve Bank undertook a series of steps towards deepening and widening the Government securities market.

(v) Institutional Measures

As an institutional mechanism to strengthen fiscal discipline, the Central Government is contemplating enactment of Fiscal Responsibility and Budget Management Bill (FRBM), 2000 (Government of India, 2000b). The Bill stresses on inter-generational equity in fiscal management and long-term macroeconomic stability. The original Bill envisaged a complete elimination of revenue deficit and reduction of the fiscal deficit-GDP ratio to 2 per cent by the Central Government by end-March 2006. The Bill also envisaged a reduction in total liabilities of the Centre to no more than 50 per cent of GDP by March, 2011. The Bill, introduced in the Parliament in 2000, was referred to the Standing Committee on Finance for examination and report. A revised Bill is expected to be introduced in Parliament soon.

State Governments

Measures initiated by the States may be broadly grouped under revenue mobilisation, expenditure containment, public sector restructuring and institutional reforms. In addition to States' own efforts, the Centre has also taken initiatives to strengthen the reform process at the State level. Further, the policy initiatives undertaken by the Reserve Bank have a bearing on State finances as well.

PERFORMANCE DURING THE 1990s

Corrective measures on the fiscal front initiated at the beginning of the 1990s produced some promising results during the first half of the decade. Expenditure growth could be curtailed leading to a decline in the fiscal deficit and the outstanding liabilities of the Government to GDP ratio. During 1990-91 to 1996-97 (excluding 1993-94), the reduction in total expenditure to GDP ratio by more than 3.5 percentage points narrowed the fiscal gap by 3 percentage points and reduced the debt-GDP ratio by over 5 percentage points. However, the fiscal consolidation even during the first half of the 1990s was brought about primarily through curtailment in capital expenditure. Decline in consumption expenditure was relatively small. From 1997-98, expenditure started rising once again, and by the year 2001-02, all the major fiscal parameters, viz., revenue deficit, fiscal deficit, and public debt rose to levels higher than those prevalent at the beginning of the reform process (Table 1).

Trends in Revenue

The efficacy of tax reforms for augmentation of tax revenue, expenditure correction, restructuring of public sector, public debt management policies and institutional reforms appears to be rather limited so far.

Trends in Tax Revenue

Tax reforms have generally led to a rise in tax revenue to GDP ratio across countries (Shome, 1992; Shome, 1995). In the Indian context, the expected increase in tax buoyancy a la 'Laffer curve effect' did not occur. Since the onset of tax reforms, the tax-GDP ratio of the Central Government has suffered a persistent decline. This has been a major drag on the reform process. The tax-GDP ratio declined from an average of 9.9 per cent during the 1980s to 9.7 per cent in the first half of the 1990s and further to 9.0 per cent in the second half of the 1990s. The pattern is, however, not the same across different types of taxes. Direct tax collection to GDP ratio rose steadily from 2.0 per cent in the 1980s to 2.3 per cent in the first half of the 1990s and further to 2.9 per cent in the latter half of the 1990s. On the other hand, the ratio of indirect tax collection to GDP declined from 7.9 per cent in the 1980s to 7.3 per cent and 6.1 in the first and second halves of the 1990s, respectively.

TABLE – 1

MAJOR FISCAL INDICATORS OF THE GOVERNMENT SECTOR*

(Per cent)

Item	*1981-82 to 1989-90*		*1990-91 to 1996-97*		*1997-98 to 2001-02*	
	Average Growth	*Ratio to GDP*	*Average Growth*	*Ratio to GDP*	*Average Growth*	*Ratio to GDP*
	1	*2*	*3*	*4*	*5*	*6*
Revenue Receipts	16.14	19.01	14.17	18.57	11.64	17.72
Total Expenditure	16.21	28.84	13.12	27 01	14.62	27.68
Capital Expenditure	12.93	8.23	6.59	4.81	16.29	3.96
Revenue Expenditure	17.78	20.62	14.61	22.20	14.43	23.73
Gross Fiscal Deficit	17.83	8.03	11.60	7.38	21.48	9.13
Revenue Deficit	31.39	1.65	19.93	3.63	31.48	6.07
Development Expenditure	15.59	18.11	11.00	15.32	13.43	14.33
Non-Developmental Expenditure	17.23	10.45	16.13	11.69	16.03	13.35

* Government sector refers to finances of Central and State Governments.
Source : Union and State Governments' Budgets.

The increase in direct tax collections despite a significant cut in marginal tax rates could be attributed to the combined effect of better compliance, broadening of the tax base and increase in income. The introduction of presumptive tax, adoption of economic criteria for identification of potential tax payers and removal of some exemptions helped in base widening. Measures such as rationalisation and simplification, both in personal tax and corporate tax, would have induced better compliance.

Unlike direct taxes, rate cuts have been important factors in reducing the indirect tax collection, as there was no commensurate gain in terms of base expansion or better compliance. It was expected that the sharp cut in custom duties from a peak rate of more than 300 per cent in the period just prior to reforms to about 30 per cent in 2002-03 would lead to a net fall in custom duty collections. Fall in excise duty collections, however, came as a surprise as the rate cuts were expected to boost growth in industrial output. The less than expected buoyancy in the excise tax seems to follow from slower than expected growth in industrial output during the major part of the reform period. The rising share of services in overall GDP which largely falls outside the tax net and progressive extension of MODVAT could have affected buoyancy estimates (Mohan, 2000). Ideally, credit extended to inputs under VAT system needs to be neutralised through increase in tax rates on end-products. Instead tax rates have been scaled back leading to a fall in excise tax collection (Shome, 1997). Another important reason for reduced revenue collection from both custom and excise duties is that the reduction in rates were not accompanied by removal of concessions and exemptions (Government of India, 2001a).

Trends in Non-Tax Revenue

A key objective of the reform process was the augmentation of non-tax revenue by way of enhancement of user charges and returns on Government investments through restructuring of PSUs. The intention of restructuring PSUs was to improve their efficiency and thereby enhance the capacity to generate returns on Government investments. Non-tax revenue of the Central Government as a proportion to GDP recorded an improvement from 2.1 per cent in 1990-91 to 3.0 per cent in 2001-02.

To sum up, the sluggishness in Central Government revenues was largely the result of lower buoyancy of indirect taxes caused by cut in tax rates without adequate expansion in the tax base. The inadequate growth in States' revenue, on the other hand, was the result of their inability to levy appropriate user charges and tax the services sector, combined with lower Central transfers due to falling tax buoyancy.

Trends in Expenditure

Government consumption and investment spending constitute an important part of aggregate demand in the economy. It influences growth through several channels. An increase in public spending on physical capital could positively influence the long-term growth. The impact of such spending in human capital formation could be larger but benefits require longer gestation period. So is the case with Government spending on research and development (R&D). As such, any programme of stabilisation-cum-adjustment, has to give considerable attention to the expenditure side of fiscal restructuring. It is important to plan expenditure reduction while improving quality of public spending to aim simultaneously at supporting growth with equity and improving fiscal balances. In India, expenditure/GDP ratio of the Centre had risen from about 12.3 per cent in 1970-71 to around 20 per cent in the latter half of the 1980s. This had placed a difficult burden on budgetary balances. With a view to narrowing down the fiscal gap, particularly by bridging the revenue deficit, a cut in current expenditure was considered essential.

TABLE – 2

TRENDS IN GOVERNMENT EXPENDITURE

(Percentage to GDP)

		1980s	*1990-91 to 1996-97*	*1997-98 to 2001-02*
	1	*2*	*3*	*4*
Centre	Total Expenditure	17.74	16.29	15.59
	Revenue Expenditure	11.49	12.28	12.70
	Capital Expenditure	6.25	4.01	2.89
States	Total Expenditure	15.90	15.64	15.77
	Revenue Expenditure	11.61	12.67	13.07
	Capital Expenditure	4.29	2.97	2.70
Combined	Total Expenditure	28.84	26.01	27.68
	Revenue Expenditure	20.62	22.20	23.73
	Capital Expenditure	8.23	4.81	3.95

Source : Union and State Governments' Budgets.

The steps taken to compress expenditure led to a reduction in the size of overall public expenditure as a ratio to GDP in the initial years of the 1990s. The combined expenditure of Centre and State Governments as a ratio to GDP declined from 28.8 per cent in 1990-91 to 25.1 per cent in 1996-97. However, the trend reversed and the expenditure to GDP ratio once again began to follow an upward movement after 1996-97 and reached 29.5 per cent in 2001-02. Furthermore, the efforts to augment investment expenditure by cutting consumption expenditure did not materialise. This was due to the fact that at, both, the national and sub-national levels of Government, expenditure correction was brought about mainly through cut in capital expenditure. Between 1990-91 to 1996-97, although combined revenue expenditure fell by 1.2 percentage points, it increased again by about 3.6 percentage points between 1996-97 and 2001-02. On the other hand, there was a steep fall of 2.5 percentage points in the capital expenditure to GDP ratio between 1990-91 and 1996-97, though it rose marginally by 0.8 percentage point between 1996-97 to 2001-02. Thus, since the beginning of the 1990s upto 2001-02, while the revenue expenditure to GDP ratio increased from 22.8 per cent to 25.2 per cent, the capital expenditure to GDP ratio declined from 6.0 per cent to 4.4 per cent, (Table 2). The deterioration in capital expenditure contributed to the decline in the share of public investment from 9.3 per cent of GDP in 1990-91 to 6.3 per cent in 2001-02.

The major contributing factor imparting a downward rigidity to the revenue expenditure relates to items of committed expenditure, of which, interest payments and expenditure on wages and salaries are prominent. Interest payments as a ratio to GDP increased from 3.8 per cent in 1990-91 to 4.7 per cent in 2001-02 for the Central Government, while for the States, the corresponding rise was steeper from 1.5 per cent to 2.8 per cent. During the phase of fiscal consolidation, even though the debt to GDP ratio for the Central and State Governments fell from 61.7 per cent in 1990-91 to 56.5 per cent in 1996-97, the rise in the weighted average interest rate on Central Government and State Governments market borrowings, following the progressive alignment of coupon rates with market interest rates, led to the rise in interest payments. On the other hand, in the latter half of the 1990s, though the cost of borrowings declined consistently due to fall in market interest rates, interest payments continued to rise unabated. This essentially reflects the impact of sizeable outstanding liabilities contracted at higher interest rates during the first half of the 1990s, and also the return to rising deficit, and consequent, increase in public debt to GDP ratio to 71.1 per cent by 2001-02.

The rising wage bill has been considered as an important element in fiscal deterioration in recent years. One view is that the rise in spending on wages and salaries and pension was the prime factor for the abnormal rise in revenue expenditure during the 1990s (Acharya, 2001; Rao, 2000). The Eleventh Finance Commission (EFC), on the other hand, notes that the surge in revenue expenditure towards the late 1990s cannot be attributed only to salary and pension revision, though it led to immediate and acute fiscal stress all round (Government of India, 2000c). A similar view is expressed by Mohan (2000) who notes that, for the Central Government, spending on salaries and pension as a proportion to GDP during the 1990s was much lower than that in the 1980s.

The growth in Central Government spending on wages and salaries and pension was restrained during the period from 1990-91 to 1996-97. As a proportion to GDP, it dropped by around 0.8 percentage point. With the implementation of the Fifth Pay Commission award towards the late 1990s, the wage bill could not be kept constricted. Though the present expenditure on salaries and pensions for the Central Government employees as a percentage to GDP is still lower than it was at the end of the 1980s, the sharp rising trend is worrisome. It may be added that with downsizing of the Government as part of the reform process, the share of its wage bill in GDP should decline substantially. As liberalisation of the economy puts upward pressure on wage rates in competitive sectors that attract fresh domestic and foreign capital, preferred strategy would be to redeploy the surplus labour from the public sector to more productive sectors. This will reduce the wage bill burden in a much more meaningful way.

Expenditure on Subsidies

Downward rigidity has also been discernible in expenditure on subsidies, which is another major constituent of the revenue expenditure. Subsidies are an important policy instrument. Apart from impacting the expenditure side of the fisc, these affect domestic resource allocation, income distribution and expenditure efficiency. Subsidies can also affect international competitiveness by introducing distortions in international trade. Apart from providing implicit subsidies through under-pricing of public goods and services, Governments also extend subsidies explicitly on items such as exports, interest on loans, food and fertilisers. Owing to the conscious efforts made by the Government, total explicit subsidies of the Central Government, which constituted 2.14 per cent of GDP in 1990-91 were reduced to nearly 1 per cent by 1995-96. Cut in subsidies in the beginning of the reform period was brought about largely through the phasing out of export subsidies (cash compensatory support) which amounted to nearly Rs. 2,750 crore (0.5 per cent of GDP) in the year 1990-91. During the second half of the 1990s, the size of subsidies again started rising and increased to 1.36 per cent of GDP by 2001-02 (Table 3).

TABLE – 3

CENTRAL GOVERNMENT EXPENDITURE ON SUBSIDIES – MAJOR HEADS

(Figures in rupees crore)

Year	Food	Fertilisers	Interest	Exports	Total
	1	2	3	4	5
1990-91	2,450 (0.43)	4,389 (0.77)	379 (0.07)	2,742 (0.48)	12,158 (2.14)
1995-96	5,377 (0.45)	6,735 (0.57)	34 (–)	318 (0.03)	12,666 (1.07)
2001-02	17,499 (0.76)	12,595 (0.55)	210 (0.01)	N.A.	31,207 (1.36)

Figures in parentheses are ratios to GDP.
– : negligible.
Source : Union Government Budgets.

The downward inflexibility in the subsidies was essentially on account of the growing size of food subsidy, which recorded nearly a six-fold rise over the reform period. It has been observed that a sizeable proportion of food subsidy is due to the carrying cost of the food stock (Balakrishnan and Ramaswami, 2000). Thus, a significant part of subsidies goes to make up for the inefficiencies embedded in institutional arrangements meant for providing subsidy rather than benefiting the targeted group. Although subsidies are extended by the Government on the grounds that the poor are benefited, evidence shows that impact on poverty and nutritional status of the population is very limited (Srinivasan, 2000; Government of India, 1997). Expressing similar concerns, it has been stated that the argument that subsidies are meant for the poor has little basis in actual practice. The better-off sections of the society consume most of such services (Mohan, 2000). It has been shown that during 1986-87, the public distribution system (PDS) and other consumer subsidy programmes accounted for less than 2.7 per cent of per capita expenditure of the poor in rural areas and 3.2 per cent in urban areas (Radhakrishna and Subbarao, 1997). This indicates that phasing out of subsidies would have a very limited impact on the poor and less so in rural areas. However, there is a need for ensuring safety-net for the poor segment of population, whose ability to adjust to areas of work in the face of restructuring is rather limited.

In sum, it seems that the reversal in expenditure correction followed from the downward rigidity in consumption expenditure, particularly, in the interest payments for both the Central and the State Governments. The pay revision in the late 1990s further compounded the problem, while provision of subsidies continued to remain inefficient. In the event, capital expenditure had to bear the brunt of restraint placed on expenditure.

It has, however, been shown that while public investment spending crowds in private investment and is expansionary in nature, consumption spending by the Government causes economic contraction (RBI, 2002). In fact, considerable scepticism has been expressed towards the success of expansionary fiscal policy, which does not consider the quality of expenditure (Chelliah, 2001). The Report of the Economic Advisory Council, Government of India, 2001 stresses that a high fiscal deficit, by raising real interest rates, crowds out private investment as Government borrowing is predominantly used to finance the revenue deficits. Relying on the reduced form evidence pertaining to the 1990s, fiscal expansion in the Indian context is observed to be contractionary (Khatri and Kochhar, 2002). It may be added that fiscal consolidation in the first half of the 1990s was accompanied by high income growth. Also, a deterioration in fiscal position in the second half of the 1990s occurred along with deceleration in income growth.

Fiscal Deficit

Between 1990/91 and 1995/96 the consolidated fiscal deficit declined by three per cent of GDP thanks mainly the Centre's efforts at fiscal prudence. This fiscal contraction made room for the investment boom of 1993-96, which took aggregate domestic investment from 22.5 per cent of GDP in 1991/92 (to which it had dropped during the crisis) to a peak of 26.8 per cent of GDP in 1995/96, without any undue stress on the external accounts. Of course fiscal rectitude was only one of the cause of investment boom. Other factors, such as the deregulation of industry and foreign trade, strong export performance and the overall reform momentum were also at work. But it does seem likely that the deficit reduction in the first half of the decade helped to nurture the rise in gross savings and investment, which, in turn, helped propel India's growth to 7 per cent plus for three successive years in the mid-nineties.

The converse seems to have happened in the second half of the decade, with a widening fiscal deficit contributing to a slowdown in investment and growth. After 1995/96 (actually after 1996/97) the consolidated fiscal and revenue deficits deteriorated steadily, with about half the worsening due to the phasing in of decisions on the Fifth Pay

Commission. Between 1995/96 and 1999/2000 both the fiscal deficit and the revenue deficit increased by three per cent of GDP. This sharp widening in deficits is fully reflected in the decline of public savings from plus 2 per cent of GDP in 1995/96 to minus 1.2 per cent in 1999/2000. This, in turn, fully explains the drop in gross domestic savings from its peak of 25.1 per cent of GDP in 1995/96 to 22.3 per cent in 1999/2000. Gross domestic investment fell by a similar magnitude over these four years (Acharya, 2003).[2]

According to Acharya "it would be hard to find more telling presumptive evidence of the adverse impact of deficits on savings and investment. Of course, other factors were also damping investment, including the slowdown in reforms, the higher uncertainties associated with coalition governance and a worsening international economic environment. But growing borrowings by government (rising deficits) and the associated high real interest rates clearly played a role in slowing private investment. The drop in aggregate savings and investment took its toll of economic growth, which slowed from 7 per cent plus of the mid-nineties to around 5 per cent in recent years".

Fiscal Deficit: Comparison between 80's and 90's

One may compare and contrast the experience with high fiscal deficits in the late eighties and the late nineties. In the eighties the high fiscal deficits "spilled" into large current account BoP deficits, which were financed by unsustainable foreign borrowing that ushered in the crisis of 1991. In the late nineties the rising fiscal deficits have taken their toll of savings and investment, and thereby, growth. What both episodes have in common is damage to sustainable economic development.

It has also been shown that in India, during the eleven year period since 1986-87, an increase in the Central Government's fiscal deficit (inclusive of oil pool account) by one per cent of GDP was associated with a reduction in private corporate investment by one per cent of GDP (Srinivasan, 2000).

It needs to be recognised that the fortuitous conditions that have restricted the adverse macroeconomic impact of high fiscal deficit are transitory in nature. With a revival of economic activity, spurred by a pick-up in the private investment demand, rise in fiscal deficit could raise the saving-investment gap and eventually raise interest rate and widen current account deficit. The problem could be compounded if

---

2. Acharya Shankar (2003), *India's Economy: Some Issues and Answers*, Academic Foundation, New Delhi.

inflationary pressures reemerge due to buoyant economic activity or some exogenous shock. In view of this, sustainability of deficit and debt and fiscal consolidation continues to be a matter of serious concern.

Worsening State Finances

The down slide in the fiscal performance of the States has assumed serious proportions. Several factors have been identified by a number of studies for the widening fiscal gap of the State Governments. Expenditure on wages, salaries and pension, growing size of interest payments, inability to levy adequate user charges and falling buoyancy in Central transfers are the prominent reasons for the deterioration of State finances.

Concluding Observations

The above analysis and assessment clearly revealed that the significant fiscal consolidation in the immediate aftermath of the fiscal reforms was essentially brought about through cut in investment expenditure, as rise in committed revenue expenditure could not be curtailed. Within a short span, it became increasingly obvious that the Indian approach to fiscal correction was not sustainable. While reduction in investment spending affected future growth prospects with consequent slowdown in revenue receipts, the interest payments and public debt continued to grow, resulting in reversal of fiscal consolidation process in the latter half of the 1990s. Downward rigidity in the revenue deficit, which amounts to dissaving by the Government sector, has significant implications for the growth target of 8 per cent set in the Tenth Five Year Plan. This would require an investment rate of about 32 per cent, whereas, over the years, the investment rate has stagnated at around 24 to 25 per cent of GDP. Acceleration of saving and investment rate would critically depend upon the efforts to restore balance on the revenue account of both the layers of Governments.

The key factors underlying the growing resource gap across the States are uneconomical level of user charges particularly in the power sector, sluggishness in the Central transfers due to low buoyancy of Central taxes and the rising interest payments. Restoration of revenue balance both at the Central and the State level would require that user charges are adequately raised, the tax collection machinery is overhauled to achieve better tax compliance, returns on Government investment in PSUs are raised through appropriate pricing policies eliminating implicit subsidies and the burden on the fisc is lowered through phasing out of unviable public sector units. The introduction of VAT should eliminate the practice of competitive tax concessions, which has seriously dampened tax buoyancies.

The elimination of automatic monetisation and reduction in pre-emption of institutional resources by the Government has provided a conducive environment to generate market liquidity and softening of interest rates in the economy. However, with a widening of the fiscal gap, it would be increasingly difficult to maintain a softer interest rate regime. In such an eventuality, it would not only crowd out the private investment initiative, but would also make public debt highly unstable given the level of returns on Government investments.

The institutional support in the form of fiscal rules should be the prime mover of future agenda of fiscal consolidation programme. Such fiscal rules could prescribe quantitative limits for elimination of the revenue deficit, reduction in the fiscal deficit and the public debt over a specific period in a phased manner. Advocates of expansionary fiscal policy have, however, cautioned against the stringent fiscal rules to avoid impairment of future growth prospects (Rakshit, 2001; Patnaik, 2001, Shetty, 2001). In a recessionary environment along with low inflation, growing forex reserves and comfortable level of food stocks, there is a definite role for the expansionary fiscal policy. The apprehension is that the stringent fiscal rules may hinder appropriate steps by the Government. However, it may be noted that such rules generally make a clear distinction between public consumption and public investment expenditure while envisaging a complete elimination of revenue deficit. Rule based fiscal policy would facilitate the path for durable fiscal consolidation through mandatory fiscal discipline, enhanced accountability and improved transparency in fiscal operations.

According to RBI Annual Reports 2000-2001 and 2001-2002, the path of durable fiscal consolidation is through fiscal empowerment i.e., by expanding the scope and size of revenue flows into the Budget. Furthermore, a fiscal strategy based on revenue maximisation would also provide the necessary flexibility to shift the pattern of expenditures and redirect them productively. Revenue maximisation requires that the tax system be reformed through widening the tax base, simplification of tax rules, review of exemptions/incentives and strict tax compliance.

12

Inflation

INFLATION is an important indicator of macro economic stability. The Indian inflation record over the past five decades can be considered satisfactory as compared with many developing economies.

Trends in Wholesale Prices: 1950's to 80's

The inflation rate (measured by variations in annual average wholesale price index, WPI) over the past five decades averaged 6.6 per cent per annum. However, decade-wise, the inflation rate accelerated steadily from an annual average of 1.7 per cent during the 1950s to 6.4 per cent during the 1960s and further to 9.0 per cent in the 1970s before easing marginally to 8.0 per cent in the 1980s. On the other hand, the volatility in the inflation rate, as measured by the coefficient of variation, which was fairly high in the 1950s (4.4 per cent), moved in a narrow range of 0.4–1.0 per cent in the subsequent decades.

The pickup in inflation from 1970s onwards coincided with a sharp rise in M_3 growth, partly reflecting fiscal dominance. At the same time, the inflationary dynamics also reflected supply shocks, such as the two wars (1962 and 1965), hike in crude oil prices (1973-74 and 1979-80) and crop failures. Demand pressures, emanating partly from the widening fiscal imbalances, sustained the inflation in the 1980s.

The Period of 90's

The first half of the 1990s saw a sharp increase in inflation. The decade began with double digit inflation attributable to the large-scale monetisation of fiscal deficits. This was intensified by hikes in procurement prices as well as supply-demand imbalances in essential commodities like pulses, oilseeds and edible oils. The severe foreign exchange shortage that the country faced at the time constrained the ability of the authorities to augment the supply position through imports and also contributed to inflationary pressures. Increases in fuel prices and other administered items also fed higher inflation. The inflationary pressures continued during 1993-94 and 1994-95 in the wake of unprecedented capital inflows and the consequent higher monetary expansion. The focus of monetary policy, therefore, shifted to the moderation of money supply with the objective of containing inflation to create an enabling environment for the process of structural adjustment.

TABLE – 1

ANNUAL AVERAGE INFLATION RATE BASED ON WHOLESALE PRICE INDEX (WPI) SINCE 1991-92

(BASED ON 52 WEEK AVERAGE INFLATION RATES)

ANNUAL AVERAGE INFLATION (%)

	All Commodities	*Primary*	*Fuel*	*Manufactured*
1991-92 to 1995-96	10.6	11.3	11.3	10.1
1996-97 to 2000-01	5.1	5.4	13.0	3.1
2001-02 to 2003-04	4.2	3.8	6.9	3.4

The second half of the 1990s was marked by a significant turnaround in the inflation outcome. The inflation rate declined from an average of 11.0 per cent during 1990-95 to 5.3 per cent during the second half of the 1990s.

In recent years, supply side factors have been more instrumental in determining the direction and magnitude of price rise, while the impact of demand side factors on inflation has been relatively weak. The occurrence of drought, decline in agricultural production, increase in global crude oil prices, supply shortages and increased international prices of imported commodities like crude oil, steel and edible oils are some of the factors that have played a crucial role in fueling inflation in the recent past. Imported inflation has therefore, a crucial role to play in setting the direction of domestic inflation.

Box 1 highlights the trends in inflation rate since the mid 1950s.

BOX 1

FIVE YEAR AVERAGE INFLATION RATE

Though on an average, inflation based on the WPI remained below the 7 per cent level through the 1950s and 1960s, it accelerated during the first half of the 1970s to touch double digit figures but decelerated in the second half of 1970s as also through the 1980s. Four out of the first five years of the 1990s registered double digit inflation, with a 13.7 per cent peak reached in 1992-93.

5 year average annual inflation rate

(Per cent)

Period	52 week annual average	Point to point (March end)
1956-57 to 1960-61	6.3	5.2
1961-62 to 1965-66	5.8	5.9
1966-67 to 1970-71	6.7	5.7
1971-72 to 1975-76	12.0	10.8
1976-77 to 1980-81	8.5	11.0
1981-82 to 1985-86	6.5	5.5
1986-87 to 1990-91	7.8	8.5
1991-92 to 1995-96	10.6	9.3
1996-97 to 2000-01	5.0	5.3

From 1995-96 onwards, there has been a continuous deceleration and the average inflation for the period 1996-97 to 2000-01 is by far the lowest since the mid 1950s in terms of the 52 week average. The point to point average inflation rate for this period is the lowest since the early 1960s. Though inflation rates may still be higher than those witnessed in some developed economies, India's performance on inflation has improved significantly since the mid 1990s.

BOX 2

DROUGHT AND INFLATION

Poor Monsoon results in lower agri/foodgrains output, shortages of primary products and uptrend in overall inflation rate triggered by rise in primary product prices.

In the 1970s, double-digit inflation characterized all the three drought/poor rainfall years, with 1974-75 registering a record inflation rate of 25.2 percent (with primary commodities also rising by 25.4 percent), reflecting the effect of not only reduced supplies but also an amplified psychology of shortages.

1974-75 was also the year when the economy was exposed to the most severe oil price shock with the formation of the OPEC cartel. The combined effect of drought and the external oil shock pushed up the inflation rate to record levels. (see table below)

Years of Drought/poor Rainfall in India

Drought/poor rainfall years	All India rainfall (percentage departure from normal)	Average inflation (percent)			Growth rate Agri prod.	percent change Foodgrain prod.
		All Comm	Primary	Fuel		
1972-73	(-)24	10.0	13.9	5.0	(-)5.6	(-)7.7
1974-75	(-)12	25.2	25.4	51.1	(-)2.8	(-)4.6
1979-80	(-)19	17.1	14.4	15.5	(-)13.4	(-)16.8
1982-83	(-)14	4.9	3.8	7.5	(-)0.5	(-)2.8
1986-87	(-)13	5.8	5.4	6.7	(-)0.6	(-)4.7
1987-88	(-)19	8.2	9.7	3.7	(-)1.4	(-)2.1
2002-03	(-)19	2.6*	2.8*	4.6*	-	-

* week ended January 18, 2003

There were three poor rainfall years in the 1980s. Agriculture (and foodgrains) growth was negative during these years and inflation rate ranged between 5 to 8 percent. In recent years, the agricultural economy has by and large moved from a shortage to a surplus situation and is thus more insulated against the vagaries of nature. Therefore, despite the failure of monsoon, average inflation rate remained low thanks to surplus stocks of foodgrains during the last three years. Reduced dependence of foodgrain production on rainfall has helped reduce the severity of the drought. The impact of the present drought could have been more severe had it not been for the fact that today 55 percent of foodgrains are being produced in irrigated areas and only the remaining 45 percent produced in rainfed areas as against only 33 percent of foodgrains produced in irrigated areas in 1987-88 and about 25 percent in the early 1970s.

Source: Economic Survey 2002-03.

The low inflation rate since the second half of the 1990s, (despite an unchanged GFD/GDP ratio, sustained external capital flows and continued double digit fuel price increases) can be attributed to a number of factors (Table 2):

TABLE – 2

INFLATION AND ITS MAJOR DETERMINANTS

(Annual averages in per cent)

Variable/Period	*1980-85*	*1985-90*	*1990-95*	*1995-2002*	*1998-2002*
	1	*2*	*3*	*4*	*5*
WPI Inflation Rate	9.3	6.7	11.0	5.3	5.0
CPI Inflation Rate	10.1	8.0	10.5	7.3	6.2
Food Articles Inflation	10.7	6.4	11.9	6.6	6.0
Increase in Procurement Prices:					
Paddy	7.6	6.3	13.0	6.6	6.3
Wheat	6.1	6.6	11.2	8.3	5.0
Fuel Inflation	12.5	6.0	12.8	11.3	12.5
M_3 Growth @	16.8	17.6	17.5	16.8 (16.3)	17.2 (16.2)
GFD/GDP @@	5.9	7.7	6.3 (5.5)	5.6 (5.1)	5.9 (5.6)
GDP Growth	5.6	6.0	5.0	6.1	5.6
Increase in Unit Value Index of Imports	5.6	8.0	7.6	6.3	5.2

@ : Figures in brackets are growth rates excluding RIBs/IMDs.
@@ : Figures in brackets exclude States' share in small savings.

- There was a perceptible deceleration in the M_3 growth rate from 17.5 per cent during 1990-95 to 16.2 per cent during 1998-2002 even as the real GDP growth accelerated from 5.0 per cent to 5.6 per cent over the same period. This was facilitated by the increased flexibility in monetary policy due to the improved monetary fiscal interface. At the same time, (as noted below), monetary policy was able to sterilise the capital flows. This also enabled a deceleration in broad money growth consistent with the objective of containment of inflationary pressures.
- Food articles inflation halved during the period from 11.9 per cent to 6.0 per cent, led by a deceleration in procurement price increases.
- External pressure on domestic prices (as measured by unit value index of imports in rupees) was lower than that in the first half of the 1990s.

- Negative output gap (as measured by the HP filter method) prevailed in the recent three years (2000-01 to 2002-03) implying that actual output trailed potential output.
- While increased capital flows and higher foreign exchange reserves have inflationary implications through monetary expansion, at the same time, they provide a greater flexibility in supply management in the face of supply shocks.

In brief, the decline in the inflation rate since the second half of the 1990s reflected a confluence of factors. These included better monetary management facilitated by improved fiscal monetary co-ordination, lower pressures from administered procurement price hikes, weakness of domestic aggregate demand, presence of excess capacities, ample food stocks and foreign exchange reserves.

Although the inflation rate witnessed a noticeable deceleration in the second half of the 1990s in India, the volatility of the inflation rate did not see a concomitant decline. This could be attributed to an increased volatility in fuel group inflation - the coefficient of variation of the fuel group increased from 16 per cent in the first half of the 1990s to 32 per cent in the period 1995-2002 reflecting volatile international crude oil prices. The primary articles inflation too was more volatile during the second half of the 1990s.

Developments during 2003-04

After the drought of 2002 and the POL price increases resulting from tension in the Gulf region, the year 2003-04 began with an inflation rate of 6.7 per cent. However, with the ebbing of hostilities in Iraq and the end of the war, the pressure on crude prices gradually eased off, giving temporary relief on the inflation front. The annual point-to-point inflation rate based on the WPI after peaking at a high of 6.9 per cent in the first week of May 2003, decelerated continuously, reaching a low of 3.9 per cent in end-August, 2003.

The interplay of different factors — increase in energy prices, rise in prices of food articles-led to a firming of the inflation rate during September-November 2003 and it hovered around the 6 per cent level in December 2003. A further firming of energy and primary product prices resulted in the inflation rate crossing 6 per cent in January 2004. However, inflation rate softened during March 2004 and fell to below 5 per cent. The year 2003-04 ended with an annual point-to-point inflation rate of 4.6 per cent, while the 52 week average inflation rate was 5.5 per cent. The high point-to-point inflation through much of 2003-04, and its sharp deceleration in March 2004, was partly because of the carry over of the price increase that took place in the last quarter of 2002-03, especially March 2003.

The manufacturing sector is the major contributor to inflation accounting for nearly 80 per cent of the inflation in 2003-04. While the year end point to point inflation rate for the primary group in 2003-04 remained below 2 per cent, the same for the manufactured and fuel products groups were 6.7 and 2.5 per cent, respectively. Non-food articles in the primary products group, including fibres, raw cotton, oilseeds and sugarcane, recorded a high price rise during the year 2003-04, consequent to the production shortfalls resulting from the drought of 2002. Within the manufacturing sector, food products, edible oils, textiles, leather and leather products, basic metal and alloys and iron and steel were the prime movers.

Inflation rate based on CPI(IW)/Consumer Inflation

Consumer Price Index (CPI) reflects changes in the retail prices of selected goods and services on which a homogeneous group of consumers spend a major part of their income. There are three distinct series of CPI - for industrial workers (IW), for agricultural labourers (AL) and for urban non-manual employees (UNME). Of these, the CPI (IW) is the most popular as the Central Government employees' wage compensation (dearness allowance) is calculated on the basis of movement in this index. CPI(IW) is constructed on a monthly basis, with a lag of one month. The base year for CPI (IW) is 1982.

Food items with a weight of 57 percent dominate the CPI(IW), and is therefore sensitive to changes in prices of food articles. (see Box 3)

BOX 3

SENSITIVITY OF WPI & CPI – A COMPARISON

The Wholesale Price Index (WPI) is the most widely used price index in India, and is an indicator of movement in wholesale prices of 435 commodities in all trade and transactions. WPI is the only price index in India, which is available on a weekly basis with the shortest time lag of two weeks. It is due to these attributes that it is widely used in business and industry circles and by Government and is generally taken as an indicator of the rate of inflation in the economy. The base year of the WPI series is 1993-94.

The Consumer Price Index for Industrial Workers - CPI (IW) is constructed on a monthly basis, with a lag of one month. CPI measures changes in retail prices of goods and services covering 260 items of consumption from 70 centres. The base year for CPI (IW) is 1982. WPI and CPI (IW) differ conceptually in terms of purpose and use, commodity coverage, weighting diagram, associated markets and the base year. Therefore, some degree of difference between the two is unavoidable. Differences in market and price behaviour of some uncommon items in the two series are responsible for creating differences in the movements of the two series. A comparison of the weighting diagram of the two series brings out this fact more clearly :

Weighting diagram of WPI and CPI (IW)

WPI	(Weight)	CPI (IW)	(Weight)
All commodities	100.00	All commodities	100.00
Primary products	22.02	Food	57.00
Food articles	15.04	Non-food articles	6.14
Pan, Supari, Tobacco	3.15	Minerals	0.48
Fuel group	14.23	Fuel & light	6.28
Coal Mining	1.75	Mineral oils	6.99
Housing	8.67	Electricity	5.48
Manufactured products	63.75	Clothing, Bedding	8.54
Food Products	11.54	Textiles	9.80
Miscellaneous	16.36	Chemicals	11.93
Basic Metals	8.34	Others	21.62

The WPI and CPI (IW) series differ significantly in terms of their weighting diagram. This implies that the degree of importance given to specific commodity groups is not the same in the two series. While food gets the maximum weight of 57 percent in the CPI (IW) series, food articles in the primary group and food products in the manufactured products group in the WPI series together have a weight of only 27 percent. The CPI (IW) series is therefore more sensitive to changes in food prices. The fuel group on the other hand gets a much higher weight in the WPI series (14.23) than in the CPI (IW) series (6.28). International price movements of crude oil would therefore have a greater bearing on the WPI series than on the CPI (IW) series in terms of their direct impact. One major subgroup in the CPI (IW) series is the miscellaneous group which includes services like transport, education, health etc. Services however do not get reflected in the WPI series. Differences in inflation rate in the two series could therefore also be on account of price movement in the services sector which gets captured in the CPI (IW) based inflation rate.

Consumer Inflation

Retail inflation, as measured by variations in the consumer price index for industrial workers (CPI(IW) or CPI for brevity), by and large, moved in tandem with WPI inflation. Although CPI inflation, at 7.7 per cent, remained lower than WPI inflation during the 1970s, it turned out higher at 9.0 per cent during the 1980s and 9.5 per cent during the 1990s. The divergence between the two inflation indicators widened during the second half of the 1990s with the CPI inflation at 8.6 per cent, almost three percentage points higher.

The wedge between the two inflation indicators largely reflects the larger weight of the food group in the CPI and a differential movement in the inflation rates of various sub-groups. For instance, in the WPI index, the 'primary articles' inflation at 6.5 per cent was higher than that of 4.1 per cent recorded by 'manufactures' in the second half of the 1990s. In addition, the divergence between the CPI and WPI could also reflect the movements in the prices of services, which are included in the CPI.

In view of the divergence between the CPI and the WPI inflation, there may be a need for monitoring a host of other indicators to obtain a more accurate assessment of expectations of inflation for a forward looking monetary policy. Pethe and Samanta (2001), for example, developed a 'composite leading indicator' for inflation and found manufacturing output, money stock, exchange rate, bank credit and raw material prices as possessing predictive capability for future inflation in India. Food prices, exchange rate and real money gap lead inflation expectations by one month each while yield spreads and fuel prices lead by two and six months, respectively (RBI, 2001b).

As the inflation rate in the short-run is often dominated by supply shocks emanating from the agricultural sector or fuel prices, the year-to-year headline (i.e., WPI) inflation rate does not necessarily reflect the underlying inflationary pressures in the economy. This brought forth the construction of 'core' measures of inflation to eliminate the noise or transient components of the headline, especially in terms of supply shocks. However, the loss of information content in the construction of core inflation and the relatively greater public acceptability of the headline inflation make the core measures useful only as indicators of the underlying inflationary process rather than as policy targets. Furthermore, in developing countries, a measure of core inflation excluding food items – which can account for more than half of the weight in the index – may not be very meaningful (Jalan, 2002b).

Inflation Targeting

In recent years, particularly given the trend of globalisation, there is increasing debate on the role of inflation targeting as a framework for implementing monetary policy. Box 4 introduces the concept of inflation targeting and explores its relevance for developing economies.

BOX 4

INFLATION TARGETING AS A TOOL FOR CONTAINING INFLATIONARY EXPECTATIONS: ITS RELEVANCE FOR DEVELOPING ECONOMIES

There is an increasing focus on inflation targeting as a framework for implementing monetary policy. Inflation targeting may be defined as a framework for policy decisions in which the central bank makes an explicit commitment to conduct policy to meet a publicly announced numerical inflation target within a particular time frame. Some countries have adopted point targets while others are following a more flexible approach of targeting inflation within a band. Inflation targeting has been adopted by a number of central banks around the world, including those in New Zealand, Australia, Canada, Finland, Israel, Spain, Sweden, and the U.K.

Rationale for Inflation Targeting

Inflation targets may help provide a clear path for the medium-term inflation outlook, reducing the size of inflationary shocks and their associated costs. Since long-term interest rates fluctuate with movements in inflation expectations, targeting a low rate of inflation would lead to more stable and lower long-term rates of interest.

Important considerations

Inflation targeting attempts to relate monetary policy implications on inflation. However, concentrating only on numerical inflation objectives may reduce the flexibility of monetary policy, especially with respect to other policy goals. Since monetary policy actions affect inflation with a lag, inflation targeting would mean that the central bank would need to rely on forecasts of future inflation. Given the uncertainties, an inflexible and undue reliance on inflation forecasts can create policy problems. Therefore inflation targets should leave room for a good deal of flexibility and should be adjusted for volatile (supply-side) components. However too flexible a target reduces the credibility of the central bank.

Pre-requisites for inflation targeting

Countries adopting inflation targeting need to fulfill some pre-requisites before adopting inflation targeting. It is imperative that the central bank should not be constrained to finance the Government Budget and must have an effective monetary policy instrument like the short-term interest rate that is fully market determined. Moreover, transparency and accountability of the Central Bank is essential to anchor inflationary expectations. The Central Bank must possess the ability to forecast inflation and to assess the impact of monetary policy on inflationary expectations.

The country adopting inflation targeting has to select the relevant price index that is to be targeted. Most countries have adopted the Consumer Price Index for this purpose. Countries which are susceptible to external shocks and supply side shocks may target their core or underlying inflation rate rather than the headline inflation. The inflation targeting framework should be forward looking as any monetary policy action has a lagged effect.

Scope of Inflation Targeting in Developing Countries

Developing countries generally have relatively higher rates of inflation. Predicting future inflation is often uncertain. Hence, missing inflation targets is more likely in developing economies than in the developed economies. Moreover, in many developing countries, central bank autonomy is more a statutory than a *de facto* situation, because its decisions are still governed primarily by the need to finance the fiscal deficit. Therefore, central banks might hesitate to raise interest rates for fiscal reasons, although they would be required to do so to contain inflation.

Inflation Targeting - Is India ready for it?

Based on the experience of some industrialised countries, there is a view that in India also, monetary policy, to be transparent and credible, should have an explicit narrowly defined objective like an inflation mandate or target. While technically this appears to be a sound proposition, there are several constraints in the Indian context in pursuing a single objective. First, the debt management function gets inextricably linked with the monetary management function while steering the interest rates. Secondly, in the absence of fully integrated financial markets, which remain still imperfect and segmented, the transmission channel of policy is yet to evolve fully. Thirdly, a fully dependent measure of inflation for targeting purposes needs to be developed. Under these circumstances, it is necessary to carefully measure and balance between possible outcomes, after taking into account movements in a variety of monetary and other indicators.

Movement of agricultural prices *vis-a-vis* manufactured prices

Agriculture accounts for one fourth of the country's GDP. Due to the sheer size of the agricultural economy, gains (and setbacks in a bad year) in agricultural production have significant potential impact on growth and poverty. A good agricultural growth provides demand stimulus for industrial products. In the post-reform period, policy emphasis shifted to liberalising trade in agriculture. Quantitative restrictions (QRs) were dismantled in April 2001. These policy changes now provide an opportunity to farmers and agro-based industries to tap the world markets. The new economic environment has created a conducive environment for improving the terms of trade for agriculture vis-a-vis the manufacturing sector. The price index of agricultural products has moved much faster as compared to the manufactured products in recent years. Trade liberalisation and removal of quantitative restrictions have helped promote greater export growth in agricultural commodities.

Issues in Price Stability

There is, by now, an emerging consensus in the literature, that while money is typically neutral in the long run, monetary policy generates short-run real effects in view of price rigidities and expectation errors. Recent research in the context of developed countries suggests that monetary policy should aim at an inflation rate of 1.5-4.0 per cent (Akerlof et al, 1996; Krugman, 1996). In view of the possibility of a inflation growth trade-off, a growth-maximising threshold inflation rate has been placed at around 1-3 per cent for industrialised countries and 7-11 per cent for developing countries

The Chakravarty Committee's observation of four per cent inflation rate as being acceptable can be regarded as the first illustrative benchmark on threshold inflation for the Indian economy. A number of studies have subsequently placed threshold inflation in the range of 4-7 per cent (Rangarajan, 1997; Kannan and Joshi, 1998; Vasudevan, Bhoi and Dhal, 1998; Samantaraya and Prasad, 2001; and RBI, 2002a). The estimate of threshold inflation has, however, a shifting perspective. With structural changes in the economy, prolonged price stability at the global level as well as in India and the credible anchoring of inflationary expectations at a lower level, the threshold inflation could also move downwards.

Finally, while there is little disagreement regarding the long-run benefits of low and stable inflation, a number of studies stress the possible short-run costs in the process of reducing inflation. This is discussed in the received literature in terms of the so-called sacrifice ratio, which is defined as cumulative output losses that an economy needs to endure to reduce average inflation, on a permanent basis, by one percentage point. The concept of sacrifice ratio focuses on reducing inflation on a permanent basis by the monetary authority rather than on a temporary reduction in inflation (say, due to beneficial supply shocks like lower food prices). Furthermore, the sacrifice ratio measures cumulative output losses, which could be spread over a number of periods. The output losses refer to deviations of actual output from its trend. Over time, as inflation expectations stabilise at a lower level, actual output gradually converges to its trend path. The sacrifice ratio measures such output losses in the process of disinflation. One study puts the estimate of the sacrifice ratio at around two for India (Kapur and Patra, 2000). It is necessary to emphasise here that for a proper interpretation of the sacrifice ratio, it is crucial to analyse the dynamics and sources of inflation. In particular, a clear distinction must be made between low inflation driven by benign supply factors and a tight monetary policy.

PART - II

Sectoral Analysis of Indian Economy

Chapters :

A. Domestic Sector

B. External Sector

13

Changing Contours of Indian Agriculture

Importance of Agriculture in National Economy

AGRICULTURE is the most important sector of the Indian economy from the perspective of poverty alleviation and employment generation. Agriculture accounts for about 25 per cent of India's national income. The share of agriculture in national income has been declining from 56.5 per cent in 1950-51 to 52.1 per cent in 1960-61, 45.7 per cent in 1970-71, 39.6 per cent in 1980-81, 33 per cent in 1990-91, 24.2 per cent in 2000-01 (Quick estimates) and 24.3 per cent in 2001-02 (Advance estimates)[1].

Agriculture as a Source of Employment

While the share of agriculture in national income has been declining, the workforce engaged in agriculture has exhibited only a marginal decline. Data provided by the Census of India reveals that whereas in 1961, 75.9 per cent of total workforce was engaged in agriculture (the absolute number being 143.2 million workers), in 1981 the percentage was 69 and further fell to 63.8 in 1993-94 and 59.9 in 1999-2000. In absolute terms, agriculture provided employment to 238.68 million persons in 1993-94. In 1999-2000 also although the percentage had declined from 63.8 to 59.9, the number of persons employed remained 237.8 million.

In the advanced countries like United Kingdom and United States, only 2 to 3 per cent of the working population is engaged in agriculture; in France, the proportion is about 7 per cent; and in Australia about 6 per cent. It is only in backward and less developed countries that the

1. Central Statistical Organisation.

working population engaged in agriculture is quite high.

Linkage between Agriculture and Other Sectors

The linkages between agriculture and industrial sectors, widely recognised in the literature,[2] focus on the role of agriculture as (i) supplier of wage goods to the industrial sector, (ii) provider of raw materials to agro-based industries which have a weight of 21.2 per cent in the Index of Industrial Production (base: 1980-81=100) and weight of 17.6 per cent in the index with base 1993-94=100, and (iii) generator of agricultural income that enables rural demand for industrial products to take place. Empirical tests show that a unit increase in agricultural output would have a positive effect on both industrial production and national income. Rangarajan (1982) estimated that a one per cent increase in agricultural output tends to raise industrial production by 0.5 per cent and augment national income by 0.7 per cent. The experience in the 'eighties and 'nineties also lends support to this. During the 'eighties, the trend growth rate of 3.2 per cent in agricultural production appeared to have had contributed to accelerated industrial production. The decelerated growth rate in agricultural production seems to have impacted on growth of industrial production in the 'nineties.

Importance of agriculture in the national economy is indicated by many facts. For example, agriculture is the main support for India's transport system, since railways and roadways secure bulk of their business from the movement of agricultural goods. Internal trade is mostly in agricultural products. Agricultural growth has direct impact on poverty eradication, containing inflation, raising agricultural wages, employment generation.

Changing Contours of Indian Agriculture

The post-Independence decades have witnessed a veritable transformation in Indian agriculture. What is most readily noticed is the increase in agricultural production, particularly the nearly four-fold rise in the production of foodgrains which saved the country from one of the gravest crisis it faced after Independence. The increase in production was made possible by expansion of irrigation, spread of new technology and additions to rural infrastructure like irrigation works, roads, market yards and warehouses. These changes in the physical features of

---

2. Rudra (1967), Chakravarthy (1974), Raj (1976), Mellor (1976), Mitra (1977), Chakravarty (1979), Krishna (1982) and Rangarajan (1982).

agriculture needed changes in the institutional structure – like new credit institutions, extension agencies, regulated markets, control of moneylenders etc. The cumulative effect of these changes has been reflected in the farmers – their perceptions, attitudes and behaviour – and in the changing features of rural communities such as stratification, diversification, commercialisation and exposure to outside influences. *The total process bringing about these wide ranging changes could be described as modernisation of agriculture.*

A striking feature of modernisation of agriculture in India is the contrasting scenarios through which it is unfolding. The aggregative physical parameters of agriculture show remarkable achievement. Listed below are a few striking indicators of improvements in the physical aspects of agriculture.[3]

- Between 1949-50 and 1996-97, Index (base 1980-81) of agricultural production increased from 49 to 176, index of foodgrains from 52 to 161 and non-foodgrains from 45 to 201. Index of per hectare yield (all crops) increased from 74 to 149. It may be mentioned that the agricultural scenario has been one of stagnancy in the decades prior to Independence.
- Between 1950-51 and 1994-95, gross cropped area increased from 132 million hectares to 188 million hectares implying a rise in cropping intensity from 111 to 132. Gross irrigated area went up from 23 million hectares to 71 million hectares.
- Between 1950-51 and 1996-97, distribution of improved seeds increased from negligible to 70 lakh quintals. Fertiliser use increased from only 69 thousand tonnes to 14 million tonnes with per hectare fertiliser use going up from negligible to 77 Kgs. Pesticides use increased from 2.4 thousand tonnes to 56 thousand tonnes. Consumption of electricity in agriculture went up from 15200 Million KWH in 1981-82 to 85736 Million KWH in 1995-96.
- Institutional credit (Cooperative Societies, Commercial Banks and Regional Rural banks) was 28653 crores in 1996-97 as compared to 10186 crores in 1989-90.

On the other hand and paradoxically, despite the good performance of agriculture, the rural communities in India have poor development

3. V.M. Rao, P.D. Jeromi, *Modernising Indian Agriculture: Priority Tasks and Critical Policies*, DRG Study No. 21, Reprinted in Uma Kapila (ed.) op. cit.

indicators. The development indicators for the rural communities given below are from a recent large scale survey conducted by National Council of Applied Economic Research.

- "About half the population of rural India is illiterate and suffers from 'capability poverty', about 40 per cent have extremely low incomes".
- "Over 50 per cent of Indian population is still vulnerable and cannot afford the cost of education and health care"
- "National policies and programmes during the last half a century have not helped the SCs and STs to emerge from the perennial poverty trap".
- "63 per cent of villages do not have pucca/all weather connecting roads. In some states this is true of over 80 per cent of villages".
- "About one-half of all villages in India do not have any source of protected drinking water".
- "Overall, 88 per cent of all villages in rural India have a primary school within the village but about a quarter of villages in Uttar Pradesh, Himachal Pradesh and Orissa do not have even primary schools. Given the relatively poor transport network in these states, implementing the goal of universal primary education in these states seems remote".
- "Only about 22 per cent of all villages have a health sub-centre within the village".

Performance of Agriculture

There has been a remarkable performance of agriculture during the 1980s. The growth rate of production of 'all crops' at 3.21 per cent per annum was the highest since independence. It exceeded the growth rate during the green revolution period (2.38 per cent per annum during 1967-68 to 1980-81) by a convincing margin. While the earlier period 1949-50 to 1964-65 also had a relatively high growth rate (3.13 per cent per annum) a major part of it was contributed by area expansion. In contrast, the growth of agriculture during 1980-81 to 1991-92 was almost entirely due to yield improvement. In fact, the growth rate of yield during this period (3.16 per cent per annum) was not only much higher than that during the earlier periods but, even more significant, it clearly exceeded the population growth rate while the reverse was true in the earlier periods, even during the green revolution years.

Growth Rates

An elaborate statistical exercise has been recently undertaken to estimate growth rates of area, production and yield by principal crops and major states[4]. This study also covered analysis of index numbers of 'foodgrains', 'non-foodgrains' and 'all crops' as well as of the national and state level series of net domestic product of agriculture which is a good indicator of its aggregate performance. The conclusions of this study are as below:

(i) There has been an upsurge in the aggregate production and productivity in Indian agriculture during the 1980s which cannot be attributed merely to favourable weather. The fact that the contribution of yield improvement has been far more important than that of expansion in area indicates that the process of growth has been technologically more dynamic (as compared to the earlier green revolution years).

(ii) Unlike in the past, yield growth has been more impressive for non-foodgrains than foodgrains and, among the foodgrains, for kharif foodgrains *vis-a-vis* rabi foodgrains. Acceleration in yield growth occurred in case of rice, maize, other pulses, rapeseed, sesame, soyabean, rubber and cotton. For many other crops yield continued to expand at the pre-1981 rates. The indication, on the whole, is that of a much wider diffusion of technology across crops than in the past.

(iii) Foodgrains output growth picked up in many less developed areas from the central and eastern regions where growth had been sluggish in the early phase of the green revolution. With fairly rapid expansion in productivity of non-foodgrains, growth in agricultural incomes too accelerated in majority of the states in the 1980s. Thus, agricultural growth has become more broad-based in recent years.

Composition of Agricultural Sector

An important aspect of the change in Indian Agriculture is the growing importance of the non-crop sectors, commonly known as sub-sectors or ancilliary sectors. For example, the share of livestock products in gross value of agricultural product (i.e. crop production *plus*

---

4. S.D. Sawant and C.V. Achuthan, *Agricultural Growth Across Crops and Regions: Emerging Trends & Patterns*, in Indian Economy Since Independence, (ed) Uma Kapila, 2000-01 edition.

livestock raising) is progressively increasing. In 1970-71, it was less than 16 per cent, by 1995-96 it has increased to 26 per cent. Same is true of the share of fisheries in agricultural GDP, which has increased from 1.7 per cent to 3.1 per cent during 1970-71 to 1995-96. This, unfortunately, is not true of forestry, where the share of the sub-sector has actually declined from 9 per cent in 1970-71 to 4 per cent in 1995-96. These changes in the composition of agricultural sector, i.e., growing importance of the sub-sectors, have significant implications for income and employment of the households depending on agriculture.

TABLE – 1

SHARE OF INCOME FROM LIVESTOCK IN TOTAL VALUE OF AGRICULTURAL OUTPUT

Year	*Value of Output (Rs. in Crores)*		*Total*	*Income from Livestock as % of Total Agricultural Income*
	Agriculture	*Livestock*		
1970-71	17306	3197	20503	15.59
1980-81	46278	10597	56875	18.63
1990-91	128657	42041	170698	24.63
1995-96	217840	76580	294420	26.01

The main engine of growth for the sub-sectors such as livestock, poultry and fishery, was the increase in income and consequent changes in the dietary pattern. The state policies aimed at encouraging these activities also helped. Other important contributing factor was the role of the producers organisations, which imparted collective strength to the small producers and contributed positively to the growth of these sub-sectors. This is particularly true of the dairying and poultry. In fishery sector also the cooperatives and the unions of small artisan fishermen played an important role. These sub-sectors also attracted private enterprises, including some multinational companies.[5]

Relative decline in the importance of forestry has serious implications for the public revenue, on the income of the households dependent on forestry and, more importantly, on the ecology of the affected regions. The declining importance of forestry in the agriculture GDP was mainly due to the stagnation in the area under forests. It was

5. V.S. Vyas, (May, 2000) *Changing Contours of Indian Agriculture*, Golden Jubilee Lecture Series of NCAER, in Rakesh Mohan (2002), Facets of Indian Economy, OUP.

also due to the failure of public policies. The main policy thrust in this sector was to encourage fuel-wood and fodder raising on the private land and using forest lands for growing trees for industrial and timber needs. Both components of policy did not succeed (Saxena, 1997). The individual producers as much as the state were losers due to shortfall in both the segments of forestry.

Livestock sector has registered an impressive growth rate of nearly 7 per cent (6.69) per year from 1980-81 to 1990-91. Milk accounts for two third of the total produce of the livestock sector. India is the second largest producer of milk in the world. Its cost of production compares favourably with the cost of production of other important milk producing countries, with the exception of New Zealand. Even though there is progressive commercialisation of livestock industry, it has remained, basically, small scale, supplementary activity to crop production. The small farmers seem to have benefitted from the growth of livestock sector as much as the large farmers.

Fishery, on the other hand provides more or less full time employment to nearly 4 million (3.84 m.) fisherman (in 1991). The share of fishery in agricultural GDP has almost doubled, from 1.97 per cent in 1980-81 to 3.7 per cent in 1995-96. Momentum has accelerated in more recent years. Fish production has increased by 6.6 per cent per year during the period 1985-86 to 1992-93. The growth in inland fishery was even higher, at 6.5 per cent per annum. India now occupies second position, next to China, in inland fish production. Although some large scale operators, including MNCs, have entered in this field fishery remains basically a small scale operation and its growth has benefitted the small man in the rural areas.

Changes in Cropping Pattern

The other major change which has taken place in the recent years is in the crop composition. We have already mentioned the growing importance of the sub-sectors of the agriculture, namely, animal husbandry, fishery, poultry raising, in comparison to the crops sector. Within the crop raising sub-sector important changes have taken place which have serious implications for agricultural producers, and which also affect relative importance of different regions.

Within the crops sector three major changes have taken place.

In the first place the share of non-food crops has increased in terms of area devoted to as well as value generated from these crops. For example, in the triennium ending 1971-72, nearly 25.7 per cent of the cultivated area was devoted to non-foodgrains. Their share increased to 32.4 per cent in the triennium ending 1992-93. In value terms the increase was not that substantial, as terms of trade tilted in favour of the foodgrains. Even then the share of non-foodgrains in the total value of crops increased from 51.3 per cent to 53.4 per cent during the same period.[6]

Second, noteworthy, development is that among the non-foodgrains, other food crops i.e., sugar, oil seeds, spices and condiments and fruits and vegetables etc., are acquiring greater importance. They are now occupying a larger part of the cultivated area and account for larger share in value of agricultural production.

The third important change has taken place in the share of so-called superior cereals among the foodgrains. Thus, the area under rice and wheat has expanded from 31.4 per cent of the area under cultivation in the triennium ending 1970-71 to 36.5 per cent in the triennium ending 1992-93. Correspondingly, the coarse cereals and pulses have declined in importance, both in terms of area and value. (Table 2).

TABLE – 2

PROPORTION OF AREA UNDER FOOD CROPS RICE AND WHEAT TO TOTAL CULTIVATED AREA

(Area 000 Hectares)

Year	*Cultivated Area*	*Area under Food-crops*	*Area under*		*Area under Non-food Crops*
			Rice	*Wheat*	
1970-71	177647	1243.2	37592	18241	334.8
		(70.0)	(21.16)	(10.26)	(18.0)
1980-81	181309	1266.7	40152	22279	369.6
		(70.0)	(22.14)	(12.28)	(20.0)
1991-92	180702	1278.3	42649	23262	599.5
		(71.0)	(23.60)	(12.87)	(33.0)
1992-93	195677	1247.1	41637	24431	468.8
		(63.0)	(21.27)	(12.48)	(23.0)

Note: Figures in parenthesis are percentage to total cultivated areas.

Many of these changes were anticipated. The farmers in this country, small and large, devote a part of the land for commercial crops in order to earn cash. In the 1970s and 1980s the policy of food self-

6. V.S. Vyas, op. cit.

sufficiency was pursued vigorously, and incentives were provided to the foodgrains production (e.g., better minimum support prices). During that period area under commercial crops stagnated. But soon this phase was over and from the mid 1970s gradual increase in the area under commercial crops began. With the globalisation of the economy, and the agriculture playing an important part in exports, incentive for raising commercial crops also improved. Fortunately, because of the improvement in the yields of foodgrains per capita availability of foodgrains remained stable even though there was fast growth in population, the latter increasing at the rate of about 2 per cent per annum. At least till the mid 1990s somewhat faster growth in commercial crops did not jeopardize the food security in the country at the macro level.[7]

The other change in the cropping pattern, namely, a larger share of non-foodgrains (i.e. sugar, edible oil, fruits and vegetable etc.) in the cropped area was a reflection of changes in the food basket. With increase in per capita income share of these items increased in the consumption pattern. This is more or less a universal phenomenon. In India the other change in food intake, i.e., the rising share of animal husbandry products, which is commonly experienced with increase in the household income was rather slow, mainly due to cultural reasons.

The shift within the foodgrains in favour of superior cereals, i.e., wheat and rice was basically an outcome of the nature of technological change. The high-yielding varieties which resulted in improving productivity in these crops further shifted comparative advantages in favour of growing these crops. The concern for food self-sufficiency helped in forging a supportive policy package along with the extension of the superior technology. In other words, the "green revolution" expressed itself in remarkable growth of wheat in the first instance and rice later on. The coarse cereals and pulses did not have the advantage of either technical or policy or institutional support for raising productivity. The area under these crops also shrunk. While the country could achieve food self-sufficiency with the growth in rice and wheat production the stagnation in coarse cereals and pulses have serious implications for the backward, rainfed, regions. It has particularly unfavourable implications for the poor consumers, especially in terms of the intake of protein. The stagnation, rather decline, in per capita availability of the pulses which is the principal source of protein for the poor, must have affected their nutritional status.

---

7. V.S. Vyas, op. cit.

The nature of diversification from farm to non-farm sector and within the farm sector in favour of commercial crops, food crops other than foodgrains and within the foodgrains in favour of superior cereals have remarkably influenced the relative economics of different regions. The gains due to faster development of commercial crops and non-foodgrains food crops benefitted the southern and the western region, including rainfed areas of Rajasthan and Madhya Pradesh (especially due to the spurt in oilseed production). Break through in rice technology gave fillip to agricultural development in the eastern part. Besides, short maturing varieties of wheat and rice made significant impact on the cropping pattern in different states. For example, Punjab emerged as an important producer of rice, while eastern region improved its share in wheat production.

Emerging Trends and Impact of Globalisation

According to V.S. Vyas "the move towards "open frontiers" implicit in the policies of liberalisation and globalization will undoubtedly affect the product mix and the input composition in agriculture sector in a significant way. Naturally the impact will vary from region to region, and will differ from one section of agricultural producers to other."

From a historical perspective, it can be observed that till the late eighties agricultural sector in India was relatively closed as the export orientation was confined to only some commercial crops like spices, tea, coffee, etc. and imports were largely restricted. However, during the period since then the degree of export orientation increased considerably with the removal of some of the restrictions/controls on export of commodities.

The share of agricultural exports in GDP (both in total GDP and GDP originated in agriculture) would indicate three major aspects, namely, i) the degree of openness or outward-orientation of the agricultural sector in regard to the export activity; ii) the nature of agricultural trade strategies adopted in the country; and iii) supply capacity of the agricultural sector as regards exports. It can be noted from the table-3 that after a marginal rise in the shares of agricultural exports in total GDP and in GDP originated through the agricultural sector during the seventies, the shares were on the decline in the eighties. However, since the beginning of the nineties there is a perceptible rise in the shares: the share in total GDP rose from 1.3 per cent in 1990-91 to 2.0 per cent in 1995-96 but since then it declined to 1.6 per cent in 1998-99. In case of the share of agricultural exports

TABLE – 3

SHARE OF AGRICULTURAL EXPORTS IN GDP IN INDIA

(Rs. crore at current prices)

	1970-71	*1980-81*	*1990-91*	*1995-96*	*1998-99*
1. GDP (Total)	39708	122427	477814	1006286	1612383
2. GDP in Agriculture*	16821	42466	135162	255613	428680
3. GDP-Rest of the Economy@	22887	79961	342652	750673	1183703
4. Total Exports	1535	6711	32558	106353	141604
5. Agricultural Exports	487	2057	6019	20344	25225
6. Exports-Rest of the Economy@@	1048	4654	26539	86009	116379
Per cent Share					
a) % of Agri.Exports in GDP (Total)	1.2	1.7	1.3	2.0	1.6
b) % of Agri.Exports in GDP Agri.	2.9	4.8	4.5	8.0	5.9
c) % of Total Exports in GDP (Total)	3.9	5.5	6.8	10.6	8.8
d) % of Exports from the rest of Economy in GDP Agriculture	4.6	5.8	7.7	11.5	9.8

Note: * : GDP originated in agriculture, forestry and fishery

@ : Total GDP minus the GDP originated in agriculture.

@@ : Total Exports minus the export of agricultural products.

Source : 1. National Accounts Statistics, various issues, CSO, New Delhi.

2. Economic Survey, various issues, Government of India, New Delhi.

in GDP originated from the agricultural sector, the rise was from 4.5 per cent to 8.0 per cent and then decelerated to 5.9 per cent, during the above period. From the above observations, it can be inferred that the degree of openness or outward orientation of the agricultural sector, with regard to exports, has increased in recent times, *albeit* a marginal decline occurred since 1995-96. It reflects the effects of the liberalisation of agricultural exports and improvement in the supply capacity of the economy in recent times. Table 3 further reveals that agricultural sector is less outward-oriented than the economy as a whole. This is evident from the share of total exports from India in GDP (total). The share was 8.8 per cent in 1998-99, which is higher than the share of agricultural exports in GDP originated from the agricultural sector at 5.9 per cent.[8]

From a phase of gradual export orientation, the agricultural sector in India is likely to enter into a new phase of globalisation with the implementation of the various provisions of WTO (as and when they are made applicable to India). Here it is worthwhile to note that there is no country in the world which has globalised its agricultural sector in the true sense of the term. Even in the advanced market economy countries, agricultural sector is relatively protected. However, with the implementation of the various provisions of WTO agreement, especially the provisions relating to removal of quantitative restrictions, it is expected that a beginning will be made in this direction.

What will be the implication of globalisation of agriculture sector? To find an answer to the above question, here we offer the findings from empirical studies on the subject[9]:

A study by Subramanian (1993) revealed that with the liberalisation of trade the movement of terms of trade against agriculture can be moderated. Trade liberalisation will lead to higher price transmission elasticities for all unprocessed commodities except coarse cereals. The author, however, cautioned against extending trade liberalisation to commodities such as edible oils, sugar and processed food as they are highly protected and in cases of those commodities whose per capita availability is low.

Parikh, et al., (1995) revealed the following:

i) trade liberalisation in the medium run increases allocative efficiency within the agriculture sector and between agricultural and non-agricultural sectors,

ii) agricultural liberalisation increases output of all agricultural commodities except coarse grains and other foods,

iii) liberalisation leads to higher volume of exports of all agricultural goods, except coarse grains and

iv) prices of several agricultural commodities, which were disprotected, would rise with trade liberalisation.

Gulati and Sharma (1997), in terms of resource use efficiency (RUE), found that area and production of rice, wheat, maize, sorghum,

8. V.M. Rao & P.D. Jeromi, Op. cit.
9. Ibid.

chickpea and cotton are likely to expand when the international trade in agriculture is completely liberalised. On the other hand, groundnut, rapeseed-mustard and sunflower may have to face deceleration in their future expansion if trade is opened up (there may even be a contraction).

Chand (1998) found that imports to India would not be attractive in case of rice, tea, sunflower oil and cotton. There was a strong possibility of rise in imports of sugar and edible oils after the removal of QRs. The study observed that dismantling the trade barriers on imports would increase volatility of Indian prices and farm incomes. On the positive side, the removal of QRs would promote competition in the domestic market, which in turn would be beneficial to the consumers.

Gulati (1998) found that globalisation of the economy, including agriculture, offers an opportunity to correct the anti-agriculture bias in Indian trade policies that have been in existence since 1950s. The study further revealed that agriculture could move on to a higher growth trajectory if supply side bottlenecks are freed, and a protective cover is accorded to the poor.

Bharadwaj, et al, (1998) found that opening up of the economy was likely to benefit the agriculture and agro-based industries.

Major Issues in the Context of Globalisation

According to V.S. Vyas, in the light of the findings of the above studies, following issues need to be addressed in the context of globalisation of the agricultural sector. They are:

i) self-sufficiency in production,

ii) price stability,

iii) cropping pattern

iv) adverse effects on weaker sections and

v) WTO commitments.

These issues are examined below.

Theoretically, if a country globalises its agricultural sector, it cannot achieve the objective of self-sufficiency in production. This is because of the fact that with globalisation, countries will be forced to concentrate on production of those commodities in which they have comparative advantage in production. For countries like India, with large population and lower purchasing power, the impact of globalisation on availability of food at relatively lower prices is of concern both politically and ethically. Hence, food self-sufficiency at the national level, not necessarily 100 per cent, is desirable so that the reliance on trade can be kept within limits (Parikh, 1999)[10]. Undue concentration on production of some agricultural commodities in the long-term may create serious consequences for the quality of land, ecological balance and employment opportunities. The experience of Punjab and Haryana on account of undue specialisation in the production of rice and wheat is an example in this respect (ICAR, 1998). In view of the likely consequences, it may not be desirable to globalise the sector entirely. Rather, we need to judiciously globalise the sector so as to avoid the undesirable outcomes.[11]

Another issue related to globalisation is the likely price instability in the domestic market due to the convergence of domestic prices with the international prices. Literature indicates that given the high level of instability of commodity prices in the international market, mainly due to variations in crop production and speculative nature of the market, it is quite likely that prices of commodities in the domestic market will be highly unstable which will adversely affect both the producers and the consumers. Hence, dismantling of trade barriers is likely to increase volatility of domestic prices and farm incomes (Nayyar and Sen, 1994). Further, domestic prices will be more volatile when there is an incidence of dumping by countries having bumper harvest (Chand, 1998). Therefore, due precaution has to be taken in case of large-scale import of agricultural commodities.

Freeing trade in agricultural commodities is likely to change the cropping pattern in the country depending upon the level of comparative advantage in the production of commodities. As India has comparative advantage in production of commodities like rice, wheat, maize, sorghum, chickpea and cotton (Gulati, et al, 1994), trade liberalisation will increase their exports, which in turn may lead to expansion of area under these crops. At present, these crops are disprotected or indirectly taxed due to the restriction on exports. However, with liberalisation of trade these commodities will be able to get higher prices and that may promote larger cultivation. However, in case of oilseeds there may be a deceleration in their future expansion as they are not having comparative advantage and they have been getting much higher level

---

10. Kirit Parikh (1999), *Food & Agricultural Policy: The Challenges Ahead*, Vikalpa, Vol. 24, No.2, April-June.
11. V.M. Rao & P.D. Jeromi, Op. cit.

of incentives than what they are likely to get under a free-trade scenario (Gulati and Sharma, 1997). With liberalisation of agricultural trade the country can import oilseeds at lower price than the domestic price. Hence, achieving self-sufficiency in oilseeds production may not be desirable given the huge cost involved in it.

Globalisation of the sector may have its adverse effects on certain areas, some crops and some group of people. It has been indicated in the literature that with export promotion and globalisation, the benefits will be accrued to only some areas which are well endowed in terms of resources, some crops which are having comparative advantage in production and some sections of the population who are producing the exporting commodities. Other areas, crops and people are unlikely to be benefited from the globalisation process (Rao, 1994). In other words, the benefits of globalisation process may not be neutral to areas, crops and people. Further, as globalisation may raise the prices of some of the essential commodities, it will have adverse welfare consequences for the people who are not engaged in the agricultural sector.

The country's commitment to WTO, which in a way may facilitate the process of globalisation, is likely to have some consequences for the sector. Currently, the commitment for reduction of subsidy may not affect the quantum of subsidy given to the farmers. However, once the exemptions provided to the developing countries are withdrawn, there can be some pressure for reduction of subsidy, especially the subsidy for food procurement and its distribution through the PDS. The commitments for removal of QRs and reducing the import duty and also for increasing the quantum of imports are likely to increase imports and depress the domestic prices, especially of those commodities in which India does not enjoy comparative advantage.

Despite some of the trade liberalisation measure, foodgrains sector still remains largely controlled and insulated from the global markets, in view of the food security objective. In case of cash crops, exports are allowed when there is enough surplus and are imported when there is a net deficit. Hence, there is a view that agricultural trade is still taking place as a 'residual' between domestic demand and supply rather than as a policy instrument to integrate domestic agriculture with the world agriculture (Gulati, 1998).[12] Ideally, agricultural export and import policies should move in tandem so as to avoid any distortions in

---

12. Ashok Gulati (1998), *Indian Agriculture in an open economy: Will it Prosper*, in India's Economic Reforms & Development, Essays for Manmohan Singh, (eds) Ishar Ahluwalia & IMD Little, OUP, Delhi, 1998.

domestic prices. However, during the last few years while the agricultural exports have been liberalised, restriction/controls on imports have remained more or less unchanged (Jeromi, 1999). While the liberalisation of exports resulted in rise in domestic prices of some of the commodities (example, onion and potato), the restriction on imports denied access to commodities from abroad. This miss-match in agricultural export-import policy was on account of the undue obsession to remain self-sufficient in all agricultural commodities. However, given the fact that no country in the world can have comparative advantage in production of all the commodities required by it, the restrictions on imports in the face of liberalisation of exports will not be beneficial in a liberalised economic environment. Hence, there is a need to continue with the liberalisation of trade in agricultural commodities so as to provide a level playing field for the agricultural sector with the industrial sector.

The following priority tasks are identified for the government to help Indian agriculture adjust to globalisation:

- Food self-sufficiency at the national level is desirable so that the reliance on trade can be kept within limits.
- Safety nets are needed to protect the interests of crops, people and regions which are likely to be affected by globalisation.
- Precautions on imports in view of the removal of quantitative restrictions.
- Agricultural export policies need to be synchronised with the import policies to avoid price fluctuations. There is a need for sequencing of measures. In view of the removal of quantitative restriction in the coming days, tariffication process needs to be done judiciously.

14

New Technology in Indian Agriculture and the Green Revolution

IT was becoming clear by the mid-sixties that there was no alternative to technological change in agriculture for achieving self-sufficiency in foodgrains. Even those countries in Asia which could carry out radical land reforms and build up adequate infrastructure for agriculture had taken to the path of modernising agriculture. Japan took the lead in this direction and China followed suit even after successfully experimenting with structural changes and mobilisation of growing labour force for capital construction in agriculture.

Characteristics of New Technology

The distinguishing characteristic of the new technology lies in the substitution of traditional robust but low-yielding varieties of seed by the so-called high-yielding variety. These seeds have the physiological attribute of being able to turn large amounts of soil nutrients into grain rather than leaf growth. This enables the plant to produce higher yields, especially so if the supply of nutrients in the soil can be increased. This in turn creates the demand for chemical fertilizers to supplement the natural fertility of the soil. Because these contain nutrients in concentrated form, they have to be applied with adequate supplies of water to enable the plant to absorb them without damaging itself. A lack of adequate water supply not only reduces the yield but may do so substantially.

Better Agricultural Practices

This seed-fertilizer-water package in turn calls for better

agricultural practices for the effective utilization of the technology.

First, the plant requires the fertilizer-water input at particular stages of growth to give the best yields.

Secondly, as fertilizers can be absorbed by weeds as well as by the plant, effective weeding is required to prevent waste of expensive fertilizer.

Thirdly, while the HYV seeds give higher yields, they are more prone to damage from excessive watering. For example, shorter-stemmed dwarf varieties are more liable to be flooded. They thus require more effective water control and better drainage. The need is for controlled and adequate water supplies.

Fourthly, being relatively new and non-acclimatized strains, they are more prone to local pests and diseases than established indigenous varieties and therefore, require a supply of germicides and pesticides.

Two further physiological characteristics of the new seeds are that they are quicker maturing than the traditional varieties and they are non-photosensitive. On the one hand, these two characteristics give rise to a shorter harvesting period, thus making it possible for farmers to practise multiple cropping, enabling them to use more intensively a given amount of land. Fertilizers, by enabling more production per acre to be achieved, and the quicker maturing HYV seeds, by making it possible to practice double cropping during the year, both act as land-saving innovations. Hence their attraction to a land-hungry south Asia. On the other hand, as the crop may be ready for harvesting during the monsoon season at a time when the cloud-cover has not yet dispersed, a possibility of loss of output due to a lack of drying and storage facilities is also opened up.[1]

Thus, the basic technological characteristic of the new technology is the application of a number of inputs which are complementary to each other. The application of these joint inputs yields much larger volumes of output of foodgrains as a result, largely by increasing yield per acre. However, in order to assess the impact of the technology on Indian agriculture, we have to also take into account some of the economic characteristics of that technology. In an economy where labour is relatively plentiful, it has low opportunity cost. Most agricultural holdings in India use either family labour or fairly low-paid agricultural labour, neither of which, generally speaking, can command high levels

1. Pramit Choudhary, *The Indian Economy : Poverty and Development*, (1978), Vikas, New Delhi, Ch.5, P. 121-123.

of alternative earnings. For traditional agriculture, the most expensive input, other than land, is bullock-power. The new inputs are mostly of manufactured origin, such as fertilizers, pesticides or pumps, and are more expensive. In non-rainfed agriculture, there are also costs attached to irrigation, in the form either of the capital costs of sinking a well or installing a pump or running costs in the form of purchase of diesel fuel or payment of water rates.

Economic Aspects of New Technology

The new practices, therefore, are much more expensive to the farmer. This has three implications. First, the extent to which the various inputs are applied in practice depends not on some technologically efficient dosage but on an economically optimum one. This depends in turn on the relative prices of inputs and outputs facing the producer. Minhas and Srinivasan have shown that fertilizer application is subject to diminishing returns, the economically optimum dose being smaller than the technical optimum. As technologically some of the inputs are complementary, the extent to which the application of a particular input can be profitably pushed depends also on the availability of, and the ability to purchase, other inputs. For example, the degree of fertilizer application that is profitable will depend on the availability of water and on the ability of a farmer to purchase the use of both inputs.

Secondly, the new technology is only worthwhile in terms of private benefits, e.g. if the farmer receives yields which are not only larger than traditional varieties but are substantially so, to make up for the additional variable costs of cultivation. This in turn requires, thirdly, a more intensive use of the fixed factor, e.g. land. The new technology opens up the possibility of multiple cropping; the economic imperative drives the farmer to it. This is compounded by the fact that while the new technology yields larger outputs, it is also more subject to risks. We have noted that the HYV seeds are prone to damage from flooding, water scarcity and pests. Moreover, because the farmer is a newcomer to these practices, he is also ignorant of how to respond if something goes wrong. Additionally, where he is involved in substantial cash outlays in order to utilize the new technology, he bears a liquidity risk. This is reinforced by the fact that very often the farmer may have to resort to borrowing in order to meet the additional costs of cultivation. A crop failure saddles him with the burden of debt.

These economic aspects of the new technology are as important as its technological characteristics to our understanding of the impact of the 'green revolution' upon the agrarian economy, especially in relation to the problems of mechanization and of unequal incidence of acceptance and use between large and small farmers. That impact can best be studied in terms of the effects of the new technology on output, employment and the regional and interpersonal distribution of gain arising from the adoption of that technology.

Green Revolution

First Phase: Increase in Public Investment in Agriculture

After the mid-sixties, apart from the introduction of HYVs of seeds for wheat and rice, public investment in agriculture was stepped up significantly. The new technology raised the profitability of investment for the farmers. Besides, in agriculture, there is a high complementarity between public and private investment. As a result, the annual gross capital formation in agriculture, public and private combined, at constant prices, rose much faster than in the pre-green revolution period. This is reflected in the accelerated increase in gross irrigated area. From less than one million hectares per annum during the pre-green revolution period, it increased to about 2.5 million hectares per annum during the seventies. However, owing to the land constraint, the growth of net sown area slowed down considerably. This explains why despite the accelerated increase in capital formation and the introduction of new technologies, the growth rate of agricultural output was no higher than in the pre-green revolution period.[2]

Nevertheless, there was a rapid increase in the marketed surpluses of foodgrains and in the stocks held by the government through internal procurement. This is due to the basic changes in the structure of agricultural production witnessed in this period. First, the breakthrough in foodgrains output occurred in the developed regions in the North-West and in certain parts of the South. The consumption of foodgrains was already high in these areas and therefore a considerably larger proportion of additions to output was marketed. Second, the use of labour per unit of output showed a significant decline, which also resulted in the generation of larger foodgrain surpluses from the rural areas.

There are two other factors responsible for the rise in marketed surpluses and availability of foodgrains. The increase in output during this period has been taking place mainly through the increase in yield

---

2. C.H. Hanumantha Rao, *Technological Change in Indian Agriculture : Emerging Trends and Perspectives*, in Uma Kapila (ed) Indian Economy Since Independence, (7th edition, 1996), Academic Foundation, Delhi.

per hectare. Therefore, there has been a decline in the ratio of seed to output, although our official estimates continue to be based on the conventional norms. Secondly, the rate of urbanisation has increased and, for various reasons, the average per capita consumption of foodgrains in the urban areas has been significantly lower than in the rural areas.

We are used to comparing the performance in the pre-green revolution period with that in the post-green revolution period as a whole. However, the mid or the late seventies mark a definite departure from the trends observed in the early phase of green revolution in several respects.

Second Phase of Green Revolution

There seems to be some improvement in the growth rate of foodgrains output in the second decade, i.e., 1978-79 to 1988-89, when compared with the first decade of green revolution. Crops such as rice, pulses and oilseeds, whose growth rates in the first decade of green revolution had fallen much below those recorded in the pre-green revolution period, are now showing higher growth rates (Table-1). There are thus clear indications that the major inter-crop imbalances in growth witnessed in the early years of green revolution are getting redressed to some extent in the recent period.

Oilseeds and pulses are grown essentially in the rainfed or unirrigated areas. Even for rice, near 60 per cent of area is rainfed. The recent experience, therefore, suggests that the disparities in growth between the irrigated and rainfed or dry areas may not be as sharp as in the early years of green revolution. It is also heartening to find that many of the states where poverty is widespread and where the growth of foodgrains output had slowed down in the first decade of green revolution, e.g., Assam, Bihar, Orissa, Madhya Pradesh and West Bengal have shown a much better performance in the last decade. Their performance is nearer, or even higher than, the all-India average. The growth of rice had slowed down considerably in the Eastern States during the seventies. All these states have experienced a step-up in the growth of rice during the last decade and some of them have recorded higher growth than the national average (Table 1).

TABLE – 1

STATEWISE COMPOUND GROWTH RATES OF OUTPUT

States	*Rice*		*Foodgrains*	
	1967-68 to 1977-78	*1978-79 to 1988-89*	*1967-68 to 1977-78*	*1977-78 to 1988-89*
(1)	*(2)*	*(3)*	*(4)*	*(5)*
Andhra Pradesh	2.66	1.70	2.56	0.41
Assam	0.88	2.12	1.27	1.63
Bihar	0.82	2.83	1.14	3.52
Gujarat	3.39	-0.43	2.23	-4.97
Haryana	11.34	5.12	2.86	3.94
Himachal Pradesh	0.04	-1.14	1.24	0.36
Jammu & Kashmir	1.73	0.09	1.47	0.36
Karnataka	-0.01	-0.44	2.50	-0.58
Kerala	0.54	-2.36	0.48	-2.30
Madhya Pradesh	0.96	5.30	1.23	4.36
Maharashtra	4.79	-0.44	4.84	-0.46
Orissa	-1.00	2.61	0.80	2.59
Punjab	18.21	7.04	5.29	4.57
Rajasthan	10.90	-1.77	3.03	1.37
Tamil Nadu	1.45	0.89	1.69	0.74
Uttar Pradesh	4.06	7.32	4.06	5.16
West Bengal	1.71	5.23	2.60	4.53
All-India	2.16	3.19	2.31	2.68
Pulses	0.27	2.32		
Oilseeds	1.39	3.86		

Source: Directorate of Economics and Statistics, Ministry of Food and Agriculture, Government of India, New Delhi.
Estimates for 1988-89 are provisional.

This encouraging performance is basically attributable to the spread of new technology to the lagging crops and regions. The special programmes for rice and oilseeds and increasing attention being given to dry farming and to the less developed state have started yielding results. This is corroborated by the increase in the consumption of fertilisers during the eighties at a faster rate in the Eastern and Western regions than in the Northern and Southern regions. What is more, fertilisers consumed in Kharif season increased at a much faster rate than in rabi season, particularly in the Eastern and Western regions, indicating the spread of new technology to the rainfed and environmentally unfavourable areas. There is also evidence of an increase in the share of the Eastern States in the total gross irrigated area of the country.

According to C.H.H. Rao although the growth rate in the foodgrains output seems to have improved because of the impact of new technology, the growth performance has by no means been smooth. The instability or the year-to-year variation in the foodgrains output has increased in the post-green revolution period. Even within this period, the instability in the last decade (1978-79 to 1988-89) was higher than in the preceding decade. The rural poor, particularly in the drought-prone areas and in the remote areas of the country, continue to suffer from fluctuations in employment and income and inadequate availability of foodgrains in years of drought.

Also the growth pattern has not been uniform with a tendency towards deceleration in the 1990s (table 2).

TABLE – 2

TREND GROWTH RATES IN THE INDICES OF AREA, PRODUCTION AND YIELDS OF FOODGRAINS, NON-FOODGRAINS AND ALL CROPS DURING 1970-71 TO 2000-01

(per cent)

Period	*Foodgrains*			*Non-Foodgrains*			*All Crops*		
	Area	*Production*	*Yield*	*Area*	*Production*	*Yield*	*Area*	*Production*	*Yield*
1	*2*	*3*	*4*	*5*	*6*	*7*	*8*	*9*	*10*
1970-71 to 2000-01	-0.03	2.52	2.13	1.46	3.31	1.66	0.35	2.83	1.93
1970-71 to 1979-80	0.44	1.91	1.06	1.10	2.15	1.00	0.59	1.99	1.03
1980-81 to 1989-90	-0.22	2.81	2.71	1.11	3.70	2.28	0.09	3.13	2.52
1990-91 to 1999-2000	0.07	1.98	1.30	1.29	2.77	1.08	0.41	2.30	1.19

Note : Trend Growth Rates are based on semi-logarithmic function.
Source : Report on Currency & Finance 2000-01.

The yield pattern in case of both foodgrains and non-foodgrains indicates that highest growth in yield levels occurred during the 1980s. Much of the growth in agricultural production in India is yield-driven as the growth in area is marginal; however, Indian agriculture suffers from lower yield levels vis-a-vis major agricultural producers in the world, despite India being one of the largest producers of most of the major crops (Table 3). The yield of 6,059 kg per hectare attained in China during 1998 in the production of paddy was more than double that of 2,890 kg per hectare in India. Similarly, wheat yield in China stood at 3,667 kg per hectare in 1998 in comparison with 2,578 kg per hectare in India.

TABLE – 3

INDIA'S GLOBAL RANK IN MAJOR AGRICULTURAL CROPS

Crop	*Rank in 2000*		
	Area	*Production*	*Yield*
1	2	3	4
Rice (Paddy)	1	2	52
Wheat	1	2	38
Coarse Grains	3	4	125
Pulses	1	1	138
Oil Crops (Primary)	2	5	147
Cotton Seed	1	4	77
Jute and Jute Like Fibres	1	1	7
Tea	2	1	13
Coffee (Green)	7	7	14
Sugarcane	2	2	31

Source : Food and Agricultural Organisation.

The Role of Technology in Indian Agriculture

One of the main reasons for the low levels of yield attained in India is the unsatisfactory spread of new technological practices, including cultivation of High Yielding Varieties (HYV) of seeds. The adoption of new technology, mainly the cultivation of HYV seeds requires intensive use of fertilisers and pesticides under adequate and often assured water supply. The use of HYV seeds entails a higher yield risk (as measured by variance in yield) as compared with the traditional seed varieties, in the absence of proper irrigation facilities. The lower spread of new technological practices to a wide variety of crops other than wheat and rice as also across regions could be attributed to the higher yield risk associated with the cultivation of HYV seeds, caused by inadequate spread of irrigation facilities. There is considerable co-movement between the area under HYV seeds and area under irrigation, probably on account of reduction in yield risk due to irrigation facilities.

It is mainly paddy and wheat, which are cultivated under the HYV seeds, while the areas under HYV seeds for other cereal crops are very low and vary across different States of the country. Low growth experienced during the past two decades in the production of coarse cereals (0.5 per cent) and pulses (0.8 per cent) in comparison to rice (2.8 per cent) and wheat (4.0 per cent) is on account of lower adoption of HYV seeds or non-availability of appropriate seeds (apart from the usual dry-land farming accorded to these crops), given the diverse soil and moisture profiles of different parts of the country. The pattern of adoption of HYV seeds across various states has accordingly been disparate (Table 4).

TABLE – 4

STATE-WISE COVERAGE OF AREA UNDER HYV SEEDS FOR CEREALS DURING 1996-97

(Lakh hectares)

State	*Paddy*	*Wheat*	*Jowar*	*Bajra*	*Maize*	*Ragi*	*Total Cereals*
1	*2*	*3*	*4*	*5*	*6*	*7*	*8*
Andhra Pradesh	36.99	0.07	5.99	0.72	3.22	-	46.99
Assam	14.22	1.03	-	-	0.12	-	15.37
Bihar	35.00	25.00	-	-	7.50	-	67.50
Gujarat	5.33	4.10	1.80	7.95	2.11	-	21.29
Haryana	5.15	19.38	-	3.58	0.12	-	28.23
Karnataka	10.16	1.34	14.01	2.70	3.53	10.45	42.19
Kerala	4.00	-	-	-	-	-	4.00
Madhya Pradesh	34.71	30.00	7.88	0.34	5.08	-	78.01
Maharashtra	12.93	7.40	47.91	18.70	2.62	-	89.56
Orissa	30.27	0.15	0.02	-	0.98	-	41.42
Punjab	20.41	32.30	-	0.03	1.47	-	54.21
Rajasthan	0.43	17.42	0.13	20.32	0.24	-	38.54
Tamil Nadu	21.20	-	5.20	1.86	0.69	1.01	29.96
Uttar Pradesh	50.18	88.83	- 4.67	6.04	-	149.72	
West Bengal	44.63	3.51	-	-	-	-	48.14
All India	**333.99**	**237.26**	**82.94**	**60.98**	**37.64**	**11.47**	**764.28**

Source : Ministry of Agriculture, Government of India.

Factor Limiting the New Technology

One significant factor limiting the adoption of HYV seeds is the generally low level of irrigation cover for most of the crops as compared with rice and wheat. Nearly 64 per cent of the total cultivated area in the country is rainfed. In fact, as compared with 79.1 per cent of the total geographical area as drought prone, the irrigation coverage of 38.2 per cent is quite unfavourable. The Ninth Plan document placed the irrigation potential at 139.89 million hectares. With this irrigation potential, the cropping intensity coefficient can be raised up to 149.0 as against the current level of 134.20. It has been found that the states of Rajasthan, Gujarat and Jammu and Kashmir have a higher probability (in excess of 20 per cent) of the incidence of drought in any given year. Moreover, agriculturally important states such as Andhra Pradesh, Uttar Pradesh, Haryana and Punjab have been found to have more than 10 per cent probability of the incidence of drought in any year. Of these, only Punjab has a good irrigation cover, while Haryana has a moderately good irrigation coverage (Table 5). Wheat and rice among foodgrains and sugarcane among non-foodgrains enjoy the maximum irrigation coverage across all states. Even in the states with lesser irrigation coverage, such as Karnataka, Madhya Pradesh, Kerala, etc., the irrigation cover for rice and wheat is much higher in comparison with other crops. Thus, in India irrigated area generally tends to be used for the growing of rice and wheat, while the other crops are grown mostly in rainfed and unirrigated conditions.

In such a scenario, the technological development in terms of the adoption of HYV seeds is mostly limited to the cultivation of rice and wheat on account of higher yield risk imparted by these seeds. It is pertinent to note in this connection that the foodgrains production in 1999-2000 was at a record high of 208.9 million tonnes despite acute drought conditions in the central stretch of India, mainly on account of record production of rice and wheat. Most of the other crops - mainly oilseeds - suffered significant fall in production in that year. This could be indicative of the disproportionate adoption of technology and irrigation benefits, underscoring the need for spreading the irrigation benefits to all crops.

Small Size of Farms

Another important factor affecting the dissemination of modern technology in general and HYV seed technology in particular is the small size of average farms in India. It has been argued that the small size of land holdings limits the adoption of new technology due to reasons other than the scale of operation. Share-cropping, which is generally undertaken by the small and marginal farmers, limits the scope for adoption of new technology as the farmer has to pay a fraction of (generally around half) the production to the land-owner, while the whole cost of adoption of the green revolution inputs such as HYV seeds and fertilisers will have to be borne by the tenant. In such an arrangement, it is imperative that the gains in marginal product due to adoption of these inputs should at least be twice that of the investment for the farmer to break even. Such dramatic increases in production are difficult to come by in the absence of other infrastructural facilities and hence, the scope for adoption of green revolution inputs by the share-cropper is clearly undermined.

TABLE – 5

STATE-WISE PERCENTAGE COVERAGE OF IRRIGATED AREA UNDER PRINCIPAL CROPS DURING 1997-98

(Per cent)

State	*Rice*	*Wheat*	*Pulses*	*Total Food-grains*	*Oil Seeds*	*Sugarcane*	*Cotton*	*All Crops*
1	*2*	*3*	*4*	*5*	*6*	*7*	*8*	*9*
Andhra Pradesh	96.4	72.7	1.2	55.1	19.7	95.2	18.9	42.5
Bihar	40.4	89.0	2.1	47.8	20.2	30.6	-	46.6
Gujarat	61.2	75.6	10.7	32.2	26.0	100.0	37.7	34.3
Haryana	99.6	98.3	22.5	77.5	70.0	97.9	98.9	78.6
Karnataka	69.2	38.2	3.9	22.5	21.3	100.0	19.3	24.9
Kerala	52.2	-	-	49.3	16.0	100.0	-	14.0
Madhya Pradesh	23.6	69.2	18.5	30.4	5.7	98.6	39.4	25.0
Maharashtra	28.1	69.6	7.3	13.3	11.1	95.0	2.8	14.5
Orissa	36.2	100.0	5.0	26.7	11.0	100.0	-	26.8
Punjab	95.0	94.8	89.8	93.8	62.2	75.1	99.6	91.7
Rajasthan	41.5	94.7	7.7	23.6	43.9	100.0	98.0	29.9
Tamil Nadu	93.2	-	6.4	62.0	40.9	100.0	34.6	53.7
Uttar Pradesh	62.7	91.7	27.7	64.7	39.5	95.0	91.7	65.9
West Bengal	25.9	73.0	4.5	27.6	63.5	30.8	-	27.1
All India	**50.2**	**85.0**	**11.8**	**40.6**	**24.4**	**92.6**	**36.3**	**38.2**

Source : Ministry of Agriculture, Government of India.

The per hectare consumption of fertilisers and pesticides is quite low in India in comparison with international standards and there is a lot of scope for improvement in this sphere. For instance, the per hectare consumption of fertilisers in India at 88.6 kg was much lower than 256.6 kg and 110.4 kg in China and USA, respectively, in 1997-98. The growth in the consumption of fertilisers during the past two decades has also quite varied across different States (Table 6). Another factor that is responsible for lower productivity of Indian agriculture is the skewed distribution of N:P:K (Nitrogen : Phosphorus : Potassium) fertiliser mix. Currently, the N:P:K ratio stands at 6.9:2.9:1.0, which is quite skewed in comparison to the optimal mix of 4:2:1. The skewed consumption of fertiliser accentuates the risk of degradation of soil, thus hampering the long-term productivity of the land. This skewed fertiliser consumption pattern is the result of high subsidies extended to the urea producers.

Instability in Output

Although the growth rate in foodgrains output seems to have improved because of the impact of new technology, the growth performance has by no means been smooth. The instability or the year-to-year variation in foodgrains output has increased in the post-green revolution period. Even within the post-green revolution period, the instability in the last decade (1978-79 to 1988-89) was higher than in the preceding decade. The rural poor, particularly in the drought-prone areas and in the remote areas of the country, continue to suffer from fluctuations in employment and income and inadequate availability of foodgrains in years of drought.

However, this increase in instability cannot be attributed to new technology. Rather, the instability arises from the adverse agro-climatic conditions in which the technology is used. The new seed-fertiliser technology has raised the response of output to water. Thus, for a given variability in rainfall or moisture conditions, the instability in output would be greater. However, when the new technology is applied under assured irrigated conditions, the increase in output would be on a stable path. This is exactly what has happened in the case of wheat where the new technology has made the maximum impact. The rise in instability is significant for crops like rice, oilseeds and pulses. This is explained by the increasing application of new seed-fertiliser technology for these crops in rainfed areas and under uncertain irrigation in the recent period. This suggests the need for stabilising consumption through larger procurement of foodgrains when harvests are good and their liberal release through public distribution system for the vulnerable groups in years of drought.

Regional Disparities and Intrapersonal Disparities

Perhaps the most widely debated issue about green revolution is the growing disparities in income between different regions and classes of farmers. The experience after the mid-seventies covering nearly a decade and half reveals trends which are typical of a diffusion process. These trends are: the spread of green revolution to new areas, the increasing adoption of new technology by the small farmers, the decline in the relative prices of foodgrains and the rise in real wages in agriculture in the less developed regions where new technology is spreading.

In the early phase of green revolution, large farmers, owing to better access to capital resources, stepped up yields per acre at a faster rate than small farmers. Because of this, in areas experiencing technological change, the inverse relationship between farm size and output per acre began to disappear. In course of time, however, the supply of institutional credit for the less developed regions and small farmers improved significantly. As a result of this and also because of improved extension services, the use of new seed-fertiliser technology among small farms caught up with that among large farms. And, because of the continued advantage that small farmers have in respect of cropping intensity, the inverse relationship between farm size and output per net operated acre has started reappearing. However, labour input per acre continued to decline sharply with the increase in the size of holding.

In-so-far as large farmers have resumed land for self-cultivation from share-croppers because of the profitability of new technology; it has led to lower labour absorption and reduced incomes for erstwhile tenants. However, in quite a few places, cost-sharing on new inputs between landowners and share-croppers has become popular resulting in the sharing of benefits from new technology by the landowners as well as tenants.

Even in the early phase of green revolution, the emerging disparities between different regions were more conspicuous than the disparities between different classes of farmers within regions experiencing technological change. The uneven regional growth was mainly responsible for low absorption of labour within agriculture. In a large number of States, especially in those regions where there was abundant availability of labour, the growth of output was too slow to generate adequate employment opportunities. In high growth regions labour was not plentiful and wage rates were high. The sudden rise in the demand for labour in these areas induced mechanisation and labour-saving practices in general. This happened despite the use of migrant labour from the less developed regions for certain operations. The net result was a significant decline in the elasticity of employment with respect to agricultural output for the country as a whole. At the same time, the inter-State disparities in the growth of output and in output per worker continued to increase from the early seventies through the early eighties. However, the inter-State disparities in agricultural wages started declining since the mid-seventies. The decline in disparities in real wages is even more significant. This is because the decline in the relative prices of foodgrains had a greater impact on the purchasing power of wage earners in low wage areas. For example, the disparities in real wages in agriculture between Punjab, on the one hand and Bihar, on the other, started coming down since the mid-seventies. The real wages in Punjab having risen significantly in the early phase of green revolution, virtually stagnated after the mid-seventies whereas the real wages in Bihar started rising. The causes for the decline in inter-State disparities in real wages are: the outmigration of labour from the less developed regions to the high wage areas; mechanisation of agricultural operations in the developed regions; the decline in the relative prices of foodgrains; the increase in employment generated in the less developed regions under the poverty alleviation programmes; and the recent pick-up in agricultural growth in these regions. An encouraging consequence of these developments is that the disparity between male-female wage rate has started declining in several states. The use of new technology may have improved the bargaining power of female labour for operations such as transplanting and interculturing on account of the rise in seasonal demand for such labour.

Low income groups, both in the rural and urban areas, would derive greater benefit from the decline in the relative prices of foodgrains, because they spend a larger proportion of their income on foodgrains than the upper income groups. Agricultural price policy has been able to ensure that the productivity gains from technological change are shared both by the consumers and producers. However, consumers seem to have benefited relatively more than the producers from the productivity gains, particularly in the case of rice and jowar. The demand for wheat has been more favourable than for other cereals. So the decline in the relative price of wheat was only about 25 per cent, while the productivity gains amounted to nearly 45 per cent of output growth.

The indirect contribution of green revolution to equity through food security and the decline in the relative prices of foodgrains has perhaps been more significant than its direct impact by way of labour absorption in agriculture. Because of slow growth of employment in agriculture, the employment and income generated under poverty alleviation programmes had to be stepped up by using surplus stocks of foodgrains.

From about 20 million man-days of employment generated annually in the mid-sixties, the employment generated under such programmes in the country as a whole amounted to 850 million man-days in 1988-89. These employment programmes together with the income generated under the Integrated Rural Development Programme (IRDP) seem to make up for about half the deficiency in employment generation in agriculture in the post-green revolution period. The relative contribution of these poverty alleviation programmes to employment generation is more significant in the poorer regions where agricultural growth has been below the national average. These programmes have been made possible because of the increased availability of foodgrains from internal procurement.

New Technology and Environmental Degradation

Pollution of environment due to the intensive use of chemical fertilisers and pesticides has become a major problem in the developed countries. In India, environmental degradation in the rural areas has arisen not so much from the high level of chemical inputs used as from deforestation and extension of cultivation to ecologically fragile areas. Land-saving technological changes by reducing pressure for extension of cultivation and by augmenting bio-mass, contribute to the conservation of fragile areas and regeneration of forests.

Across different States in India, the extension of area under cultivation and the denudation of forests seem to be high where the progress of yield-increasing technology is slow. In such regions, the levels of agricultural income and wages are low and poverty levels are high. Similarly, the pressure from animals such as goats and sheep on forests and common lands has been increasing in regions where growth in crop production is slow. This is because the rural poor supplement their incomes by rearing these animals (Rao, forthcoming; Mellor, 1988). Apart from yield-increasing technology for crops, the use of new technologies in forestry and animal husbandry to raise the yields from trees and animals and to improve management practices are likely to contribute significantly to the protection of environment. The emerging biotechnologies are opening up opportunities for environmentally sound management of agriculture.[3]

---

3. C.H. Hanumantha Rao and Ashok Gulati, *Indian Agriculture : Emerging Perspectives and Policy Issues,* in Uma Kapila (ed) Indian Economy Since Independence, 2000-01 edition.

Prime Movers of Growth

Development and Diffusion of Technology

Adequate funding of public research; appropriate economic signals for setting right priorities in research, whether public or private; and a favourable institutional framework providing for the absorption of new technology are the three basic pre-requisities for the proper development and diffusion of new technology.

So far, achievements of the Indian agricultural system in raising yields in the unirrigated and unfavourable agroclimatic regions are not comparable with those realised for the irrigated areas in the early years of the Green Revolution. Even in irrigated areas, yields from the seed-fertiliser technology have hovered around their peak for some time. The tools of emerging biotechnology, including genetic engineering and tissue culture, seem to offer significant possibilities for breaking these barriers. Although some advanced centres of research in biotechnology have been established in India, it is not clear how such priorities find their place in the existing agricultural research system. A fresh look at the priorities of the Indian agricultural system is necessary in light of these emerging prospects, adequately taking into account the socio-economic factors relevant in the evolution of new technologies. India is currently investing only about 0.3 per cent of its agricultural GDP to agricultural research, as against 0.7 per cent in the developing countries as a whole and 2-3 per cent in the developed countries. Therefore, there is considerable scope for diverting incremental outlays to the priority areas in research.

Irrigation

Irrigation was the cradle where HYV seeds and fertiliser consumption thrived, bringing about the green revolution in Indian agriculture during the late 1960s and early 1970s. But even before that, development of irrigation was assigned a high priority by the government in its successive plans. In the early 1970s, north-west India experienced a 'tubewell explosion' in response to the first flush of profits accruing to farmers from the introduction of new technology in wheat production.

Between 1951 and 1990, India added about 55 million hectares of irrigated land to its existing 23 million irrigated hectares, taking the total to 78 million hectares in 1990. About 40 per cent of this additional irrigation was through major and medium schemes and the rest through minor schemes. This is only about half the ultimate irrigation potential of the country, indicating that the country has a long way to go on irrigation. In the 1990s, looking ahead to the future growth of Indian agriculture and what role the irrigation sector will play, the following questions have to be addressed:

(1) Should more investment funds be allocated to major and medium irrigation schemes than has been the trend in the last decade and a half? During the 1980s, the irrigation potential created through major and medium schemes decelerated sharply in response to the shrinking real government expenditure on this sector. This has long-term implications for the growth of Indian agriculture.

(2) Should investments in major and medium irrigation works go to new schemes or to complete those already at hand? This is important because spreading resources too thin leads to long lags in completion of projects.

(3) Should canal waters be priced to cover at least operational and maintenance costs (and a part of the capital cost)? Cost recovery from the canal network has reached extremely low levels, leading to suboptimal use of water on the one hand and a financial crisis on the other. Research reveals that capital costs of major and medium irrigation schemes rose sharply during the 1980s due to larger concerns about rehabilitation and the environment and because more difficult sites were taken up. Operation and maintenance expenses have also gone up in real terms, and the share of management and administration costs has been increasing. As a result, a financial crisis is adversely affecting not only new construction activity but also proper maintenance of the existing systems. To improve the efficiency and financial sustainability of major and medium schemes, drastic institutional reforms in management and ownership are needed in addition to corrections in the price of water.

(4) What institutional reforms need to be initiated in major and medium schemes to improve efficiency in resource use?

(5) How can the overexploitation of groundwater be curtailed? An important cause is the inappropriate pricing of electricity, which encourages excessive pumping.

In terms of policy responses to these questions, the highest priority should be given, first, to maintaining the existing irrigation facilities and then to developing the rest of the irrigation potential in the country. This cannot be done without significantly stepping up the rate of investment in this sector. The largest chunk of this investment, however, should be directed to operating and maintaining the existing facilities and completing the projects already started. At current levels of investment, it is estimated that the projects in hand will take about 28 years to complete. This time span needs to be brought down to 10-15 years. To accomplish this, the rate of investment would have to almost double. In order to generate resources to accomplish the above task, it is essential that pricing of canal waters be given due importance, along with institutional reforms in operation and management (O&M). Granting irrigation departments financial autonomy provided they recover O&M expenses from the beneficiaries is one way to proceed with reforms in this sector. Also, involvement of water users' associations (WUAs) in ownership and management of canal networks (starting with distributaries) through 'water bonds' or other mechanisms to transfer ownership should be placed high on the agenda for reforming the irrigation sector.

Fertilisers

Empirical studies pertaining to the Indian fertiliser sector reveal that diffusion of fertiliser consumption has been quite widespread. Fertiliser was used on more than 85 per cent of irrigated land and about 50 per cent of unirrigated lands by 1988-89. During the last two decades (1970-71 to 1988-89), the growth rate of diffusion to the unirrigated land was much higher, taking the unirrigated land fertilised from 9 per cent to about 50 per cent, thus narrowing the irrigated-rainfed differential in fertiliser diffusion. Unirrigated areas, however, still suffer from discontinuity in the use of fertilisers.

The intensity of fertiliser use has gradually gone up from about 3 kilograms per hectare in the early 1960s to about 16 kilograms per hectare in the early 1970s to 34 kilograms per hectare in the early 1980s to more than 70 kilograms per hectare in the early 1990s. It has been relatively higher in irrigated regions (129 kilograms per hectare by 1988-89), which leads to skewed consumption of fertiliser in the country in favour of irrigated areas. Irrigated areas, which accounted for about 30 per cent of total crop area, used 69 per cent of fertilisers consumed in the country. Gujarat is perhaps the only state that, despite its low rainfall and low irrigation, had adopted fertiliser consumption on a sufficiently wide scale by the early 1980s. This success was primarily due to an efficient state machinery, which, in seeking to develop the fertiliser industry, streamlined transportation and stocking of fertilisers, and co-operative agencies, which distributed fertilisers.

The studies find that the rate of adoption of fertiliser use is somewhat lower among small farmers than large farmers, owing mainly to credit constraints, but those small farmers who do adopt tend to use higher doses of fertilisers than the large farmers. This relationship is more pronounced on unirrigated and partially irrigated plots, but breaks down on irrigated plots, where, in fact, farmers use higher doses of fertilisers. It is possible that small farmers improve the quality of their unirrigated plots through the use of surplus labour, whereas the quality of irrigation is better on large farms on account of higher investment in minor (controlled irrigation).

The domestic production of fertilisers increased substantially from less than 1 million tons in 1960 to more than 10 million tons by the early 1990s, thus India achieved a high degree of self-sufficiency. Growth was very rapid, especially during the 1980s, primarily for two reasons. First, the Retention Price Scheme launched in 1977 provided a good incentive environment for the industry, and second, the discovery of oil and gas fields at Bombay High contributed to the growth of gas-based fertiliser plants. However, by the late 1980s, it was increasingly realised that the cost of fertiliser production was becoming high at the margin, and that the Retention Price Scheme was inducing overcapitalisation of plants. This led to rapid growth in the fertiliser subsidy, making it an almost financially unsustainable part of the central budget.

Implications of research findings for policy are clear :

(1) Wider distribution of fertilisers need to be prompted by covering the regions that previously have used very low doses of fertilisers (for example, central and eastern regions and Uttar Pradesh in the case of wheat and rice).

(2) Subsidies are not required to promote improved fertiliser management; if subsidies have to be given, they should be targeted to low-consumption areas where response is highest (for example, eastern and central regions, and Uttar Pradesh, especially for wheat and rice).

(3) Production of fertilisers has to be made efficient by gradually withdrawing the Retention Price Scheme and exposing domestic production to foreign competition by freeing imports of fertilisers.

Major Factors Affecting the Growth Potential

A number of factors are constraining the growth potential of the sector. Here, we identify four major factors responsible for limiting the growth potential of the sector. They are i) lack of long-term policy perspective, ii) decline of public sector capital formation, iii) inadequate research and development efforts, and more importantly, iv) inefficient management of natural resources like land and water.

i) Lack of Long Term Policy Perspective

On the policy front, there was lack of long-term strategy for agricultural development. One will be surprised to find that only recently the Government has come out with a national agricultural policy. From the very beginning of the planning process in India, especially from the Second Five Year Plan with the sectoral priorities of Mahalanobis model favouring industry, the emphasis has been placed on industry relative to agriculture (Bhide, et al, 1998). Broadly, the two basic objectives of agricultural policies have been i) self-sufficiency in production and ii) stability in price. As the objective of higher production and thereby achieving self-sufficiency in production (which required incentives through higher prices) is inherently inconsistent with the objective of achieving stability in prices, there was a policy dilemma. The policies followed for agricultural development suffers from a number of weaknesses.

First, though there was no significant direct taxation of the sector, agricultural sector has suffered from a typical anti-agricultural bias due to the nature of policies followed in other sectors like industry, trade, exchange rate, etc. (Gulati, 1998). Agricultural policies provided little incentives for the farmers, as the agricultural prices were depressed (Indian farmers received lower price than international prices). As there were numerous controls and restrictions, the sector was disprotected vis-a-vis other sectors of the economy. The restrictions on agricultural exports were believed to be one of the prime reasons for the disprotection of the sector as compared to the industrial sector (Gulati and Pursell, 1990, Singh, 1995, Economic Survey 1996-97, Parikh, 1999).

Second, the nature of the policies was inward-looking as it was driven less by comparative advantage. In general, agricultural policies gave little emphasis on agricultural exports as a means of stimulating domestic production (Jeromi, 1997).

Third, it has excessive price-based focus than non-price factors like water, infrastructure, research and development (R&D), extension services, etc., which are important determinants of agricultural production in India, a fact highlighted more than three decades back by Dantwala (1967) and recently by Pulapare (2000) and Vaidyanathan (2000). These weaknesses of agricultural policies, inter alia, affected the faster growth of the sector and in creating a sound infrastructure base for future growth.

ii) Neglect of Capital Formation

Lack of long-term perspectives on the development of the sector is clearly reflected in the poor state of capital formation in the sector, which is likely to affect the future growth. In fact, one of the most disquieting developments in the agricultural sector during the last two decades has been the neglect of capital formation, particularly in the public sector. Gross Capital Formation (GCF) in agriculture as per cent of total gross capital formation in the economy, after rising during the 70's, declined during the eighties and nineties. In 1999-2000 it was just 5.8 per cent as against 16.3 per cent in 1980-81. Further, GCF in agriculture as per cent of GDP in agriculture also declined during the last two decades from 10.9 per cent in 1980-81 to 7.0 per cent in 1999-2000. What is more disturbing is the fact that GCF in the agricultural sector by the public sector declined at an annual average rate of 4.0 per cent during the 1980s. As a result, the share of public sector in total capital formation in the sector declined to around 23.0 per cent during the nineties as against 32.0 per cent during the seventies. However, in the private sector, the decline was only marginal during the eighties (-0.1 per cent) and it picked up at a moderate of 6.7 per cent in the nineties (Table 6).

There is a lively debate in the literature on complementarity between public and private sector capital formation in agricultural sector. Here we take the view that public sector investment has a crucial role to play in creating infrastructure in terms of irrigation, roads, markets, storage facilities, rural electrification and technology development. Private sector capital formation is hard to come in these areas. Private sector capital formation is essentially taking place for short-term asset building and it is mainly in the areas of mechanisation, ground levelling, private irrigation, etc. Therefore, public sector capital formation needed to be augmented with a definite content and targeted focus, especially in case of rainfed areas, which lack not only in irrigation facilities, but also in other infrastructural facilities. Here it may be mentioned that public spending in agriculture is a common feature in both the developed and developing countries. In a World Bank study, Blarcom, et al, (1993) found that in case of 40 developing countries, total central government expenditure during 1972 to 1988 formed around 10 per cent of net value of agricultural production. In case of a group of 15 developed countries, it formed around 20 per cent of their net value of agricultural production. The comparative figure for India is far too low.

TABLE – 6

GROSS CAPITAL FORMATION IN AGRICULTURE

Year	*GCF in Agriculture*			*GCF as %*	*GCF as % of Total*
	Public	*Private*	*Total*	*Of GDP in Agriculture*	*GCF in Economy@*
		At 1980-81 Prices			
1970-71	789	1996	2785	7.8	14.7
1980-81	1796	2840	4636	10.9	16.3
1990-91	1154	3440	4594	7.5	8.1
		At 1993-94 Prices			
1995-96	4848	10242	15690	6.8	2.9
1996-97	4668	11508	16176	6.4	6.7
1997-98	3979	11974	15753	6.5	5.9
1998-99	3846	12538	16384	6.2	5.9
1999-00**	4668	13988	18656	7.0	5.8
		Annual Average Growth (%)			
1971-79	10.0	7.2	7.9		
1980-89	-4.0	-0.1	-1.5		
1990-99	1.0	6.7	5.0		

Note : @ : Gross Capital Formation adjusted for errors and omissions
** : Provisional.

Source : 1. National Accounts Statistics, various issues, CSO, Government of India.
2. Agricultural Statistics at a Glance, Various Issues, Government of India.
3. Economic Survey 2000-01, Government of India.

There is a view among the agricultural economists that the lagged effect of decline of capital formation during the eighties has been one of the major reasons for the decelerated growth of the sector during the nineties (Mahendra Dev, 1998). Therefore, the subdued level of capital formation during the nineties can have an impact on agriculture production in the coming years.

According to B.B. Bhattacharya committee on Capital Formation in Indian Agriculture, there has been a long-term deceleration in the share of capital formation in agriculture in GDP at both aggregate and Public Sector level. In fact the shares of GFCF in agriculture and for agriculture in GDP have declined much more sharply in the Public Sector, as would be evident from the Table 7.

TABLE – 7

GROSS FIXED CAPITAL FORMATION IN AND FOR AGRICULTURE AT 1993-94 PRICES (PUBLIC SECTOR)

(Rs.Crore)

Year	*GDP*	*GFCF*		*Percent Share in GDP of GFCF*	
		in Agriculture	*for Agriculture*	*in Agriculture*	*for Agriculture*
(1)	*(2)*	*(3)*	*(4)*	*(5)*	*(6)*
1980-81	401128	7358	9855	1.8	2.5
1985-86	513990	6005	9224	1.2	1.8
1990-91	692871	4871	8706	0.7	1.3
1995-96	899563	5318	9631	0.6	1.1
1999-00	1148442	4637	9902	0.4	0.9

Currently, GFCF for agriculture at 1993-94 prices account for about 12 per cent of aggregate capital formation. As against this, the share of agriculture in GDP is currently about 24 per cent. Clearly there is a strong case to increase the share of agriculture in total capital formation in the economy. Even in the case of Public Sector, the share of agriculture in total Public Sector capital formation has declined over the years.

As agriculture is getting diversified, there is a need to not only augment but also re-structure the pattern of investment in agriculture. Historically, the Public Sector has taken the lead in directing the growth and pattern of agriculture investment. The Committee recommended that immediate steps should be taken to improve capital formation for agriculture in both Public and Private Sectors. Otherwise, it may be difficult to sustain the agriculture growth and rural purchasing power. Currently, irrigation accounts for the bulk of public investment in agriculture (above 90 per cent). The new strategy of agriculture growth and diversification of agriculture from traditional crop cultivation to horticulture etc. would require more investments on cold storage, rural roads, communication, marketing network and facilities, warehouses etc.

iii) Lagging Research and Development Efforts

Another important factor limiting the growth potential of the sector is the lack of breakthrough in research and development after the green revolution. Perhaps, it may be one of the reasons for the decline of productivity in the nineties. India compares poorly with the productivity levels in major producing countries. Though India is one among the major producers of agricultural commodities in the world, the yield levels, here, for a number of commodities like paddy, wheat, groundnut, cotton, jute, etc., were far lower than the yield levels in major producing countries and in case of some crops it was even lower than the world average (Table 7).

India is considered as having the largest public agricultural research establishments in the world (Evenson, et al, 1999). Indian Council of Agricultural Research (ICAR) and agricultural universities constitute the main part of governmental agencies. However, agricultural research in India suffers from several weaknesses like

i) uneven progress of varietal improvement across crops and regions,
ii) neglect of crop systems research,
iii) unimpressive results of local adaptive research,
iv) inadequacy of collaborative multi-disciplinary research,
v) weak interaction between researchers, extension workers and farmers;
vi) excessive centralisation of planning and monitoring,
vii) lack of accountability for performance, etc. (Vaidyanathan, 2000).

Compared to other countries, India's efforts in research and development, in terms of provision of resources, is insufficient. India is investing only around 0.3 per cent of GDP in agriculture for agricultural research, as against 0.7 per cent in the developing countries and 2-3 per cent in case of developed countries (Evenson, et al, 1999). Expenditure on agricultural research and education accelerated during the post-green revolution period of the 1970s, but slowed down since the mid-80s and it hovered around 0.49 per cent of agricultural GDP in the early 1990s, which was lower than the requirement of 1.0 per cent projected by the ICAR. Further, the level of research expenditure was sub-optimal or significantly lower than desired in states like Bihar, Orissa, Madhya Pradesh, Uttar Pradesh and West Bengal where

TABLE – 7

YIELD OF IMPORTANT CROPS IN MAJOR PRODUCING COUNTRIES IN 1997 (KG./HA.)

Country	*Paddy Yield*	*Country*	*Wheat Yield*	*Country*	*Groundnut Yield*	*Country*	*Sugarcane Yield*	*Country*	*Cotton Yield*	*Country*	*Jute Yield*
China	6331	China	4087	China	2574	Brazil	69021	China	943	Banga.	1577
Indonesia	4561	France	6530	Nigeria	1124	China	75982	USA	769	China	2517
Pakistan	2827	USA	2673	USA	2828	Thailand	55878	Pakistan	552	Thailand	3548
Philippines	2933	Australia	1712	Indonesia	1519	Mexico	72734	Turkey	1065	Myanmar	939
Thailand	2143	Canada	2128	Sudan	762	Australia	97337	Argentina	368	Brazil	1714
India	2915	India	2654	India	988	India	69737	India	321	India	1830
World	3827	World	2686	World	1273	World	63324	World	584	World	1734
India % Of World	**76.2**		**98.8**		**77.6**		**110.1**		**55.0**		**105.5**

Source: Production Yearbook, Food and Agricultural Organisation, 1997.

productivity is low. Crop-wise, research expenditure was low in case of rice, certain coarse cereals, pulses and oilseeds (Pal, et al, 1997).

Since there is hardly any scope for further expansion of area under cultivation, the future production prospects depends largely on the improvements in the yield levels. Here what we need is to break the yield barrier and bridge the gap between the potential and actual yield through research and development (R&D) efforts. ICAR studies reveals that there is vast unexplored technological potential for improvement in the yield of crops. In this context, Swaminathan (1999) noted that the "low yield phenomena" in India should be considered as a "yield reservoir" and it should be treated as an asset for future development of the sector. Exploiting the "yield reservoir", inter alia, require substantial investment and development and deployment of high yielding seed varieties. So far the emphasis has been on the use of HYV seeds, but it loses it vigor with time. Therefore, new varieties need to be developed periodically to expand production possibilities. However, agricultural research established could not come up with improved varieties of seeds, which are suited to different regions of the country, especially in drought prone areas. Therefore, it is imperative for the country to build up a sound agricultural research system, which is responsive to the changing needs and circumstances. As the agricultural growth reduces rural poverty directly, and it fosters the conditions for pro-poor growth in the non-farm sectors, it is imperative to overcome the limits to growth by increase in productivity of the sector.

iv) Rising Soil Degradation and Over-exploitation of Ground Water

Large-scale soil degradation and over-exploitation of ground water are other important factors putting limits on growth of the sector. Around 40 per cent of India's total geographical area are officially estimated as degraded (some other estimates put the figure at 50 per cent). Using the guidelines of the Global Assessment of Soil Degradation (GLASOD), Sehgal and Abrol (1994) estimated the extent of soil degradation in India. The area under degradation is quite large and the severity is high with significant loss of yield in case of around 68 per cent of the total area degraded.

The emergence of rice-wheat crops system in states like Punjab and Haryana, on account of continuous increase in procurement prices, has resulted in overexploitation of natural resource base. An ICAR study found that soil health is deteriorating in Punjab and Haryana and this is a major cause of decline or stagnation in productivity of cereals, particularly of rice and wheat. The study revealed that the organic carbon content in the soils in Punjab and Haryana has declined to 0.2 per cent in 1995 from 0.5 per cent in the sixties. Soils with low phosphorus content have also increased to 73 per cent from only 3.5 per cent in 1975 in Haryana. Similarly, soils with high potash category have scaled down from 91 per cent in 1975 to 62 per cent in 1995. Further, consequent to the decontrol of prices of phosphorus and potash, there was decline in the application of these fertilisers. This caused nutrient imbalance in the soils. Now farmers have to apply more fertilizers to get the same yield as they were getting with less fertilizer 20-30 years ago. In case of ground water, the study found that the rapid increase in the number of tube wells during last three decades in the region has resulted in over-exploitation of ground water. This decline forces the farmers to lower the pumps further deeper in the wells, which results in the use of irrigation with saline water.

The irrigation potential in the country has been estimated at 85 million hectares, of which 76 million hectares have been already utilised by 1993-94. The average cost per hectare of irrigation potential created has risen sharply from Rs. 8,620 during the First Five Year Plan to Rs. 29,587 in the Seventh Five Year Plan at 1980-81 prices. This acts as a constraint to further augmentation of irrigation potential. Even after full utilisation of the irrigation potential, nearly 45 percent of the net cultivated area will have to depend on rainfall. As the present agricultural development strategy in India is centred mainly on the irrigated areas and the yield levels of crops in many irrigated areas are plateauing, there is a growing realisation that agricultural production cannot be increased beyond a point (Planning Commission, 1997).

Is Indian Agriculture approaching limits to growth?

Thus, the indications provided by the deceleration in growth of area, production and productivity, over-use of water resources, degradation of soil, decline of capital formation in the public sector, etc., tend to suggest that Indian agriculture is approaching limits to growth in the near future.[4] The estimation of potential output also suggests that the scope for higher growth is limited. To overcome limits to growth and put the agricultural sector on an ambitious growth curve, there is a need to correct the policy bias against agriculture, make higher investments, develop new varieties of seeds, conserve natural resources like land and water and provide incentives to the farmers to adopt modernisation.

---

4. Jeromi, P.D. (2003), *Is Indian Agriculture Reaching Limits to Growth* in Economic Developments in India, Vol.62, Academic Foundation, New Delhi.

Strategy and Thrust in the Tenth Plan

The National Agriculture Policy (NAP), 2000 envisages a growth rate exceeding 4 per cent per annum in the agriculture sector. The Tenth Plan also targets a 4 per cent growth. The NAP envisaged the following type of growth :

- Growth that is based on efficient use of resources and conserves our soil, water and bio-diversity.
- Growth with equity, i.e., growth which is widespread across regions and covers all farmers.
- Growth that is demand driven and caters to domestic markets as well as maximises benefits from exports of agricultural products in the face of the challenges arising from economic liberalisation and globalisation,
- Growth that is sustainable technologically, environmentally and economically.

Regionally Differentiated Strategy

The Regionally Differentiated Strategy based on agro-climatic conditions and natural resources envisaged for the Ninth Plan, for increasing the pace of growth in every region of the country, will be continued during the Tenth Plan. The three-pronged strategy envisaged for the Ninth Plan to meet the basic food requirements for all will be continued. This strategy involved: (i) increase in overall employment and incomes by raising farm productivity and the growth of other economic activities in the rural areas; (ii) provision of gainful supplementary employment through poverty alleviation schemes; and (iii) distribution of food grains through the public distribution system at subsidised prices to those living below the poverty line.

Sustainable Development of Natural Resources

The biotic pressure on the natural resources, especially land, water and biodiversity, is increasing resulting in their decrease in per capita availability. With the increasing population, the fragmentation of holdings has increased, resulting in smaller and unviable units of land holdings. To address the issue of fragmentation and small holdings, a clear policy with regard to transfer of agricultural land has to be formulated and implemented. The transfer of land has to be made easier to enable the farmers to augment their holdings to viable units. The rationalisation of stamp duty will facilitate the transaction of land. Besides, freedom in leasing of land, both 'leasing in' and 'leasing out' will help generate income for both lessee and lessor/contractor. A legislation needs to be enacted to facilitate the land utilisation by making land transactions easier and facilitating leasing and contract farming. Besides, to increase the productivity of small and marginal holdings, which constitute 78.2 per cent of all holdings and operate about 32.4 per cent of total area, the technologies suited for such holdings have to be developed.

BOX 1

THRUST AREAS FOR THE TENTH PLAN

- Utilisation of wastelands and un-utilised/under-utilised lands.
- Reclamation/development of problem soils/lands.
- Rainwater harvesting and conservation for the development of rainfed areas.
- Development of irrigation, especially minor irrigation.
- Conservation and utilisation of biological resources.
- Diversification to high value crops/activities.
- Increasing cropping intensity.
- Timely and adequate availability of inputs.
- Strengthening of marketing, processing/value addition infrastructure.
- Revamping and modernising the extension systems and encouraging private sector to take up extension services.
- Bridging the gap between research and farmer's yields.
- Cost-effectiveness while increasing productivity.
- Promotion of farming systems approach.
- Promotion of organic farming and utilisation of organic waste.
- Development of eastern and north-eastern regions, hill and coastal areas.
- Reforms to introduce proactive policies for the farm sector.

Besides, consolidation of holdings has to be taken up on a priority basis and completed speedily by the States which have not yet taken up the work. The consolidation of holdings in the northern states has shown promising results in terms of per unit area productivity, adoption of production technologies and returns to the farmers. Preparation of land records would also be given emphasis. States would be asked and helped to take up computerisation of all land records.

Out of the estimated area of about 107 m ha of degraded land, 64 m ha are categorised as wastelands. These wastelands and other degraded areas are either un-utilised or under-utilised. Being a common property resource, individuals do not have the right to utilise these lands for any productive purposes. All such lands under the control of Government or panchayats, would be parceled out in viable units and allotted to landless, scheduled caste and scheduled tribe farmers, small and marginal farmers, retired defence personnel and educated rural youth for cultivation. A condition that a certain percentage of allotted land (say 40 or 50 per cent) must be utilised for tree cover can be stipulated so as to increase the crown area for improving the environmental and ecological conditions. The highly degraded wasteland could exclusively be used for forestry, tree cropping or agro forestry.

Rainwater harvesting and conservation will continue to get attention so as to increase productivity of rainfed farmlands. Besides, minor irrigation development, which is more cost-effective will also be emphasised, especially in the eastern region where huge groundwater potential has remained unharnessed. Investments in the development of minor irrigation facilities will be enhanced. Besides, the utilisation of under-utilised irrigation potential will be improved by encouraging the conjunctive use of water, adoption of improved on-farm water management practices and also the use of water saving devices such as sprinkler irrigation system, drip irrigation system, etc., especially in the low rainfall areas.

Vast areas are in need of Watershed Development Programmes, which call for urgent attention. Both the Central and State Governments should provide maximum possible budgetary support for the development of degraded rainfed lands on a priority basis. In watershed development there is need to move from the conventional soil conservation approach of safe disposal of run-off to rainwater harvesting and conservation based on indigenous systems and practices. Rainwater conservation and harvesting hold the key for sustainable development of rainfed areas. The watershed development must ensure that the minimum basic water needs of the rural communities in the project areas are met.

Strategies for Unfavourable Agro-climatic Regions

In the first decade of the Green Revolution, the new seed-fertiliser technology spread rapidly in agro-climatic regions with medium-to-low rainfall that had an adequate physical infrastructure (irrigation, roads, and marketing network) as well as a favourable institutional framework (land tenure systems and credit institutions). Favourable agro-climatic factors such as an abundant sunshine, irrigation, and low incidence of pests and diseases were extremely important in triggering the Green Revolution in these regions. On the other hand, regions with unfavourable agro-climatic factors such as too much, too little, or too variable rainfall; waterlogging; salinity; soil erosion; or moisture stress could not experience technological breakthrough.

The initial success of the Green Revolution in the favourable agro-climatic regions has undoubtedly led to the neglect of unfavourable areas, both with respect to the evolution of technologies suited to such regions and conservation of land and water resources. Moreover, the slow growth of income and widespread poverty in the dryland areas and the defective pricing of electricity for pumping water exerted further pressure on already fragile ecosystems, thus accentuating the depletion of land and water resources.

Experience has shown that a critical minimum of favourable soil moisture is necessary to adopt technologies suited to the climatic conditions of these regions. Since favourable areas at present account for a small proportion of cultivated area in the country, broadening the geographical base of agricultural growth through the development of natural resources, infrastructure development, and the evolution of location-specific technologies for the hitherto unfavourable regions is essential for sustaining growth, improving the overall efficiency of resource use, reducing poverty, and protecting the environment.

Among the degraded areas, dryland areas with very low and uncertain rainfall and with low irrigation potential need to be given a high priority for soil and moisture conservation in view of their high geographical coverage, high rate of degradation, widespread poverty, and their comparative advantage for producing high value crops for export. The existing programmes for soil and moisture conservation have failed to make an impact because they are inadequately planned on a watershed basis; they have failed to integrate employment generation programmes into their works; they have failed to involve the beneficiaries and the voluntary organisations in the planning and implementation of programmes; and they lack co-ordination among the various departments concerned with these programmes. Therefore, to give high priority to soil and moisture conservation in the dryland areas, present strategies have to be revamped to create the necessary conditions for the adoption of improved practices.

Infrastructure

If Indian agriculture is opened up to international trade, and if the future growth of Indian agriculture is to be yield-based, requiring intensive use of inputs, development of infrastructure is necessary to support this growth. Infrastructure plays a critical role on both input and output sides. On the input front, it helps ensure timely and adequate delivery to farmers, which is essential in raising the aggregate supply response. On the output front, it helps integrate local markets with national and international markets so that the benefits of trade can percolate down to farmers. Without an adequate and efficient system of infrastructure, the real potential of Indian agriculture under the changing incentive environment cannot be realised.

TABLE – 8

PROGRESS OF SELECTED AGRICULTURAL DEVELOPMENT PROGRAMMES

Programme	*Unit*	*1970-71*	*1980-81*	*1990-91*	*1996-97**	*1999-2000**
1	*2*	*3*	*4*	*5*	*6*	*7*
High yielding varieties	Million hectares					
Paddy	”	5.6	18.2	27.4	33.4	NA
Wheat	”	6.5	16.1	21.0	23.7	NA
Maize	”	0.5	1.6	2.6	3.8	NA
Jowar	”	0.8	3.5	7.1	8.3	NA
Bajra	”	2.0	3.7	5.7	6.1	NA
Ragi	”	-	-	1.2	1.1	NA
Total HYV	”	15.4	43.1	65.0	76.4	NA
Irrigated Area*	”	38.0	54.1	70.8	80.7	84.7
Major & medium	”	17.3	22.7	26.0	28.4	30.5
Minor @	”	20.7	31.4	44.8	52.9	54.2
Soil conservation+	”	13.4	24.4	34.9	NA	NA
Fertiliser consumption	Million tonnes	2.2	5.5	12.5	14.3	18.1
Nitrogenous	”	1.5	3.7	8.0	10.3	11.6
Phosphatic	”	0.5	1.2	3.2	3.0	4.8
Potassic	”	0.2	0.6	1.3.	1.0	1.7

* Provisional.

NA : Not available.

@ The figures for minor irrigation indicate the net benefit after allowing for seepage.

\+ Cumulative level at the end of the year.

Sources : Economic Survey, 2000-01, (Table 1.16), S.22.

15

Farm Mechanisation and Choice of Appropriate Technology

FARM mechanisation means the use of mechanical implements for farming instead of the traditional simple methods involving human and animal labour. This will mean a transformation from biological sources of energy (human and animal) to mechanical sources of energy (tractors, threshers, pumpsets, harvester combines, etc.)

Farm mechanisation can be partial or complete. When machines are used along with traditional implements mechanisation is partial. But when all farm operations are mechanised, animal labour is completely eliminated and human labour is reduced to the minimum, there is total mechanisation. In many developed countries of the West the factor endowments are such that labour is scarce and capital is abundant. This provided a favourable environment for mechanisation. In third world countries like India having scarcity of capital and abundance of labour only partial mechanisation has been accomplished. In India, there is a heavy pressure of population on land; holdings are small and fragmented; the average farmer is too poor to purchase machines; and there is an acute shortage of diesel and power.

Arguments for Mechanisation

Mechanisation Promotes Productivity

A number of field studies have been conducted to determine the relationship between mechanisation and productivity. Almost all the studies have indicated that mechanisation promotes productivity. The reasons are not far to seek. Depending on the nature of operations, sowing, ploughing, fertilisation, irrigation and harvesting can be done more efficiently and with less wastage with the help of machines. For example, the use of machines permits a better distribution of seeds and fertilisers all over the farm than can be achieved in a manual operation.

Coping with Peak Period of Labour Requirements

Since agriculture in many developing countries is seasonal in nature it involves a peak requirement of labour of two or three months' duration. Therefore, a 'labour bottleneck' (especially in areas under new high-yielding varieties) emerges. Mechanisation helps to overcome this bottleneck by reducing requirements during peak periods.

Mechanisation and Reduction in Costs

It has been argued that mechanisation helps in reducing the cost of production in agriculture. As far as developed countries of the West are concerned, there is no doubt that machines help in keeping the cost of production low. On the face of it, one gets the impression that labour is the cheaper factor of production in this country. However, the study of Hanumantha Rao does not support this contention. In his opinion the cause of increasing use of tractors in farm operations in Punjab and Haryana is that tractor is the relatively cheaper input. According to Rao, rapidly increasing population has pushed up the prices of foodgrains substantially and this factor has accounted for an increase in labour wages (both in cash and kind).[1]

Multiple-cropping

Mechanisation makes adoption of multiple-cropping practices possible. Completion of harvesting operations in optimum time and quick vacation of fields from the standing crops has enabled the farmer to undertake multiple cropping with ease and facility.

Multiple cropping will lead to increases in farm income and transformation of traditional agriculture into commercial agriculture.

Use of machines on farms increases the income of farmers. It is often observed that under traditional agriculture based on wooden (or iron) ploughs, bullocks and other primitive implements, agriculture is a mere subsistence occupation (even though the farmers might sell a portion of their produce in the markets). Introduction of tractors, harvesters, threshers, pumpsets for irrigation etc. changes the very nature of traditional agriculture and transforms it into a commercial occupation.

---

1. C.H. Hanumantha Rao, *Farm Mechanisation* in C.H. Shah (ed.) Agricultural Development in India: Policies and Problems (Bombay 1979) p. 293.

Improvement in General Well-being

Introduction of machines reduces the drudgery and hard work that accompanies traditional agriculture. Farmers can now avail themselves of more leisure time and work under more agreeable circumstances. As noted by Rao, "It may even raise the participation rate among those who could afford to abstain from drudgerous manual work. Not only this. It is often observed that farm mechanisation is accompanied by a change in the general outlook of farmers. They become more sensitive to changes in their socio-economic environment and to factors affecting their general well-being."

Case Against Farm Mechanisation

Impact of Mechanisation on Agricultural Employment

The main argument advanced against mechanisation is that it reduces agricultural employment and is unsuitable in the conditions of factor endowments prevailing in a labour-abundant economy like India.

It has been observed that introduction of tube well irrigation in certain pockets of the country has helped to increase per hectare employment by making multiple cropping possible. However, the use of tractors displaces labour mainly for ploughing and transportation. On the basis of study conducted for Ferozepur (in Punjab), C.H. Hanumantha Rao estimates that tractorisation displaces 20 to 30 per cent of the total human labour-days per cropped acre on account of tillage and transportation. Use of other agricultural machinery like threshers and harvesters also promotes unemployment. According to Rao, a mechanical thresher displaces around 15 per cent labour and harvester combines around 25 per cent in addition to that displaced by mechanical threshers. This would make it clear that the use of tractors, mechanical threshers and harvester combines will displace labour on a very large scale. A large number of rural poor will, therefore, be left without employment as a result of mechanisation of farm operations.[2]

However, off-farm employment generated by machines should also be taken into account. Mechanisation generates employment through the manufacture of farm machinery, distribution of spare parts, fuels and lubricants, repair of equipment, etc. Thus, at the present stage of development, the marginal loss in direct farm employment resulting from mechanisation can be more than offset by off-farm employment in

---

2. C.H. Hanumantha Rao, *Technological Change in Indian Agriculture*, in M.L. Dantwala, Indian Agriculture Development Since Independence (1991, New Delhi).

agro-industrial commercial complexes and secondary and tertiary sectors of the economy.

Existence of Small Farms

Critics of farm mechanisation point to the existence of a large number of small and marginal holdings and question the feasibility of mechanisation on this account. According to them, machines can be used profitably only when the size of farms is sufficiently large as in advanced countries. The average size of holdings was 145 hectares in Canada in 1961, 122 hectares in the U.S.A. in 1959 and 124 hectares in Mexico in 1960. As against this, the size of holdings was a meagre 2.63 hectares in India in 1961-62. A large number of farms are even smaller than this already small average size. For example, in 1990-91, 59.0 per cent of operational holdings in India were less than one hectare in size and 19.0 per cent had a size between 1.0-2.0 hectares. Obviously full scale mechanisation is not possible on such small farms. Not only this, even the small holdings are split up into tiny plots scattered all over the village.The classic example is that of Japan where the size of holding was only 1.18 hectares in 1960 (less than that in India) but which practised large-scale mechanisation. As the discussion clearly shows, existence of small farms' is not an argument against mechanisation as such, it only points to the hurdles in adopting mechanisation. Undoubtedly, the poverty of small and marginal farmers comes as a big obstacle to programmes of mechanisation.

It is pointed out that India depends to a large extent on fuel supply from abroad, her own production being inadequate to meet her requirements. A widespread mechanisation may cause more pressure on the fuel situation. This may be correct. But on that account alone the agricultural sector cannot be denied the use of yield-increasing machinery.

Scope for Farm Mechanisation and the Question of Appropriate Technology

In Indian agriculture, broadly speaking the following four technologies are being used in the different parts of the country :

(i) Traditional Technology based on the use of wooden/iron plough and animal labour with no use of fertilisers, HYV seeds etc.

(ii) Land augmenting technology which uses traditional implements but makes ample use of fertilisers, irrigation,

HYV seeds etc.

(iii) Labour substituting technology where production is carried on with the help of machines like tractors, threshers, harvesters etc.

(iv) Land augmenting technology in conjunction with labour substituting technology which is used in most of the developed countries of the world.

Out of these four, what is the most appropriate technology for India? Obviously not the first, because it keeps productivity low, nor the third because of abundance of labour in Indian economy.

In an effort to increase agricultural productivity in the country, the Government of India adopted a new agricultural strategy wherein main attention was focussed on increased application of fertilizers and high-yielding varieties of seeds in areas of assured water supply. Though this land augmenting technique has not been successful in all areas where practised, yet there is no denying the fact that it has proved to be immensely successful in wheat growing areas. Another advantage of this technique is that it leads to an increase in the demand for labour thereby creating new avenues of employment. In India where a considerable number of people are either totally unemployed or partially employed, this technique is proving very beneficial.

In areas like Punjab, Haryana, western Uttar Pradesh, Deltaic belts of Tamil Nadu and Andhra Pradesh, large farmers have opted for a mixture of land augmenting and labour substituting techniques with considerable success. However, while resorting to this technique, care has to be taken to find alternative employment opportunities for persons who are displaced from the land.

Introduction and adoption of agricultural machinery is largely confined to the North and North-West regions of the country. However, with the increase in irrigation and modernisation of cropping practices, the demand for agricultural machinery has also shown an increasing trend in southern and western parts of the country.

Development of energy and time saving efficient machines and implements and their adequate production and supply would be given special attention.

Special focus will be made on small farm mechanisation. Specific efforts will be devised for developing and popularising hand held tillers, small tractors etc. with appropriate tie-up arrangements with institutional finance.

Implements and machinery used in countries like Japan which are specially suited to small farms will be adapted for use in India.

Though the country is self-sufficient in meeting the indigenous demand for conventional agricultural implements, the quality is not up to the desired standards due to limited know-how and resource constraints faced by the small scale manufacturing units. The State Agro-industries Corporation are engaged in manufacture and distribution of agricultural machinery improved implements and tools etc.[3]

There has been de-reservation of large number of farm implements but 25 items still remain reserved. These include items like animal drawn implements, cultivators, disc harrows, harvesters, rice and dal mill machinery, diesel engines up to 15 HP, etc. The tenth plan recommends all the implements/machines used for agriculture operations need to be de-reserved.

---

3. Planning Commission, Tenth Five Year Plan, Vol.2, page 534.

16

Institutional Factors

Land Reforms

Feudal Agrarian Structure

AT the time of Independence, India inherited a semi-feudal agrarian structure. The ownership and control of land was highly concentrated to a relatively few landlords and intermediaries. The principal interest of this controlling group in agriculture was to extract maximum rental from tenants, either in cash or in kind. Often tenants of land under intermediary and landlord control sublet their lands in smaller plots to working cultivators, thus smaller holdings increased. Under this arrangement, economic motivation to develop farm land for increased production or to improve the economic conditions of cultivators was lacking. At the same time, working cultivators after paying high rent had no surplus to invest in farm improvement. They had neither resources nor knowledge for increasing agricultural production. Thus the agricultural land resource of India, along with its operators was gradually improverished because economic motivation tended toward exploitation rather than toward investment and improvement.

With increasing pressure on land, the operating land base of many working cultivators was further reduced. Land occupancy rights became increasingly insecure. Often cultivators were continuously shifted from one plot to another according to the whims of superior holders. Land was divided into small fragments, each owned or leased by cultivators whose objective was subsistence. Over time, a large number of farms became disincentive-ridden due to size disability. A substantial portion of such cultivators sought to supplement their farm income by working as hired labourers, competitive with even poorer landless workers. Independent India thus emerged with serious imbalances in man-land relationship among the three principal groups in the agricultural sector, viz., proprietors, working cultivators and labourers.

Objectives of Land Reforms

It was basically to stop the exploitation of the actual tillers of the soil and pass on the ownership of land to them that land reforms were introduced in the Post-Independence period in India. The government has defined the objectives of land reforms as follows :

(i) to remove such impediments to increase in agricultural production as arise from the agrarian structure inherited from the past; and

(ii) to eliminate all forms of exploitation and social injustice within the agrarian system, to provide security for the tiller of soil and assure equality of status and opportunity to all sections of the rural population.

Measures contemplated to achieve the objectives were as given below :

1. Abolition of Intermediaries
2. Tenancy Reforms
3. Reorganisation of Agriculture.

Reorganisation of Agriculture included the following policies:

(i) Redistribution of Land,

(ii) Consolidation of Holdings and

(iii) Cooperative Farming.

Abolition of Intermediaries

The process of initiating, debating, amending and finally passing the bill for zamindari abolition mostly took a very long time. For example, in Uttar Pradesh, the Zamindari Abolition Act took four and a half years to become law. However, it goes to the credit of the government that most of the States had passed such Acts before the end of the First Five Year Plan. This possibly reflected the popular sentiment against the zamindars and their exploitative practices. Once the stage of legislation was completed and the stage of implementation started, fresh difficulties had to be faced. Zamindars were not willing to lay down their rights and privileges and turned to courts. As was to be expected, the legal battle between the zamindars and the State governments took an unduly long time. When the zamindars ultimately lost the battle they turned to other delaying tactics by refusing to hand over land records and other related documents.

The policy laid down in the First Plan was that zamindars could assume land for personal cultivation up to the ceiling limit and tenants could acquire permanent and heritable rights in land only over and above the ceiling limit. With a view to bringing about uniformity in the definition of personal cultivation as adopted in different States, the Second Five Year Plan specified that personal cultivation should have three elements: (i) risk of cultivation, (ii) personal supervision, and (iii) labour.

Though the official documents claim that zamindari has been completely abolished, yet the fact is that it has only changed its 'garb' The previous zamindars have acquired large areas for personal cultivation on which cultivation is done with the help of hired agricultural labour. They are now designated as 'big landowners' and along with the rich peasantry, have formed "a new and dominant class of rural capitalists." In the States where a ceiling has been fixed as to the amount of land a former zamindar can hold, the ceiling has been kept so high that very few zamindars have been affected. Flaws in the legislation have also enabled them to transfer their land to other members of their families and thus escape the ceiling law. For example, Daniel Thorner found that in post-reform Bihar, there existed estates of 500, 700 or even 1,000 acres and the older structure of landowner, occupancy raiyat, non-occupancy raiyat, under-raiyat, and bataidar (cropsharer) continued even after the so-called zamindari abolition. Bihar remained a stronghold of large landholders and hierarchical property rights, where "leasing, subleasing and evictions are all common."

Tenancy Reforms

Under the Tenancy Reforms, the following three measures were undertaken (i) Regulation of Rent, (ii) Security of Tenure, and (iii) Conferment of Ownership Rights on Tenants.

Regulation of Rent

In the pre-Independence period, the rent charged by zamindars from the tenants was exorbitant. The British government was merely interested in its share and consequently gave unlimited powers of suppression to the zamindars to squeeze the tenants.

These highly exploitative rates spelt misery on the toiling tenants who could hardly make both ends meet. As a consequence, legislations were enacted after 1947 to regulate the limits of rents and reduce the burden on tenants. The First Five Year Plan stated that maximum rent should be fixed at one-fourth or one-fifth of the total produce. Except Punjab, Haryana, Jammu and Kashmir, Tamil Nadu and some areas of Andhra Pradesh, this limit has been generally observed by all the states. In Punjab and Haryana, fair rent is fixed at one-third of total produce. In Tamil Nadu it is 40 per cent of gross produce for irrigated lands, 35 per cent where irrigation is supplemented by lift irrigation, and 33.33 per cent in other cases. In Jammu and Kashmir, landowners have been divided into two categories — (i) those holding less than 12.5 acres and (ii) those holding more than 12.5 acres. For the former fair rent has been fixed at one-half of total produce while for the latter it has been fixed at one-fourth of total produce for wet lands and one-third for dry lands. In some areas of Andhra Pradesh, fair rent is 30 per cent of total produce for irrigated land and 25 per cent for dry land.

However, legislations fixing maximum limit of rent have been often violated. Because of the strong socio-economic and political hold of the landowners in the countryside, they have been able to extract considerably more rent from the peasants than the rent fixed by the legislations. For example, while in Bihar the maximum limit is 25 per cent of gross produce, sharecroppers are usually required to pay 50 per cent. In Balasore District of Orissa, it was found that sharecroppers had to hand over 50 per cent of gross produce as late as in 1972. Similarly, while, law had fixed the maximum rent at 25 per cent of gross produce in West Bengal, sharecroppers continue to pay 50 per cent.

Security of Tenure

To protect tenants from ejectment and grant them permanent rights in land, legislations have been passed in most of the States. Legislation for security of tenure had three essential aims:

(a) Ejectments do not take place except in accordance with the provisions of the law;

(b) Land may be resumed by an owner, if at all, for 'personal cultivation' only; and

(c) In the event of resumption, the tenant is assured of a prescribed minimum area.

However, as pointed out by P.S. Appu, the degree of protection to tenants afforded by the law in a particular area, depends upon the following important factors:

1. Definition of the term tenant;
2. The circumstances in which landowners are allowed to resume tenanted land for cultivation;
3. Definition of the term 'personal cultivation';
4. Status of land records.

In all tenancy laws of the country, persons cultivating the lands of others on payment of rent (either in cash or kind or both) are treated as tenants. However, in some states like Uttar Pradesh and West Bengal, sharecroppers (who pay rent by division of produce) are not regarded as tenants. Thus all laws aiming at protecting tenants do not, in any way, help them. A limited right of resumption of land by landowners for personal cultivation was granted in all states excepting Uttar Pradesh and West Bengal. In some states landowners were permitted to resume land right up to the ceiling limit while in others the permissible limit was below the ceiling limit. Several states also passed laws requiring the landlord to leave a certain minimum area with the tenant as and when he assumes land for personal cultivation. For example, the laws in Kerala, Gujarat, Himachal Pradesh, Maharashtra, Karnataka, Orissa and Tamil Nadu provided that one-half of the tenanted land should be left with the tenant.

The right of resumption combined with flaws in the definition of personal cultivation rendered all tenancies insecure. The landlord could eject any tenant on the plea of personal cultivation. It was on account of this fact that the Fourth Five Year Plan recommended that all tenancies should be declared non-resumable and permanent (except in cases of landholders who are serving in the defence forces or suffering from a specified disability) and penalty should be imposed for wrongful evictions.

Another serious problem that had to be faced related to 'voluntary surrenders'. Many landlords compelled their tenants to give up the tenancies on their own accord. In this manner they succeeded in circumventing the tenancy laws because no laws can help the tenants if they give up their right voluntarily. Experience has shown that most of the 'voluntary' surrenders were anything but voluntary. In fact, landlords applied various kinds of threats and pressures on the tenants to surrender their land. Because of their weak socio-economic conditions and abject poverty, the tenants easily succumbed to these pressures. It was on account of this reason that the Fourth Plan recommended that "voluntary surrenders" should be regulated by the state in such a way that landowners are prohibited from taking possession of surrendered land which could be given over to other eligible tenants selected by the government. This means that all surrenders should be in favour of the government only. However, this provision has been enacted only in the states of Gujarat, Himachal Pradesh, Kerala, Orissa, Karnataka and West Bengal.

Laws relating to security of tenure can be implemented effectively only if correct and up-to-date land records are available. A person can claim that he is a tenant only if his name appears as such in the land records. However, it has been observed that in many states either no records of tenancy exist or (in areas where they exist) are incomplete and out-of-date.

Ownership Rights of Tenants

It has been repeatedly emphasized in the Plan documents that ownership rights should be conferred on tenants, that is, they should be made owners of the land they cultivate. Accordingly, some states have passed legislations to confer right of ownership on tenants. However, while some states did not adopt legislations for conferment of ownership right, in some other states the laws fall short of expectation. On tenancy reform, Appu found that "...it has not put an end to absentee ownership of land nor has it led to the disappearance of tenancies. It has only resulted in tenancies being pushed underground...". Summing up the performance on this front, he wrote:

"...Taking country as a whole, by 1992 ownership rights had been conferred on (or tenancy rights had been protected of) some 11 million tenants on 14.4 million acres of land. That constituted no more than 4 per cent of the operated area. It is interesting to note that the seven states Assam, Gujarat, Himachal Pradesh, Karnataka, Kerala, Maharashtra and West Bengal account for 97 per cent of the beneficiaries. Practically, no benefits accrued to the tenants in the other states. Even in these seven states tenancy reform led to the large scale eviction of tenants. Except in West Bengal, sharecroppers by and large remained beyond the pale of tenancy reform everywhere. Only in West Bengal and Kerala did those in the lowest rungs of the peasant society received solid benefits on the implementation of tenancy reform. The rights of some 14 lakh sharecroppers were protected in West Bengal and in Kerala some 2.84 lakh rural poor, mostly agricultural labourers, became owners of tiny homesteads. As a result of tenancy reform there has been a sharp fall in the area of land under tenancy. From over one-half of the operated area on the eve of the reform, the area under tenancy has come down to about 15 per cent of the operated area now. The tenants acquired ownership rights or were made secure in only about 4 per cent of the operated area. Thus the reform led to the rural poor losing access to some 30 per cent of the operated area."[1]

Ceiling on Land Holdings

An important aspect of Land Reform measures has been ceiling on land holdings. Justifying ceiling on holdings Gadgil observed "among all resources the supply of land is the most limited and the claimant for its possession are extremely numerous. It is therefore obviously unjust to allow the exploitation of any large surface of land by single individual, unless other overwhelming reasons make this highly desirable. Moreover, in the context of current socio-political climate, redistribution of land would rather appear to be imperative."

Ceiling on land holdings were designed to offset the extremely uneven distribution of agricultural land. The policy implications of this measure were (i) to meet the land hunger of working cultivators, (ii) to reduce disparity in agricultural incomes, in ownership and in the use of land, and (iii) to increase employment opportunity in the rural sector.

Legislation for ceiling was enacted in two phases. The first phase upto 1972 and the second phase after 1972. In the first phase individual land holding was treated as the unit of application. After 1972 it was decided to have family as the basis of holding. Further ceiling limit was also reduced to bring about a more equitable distribution of this scarce asset. Also the exemption list was reduced in the new ceiling laws.

The performance regarding the implementation of ceiling on agricultural holdings has turned out to be more disappointing. Appu observed :

"...As a result of the implementation of the old and the new laws, by 1992 only about 2 million hectares of surplus land could be distributed to some 4.76 million beneficiaries. Thus the efforts spread over a period of three and a half decades to enforce ceilings and take over of surplus land led to the redistribution of less than 2 per cent of the operated area. If we look into the performance of individual states, we find that the area distributed as a percentage of the total area operated is 17.4 for Jammu and Kashmir, 6.3 in West Bengal and 5 in Assam. In all the other states only less than one per cent of the operated

1. S.K. Ray, *Reforms in Land System in Post Independent India*, in Uma Kapila (ed) op. cit.

area could be distributed. Obviously, the imposition of ceilings and the redistribution of surplus land made no impact on the agrarian structure in most states."[2]

On balance, there seems to be some reasons to conclude that agrarian reorganisation in India has failed to make any considerable impact on the socio-economic conditions of the working cultivators. Indeed, the record so far is so depressing and frustrating that even an able administrator like Appu, who championed and spent a considerable part of his career in administering land reform programmes noted :

"Thus the programmes of land reform implemented since Independence did not lead to any significant re-distribution of land, or, the removal of all the obstacles to increasing agricultural production. Of the three programmes considered in this study, the laws for the abolition of intermediary interests were implemented fairly well. But in the case of tenancy reform and ceilings on holdings, the policies adopted were ambivalent and there were large gaps between policy and legislation and between legislation and implementation. We have seen that as result of the implementation of the tenancy laws, tenants became owners of or acquired rights in only about 4 per cent of the operated area. The enforcement of ceilings led to the redistribution of less than 2 per cent of the operated area. Thus these two measures taken together led to the redistribution of only about 6 per cent of the operated area."[3]

Consolidation of Holdings

The national policy on land reforms right from its inception has continued to press the need for consolidation of holdings. Consolidation means bringing together the scattered holdings of a farmer in one compact block. The Sixth Five Year Plan states, "Consolidation is achieved by first pooling all land in the village into one compact block and then dividing it into compact blocks among all the farmers in the village. Most of the States in the country have enacted legislation to undertake consolidation of holdings. It is estimated that by now, nearly 45 million hectares of land, i.e., about 1/4th of the consolidable land has been consolidated all over the country. However, the implementation has been extremely patchy and sporadic. Only in Punjab, Haryana and Western Uttar Pradesh, the work is complete. Even a beginning has not been made in the Southern States and Rajasthan. In the Eastern States, some work has begun only in Orissa and Bihar."

2. S.K. Ray, op. cit.
3. S.K. Ray, op. cit.

Major difficulties coming in the way of consolidation are the unwillingness of the farmers to join consolidation because of strong attachment to their ancestral land as well as the fear that they may not get in return inferior quality of land after consolidation. The Fifth Plan stated, "A major weakness of the programme was that the consolidation was done without taking effective steps to ensure security of tenure to tenants, particularly share-croppers. As a result, consolidation of holdings has often led to the large-scale ejectment of insecure tenants."

Co-operative Farming

In the initial phase of planning, Government of India accepted co-operative farming as the official policy in the scheme of agarian reorganisation. The Congress Agarian Reforms Committee in its Report (1949) came to the conclusion : "Without various co-operative moulds co-operative better farming for family farms and co-operative joint farming for holdings below basic – the efficiency of agriculture cannot be substantially increased."

However, the story of co-operative farming in India is a story of complete failure. Co-operative farming was used as a convenient device to by-pass land reforms – (to escape ceiling on land holdings as no ceiling was applied to co-operative farms) and also to use it for receiving preferential treatment in the provision of credit, irrigation, HYV Seeds etc.

Emerging Perspectives and Policy Issues

Appu observes, it is against the background of the last four decades experience that the need to reformulate the land policy of India should be considered. Even persons emotionally attached with land reform programmes agree that the scope for improving implementation through legislative measures is now very limited. They point out, the socio-economic and political environment in which these programmes were introduced have changed so dramatically, that it would be almost impossible to carry out the reforms. Appu described the changed environment as follows :

"...If the political will in favour of meaningful land reform was weak at independence and weaker still later on, it is non-existent today. Land reform has practically disappeared from the agenda of most political parties. This, in my view, is the inevitable consequence of the great changes that have taken place in the social and economic fields. With the abolition of intermediary interests the erstwhile superior tenants belonging mostly to upper and middle castes acquired a higher social status. Rise in agricultural productivity, rising land values and higher incomes from cultivation have added to their economic strength. Substantial landowners who wield great authority in rural India are bitterly opposed to ceilings on agricultural holdings. They are able to have their way because no serious efforts have been made to organise the landless and the land poor, and enlist their support in favour of reforms. As for tenancy reform is concerned, there is a certain commonality of interest between all landowners - large, medium, small and even marginal. They are all passionately attached to their land and all of them are opposed to conferring benefits on insecure tenants. In the first round of land reform only the intermediaries were adversely affected. They were few in number and were weak politically. they had also made themselves obnoxious by aligning themselves with the colonial power. So it was easy enough to abolish intermediary interests. And it was done without hurting them much. But injuring the interests of the present class of landowners is an entirely different proposition. No political party that wishes to win elections and come to power can afford to do that. At the time of independence this class of landowners did not wield much political and economic power, and with a modicum of political will the reforms could have been implemented. But now it has become almost impossible to carry out the reforms."[4]

4. P.S. Appu, (1995), *Land Reforms in India: A Survey of Policy, Legislation and Implementation, Land Reforms Unit*, Lal Bahadur Shastri National Academy of Administration, Mussoorie, U.P. (mimeo), P. 232-233.

17

Agricultural Credit

Credit Requirements of Cultivators

THERE are two types of credit requirements of the farmers. First, the purpose for which the credit is required, and then the period for which it is required i.e., short-term, medium-term, or long-term.

The credit requirement of the farmer can be for the purchase of additional piece of land or to make some permanent improvements in the land as digging or deepening of wells or fencing on the land, or to acquire costly agricultural implements, etc. Such requirements are for medium-term or long-term i.e., for one year or for over five years. There is also the short-term requirement of funds for buying seeds, fertilisers, cattle-feed, etc. During bad crop years the farmers require short-term funds for household expenses. The short-term loans are generally repaid after the harvest.

The credit requirements can be for productive purposes or unproductive purposes. Productive purposes include loans to buy seeds, fertilisers, implements, etc, or even to pay taxes to the Government and for carrying out permanent improvements on land. The productive credit helps the farmer in agricultural operations. But the farmer also borrows for unproductive purposes, such as for marriage, birth or death, or for litigation, etc.

Sources of Agricultural Finance

There are mainly two sources of finance available to the farmers : institutional and non-institutional. The institutional sources include the Government, the Co-operatives, and the Commercial Banks including the Regional Rural Banks (RRBs). The non-institutional sources include money-lenders, traders and commission agents, relatives and landlords.

TABLE – 1

INSTITUTIONAL AND NON-INSTITUTIONAL SOURCES OF FINANCE

(Percentages)

	1951-52	*1961-62*	*1981*	*1991*
A. Institutional	**7.3**	**19.7**	**61.2**	**56.6**
Government	3.1	15.5	3.9	5.7
Co-operatives	3.3	2.6	28.6	18.6
Commercial Banks	0.9	0.6	28.0	29.0
B. Non-Institutional	**92.7**	**81.3**	**38.8**	**39.6**
Money-lender	69.7	49.2	16.9	15.7
Landlord and others	23.0	32.1	21.3	23.9
Total (A+B)	100.0	100.0	100.0	100.0

In 1951-52 the institutional sources of finance, including the Government, accounted for only 7 per cent whereas the non-institutional sources accounted for 93 per cent of the total credit. This share of non-institutional sources declined sharply to about 39 per cent in 1991, money-lenders accounting for only 16 per cent.* The share of institutional credit, on the other hand, has gone up to 57 per cent, the co-operatives accounting for 18.6 per cent and commercial banks for 29 per cent. Thus, the emphasis now is on strengthening the co-operatives and expanding the commercial banks' network to meet the increasing demand for agricultural credit.

Institutional Sources of Finance

State Governments also provide "Taccavi loans" to farmers and extend financial support to State Co-operative Banks (SCBs) and Land Development Banks (LDBs). The Primary Agricultural Credit Societies (PACs) provide mainly short and medium term loans and Land Development Banks (LDBs) provide long-term loans to the farmers. The commercial banks, including Regional Rural Banks (RRBs), provide short-term as well as long-term loans for agriculture and allied activities. At the national level, the National Bank for Agriculture and Rural Development (NABARD) is the apex institution for agricultural finance and also provides refinance assistance to the agencies mentioned above.

* All India Debt and Investment Survey (1981)

The Reserve Bank of India plays a crucial role by giving overall directions for rural credit and provides financial support to the National Bank (NABARD).

Co-operative Societies

Co-operative credit is the cheapest and the best source of finance for agriculture. The rate of interest is low. The Government has come to rely on co-operatives as the most appropriate institutional arrangement for catering to the financial requirements of the farmers. Directly helped by the Government, the co-operative societies have made spectacular progress in the last two decades : notably in Tamil Nadu, Andhra Pradesh, Karnataka, Punjab and Himachal Pradesh. The primary credit societies cover over 85 per cent of the villages, and account for 36 per cent of the rural population. The credit provided by the co-operatives is 33 per cent of the total requirements for agriculture and this was only 3 per cent in 1951-52. However, the stranglehold of money-lenders on the peasants is not completely eliminated as all the financial requirements of farmers are not met by the co-operatives. Moreover, there are vast areas and regions in West Bengal, Bihar, Orissa and Rajasthan where the co-operative movement has not spread adequately.

Commercial Banks

The commercial banks were not concerned with the provision of short-term and medium-term credit for agricultural purposes as these were met by the co-operative credit societies and land development banks. Moreover, the uncertain character of Indian agriculture, lack of proper accounting of agricultural transactions, small amount of individual loans, inadequate security for loans, difficulty of collection from farmers – these were some of the factors which prevented the commercial banks from taking interest in agricultural finance. However, after the nationalisation of banks in 1969, the commercial banks started giving loans to farmers. Direct credit is given for short-term and medium-term periods. Indirect finance is provided by way of advances for the distribution of fertilisers and inputs, etc., and also through financing primary agricultural credit societies. The financial requirements of service units catering to warehousing, processing, marketing, transporting, and repairing of tractors, etc. form part of the bank's credit for infrastructure. The banks finance the operations of Food Corporation of India, the State Governments and their agencies for food procurement. Stocking and distribution of agricultural inputs is another sector served by banks. Along with SBI group, they are implementing the "village adoption scheme" under which the credit and other needs of farmers are fully met by banks. They have sponsored regional rural banks to extend credit to small and marginal farmers and rural artisans to save them from the clutches of the moneylenders. The advances extended by scheduled commercial banks totalled Rs. 44 crores in June 1969. During 1998-99 commercial banks, along with Regional Rural Banks, provided credit amounting to Rs. 19,499 crores.[1]

Land Development Banks

The requirement of long-term finance is being satisfied by land development banks which were formerly known as land mortgage banks. These banks provide long-term credit to farmers against mortgage of their lands. The loans from the land development banks are relatively cheap and are spread over long periods of 15 to 20 years. Farmers find it convenient to borrow from these banks whenever previous debts have to be cancelled or when additional land is to be purchased or when permanent improvements, like digging of wells, have to be made. As the land development banks lend against the security of land, the big landlords take advantage of them so much so that, by and large, small peasants have not benefitted from them.

Regional Rural Banks

Set up in 1975 to give direct loans and advances to small and marginal farmers, agricultural labourers, rural artisans, etc. the 196 Regional Rural Banks (RRBs) have been lending around Rs. 5,500 crores annually. Over 90 per cent of the loans of RRBs are given to the weaker sections.

Institutional Credit Disbursement in 90's

There has been an appreciable increase in the flow of credit from the institutional agencies. For instance, the co-operatives and the commercial banks (including the RRBs) tremendously increased the disbursement of rural credit : from Rs. 24 crores in 1960-61 to Rs. 880 crores in 1970-71 and Rs.38,054 crores in 1998-99. The major problem faced by the lending institutions, particularly the co-operatives, is the most unsatisfactory level of overdues. The ratio of overdues to demand is around 40 per cent in the case of co-operatives and 47 per cent in the case of regional rural banks. Accordingly, the health of agricultural

1. Reserve Bank of India, Report on Currency and Finance, 1998-99.

credit institutions, both co-operative and commercial banks, is in a very sad state. The Planning Commission regretfully admits: "Willful default and overdues are mounting in a number of states, including some co-operative progressive states like Maharashtra and Gujarat. By writing off agricultural loans and providing subsidies out of the state exchequer, some of the states have set a bad example to the entire country. If this trend is not reversed and if banks are reduced to institutions providing grants rather than recycling scarce resources to get the maximum benefits for the country as a whole, the banking system will be unable to provide more credit to meet the growing needs of the farmers."[2]

Non-Institutional Sources of Credit

Rural Moneylenders

There are agriculturist moneylenders who combine farming with moneylending. The village shopkeeper also acts as a moneylender. Besides, there are professional moneylenders also whose only occupation is money-lending.

The farmers depend upon the moneylender for their requirements of cash. The importance of moneylenders as suppliers of cash to the cultivators is, however, declining rapidly. According to the All-India Rural Credit Survey undertaken in 1951, the moneylenders accounted for about 70 per cent of all rural credit. In 1991 they accounted for only 16 per cent of rural credit. The moneylenders are, thus, losing ground to institutional agencies. But even now however, there are many reasons for the preponderance of the village moneylenders: (i) the village moneylender is easily accessible and maintains a close and personal contact with the borrower, often having relations with the family extending over generations; (ii) his methods of business are simple and elastic; (iii) he has local knowledge and experience and, therefore, can lend against land as well as against promissory notes. He knows how to protect himself against defaults; and (iv) the moneylender supplies credit for productive as well as non-productive purposes, and also for short-term and long-term requirements of the farmers.

There are, however, many malpractices which are associated with the village moneylenders. They obtain bonds and promissory notes from their debtors on false pretences, and enter in them sums larger than actually lent. They deduct exorbitant premiums. They give no receipts for repayments and often they deny such repayments. They charge high

2. Planning Commission, *Seventh Five Year Plan* (1985-90), Vol.2, P.17.

rates of interest, over 24 per cent.

Landlords, Traders and Relatives

The village cultivators generally borrow from their relatives in order to tide over temporary difficulties. These loans are generally contracted in an informal manner. This source of finance has all the defects associated with moneylenders, traders and commission agents. Interest rates are exorbitant. Often the small farmers are cheated and their lands are appropriated. The landless labourers are forced to become bonded slaves. Then, there are traders and commission agents who supply funds to farmers much before the crops mature. They, in turn, force the farmers to sell their produce at low prices and they charge a heavy commission for themselves. This source of finance is particularly important in the case of cash crops like cotton, groundnut, tobacco, etc.

There are, however, many defects in the system of private sources of agricultural finance : the use of credit for unproductive consumption purposes, high rates of interest and hence inability of farmers to meet the high interest charges and return the principal.

Have the Institutional sources of credit replaced the Non-Institutional sources in Rural India ?

Despite having a wide network of rural branches in the country and implementation of many schemes and programmes for expansion of credit (targeted lending) for agriculture and rural development, a large number of the very poor people still continue to remain outside the fold of the formal banking system. The All India Debt and Investment Survey 1991-92 shows that during the eighties there was a decline in the share of institutional agencies in cash dues of rural households by 4.6 percentage points to 56.6 per cent as against a rise of 32 percentage points to 61.2 per cent during the seventies. In case of non-cultivators, the share of institutional agencies was only 49.9 per cent in 1991. What is more revealing is the fact that the share of institutional agencies declined at a time when the proportion of rural households reported debt in 1991 increased to 32 per cent from 19.4 per cent in 1981. Thus, the rural households still seem to depend on money lenders, landlords and relatives for a significant par of their credit. In case of non-cultivators, the share of institutional agencies was only 49.9 per cent in 1991. The decline in the institutional outreach during the eighties is mainly on account of decline in the share of co-operatives from 28.6 per cent in 1981 to 18.6 per cent in 1991. Correspondingly, the shares of traders and professional money lenders have increased.

Weaknesses in Rural Credit System

Over the years, rural credit system has been suffering from a number of weaknesses like, limited outreach, skewness in the availability of credit in different regions, sectors and sections of the farming community, lower recovery of loans and growing non-performing assets, loss making institutions, etc.

A World Bank study carried out in a district in Eastern Rajasthan reveals that the share of institutional agencies in the provision of credit was just 16 per cent among the surveyed people below the poverty line (World Bank, 1995). Further, during the nineties, public sector banks could not meet their agricultural credit target of 18 per cent of net bank credit. Their achievement was only 15.7 per cent during the nineties. The Report of the High Level Committee on Agricultural Credit Through Commercial Banks (1997) (Chairman: Shri. R.V. Gupta) also found that there is a substantial unfulfilled demand for crop loans, which is being met either by the money lenders or leading to the usage of lower inputs. However, the Committee recommended for non stipulation of credit targets. Once the recommendation is accepted it will make agricultural credit on equal par with credit to other sectors. Given the inherent weakness of the agricultural sector (susceptible to the vagaries of monsoon, operation of the law of diminishing returns and the general policy bias against the sector), it may not be appropriate to treat the sector on equal par with other sectors where returns are much higher than agriculture. Further, if this recommendation is accepted, the Government and the Reserve Bank will be left with no policy instrument for increasing the flow of credit to the agriculture. As informal credit is very costly as compared to the institutional sources and the existing set-up largely serves well-off farmers, the reach of the institution needs to be further improved especially to small and marginal farmers. Credit targeting can ensure the availability of credit to those sections of the society.

Along with credit targeting, concessionality in interest rates has been an instrument for increasing the flow of credit to the agricultural credit. There is a valid reason for following such a policy: "principal justification for charging lower interest rates to certain category of borrowers was that the farm based investment activity in the short-run does not always yield a return which enables regular servicing of loans and at the same time meet the minimum consumption requirements" (Reserve Bank of India (1971). However, the Report of the Committee on the Financial System (1991) suggested that *it is timely and adequacy of the credit that is more important than the cost of credit.* Subsequently, following the financial sector reforms and de-regulation of interest rates in the economy, the concessional element in agricultural credit has been gradually wiped out. This is done by giving freedom to commercial banks, RRBs and co-operatives to fix their own interest rates on loans of amount. The only stipulation now is in respect of commercial banks that the rate of interest on loans below Rs.2 Lakhs should not exceed the Prime Lending Rate (PLR) of the respective banks. As PLR of banks are decided purely in terms of commercial considerations, the above stipulation does not provide any concessionality in lending to the agriculture sector.

With the rising rural income and agricultural exports, agricultural output mix is likely to undergo radical changes in the coming years which would substantially increase the demands for rural credit. The investment needs for the production of highly income elastic agricultural products such as dairying and livestock, horticulture, farm-forestry and agro-forestry, which are more land saving and capital intensive, would rise much faster than before. Similarly, with the liberalisation of agricultural exports, the agriculture sector will be more commercialised and capital intensive, particularly in area like horticulture, floriculture, aquaculture, agro-industries, etc. Since many of the emerging activities are land saving in character, the income earning prospects for small and marginal farmers can be improved by providing requisite credit and technical expertise. Owing to these factors rural credit has to expand at a rate faster than in the recent past.

Findings and Recommendations of the Report of the NABARD Expert Committee on Rural Credit

(Chairman V.S. Vyas, July 31, 2001)

Challenging Tasks

Changes in Rural Economy: Changes in the livelihood pattern (diminishing dependence on agriculture), pattern of holdings (increasing proportion of smaller units) and input and activity mix (greater use of purchased inputs, preference for higher value crops, and growing importance of animal husbandry, fishery, forestry etc.) are the features of the emerging scenario. These and similar changes may also necessitate involvement of newer financial agencies or groupings such as self-help groups, non-banking financial companies, etc, in rural credit. A progressive integration of financial markets will be accompanied by autonomy to institutions and corresponding stress on self-regulation and on accountability. State governments will be the most influential players, but their financial difficulties and populist policies are impairing this capacity.

Financing Assetless Poor: Target-oriented subsidy-driven programmes can have only a limited impact on asset creation and income generation on a sustainable basis. Sometimes they do more harm than good. Successful experiences of forming self-help groups of the poorest, especially rural women, encouraging them to save, and providing micro-finance has proved that the poor are bankable even without subsidies. This approach, with support in capacity building, is the best. In schemes such as the Swarnajayanti Gram Swarojgar Yojana (SGSY), which target subsidies towards self-help groups, it is important to ensure that the subsidies do not impair functioning of the groups themselves. *Subsidies should go to the group rather than to individuals and the subsidies should not limit the ability of the group to choose its activities.*

Financing Small Farmers and Tenants: The share of small farmers in cultivated area is steadily increasing. A holistic approach to lending, which will cover all their various sources of livelihood and consumption requirements is best suited to meet their needs. Since the security they offer is inadequate according to present norms, *new innovations in risk management, such as formation of joint liability groups should be tried. Freeing the lease market would help meet the credit needs of tenants. The prevailing situation in land holdings and leasing should be recognised and appropriate procedures designed to incorporate these rights in collaterals. Contract farming, with adequate safeguards for both parties, should also be encouraged.*

Financing Agricultural Sub-Sectors: Activities other than crop production, such as animal husbandry, inland and marine fisheries, silviculture including farm forestry, will also grow significantly. These activities offer a large scope for credit support. RFIs are mainly geared to finance crop production loans. Special efforts are needed to finance these non-crop activities. Hurdles such as inadequacy of feed and fodder, poor quality livestock, insufficient veterinary services and limited processing facilities hamper animal husbandry, poultry and fisheries. Successful pursuit of forestry requires public participation as well as technical support. Credit institutions can play their important role in the progress of these activities only after these initial hurdles are removed.

Financing Private Capital Formation: Productive agriculture requires investment in complementary assets such as irrigation structures and devices, as well as farm machinery, mainly tractors and power tillers, wherever possible. While public funds have created the bulk of irrigation facilities so far, further exploitation of irrigation will be primarily by way of minor projects - wells, tanks, their energisation, on-farm devices and so on. The current approach to financing minor irrigation on private lands also depends to an extent on subsidies. A more sustainable pattern of private investment will require better technical support from ground water departments and rural electrification agencies. This is essential for fruitful investment in this area, which must address the issue of the vast untapped groundwater potential in the Eastern states. *With the decline in public capital formation and growing importance of private investment, financial institutions must prepare for a more proactive role, shedding excessive caution and exploring alternative methods of providing insurance.*

Strengthening the credit delivery system

Co-operative Credit Institutions: The scale of operations and reach of rural financial co-operatives are truly outstanding. They cover geographically the entire country and functionally all economic activities of both short and long-term nature. Their operations have been reviewed many times and extensive recommendations following from these reviews have been implemented to varying extents. Co-operatives are supposed to embody the democratic ethos, while financial prudence and accountability are the governing principles of banking. Yet there are distortions. They do not try hard enough to mobilise funds; instead they act more as channels of disbursement of funds from various sources. Strict state controls compromise their democratic character severely. The RBI is not at present fully empowered to supervise and regulate their banking function. Their overall financial position is precarious. Most district and primary bodies have incurred heavy losses, as has the entire long-term structure.

Revitalisation of Co-operatives: A collapse of the co-operative credit system will leave an unbreachable gap in credit availability in rural areas. Co-operatives need to be revitalised at the earliest, as delays would be detrimental to the interests of the rural population. Central and state governments will have to provide the required resources, since co-operatives obviously do not possess them. Government of India should act expeditiously on the recommendations of the Jagdish Capoor Task Force on revitalisation and place Rs 500 crore with NABARD for the purpose. State governments may be allowed to borrow from the

Rural Infrastructure Development Fund (RIDF) at concessional terms to meet their share, since they are also financially weak.

Strengthening PACS: Expeditious steps are needed to restore the health of PACS. District and state level co-operative banks should exercise oversight function with regard to PACS and develop rules and manuals of business and accounting procedures for them. They should also train staff, management committees and other members of PACS in prudential financial norms. Greater professionalism should be introduced through audits by chartered accountants and replacement of the cadre of secretaries by recruitment of professional staff. Also, Co-operatives should take initiative in forming and nurturing SHGs.

Commercial Banks: Waning Enthusiasm: Commercial banks were made to expand their rural operations substantially after nationalisation. They were also required to maintain 40 per cent of their net credit to priority sector activities, of which 18 per cent was for agriculture. They now seem to have turned shy, as they find servicing vast numbers of small accounts - both deposit and borrowing - costly and cumbersome. They prefer instead the safer (and remunerative) alternative of meeting targeted levels of lending to agriculture, investing the shortfall from the target in RIDF. They also face problems of some non-viable branches, unmotivated or unwilling staff posted to rural branches with inadequate training and sensitisation, and some procedural problems, which place them at a disadvantage as compared to co-operatives.

Continued Involvement in Rural Lending: Commercial banks cannot, however, be allowed to withdraw from rural credit, as this would leave an enormous gap. Nor will it be in the interest of banks, which have already established a wide network of rural branches and now face competition from foreign and new-generation private sector banks for urban business. They should offer value-added services, (e.g. insurance) through their rural branches either on their own or by tying up with others, to improve viability of rural branches.

Regional Rural Banks: Re-capitalisation and Reforms: Although restricted to five institutions at the conceptual stage in 1975, the number of Regional Rural Banks (RRBs) grew to 196 by 1987. This proliferation notwithstanding, RRBs ceased to enjoy their original advantage of low costs by the late 1980s, which affected their viability. Only two RRBs did not need re-capitalisation to cleanse their balance sheets in the early 1990s; 187 were selected for the programme, of which 158 have been fully re-capitalised. Various reforms (deregulation of interests, prudential norms, lending beyond target groups and taking up diverse banking functions, among others) were also introduced to improve their prospects.

Planning, Supervision and Co-ordination

Effective Co-ordination Required: Reforms in the financial sector are motivated to a significant extent by a desire to create greater confidence in the institutions through closer supervision, better reporting and transparency in their administration. Rural credit, which involves an enormous amount of money and covers vast sections of the population, also needs such assurances and confidences. External agencies, starting with Government of India and RBI/NABARD, need to be pro-active in their promotion of rural credit and supportive of the institutions involved in actual disbursements. Reforms in regulatory and supervisory areas in the financial sector are motivated to a significant extent by desire to create greater confidence in the institutions through closer monitoring, mid season correction, better reporting, and transparency in administration. In performing these functions, governments at all levels, apex financial institutions, as well as civil society institutions can play effectively advocacy as well as developmental roles. They can provide a supportive institutional environment for improved performance of rural financial agencies.

Role of Reserve Bank of India: The RBI Act envisages an important role of development bank for rural India in addition to its basic function as the central bank of the country. To discharge these dual obligations, RBI should:

- Announce rural credit policy and review achievements in the year past, at an Annual Rural Credit Conference, with NABARD monitoring progress on decisions taken;
- Advocate revitalisation of co-operatives;
- Ensure greater involvement of commercial banks in rural credit, through cuts in RIDF interest rates and removal of ceiling on interest rate in small borrowal accounts;
- Monitor lead bank performance actively in consultation with NABARD. RBI/NABARD must secure commitments to action within a given time frame from concerned government agencies and banks;
- Include information on co-operative banks in banking statistics;

- Extend greater credit support to NABARD, with an increase of 10 to 15 per cent annually in its General Line of Credit to NABARD for another five years and allow it access to National Industrial Credit.

National Bank for Agriculture and Rural Development: Its role as currently defined includes development as well as supervisory functions for rural credit. To comply with these directives, it should:

- Play a more active role in financing critical sub-sectors of agriculture, sharing the credit risk along with refinance;
- Form a venture capital subsidiary to provide assistance for innovative high risk, hi-tech agricultural ventures;
- Allow preferential interest rate on its refinance to sectors such as dry and waste land development and banks in the North-East and hilly/tribal areas, as also states with high concentration of population below poverty line;
- Make its Co-operative Development Fund, set up out of its profits. NABARD may enhance its annual contributions to Rs. 50 crore to make its impact significant and visible;
- Sharpen development action plans and Memoranda of Understanding, with automatic suspension of credit facilities from higher level institutions (SCB/SCARDB/NABARD) on non-submission of progress report by stated dates;
- Spread district development offices by appointing more and better trained DDMs;
- Incorporate greater disclosures in balance sheets of co-operative banks and RRBs, by asking RBI to amend proforma of balance sheets and profit and loss accounts;

Government of India: As the ultimate supervising and funding authority, the Government of India should:

- Support revitalisation of co-operatives and RRBs;
- Professionalise RRB boards through careful selection of its nominees;
- Legislate enabling measures (extension of B R Act to co-operatives, amendments to RRB Act, and other acts relating to mortgages, law of limitations etc);

- Use annual rural credit conferences to discuss credit requirements of central sector schemes which receive budgetary support from central and state governments;
- Defer incidence of corporate income tax on NABARD by five years.

State Governments: They exercise possibly the greatest influence on rural areas and hence have a special responsibility in improving availability and use of rural credit. They would have to:

- Take greater interest in RRBs and co-operatives as recommended variously above;
- Devise internal systems to make the best use of district credit planning as an instrument of development;
- Promote private sector participation in rural development by creating better facilities, out of possibile borrowings from NABARD out of RIDF.

Panchayati Raj and Civil Society Institutions: This bottom tier of elected government bodies can be very effective partners and helpmates to credit bodies in various pursuits, such as deposit mobilisation, awareness creation and recovery. They could interface between government and non-government agencies. Social and religious opinion leaders could facilitate development tasks in general, and those addressed to the poor in particular. Associations of Commercial Banks and Co-operatives could gather and disseminate information and analyses of various aspects of rural financial services. They could also commission professional studies and help in computerisation, etc; NGOs could help empower the poor and act as catalysts for effective delivery of credit to them, help form SHGs, provide models or alternative approaches for action and also act as social auditors and watchdogs on behalf of the poor.

18

Agricultural Price Policy

Objectives of Agricultural Price Policy

THE objectives of price policy as propounded from time to time are multiple and often conflicting. The price policy was evolved in the context of relative shortage of agricultural products, particularly of foodgrains. Thus we had the overriding objectives of the price policy as achieving self-sufficiency in foodgrains (understood as the availability of adequate foodgrains from domestic production) and protection of consumer from scarcity-induced speculative price rise. As V.S. Vyas points out "the main function of prices, i.e., to act as signals for allocation of resources has been made subservient to income parity and food security objectives."

Apart from the consideration of income transfers, the policy is also directed to increase agricultural production by offering higher 'incentive' prices. A discriminatory price policy can be used to encourage inter-crop shifts in resource use. However, when it comes to aggregate agricultural output, greater reliance has to be placed on 'non-price' factors, e.g., generating and extending more efficient technologies. The available studies clearly bring out that aggregate supply response of agriculture is very weak. Thus, any attempt to use high prices to encourage agricultural production can bring in its wake irreparable distortions in the price structure.

These limitations of price policy are not very often recognised. Also the strength of price policy in affecting desirable shift in cropping pattern fully exploited. As Vyas remarks "in a mixed economy like ours an important objective of the price policy could be to give directions to the cropping pattern not only on the basis of the existing demand supply situation but also to take into account a qualitatively superior crop mix, e.g., to provide a price advantage to nutritionally superior crops or to the crops where the country may have comparative advantage. In fact, in this respect we seem to be regressing. In the 1970s price policy was used as an effective tool to encourage production of crops where superior technology was available." [Vyas 1989]. In recent years we have largely neglected this aspect of price policy.

Further, there has been no clarity on the priority to be assigned among these numerous objectives, or the trade-off involved in pursuing these objectives simultaneously. If we are to go by the public pronouncements, the objectives sought to be achieved by the price policy include, ensuring

(i) reasonable prices for the growers,

(ii) reasonable prices for the grains released from public distribution system, and

(iii) reasonable prices in the open market.

A moment's reflection will show that in most of the circumstances these aims conflict with each other. The price policy cannot resolve all conflicts in the society.

It must be recognised that price policy taken by itself is a weak instrument in giving directions to agricultural economy, more so as an instrument of income transfer. While the objective of providing an insurance cover in terms of guaranteed minimum prices to a large section of agricultural producers could be a worthy objective but until and unless required resources are available and administrative machinery is in place, mere announcement of minimum prices for a large number of commodities may not serve any purpose. It may, infact, do more harm with an erosion of the credibility of the government. In view of this it is suggested that the support prices should be applicable only for a limited number of crops. Crops which can be considered as price leaders or the crops, for which technological break through is imminent ought to be covered under the price guaranties. The other crops to be considered for support are the crops grown under high risk environment and there also it should be a transient measure i.e., till a viable crop insurance programme is evolved.

Along with limiting the scope for price policy is the need for a discriminatory and flexible approach to price interventions. By covering a large number of commodities on the one hand and by ensuring minimum prices in the guise of procurement prices on the other, not only government's commitment has enhanced to an unmanageable extent, it has also led to serious distortions in agricultural economy.

V.S. Vyas remarks *"the time has come to take a serious look at the scope, instruments and institutions of agricultural price policy. There is a need to recognise that the price policy is a weak instrument for income transfers; our capacity to offer minimum support prices for a large number of commodities is limited; need for dovetailing agriculture and trade policies is urgent. instrument of minimum support prices has to be used sparingly; procurement operations need to be made more business like; CACP should retain its expert character rather than trying to be representative of various interests, FCI should be decentralised and debureaucratised and the states should be made major stakeholders."*

According to N. Krishnaji,[1] the objectives as laid down in the terms of reference of the APC are to some extent mutually conflicting, and difficult to realise for other reasons as well. One may thus say that the APC was given an impossible task. Let us elaborate.

(a) If the sole objective is to promote agricultural growth — whether or not broad based with respect to crops and regions — through subsidies and price incentives, there is a clear possibility that the implied policy would hurt the interests of the buyers of food and agricultural raw materials. A resolution of the conflict of interests between producers and consumers — or between net sellers and net buyers, and between 'surplus' and 'deficit' areas, as some have described it in the case of foodgrains — thus becomes a necessary element of overall policy making. It is a recognition of this necessity that is reflected in the expressed concern about the impact of policy on cost of living etc, and has led to the conversion of price policy into an approach which seeks to integrate in some measure production objectives with those of distribution. In the case of foodgrains this meant that price policy had to be combined with the operations of a public distribution system (PDS) to ensure supply of foodgrains at subsidised prices to at least some of the poorer sections of the population. However, to the extent that subsidising both the producer and consumer is severely limited by financial constraints, it cannot be sustained on either a short or long-term basis without being supplemented by compensating measures of taxation. All this makes the design of price policy

1. N. Krishnaji, *Agricultural Price Policy: A Survey with Reference to Indian Foodgrains Economy,* in Indian Economy Since Independence op. cit.

difficult, especially by a body with no decision-making powers; more importantly, the difficulty leads to politically expedient measures which exacerbate rather than resolve conflicts.

(b) The difficulty is compounded by two other obvious factors. First, if relative prices are to play an efficient allocative role and not lead to undesirable cropping pattern shifts, policies must be designed to cover all the major crops on a country-wide basis, an impossible task to accomplish. Second, since public distribution of subsidised grain cannot hope to meet the entire market demand (of both the rural and urban consumers), the impact of policies on market prices assumes importance. Thus, with the government handling only a fraction of the marketed surplus, the pricing objectives may in the end be defeated by market forces. The design of price policies with only a limited control over the market thus not only involves an appropriate combination of procurement, stock accumulation and depletion policies but must necessarily be based on a sound knowledge of the implied working of dual markets. The biggest hindrance in this respect is not lack of knowledge about production trends and demand elasticities but our virtual ignorance about the operations of private traders at the different tiers of the grain markets and their impact on prices.

(c) Finally, it must be noted that the objectives are not only conflicting — the fact that there is no indication in policy formulations whether it is only in short-run but also in the long-run, these conflicts could be left unresolved is also important — they are also incomplete and imprecise in some respects. For example, income and price stabilisation are common objectives of price policy; maintenance of some form of parity between the agricultural and industrial sectors and prevention of the erosion of purchasing power of agricultural incomes is a related concern, and all these are adequately discussed in the literature. Indeed they can be stated with some precision; unlike the vague 'protection' of producer and consumer 'interest'; but it is doubtful if multiple objectives are realisable.

Also refer to Ch.19, P. 270-71.

19

Reform Agenda for Agriculture

THE incentive framework for Indian agriculture improved considerably as a result of trade and exchange rate liberalisation and a significant reduction in the protection to domestic industry, following economic reforms introduced in the country in the early 1990s. The terms of trade for agriculture have improved and there has been a record rise in agricultural exports. On the whole, farmers' expectations have been aroused for better prospects from the opening up of the economy. This is reflected in a big rise in private investment in agriculture in the 1990s. The full benefits for agriculture from the macroeconomic reforms introduced so far can be expected to materialise, in course of time, when reforms directly affecting agriculture such as removal of restrictions on domestic trade and processing, stepping up public investment in agriculture, reforms in the management of infrastructure, etc, are put in place. Indeed, the slowing down of agricultural growth in the post-reform period, despite favourable macroeconomic environment, is explained by the neglect of such reforms directly affecting agriculture.

The basic objectives of reforms in agriculture should be:

First, stepping up agricultural growth to at least 4 per cent per annum to sustain the overall growth rate in GDP at a high rate, say, 8 per cent.

Second, diversifying agriculture with a view to promoting, among other things, the growth of rural non-farm sector such as agro-processing thus facilitating a significant shift of labour force from agriculture to non-agriculture.

Excerpted from C.H.H. Rao, '*Reform Agenda for Agriculture*', EPW, February 15, 2003.

Third, increasing application of cost-reducing technologies for making agriculture competitive.

Fourth, reducing rural poverty and inequality through broad-based growth of agriculture by reducing disparities between different regions and classes of farmers and by strengthening the role of women in farming.

Fifth, protecting environment by reversing the ongoing degradation of natural resources like land and water and by preventing the excessive chemicalisation of agriculture.

Reforms needed for achieving these objectives are outlined below within the framework of a two-pronged strategy to improve the performance of agriculture:

(a) to release the initiative and enterprise of farmers and the private sector in general by removing restrictions on agricultural trade, processing etc; and

(b) to facilitate adequate supply response to the incentives so created by strengthening infrastructure, agricultural research and extension and delivery of credit, while protecting environment.

I

REMOVAL OF RESTRICTIONS ON DOMESTIC TRADE AND PROCESSING

(a) Removal of Restrictions

The prevailing restrictions on domestic trade and processing of agricultural commodities are inherited from the post-war, pre-green revolution era of shortages. With the achievement of self-sufficiency in foodgrains, increasing trend towards diversification of agriculture, globalisation of trade and WTO commitments, such restrictions on movement, storage and processing have out lived their utility and have become counter-productive, denying fair prices to producers as well as to consumers and inhibiting much needed investments in the technological upgradation and modernisation of processing, storage and marketing.

The Essential Commodities Act (ECA), Agricultural Produce Marketing Act, the Small Scale Industry Reservation, and so on, need to be thoroughly reviewed and revamped with a view to abolishing all legal impediments under these Acts that restrict the entry of big private sector, including FDI, in marketing, storage and processing.

While revamping these Acts, care has to be taken to see that some of the positive features in them are retained and strengthened. Given unscrupulous practices by certain sections of traders and middlemen, some regulations, including regulated markets, are necessary. Further, in states such as Punjab and Haryana, markets and road infrastructure were developed through taxes collected via APMC Acts. However, there is a need to rationalise these taxes. For example, Commission Agents' charges could be removed and Mandi fees could be waived when processors buy directly from the farm gate (such as through contract farming) and commission charges are not levied.

(b) Minimum Support Prices and Public Procurement of Foodgrains

The mounting stocks of foodgrains with the FCI are explained by the steep rise in procurement prices (acting as minimum support prices), and the open ended procurement by the FCI even when market conditions were adverse. A good part of the large amounts of grain procured is off-loaded at a price almost half its 'economic cost'. Such market operations at huge discounts drove out the private sector from grain trade, and consequently government is saddled with even more stocks.

In principle, since MSP is intended to provide an element of insurance against precipitous fall in prices, it should preferably be based on the average paid-out cost, while the procurement price should be set by the market conditions in competition with the private trade. However, sudden and drastic changes in the existing system of pricing and procurement of foodgrains carry the risk of undermining food security so painstakingly built over a long period. In the medium term, therefore, the objective should be to consolidate the food security achieved so far and simultaneously move towards diversification of agriculture in consonance with the changing demand and resource endowments.

Towards this end, the government should, as a rule, accept the recommendations of the Commission on Agricultural Costs and Prices (CACP) while deciding the level of MSP. Moderation on the price front for foodgrains by tilting the relative prices in favour of non-foodgrains needs to be combined with vigorous non-price interventions for making the cultivation of non-foodgrains attractive to farmers such as through research and extension, infrastructure development for agro-processing and marketing, and measures for promoting exports. Since diversification leads to risk and uncertainty for higher value added products, their risk management can be subsidised. In the meantime, the foodgrain surpluses available with the FCI provide an opportunity to generate rural employment for productive works like watershed development, afforestation and for building up other community assets. They should also be used for providing mid-day meals to the children in schools for improving their nutrition and reducing drop-out. Over and above this, the BPL (below the poverty line) families, whose children go to school, can be compensated for their children's earnings foregone by giving them 5 to 10 kgs of grain per month free, so as to induce them to send their children to school.

A major element in the new dispensation should be to allow the private sector to operate in the market without any restrictions in terms of the movement of grain, stocking limits, levy to the government agencies, exports, etc. This necessitates that the public agencies (FCI) should not be reimbursed for their losses due to their open market operations (beyond what is absolutely necessary on account of the maintenance of buffer stocks and the operation of the PDS) at a price much below their cost. Otherwise the private sector will be driven out of the market.

(c) Trade and WTO Related Issues

There is a need to formulate a consistent policy for export of agricultural products and processed agro-products in which the country has a comparative advantage. Most agricultural commodities (cotton, onions, sugar, etc.) continue to be under severe export controls and quotas. These destroy any chance of building up a sustained international market. Exporters should have the freedom to enter into long-term contracts. They should be allowed to buy from the farm-gate or from the market at minimum support prices and stocking and handling should be freely allowed.

India should argue at the WTO that all the subsidies need to be clubbed together, instead of being placed in separate boxes (green, blue, amber), as some of the developed countries have been claiming large exemptions by using such provisions and also by interchanging subsidies shown from one box to the other. India would not be adversely affected if these are clubbed together, as the aggregate measure of support (AMS) to Indian agriculture is still well below the de-minimis of 10 per cent.

II

AGRICULTURAL RESEARCH AND EXTENSION

(a) Agricultural Research

India is endowed with one of the most advanced agricultural research systems among the developing countries in terms of scientific skills as well as its reach, even though a great deal of restructuring is needed for its efficient functioning. Indian farmers, despite low literacy levels, have responded exceptionally well to the opportunities opened up by new technologies. Also, frontier technologies like biotechnologies remain underexploited in the country. Therefore, the returns from investment in agricultural research and extension in the country can be expected to be very high, relatively quick, and assured.

The existing public outlay on agricultural research and education, stagnating around 0.3 per cent of agricultural GDP in the country, is too meagre and needs to be stepped up substantially. At the same time, there is considerable potential for raising the effectiveness of these outlays by reordering the priorities in agricultural research and redefining the relative roles of public and private sectors in research and extension.

There is a need for a shift away from individual crop-oriented research focused essentially on irrigated areas towards research on crops and cropping systems in the dry lands, hills, tribal and other marginal areas. In view of high variability in agro-climatic conditions in such unfavourable areas, research has to become increasingly location-specific with greater participation or interaction with farmers. Greater attention to research on horticultural products that are land-saving as well as water-saving, animal husbandry and dairying integrated with crop production, and on small ruminants can benefit resource-poor farmers and women, besides being environmentally sustainable.

Progress in post-harvest technology is essential to promote value addition through the growth of agro-processing industry.

Private sector participation in agricultural research, extension and marketing is becoming increasingly important, especially with the advent of biotechnology and protection being accorded to intellectual property. However, private sector participation tends to be limited to profitable crops and enterprises undertaken by the resource-rich farmers in well-endowed areas. Public sector research has to increasingly address the problems facing the resource-poor farmers in the less-endowed regions.

(b) Extension

There is an immediate need for revamping and revitalising the existing agricultural extension system in the country, so as to conform to the new priorities in agricultural research, with adequate financial support from the centre and the states. The main ingredients of this reform should be:

(1) Active involvement of farmers through user groups and Self Help Groups (SHGs), and accountability to them,

(2) Enabling participation by the private sector, farmers' associations and the NGOs, to complement public services, by putting in place an independent regulatory body, to which samples can be submitted for quality checks, encompassing inputs like fertilisers, pesticides, and seeds.

(3) Increasing use of media and Information Technology, including cyber kiosks, to disseminate knowledge on new agricultural practices and the information on output and input prices for improving the effectiveness of agricultural services in general. The use of information technology will reduce the requirement of a large number of extension workers at the block level and would indeed complement, to a considerable extent, the services rendered by the extension workers in remote areas.

(4) Building gender concerns into the system, for example, by manning the extension services predominantly by women in hill and tribal areas where farming is managed essentially by women.

(5) Capacity building of extension functionaries and farmers, among other means, through distance education.

III

MANAGEMENT OF INFRASTRUCTURE

(a) Exploiting the Available Irrigation Potential

Public investment in basic infrastructure, especially roads, irrigation and power, where private sector is still reluctant to enter, will have to be stepped up. Government programme on highways and rural roads has made some progress, but major institutional and price reforms are required in irrigation and power sectors to raise efficiency, and generate resources at least for the proper upkeep and maintenance of the systems.

Nearly 40 per cent of the available irrigation potential of 58.5 million hectares from major and medium irrigation projects in the country still remains to be exploited. Over 400 such projects were in the pipeline at various stages during the Ninth Plan period. When these ongoing projects are completed, bulk of the remaining irrigation potential would have been exploited. Decline in public investment and the thin spread of resources over a large number of projects are responsible for the delay in the completion of these projects. This underlines the need for stepping up public investment for the speedy completion of the ongoing major and medium irrigation projects by the states, as the latter account for over 95 per cent of public investment in irrigation in the country. The resource-poor states in the eastern and central regions account for the bulk of the irrigation potential remaining to be exploited. There may, therefore, be a need for special central assistance to enable such resource-poor states to speedily execute the ongoing irrigation projects.

(b) Raising Water-Use Efficiency

Since water-use efficiency for irrigation is very low in the country, achievement of water security depends not only on the exploitation of the remaining potential but increasingly on the efficient and productive use of available irrigation water. There exists a vast gap now between the knowledge available for improving water-use efficiency and its actual application in the country. This is explained by the lack of incentives to follow improved practices under the existing system of management and pricing of water. However, reforms in management and pricing are inter-linked as farmers would be willing to pay higher charges only if the efficiency of services improves.

Involvement of user-farmers in the management of irrigation systems at various levels is accepted the world over as an effective alternative to the present system of management by the government, as well as to privatisation. Participatory Irrigation Management (PIM) being experimented in the country towards this end has thrown up certain useful lessons; Unwillingness to devolve adequate powers to the Water Users' Associations (WUAs) and insufficient infrastructure for capacity building at grassroots level have inhibited the participation of user-farmers and impeded the growth of leadership at the local level, India has been very much lagging behind several south east Asian countries in respect of coverage by WUAs as well as effectiveness of their performance. Therefore, there has to be a vigorous drive towards the empowerment of Water Users' Associations in the country by putting in place an adequate infrastructure for capacity building.

(c) Input Subsidies and Pricing of Irrigation Water and Rural Electricity

The rising subsidies on irrigation water from canals and on electricity for pumping water have benefited the large farmers as well as the consumers at large on account of the food security achieved and the decline in the relative prices of foodgrains for quite some time. However, these subsidies caused severe deterioration of the systems due to the neglect of their maintenance in addition to becoming fiscally unsustainable. Further, they have led to the highly wasteful use of canal water, ecological degradation from waterlogging, salinity and pollution, excessive consumption of electricity, and overdrawl of ground water resulting in the shortage of drinking water in several parts of the country. There is, therefore, an immediate need to reverse this process.

Awareness on the part of the farmers about the harmful consequences of rising input subsidies and their cooperation in pricing the inputs on a volumetric basis is essential for making the change-over politically feasible and sustainable. A possible solution is to evolve a system where the village communities develop a stake in the conservation of resources. As an experiment, Water Users' Associations and panchayati raj institutions (PRIs) can be fully empowered and induced to charge and collect water and electricity rates from the farmers on the basis of the volume of actual consumption where metering is possible, or, on the basis of the quantities of water received or electricity consumed as estimated by the farmers' associations where metering is uneconomical or otherwise infeasible. In such situations, panchayats can regulate the cropping pattern and the use of water for raising water-use-efficiency and productivity. The revenues so collected should be allowed to be retained partly or wholly by the WUAs under the aegis of panchayats for maintenance and development of irrigation and rural electricity services. Since agricultural income has not been taxed, this should be made the fiscal domain of PRIs through a land-based tax.

The prevailing heavy subsidy on nitrogenous fertilisers perpetuates inefficiencies in the domestic fertiliser industry. The benefit flowing to the farmers and consumers of food is illusory, as it is leading to the degradation of soil on account of excessive chemicalisation and adverse NPK ratio. As in the case of water and electricity discussed above, a fixed quantity of fertilisers sufficient for one or two hectares may be subsidised for all the farmers, if necessary through a system of input stamps, requiring them to purchase the remaining quantities in the market at the going rates.

IV

CREDIT REFORMS

About 60 per cent of the credit requirements of farmers are now met by the institutional sources, and the remaining 40 per cent by informal sources like money lenders who charge very high interest rates. However, small and marginal farmers (less than 2 ha), including tenants, who account for nearly 80 per cent of holdings and one-third of area operated, depend far more heavily on informal sources. Among the formal credit institutions, the commercial banks have emerged as a major player in agriculture credit (about 50 per cent) followed by cooperatives (about 43 per cent) and RRBs (about 7 per cent).

In the post-reform period, despite the rise in capital-intensity of agriculture in the wake of its diversification, and despite broadening the definition of 'priority sector' by adding a number of activities hitherto financed outside the priority sector, the direct agriculture advances by the commercial banks declined to 11-12 per cent of net bank credit as against the original target of 18 per cent. The position is much worse in the eastern and north-eastern states, even though the commercial banks are saddled with excess liquidity. The Rural Infrastructure Development Fund (RIDF), started a decade ago presumably as a temporary measure to provide infrastructural support to agriculture in lieu of its falling share in commercial bank credit, seems to have been turned into an easier route for meeting part of the stipulated obligations. In the process, individual needs of the farmers for investment and production credit are not being adequately met. This declining priority to agriculture is apparently explained by the efforts on the part of the banks to reduce 'transaction costs' and minimise 'risks'. Nothing short of a major change in the mind-set, and a new code informed by social purpose, initiated and monitored by the authorities in the banking system, can remedy the situation.

The share of Cooperative Banks in the institutional credit for agriculture and allied activities has declined from 45 per cent in 1996-97 to 41 per cent during 2000-01. Under the prevailing economic scenario of liberalisation and globalisation, the cooperatives have to be strong enough to compete in the open market. They may need to be assisted in recapitalisation and also by substantially increasing the quantum of refinance by NABARD. Also, the proposals initiated by the centre for amending the cooperative laws of the states with a view to inject professionalism, autonomy and transparency in the functioning of these societies need to be followed up expeditiously.

The Kisan Credit Scheme, aimed at providing adequate and timely support to the farmers from the banking system in a flexible and cost effective manner, does not seem to be succeeding in its avowed purpose because of various stipulations and restrictions. Its operation seems to be limited to only fertilisers from fixed shops. A more farmer-friendly credit card system needs to be operated so as to realise the objectives of the scheme.

High value agriculture needs higher working capital and also entails higher risks. Facilitating credit through processors, input dealers, NGOs, etc, that are vertically integrated with the farmers, including through contract farming, for providing them critical inputs or processing their produce, could increase the credit flow to agriculture significantly. These dealers/processors can act as non-banking financial intermediaries, who can get refinance from the banking sector and can give loans to agriculture, and bear the risk of default. Such arrangements would reduce transaction costs and ensure good recovery. Policy changes are needed to facilitate such intermediation by freeing up interest rates within a band.

Self-Help Groups of women for providing micro-credit have been a success story in the country. Such households being essentially landless, credit by SHGs has been confined mainly to activities falling outside agriculture. However, their experience does point to the promise that groups comprising small and marginal farmers, especially women farmers, hold in managing credit for land-saving activities like animal husbandry, dairying, horticulture, agro-forestry, etc, provided there are contractual arrangements with dealers and processors for the provision of inputs and services for marketing. As capital assets of these farmers are limited, community/group collateral and the produce on farmers' land, including that of tenants, should be considered as collateral in granting credit.

V

MEASURES TO CONSERVE LAND AND WATER RESOURCES

(a) Watershed Development

The experience from the on-going watershed development programme for drought proofing of rainfed agriculture by conserving land and water resources has been encouraging. The single most important factor accounting for the positive impact of this programme is community participation and decentralisation of programme administration made possible under the new guidelines. Yet, the present level of participation is inadequate for sustaining this development, especially in areas where the programme has proceeded too fast by fulfilling the targets for completion of works without the required institution building and leadership formation at the grass roots level. The coverage has, nevertheless, to expand through increased outlays, as only about 25 per cent of around 107 million hectares of degraded land in the country is estimated to have been treated so far.

Certain policy changes are needed for the movement to become self-sustaining as and when the assistance under the current officially sponsored programme ceases. The foremost among these requirements being institution-building and leadership formation, it calls for empowering people inhabiting the watersheds by delegating authority to their committees and user-groups. Mobilising adequate contribution from the land owning households on a regular basis for the maintenance of assets created, and ensuring equitable benefits to weaker sections, especially the landless poor, are essential for sustaining the movement. The second major task is creation of awareness and capacity building through training at various levels by entrusting this to an autonomous nodal agency at the national level and by guaranteeing adequate funding. Third, a major shift is needed in the existing policy for dry land or rainfed agriculture by according greater priority to agricultural research and extension, supply of inputs, infrastructure development like roads and marketing and price and credit policies. Because of the emerging shift of consumer demand towards water-saving products which also have a good export potential, greater priority to dry land agriculture can provide the necessary incentives to the local communities to sustain their interest in the conservation of land and water resources and indeed for easing pressure on such resources.

(b) Joint Forest Management (JFM)

JFM is a programme for the regeneration and conservation of forest resources in partnership with the local people consisting largely of tribal population. This programme has, on the whole, made a much better impact in a relatively short period when compared to the watershed development programme. Apart from the absence of problems arising from individual property rights as in areas under watershed development, the returns to the participating farmers from the regeneration of forests are quick and assured. Also, the institutions of forest dwellers, especially of tribals, are conducive to community participation.

Some of the major problems still to be addressed are : permitting JFM in good or high productivity forest areas, encouraging profitable enterprises like agro-forestry, increasing the participation of women, greater security to the poorer segments of the participants, recognising self-initiated or spontaneously formed groups, and clarifying the use rights of the dwellers so that those living nearer the forest area develop a greater stake in protecting the forests. Relaxation of existing restrictions on marketing and processing of forest produce will increase the returns to the participating farmers by ending the privileged position now enjoyed by the government and the industry.

(c) Hill and Tribal Areas

The protection of fragile ecology of hills requires a major shift from short duration crops like foodgrains to forestry, animal husbandry, pasture management and horticulture. This calls for effective interventions by way of research and extension, and development of transport and marketing infrastructure. Since farming is done essentially by women in hill areas, greater interaction with them would be necessary for developing technologies and programmes suited to these areas. Also, access to technology, inputs and credit has to be ensured predominantly through women extension workers.

(d) Flood-Proofing of Flood-Prone Agriculture

About 4 per cent of the crop area in the country, located mainly in the eastern states, is affected by the recurring floods. The traditional land use and cropping patterns are closely adapted to the seasonal flooding cycle, emphasis being on flood management rather than on flood control as such. Farmers usually harvest bumper rabi crops in the post-flood season, thus compensating kharif losses to some extent. The strategy for flood-proofing through embankments, dams, etc, combined with the use of high yielding varieties for irrigated rabi crops have led to significant and positive changes in the farming systems, diversified employment opportunities and better food security. In the light of this experience, research has to be designed to adjust cropping systems to the flooding cycle, harvest flood water for irrigation in the post-flood season and to evolve yield-raising technologies.

VI

LAND CEILING AND TENANCY LAWS

In view of the continued pressure of population on land, it may not be advisable to remove, at the present juncture, the ceiling on the ownership of agricultural land. Ceiling on the ownership of land has in general made land market favourable to the small and marginal farmers who can augment their ownership as well as operational holdings. However, tenancy laws guaranteeing security of tenure and prescribing the rental share have led to the growth of concealed tenancy which discourages investment by the tenants and restricts the flow of credit to them. Since such tenants are in any case paying market rents, liberalisation of tenancy laws can help to increase their employment and income by augmenting their operational holdings, stepping up investment and getting better access to credit and inputs.

Conclusion

It is clear from the above that the role of government by way of public policies, programmes, and investment is going to be extremely important. Success depends crucially on effective governance at the grass roots level, as many of these programmes are going to be location specific. Interaction with farmers is essential for ensuring relevance and quality of the programmes designed, and accountability to them is necessary for effective implementation. The key to the success is the effective functioning of the Panchayati Raj Institutions as enjoined by the 73rd and 74th amendments to the Constitution. As it is, most state governments have been reluctant to transfer functions, finances and functionaries to the Panchayats, as indicated in the Eleventh Schedule to the Constitution. Major initiatives are needed from the centre to persuade the states to devolve these powers and, if necessary, bring about consensus for directly transferring from the centre to the panchayats resources allocated to schemes falling under the subjects listed in the Eleventh Schedule.

20

Industrial Growth and Policy

Extent and Pattern of Industrialisation During the British Rule

INDIAN manufacturers had a world-wide market prior to industrial revolution and the rise of modern industry. The exports consisted chiefly of manufactures like cotton and silk fabrics, calicoes, artistic ware, silk and woollen cloth. The impact of the British rule and industrial revolution led to the decay of Indian handicrafts. Machine-made goods started pouring into the country. The decline of handicrafts was not followed by the rise of modern industry in India because of the British policy of encouraging the import of manufactures and export of raw materials from India.

The British government in India followed the policy of discriminating protection to some selected industries since 1923. This protection was accompanied by the most favoured nation-clause for British goods. Despite this factor, some industries such as cotton textiles, sugar, paper, matches and to some extent iron and steel did make progress. But one thing was quite obvious that during the British period, no effort was made to foster the development of capital goods industries. The main features of the industrial scene in India on the eve of planning (1950) were as under :

(i) There was the preponderance of consumer goods industries *vis-a-vis* producer goods industries resulting in lop-sided industrial development. In 1953, the ratio of consumer goods to producer goods worked out to be 62:38.

(ii) The industrial sector was extremely underdeveloped with a very weak infrastructure.

(iii) The lack of government intervention in favour of the industrial sector was considered as an important cause of underdevelopment.

(iv) Export orientation had been against the country's interests.

(v) The structure of ownership was highly concentrated and

(vi) Technical and managerial skills were in short supply.

As a result, the national consensus was that economic sovereignty and economic independence lay in rapid industrialization including particularly the promotion of industrial infrastructure.

Organized thinking concerning the direction of industrial development in India may be traced to the Statement of Industrial Policy, 1945, the Industrial Policy Resolution of 1948, the enactment of the Industries (Development and Regulation) Act, 1951, the First and Second Five Year Plan documents, and the Industrial Policy Resolution of 1956.

The First Five Year Plan stated that the objective of industrial planning was to make good the deficiencies in production of key industrial items and to initiate development which would enable the cumulative expansion of such basic production. The scope and need for the development of India's industries was felt to be so great that it was necessary for the public sector to develop those industries 'in which private enterprise is unable or unwilling to put up the resources required and to run the risk involved.' The idea was that the rest of the field could be left free for private enterprise.

The Industrial Policy Resolution of 1948 had identified a small number of industries to be reserved for production by the public sector. The production of arms and ammunition, production and control of atomic energy and ownership and management of railways were to be the sole preserve of the central government. However, coal, iron and steel, aircraft manufacturing, ship-building, manufacture of telegraph and wireless equipment (except radios) and minerals were reserved for production by central or state government undertakings.

The 1956 list of industries reserved for the public sector is obviously based on this 1948 list but includes a number of additional industries. The thinking concerning the public sector had changed during the course of the 1950s. As far as can be ascertained, the original thinking was concerned with the use of the public sector investment in industries which the private sector would find difficult to invest in. By 1956 this had changed towards an explicit preference for state ownership of industries that were termed as capturing the 'commanding heights of the economy'

Although the Second Five Year Plan is always seen as the conceptual basis of Indian planning, a close reading of the First Five Year Plan suggests that the difficulty of directing a mixed economy was better appreciated by the earlier planners and policy makers. There was better appreciation of the need for indicative planning in the First Plan and the need for coordination of industrial planning with the formulation of other economic policies such as customs and excise tariff structure, import and export policy, investment and technology policy, monetary and financial policy. The Second Plan and later plans have been increasingly concerned with the allocation of public resources and much less with indications and policies to direct the whole economy in desired directions. (Rakesh Mohan, 1992).

Industrial Control Regime

The system of Indian industrial licensing, therefore, has its origins in a combination of thinking resulting from the exigencies and requirements of a war situation, Indian nationalistic aspirations and the socialistic leanings of some of the founding fathers of the country. The leaders of the private sector of the time were also in favour of strong governmental assertion. The industrial licensing system has operated in the country with the simultaneous operation of other schemes of governmental allocations and controls such as:

(i) Five Year Plan documents

(ii) Import and export controls

(iii) Control of capital issues

(iv) Control of foreign exchange

(v) Transport controls including allocation of raw materials

(vi) Price controls

(vii) Allocations of credit

This suggests that the planners and policy makers in India understood the need for using a wide variety of instruments and controls to steer Indian industrial development in a desired direction. However, there has always been a mismatch between the intentions expressed and the licensing instruments available for realizing these planning intentions. It should also be noted that, whereas the original intention of licensing was to use this power selectively for the promotion of selected important industries, it was later used to control almost all industries with the result that *regulation rather than development became the more important feature of the system.*

Performance of the Industrial Licensing System

Until the recent industrial and trade policy reforms, the establishment and operation of an industrial enterprise in India required approvals from the central government at almost every step (see Paranjape, 1988). Before making an investment, an entrepreneur had to first obtain approval in principle from the Ministry of Industry. The granting of this approval resulted in the issuance of a Letter of Intent (LOI). Armed with this LOI, the entrepreneur could then tie up other requirements for setting up the project. If he needed to import a capital good, he had to obtain a capital goods import licence from the Chief Controller of Imports & Exports (CCI&E) in the Ministry of Commerce. The approval for the import, however, was given by a committee set up in the Ministry of Industry. If there was also need for a foreign technology collaboration agreement, the entrepreneur had to obtain a specific approval for this (a Foreign Collaboration–FC–approval) from a committee chaired by the Finance Secretary but serviced by the Ministry of Industry. In order to raise funds for the project, if an entrepreneur wanted to go to the capital market, he needed separate approval from the Controller of Capital Issues in the Ministry of Finance. For imports of raw material and components, separate licences had to be obtained on an annual basis from the CCI & E. In each case, an 'essentiality' and indigenous non-availability clearance had to be given by the technical wing of the Ministry of Industry (the Directorate General of Technical Development – DGTD). Once everything was tied up and the unit was about to go into production, the entrepreneur had to go back to the Ministry of Industry for an 'Industrial Licence'.

In addition to these approvals, since the enactment of the MRTP Act in 1969, the firms covered under this needed to obtain separate MRTP clearances from the Department of Company Affairs. Further, resulting from the desire to promote small-scale industries, 836 items have been reserved for production in small-scale enterprises. Since 1956, there has also been a list of industries reserved for exclusive production in the public sector. Since 1977, there has also been a ban on the location of industries in the largest twenty to thirty cities. In 1988, this ban was extended to include municipal areas of all towns and cities and to specified areas of influence around the largest twenty-one cities.

That this system was unsuited for directing investments has been well understood since the early 1960s. The most comprehensive description, evaluation and indictment of this system is that by Bhagwati and Desai (1970). The government appointed one committee after another in the 1960s to examine the industrial licensing system (The Swaminathan Committee, 1964; the Mahalanobis Committee, 1964; the Hazari Report, 1967; the Dutt Committee Report, 1969; and the Administrative Reform Commission, 1969). Despite the findings of most of these early committees, that the licensing mechanism was not serving its purpose of channelizing investments into desired directions, there seems to have been a continuing inability of the government, until recently, to bring any substantative changes to the industrial licensing system.

It seems the promotion of a sheltered home market had a common appeal to the bureaucratic authoritarian state, urban manufacturers, and multinationals that supplied technology and capital. Protection also met the state's objectives pursuing revenue and expenditure maximising activities through maximum revenue tariffs and export tariffs.

Thus the interests of politicians, bureaucrats, multinationals, as well as domestic industrial houses all coincided to keep Indian industry sheltered through the operation of the industrial control system.

The stagnation of Indian industrial production between the mid-1960s up to the late 1970s induced some serious new thinking. Towards the end of the 1970s and by the early 1980s there emerged a growing consensus that Indian industry was exhibiting a slow-down in industrial growth due to low productivity, high costs, low quality of production and obsolete technology (Ahluwalia, 1985). Three important committees were set up in the early 1980s – the Abid Hussain Committee on trade policy, the Narasimham Committee on the shift from physical to fiscal controls and the Sengupta Committee on the public sector. These committees clearly recommended an easing up of trade policy, the substitution of physical and quantitative controls by fiscal and other means of macroeconomic management, the promotion of greater public sector autonomy in business and operating decisions and the need for measures for enhancing productivity efficiency and modernization.

The result of such thinking was that there was some progress in the process of de-regulation during the 1980s, though perhaps not as significant as is often believed. Two kinds of delicensing activity took place. First, thirty-two groups of industries were delicensed without any investment limit. Second, in 1988, all industries were exempted from licensing except for a specified negative list of twenty-six industries. This exemption from licensing was, however, subject to investment and location limitations. As has often been done in the past, this announcement also contained further restrictions which reduced significantly the effectiveness of exemption from licensing that was provided in this announcement. On the trade policy front, the key change was increasing access of exporters to inputs at international prices. However, it seems that tariff protection to industry increased significantly during the 1980s relative to previous decades.

While the industrial licensing system underwent some changes in terms of threshold levels and types of products, it formed an essential part of Government policy until the end of the 1980s.

New Economic Policy

As Rangarajan has rightly stated, the year 1991 is an important landmark in the economic history of post-Independent India. The country went through a severe economic crisis triggered by a serious balance of payments situation. The crisis was converted into an opportunity to introduce some fundamental changes in the content and approach to economic policy. The response to the crisis was to put in place a set of policies aimed at stabilisation and structural reform. While the stabilisation policies were aimed at correcting the weaknesses that had developed on the fiscal and the balance of payments fronts, the structural reforms sought to remove the rigidities that had entered into the various segments of the Indian economy. The structural reforms introduced in the early 1990s broadly covered the areas of industrial licensing, foreign trade, foreign investment, exchange rate management and the financial sector. From the point of view of industrialisation, changes in the areas of licensing and foreign trade and investment had important implications. Even before the onset of reforms, the problems associated with industrial licensing were well recognised. The approach document of the Eighth Plan (1991-1996) submitted in May 1990 had remarked: "A return to the regime of direct, indiscriminate and detailed controls in industry is clearly out of question. Past experience has shown that such control system is not effective in achieving the desired objective. Also the system is widely abused and leads to corruption, delays and inefficiency" (Government of India: 1990). One early step that was undertaken as part of the structural reform process was to dispense with licensing. Changes in foreign trade policy focussed on reducing the tariff rates and dismantling quantitative controls over imports. The tariff rates have been brought down in stages. Some caution in this regard had become necessary to enable the Indian industries set up behind high protective tariff walls to adjust to the changed situation. The policy towards foreign investment underwent a significant change with foreign investors given the freedom to own majority shareholding over a wide spectrum of industries.

Without going into details, the common thread running through the various policy measures introduced since 1991 has been the improvement of the efficiency of the system. The thrust of the New Economic Policy has been towards creating a more competitive environment in the economy as a means to improving the productivity and efficiency of the system. This was to be achieved by removing the barriers to entry and the restrictions on the growth of firms. While the Industrial Policy of 1992 sought to bring about a greater competitive environment domestically, the counterpart Trade Policy set out in the same year, sought to improve international competitiveness subject to the degree of protection offered by the tariffs. The private sector was to be given a larger space to operate in as much as some of the areas, reserved exclusively earlier for the public sector were now to be opened to the private sector. In these areas, the public sector would have to compete with the private sector, even though the public sector might continue to play the dominant role in the foreseeable future. What was sought to be achieved was the improvement in the functioning of the various entities, whether they were in the private or in the public sector.

In the New Industrial Policy 1991, industrial licensing will henceforth be abolished for all industries except these specified irrespective of level of investment (Ch. 21)

These specified industries will continue to be subject to compulsory licensing for reasons related to security and strategic concerns, social reasons, problems related to safety and overriding environmental issues, manufactures of products of hazardous nature and the articles of elitist consumption. The exemption from licensing will be particularly helpful to the many dynamic small and medium entrepreneurs who had been unnecessarily hampered by the licensing system.

Industrial Growth

Having looked into the industrial control regime and the performance of the industrial licensing system. Let us now look at the industrial growth since independence – the rate and pattern of growth and the structural changes.

Since independence, the share of industry has increased substantially from 11.8 per cent of GDP in 1950-51 to 24.6 per cent in 1990-91. Secondly, the composition of industry has undergone great transformation. The share of Capital Goods in industrial value added increased steadily at a high pace from 4.7 per cent in 1956 to 23.7 per cent in 1990. The share of Basic Goods increased relatively moderately, from 22.3 per cent to 38.4 per cent. Consumer Goods group declined considerably in relative importance, with the share in industrial value added falling from 48.4 per cent in 1956 to 20.5 per cent in 1990.[1]

Phases of Industrial Growth

One can identify three distinct phases of industrial growth in India since the planning era. The first phase of rapid growth ends from 1956-1965. The second phase of slow growth or deceleration extends from 1965-66 to 1979-80. The third phase is a phase of recovery and revival of growth since 1980s. Krishna has summarised the various explanatory hypotheses and has also reviewed the available empirical evidence bearing upon the alternative hypotheses.

During the period 1959-60 to 1965-66, value added in organised industry grew at the rate of 8.0 per cent per annum. The growth rate declined to 5.7 per cent in the period 1966-67 to 1989-90. The corresponding growth rates for the registered manufacturing were 7.6 and 5.5 per cent. In capital goods and basic goods the decline was very pronounced from 15.4 to 6.6 and 11.0 to 5.0 per cent per annum, respectively. Consumer goods and its sub-category consumer non-durables experienced slight acceleration. In Intermediate goods and consumer durables, there was mild deceleration. Thus deceleration was largely confined to heavy industry which accounted for about 50 per cent of value added in industry in 1979-80.

Ahluwalia (1985) after empirically examining different hypotheses identified four factors:

(i) slow-down in public investment

(ii) poor management of the infrastructure sector

(iii) slow growth of agricultural incomes, and

(iv) restrictive industrial and trade policies.

---

1. Krishna, K.L., Industrial Growth and Diversification in Uma Kapila (ed.), op. cit.

However, Ahluwalia did not carry out any econometric exercise to establish her thesis. Rangarajan (1982), Lahiri et al (1984), Ray (1991) Mukhopadhyay (1992), Kavita Rao (1993) and Balakrishnan (1995) conducted econometric exercises to verify the various hypotheses. These exercises established that one or more of the following factors, public investment, agricultural performance, infrastructure, the policy of import substitution and domestic terms of trade turned out to be significant for the different industry groups. The over all inference from the various studies is that the demand constraints were more important than supply constraints.

In the 1980s, the industrial sector fared impressively in this decade, compared to the preceding 15-year period. The annual rates of growth for manufacturing, registered manufacturing and unregistered manufacturing were 7.0, 8.1 and 5.8, respectively.

In the first six years of the eighties, consumer durables recorded a growth rate of 14.2 per cent, while capital goods recorded a relatively modest growth of 7.8 per cent per annum.

Empirical evidence suggests that the explanations for the resurgence of growth in the 1980s are similar to those for the deceleration after the mid-sixties.

Industrial Growth in the 90s

The manufacturing sector witnessed an upward trend in growth rates registering growth rate of 8 to 9 per cent in the second half of 80s. In the 90s, the period immediately following the reforms was marked by low growth rates. However, the growth rates quickly recovered. After a decline of 0.8 per cent in 1991-92, the rate of growth climbed to 2.2 per cent in 1992-93, 5.5 per cent in 1993-94, 8.6 per cent in 1994-95 and an estimated 12 per cent in 1995-96. However since 1996-97, deceleration in industrial sector has set in.

The major policy changes initiated in the industrial sector since July 1991 viz removal of entry barriers, reduction of areas reserved exclusively for public sector, rationalisation of the approach towards MRTP, liberalisation of foreign investment policy, far reaching liberalisation of import policy with respect to intermediates and capital goods may have all contributed to the upsurge in industrial growth.

Industrial production registered a higher growth of 6.6 per cent in 1997-98 compared to the 5.6 per cent in 1996-97. The improvement in 1997-98 was due to better performance of mining and electricity generation, which recorded higher growth rates of 5.9 per cent and 6.6 per cent compared to 2.2 per cent and 4 per cent respectively in 1996-97. Higher growth of mining could be attributed to improved performance of crude oil (2.9 per cent in 1997-98 compared to -6.5 per cent in 1996-97) and that of electricity generation to improved performance of hydro-electricity (8.2 per cent in 1997-98 compared to -5.4 per cent in 1996-97). The growth of manufacturing in 1997-98 at 6.6 per cent remained almost at the level of the previous year. In 1998-99 year, industrial production has registered a growth rate of 3.9 per cent during April-December 1998, lower than the 6.8 per cent growth in April-December 1997. The low growth is noticeable in mining and manufacturing sectors. Electricity generation has posted a higher growth in the current year (Table–1).

After a relatively modest performance in 1998-99, the Indian industry experienced a turnaround. Several macroeconomic and business indicators were showing signs of a broad-based industrial recovery. The cumulative growth of industrial production, as measured by the Index of Industrial Production (IIP), was 6.2 per cent for April-December 1999, significantly higher than the 4.0 per cent of April-December 1998. The higher growth in the 1999-2000 has been largely contributed by the 7.0 per cent growth in manufacturing and the 7.7 per cent growth in electricity. (Table 1)

After a turnaround in 1999-2000, Industrial growth (measured by the Index of Industrial Production) has again slowed down during the year 2000-01 and in 2001-02 registered 2.1 per cent rate of growth against 6.2 per cent in 2000-01.

The industrial deceleration was due to a number of structural and cyclical factors such as:

(i) normal business and investment cycles,

(ii) a lack of both domestic and external demand,

(iii) continuing high real interest rates,

(iv) infrastructure bottlenecks in power and transport,

(v) lack of reforms in land and labour markets,

(vi) inherent adjustment lags resulting from industrial restructuring through merger and acquisitions,

(vii) and delays in establishing appropriate institutional and regulatory frameworks in some key sectors.

TABLE – 1

ANNUAL GROWTH RATES OF INDUSTRIAL PRODUCTION IN MAJOR SECTORS OF INDUSTRY

(BASED ON THE INDEX OF INDUSTRIAL PRODUCTION)*

BASE: 1993-94=100

(per cent)

Period	*Mining & Quarrying*	*Manufacturing*	*Electricity*	*Overall*
Weight	**10.4**	**79.4**	**10.2**	**100.0**
1995-96	9.7	14.1	8.1	13.0
1996-97	-1.9	7.3	4.0	6.1
1997-98	6.9	6.7	6.6	6.7
1998-99	-0.8	4.4	6.5	4.1
1999-00	1.0	7.1	7.3	6.7
2000-01	2.8	5.3	4.0	5.0
2001-02	1.2	2.9	3.1	2.7
Apr-Nov.				
1995-96	11.6	13.7	9.6	13.1
1996-97	-1.0	9.8	3.7	8.0
1997-98	6.1	6.9	6.4	6.8
1998-99	0.5	4.1	6.2	3.9
1999-00	0.5	6.6	8.2	6.2
2000-01	3.6	6.3	4.9	6.0
2001-02	0.7	2.6	2.5	2.5
2002-03	5.7	5.4	4.0	5.3

* Revised index of industrial production

Source: Economic Survey 2002-03.

The difficulties caused by internal constraints were accentuated by the slow growth in the world economy, which contributed to a substantial slowdown in manufactured exports. While the government was in the process of seeking a consensus for further reforms, external factors such as the attack on the World Trade Centre in September 2001 and related events slowed down the recovery through lack of external demand and adverse impact on air transport, communications and tourism.

Comparative Growth Rates in the '80s and the '90s

The average growth rate of Industrial sector (measured by the Index of Industrial Production) during the period 1992-93 to 1999-2000 was lower than that observed during the period 1980-81 to 1991-92. The growth rate was lower in all the three sectors i.e. manufacturing, mining and electricity. In terms of use-based classification also there was a lower growth rate in basic and capital goods. However, the GDP from manufacturing sector at constant prices showed higher growth rates during the period 1992-93 to 1999-2000 when compared to the period 1980-81 to 1991-92 at the aggregate (total) level and amongst both registered and unregistered segments (Table 2).

TABLE – 2

COMPARATIVE GROWTH RATES IN THE INDUSTRIAL SECTOR 1980-2000

Parameter	*Avg. Annual growth rate (1980-81 to 1991-92)**	*Avg. Annual growth rate (1992-93 to 1999-2000)**
Index of Industrial Production		
General	7.8	6.0
Manufacturing	7.6	6.3
Mining	8.4	3.3
Electricity	9.0	6.6
Use-based classification		
Basic goods	7.4	6.1
Capital goods	9.4	5.9
Intermediate goods	4.9	9.1
Consumer goods	6.0	6.3
of which		
(i) Consumer durables	10.8	11.2
(ii) Consumer non-durables	5.3	5.1
GDP-Manufacturing at 1993-94 prices		
Total	6.1	7.4
Registered	6.8	8.1
Unregistered	5.0	6.2

* Simple average of the annual growth rates.
Source : Economic Survey, 2000-01.

The use-based classification, shown in Table 3, shows that in addition to capital goods, consumer non-durables were also an area showing sharp growth: an acceleration from 3.2 per cent in April-November 2001 to 12.7 per cent in 2002-03. However in 2003-04 the growth rate is 5.7 per cent.

TABLE – 3

GROWTH RATES OF INDUSTRIAL PRODUCTION BY USE-BASED CLASSIFICATION

(per cent)

Sectors	*(Weight)*	*1996-97*	*1997-98*	*1998-99*	*1999-2000*	*2000-01*	*2001-02*	*2002-03*	*2003-04*
Basic Goods	35.5	3.0	6.9	1.6	5.5	3.7	2.6	4.9	5.4
Capital Goods	9.3	11.5	5.8	12.6	6.9	1.8	-3.4	10.5	12.7
Intermediate Goods	26.5	8.1	8.0	6.1	8.8	4.7	1.5	3.9	6.2
Consumer Goods	28.7	6.2	5.5	2.2	5.7	8.0	6.0	7.1	7.1
of which									
Consumer Durables	5.4	4.6	7.8	5.6	14.1	14.5	11.5	-6.3	11.6
Consumer Non-Durables	23.3	6.6	4.8	1.2	3.2	5.8	4.1	12.0	5.7
IIP (Index of Industrial Production)	100.0	6.1	6.7	4.1	6.7	5.0	2.7	5.7	6.9

Note: The indices are based on revised itemwise weights.
Source: Economic Survey 2003-04.

This recovery in industrial output appears to reflect a variety of factors, including: the lagged effect of the strong rabi harvest of the previous year, improvements in infrastructure, the demand impact of public investment, and improvement in exports through the recovery of the US and EU markets after the September 11, 2001 incidents in the United States.

Relative Contribution of Sectors to Total Production

Changes in the relative contribution of different sectors to the general Index of Industrial Production reflect another dimension of the structural changes in industrial production. Data presented in Table 4 reveal that the relative contribution of the manufacturing sector rose from 70.0 per cent during the 'eighties to 81.6 per cent during the 'nineties. However, in case of mining and quarrying, there was a noticeable decline. This was reflected in the changes in the weights assigned to different sector in the construction of IIP series. The weight for the manufacturing sector rose from 77.1 per cent in the earlier series of IIP with base 1980-81=100, to 79.36 per cent in the current series with base 1993-94=100. Correspondingly, the relative weights of mining and quarrying and electricity sectors declined from 11.46 per cent and 11.43 per cent in the old series to 10.47 per cent and 10.17 per cent, respectively, in the new series (Table 5).

TABLE – 4

RELATIVE CONTRIBUTION OF SECTORS TO THE INDUSTRIAL PRODUCTION

(Per cent)

Sector	*1981-82 to 1990-91 (Average)*	*1992-93 to 1998-99* (Average)*
1	*2*	*3*
i) Manufacturing	70.0	81.6
ii) Electricity	14.4	14.4
iii) Mining and Quarrying	15.6	4.0
General Index	**100.0**	**100.0**

* The data relating to 1991-92 were excluded in this period because production was almost stagnant.

TABLE – 5

SECTOR-WISE WEIGHTING PATTERN

NIC Division	*Sector*	*Base: 1970=100*	*Base: 1980-81=100*	*Base: 1993-94=100*
1	*2*	*3*	*4*	*5*
Division 1	Mining & Quarrying	9.69	11.46	10.47
Division 2&3	Manufacturing	81.08	77.11	79.36
Division 4	Electricity	9.23	11.43	10.17
Total	**General Index**	**100.0**	**100.0**	**100.0**

During the 'nineties, while the relative contributions of basic and capital goods sectors declined, there was a rise in those of intermediate and consumer goods sectors (Table 6). In the new series (Base: 1993-94=100), the weights of basic and capital goods sectors were reduced and those of intermediate goods and consumer goods sectors were raised.

TABLE – 6

RELATIVE CONTRIBUTION OF SECTORS TO INDUSTRIAL PRODUCTION (USE-BASED CLASSIFICATION)

(Per cent)

Sector	*1981-82 to 1990-91 (Average)*	*1992-93 to 1998-99* (Average)*
1	*2*	*3*
i) Basic Goods	43.6	35.8
ii) Capital Goods	25.0	7.1
iii) Intermediate Goods	14.6	35.2
iv) Consumer Goods	16.8	21.9
General Index	**100.0**	**100.0**

* The data relating to 1991-92 were excluded in this period because production was almost stagnant.

The relatively low contributions of the basic and capital goods sectors to overall industrial output in the 'nineties reflect, among others, the impact of trade liberalisation, particularly imports, and of financial liberalisation that enabled the corporate sector to make financial gains through 'other income', as also the lack of competitiveness requiring industrial restructuring and modernisation of technologies in a number of industries.

Profile of Industrial Growth

Fall in Potential as well as Actual Industrial Growth

As per the analysis given in RBI Report on Currency and Finance 2001-02 the actual industrial growth during the latter phase of the reform period fell below the potential growth, indicating a decline in the capacity utilisation over the medium-term. Besides, there have been distinct signs of the potential growth itself slowing down compared with the first phase of the reform period and the latter half of the preceding decade. This can be attributed to a deceleration in growth across all sub-sectors, i.e., registered manufacturing, mining and quarrying as well as electricity, gas and water supply. An analysis of industrial slowdown as per the use-based classification reveals that while the consumer goods industries sustained growth momentum to some extent during the latter part of the reform period, substantial decline in growth was witnessed in basic and intermediate goods segments. The demand for these goods in the face of sustained consumption demand in the latter period of the reforms implies that industry may be undertaking inventory adjustment created by the initial phase of capacity creation and overproduction. Although production of capital goods witnessed an improved average growth during the latter phase of the reform period, a rapid decline was observed from 2000-01 onwards, indicating the impact of weakening investment demand in the economy.

Shift in Favour of Registered Manufacturing

The 1990s witnessed a shift in the production structure in favour of the registered manufacturing as against the unregistered one. While the share of registered manufacturing in industrial GDP increased from 38.6 per cent in 1990-91 to 41.5 per cent in 2001-02, the share of unregistered manufacturing declined from 22.5 per cent to 21.6 per cent during the same period. Even within registered manufacturing, traditional industries such as textile, jute and other vegetable fibre textiles witnessed a decline in their respective shares in the reform period while the modern segments like metal products and electrical machinery forged ahead. The relatively low growth in productivity, lack of technological improvements and reduced access to credit have, inter alia, possibly acted as a more binding constraint in respect of the traditional segment vis-a-vis the modern one.

Decline in Employment Growth in Organised Manufacturing

During the 1980s, although the average growth in value added in the manufacturing sector was relatively high at 7.3 per cent, it was not reflected in the commensurate growth in employment mainly on account of reduction in employment in cotton textiles and jute textiles, which were high employment generating industries. The employment growth in the organised manufacturing sector rose to 2.3 per cent in the first half of the 1990s from 0.8 per cent in the 1980s. This may be attributed to increased employment in small and medium size factories as a result of liberalisation of industrial and trade policies (Goldar, 2000). The deceleration in the manufacturing growth rate in the latter half of the 1990s had, however, adverse implications on employment growth. This was visible in employment growth turning negative (-2.1 per cent) in the latter half of the 1990s.

The Stagnant Share of Manufacturing Sector

While the emerging production structure of industry bodes well for the economy, the stagnant share of manufacturing at around 17 per cent of GDP during the 1990s is a matter of concern. Other emerging market economies have exhibited a rising share of manufacturing and industry at similar levels of developments, with these sectors being the lead growth centres. The contribution of industry to GDP in such developing countries is placed in the range of 28 per cent to 51 per cent in 2000, much higher than 25 per cent in India. As a matter of fact, the fast growing East Asian countries witnessed a rise in the share of industry in GDP between 1990 and 2000 (Table 7). The differences in the nature of industrial policy and their implementation are found to be critical to the industrial success of such countries. Important elements of industrial policy in these countries included flexibility of labour use, build up of large and efficient social infrastructure, favourable attitude towards international technology transfer, substantial investment in public technology institutions and competitive pressures resulting from exports. Given the stagnating share of industry in GDP in India, the issues of manufacturing slowdown, productivity and competitiveness need further examination, which is attempted next.

TABLE – 7

SHARE OF INDUSTRY IN GDP: CROSS-COUNTRY COMPARISON

(Per cent)

Country	*1990*	*2000*
	1	*2*
India	24	25
China	42	51
Indonesia	38	47
Korea, Rep.	43	43
Malaysia	42	45
Thailand	37	40
Brazil	39	29
Argentina	36	28
Mexico	28	28

Source : World Development Indicators 2002, World Bank.

The Manufacturing Slowdown

The loss of momentum in manufacturing growth, which occured in the latter part of 1996, has since continued during the second phase of the reform period. At the disaggregated two-digit level, the manufacturing sector witnessed substantial deceleration in 11 industry groups with a combined weight of 64 per cent in the manufacturing production. Six industry groups with a combined weight of 36 per cent withstood the slowdown and posted an accelerated growth during 1996-2002. However, in view of their relatively low weight, the manufacturing sector, as a whole, registered a slowdown.

Factors Causing the Industrial Slowdown: Some Hypotheses[2]

A number of hypotheses in terms of cyclical and structural factors have been put forward to explain the slowdown in the manufacturing activity during the latter phase of the reform period. The explanations provided, however, fall short of giving a satisfactory answer to what has led to the manufacturing slowdown and its persistence. The onset of slowdown is often attributed to the saturation of the pent-up domestic demand of 'once-for-all' nature for a host of import-intensive goods, which could be domestically assembled or produced following trade liberalisation (Chandrasekhar and Ghosh, 2002). The short-run increase in domestic demand was seemingly facilitated by easy access to credit, including consumer credit in the wake of financial liberalisation. Once that pent-up demand of transitory nature was satisfied, industry entered the phase of slowdown in the absence of demand support - domestic or exports. However, the huge capacity-build up noticed in the first phase of the reform period runs counter to the momentary surge in demand that was not likely to be sustained in the long run.

Another hypothesis on the onset of slowdown relates to the 'credit crunch' which, it is argued, triggered off the manufacturing slowdown (Sen et al, 1997 and Desai, 2001). The unexpected and temporary tightening of liquidity in money markets during 1995-96, resulting from large dollar sales by the Reserve Bank to contain volatility in the forex market, was mistaken to be an expression of deflationary credit policy (Acharya, 2002).

Yet another factor was the role of the corporate sector. The proportion of corporate funds locked up in inventories and receivables went up steadily, leading to a scarcity of working capital (Sen et al,

---

2. This section draws from RBI Report on Currency and Finance 2001-02.

1997). Further, the proportion of funds invested in financial instruments, which had hovered around 5 per cent during 1985-1993, crossed the level of 10 per cent subsequently. The depressed stock market conditions in 1995-96 inhibited the redemption of financial instruments. The rising interest rates may also have been prohibitive for new projects and investment, particularly, in the informal sector which has limited access to funds (Shetty, 1997a and 2001b). Reinforced by the increased borrowings by the Government, the weighted average lending rate of scheduled commercial banks rose to 17.1 per cent in 1995-96 from 16.1 per cent in 1994-95. In real terms, the rate shot up to 8.5 per cent in 1995-96 from an all-time low (for the 1990s) of 3.9 per cent in the preceding year.

Infrastructure Constraints in the Industrial Sector

The industrial performance continues to be hampered by physical infrastructure bottlenecks with the demand-supply imbalances persisting and growing during the reform period. A worrisome feature of infrastructure development has been the declining trend in potential output of a number of basic activities such as steel, coal, cargo handling and freight loading. There are, however, signs of improvement for a few sectors, like power and communication. With the initiation of power sector reforms, the demand-supply gap for power has witnessed a decline to 7.9 per cent during the reform period from 8.9 per cent during the pre-reform period. Notably, the power deficit remained high at around 9 per cent during the mid-1990s when the industrial sector was growing at a faster rate. The downtrend in demand-supply gap for telecommunications accompanied by a decline in unit cost reflects the regulatory reforms and increased competition arising from private sector participation.

The deteriorating infrastructure services represent a direct fall out of shrinkage in infrastructure investment in the context of grossly inadequate internal resources of public infrastructure entities and dwindling Plan outlay for infrastructure. The real capital formation in electricity, gas and water supply declined to 2.6 per cent of GDP during the 1990s from 2.9 per cent during the preceding decade (Table 8). A similar trend was observed for railways. Within the 1990s also, there was a decline in the real gross capital formation in sectors like electricity, gas and water supply, and the railways between the first and the second half. In contrast, communication witnessed an improvement in the reform period following the market based pricing of services and better regulatory framework. The investment in infrastructure sector as a whole has shown clear decline of one percentage point of GDP between the first and the second halves of the 1990s. This decline can be attributed to declining government investment on infrastructure – a fall out of the prevailing fiscal situation – which was a major contributing factor for the economic slowdown in the latter part of the 1990s.

The pace of public investment in infrastructure slowed down substantially during the reform period on account of rising fiscal imbalances of the Government, both at the Centre and the States. As a result, public investment in major infrastructure sectors declined in real terms during the reform period. The rates of return from infrastructure services extended by the Government continue to be abysmally low, constraining the ability to generate internal resources for investment. For instance, the rate of return on investment for the State power sector deteriorated from (-)12.7 per cent in 1991-92 to (-)32.8 per cent in 2001-02. These essentially indicate lack of required structural reforms in the power sector in India, notably the near absence of market based pricing.

TABLE – 8

REAL GROSS CAPITAL FORMATION IN INFRASTRUCTURE SECTORS

(Per cent of GDP)

Period Averages	*Electricity Gas and Water Supply*	*Construction*	*Transport, Storage and Communication*	*Of which: Railways*	*Communication*	*Total Infrastructure*	*Total Gross Capital Formation*
	1	*2*	*3*	*4*	*5*	*6*	*7*
1980-81 to 1984-85	2.8	0.5	2.5	0.6	0.4	5.8	25.5
1985-86 to 1989-90	3.1	0.4	2.9	0.7	0.5	6.4	25.4
1990-91 to 1994-95	2.9	0.4	3.0	0.6	0.7	6.3	24.7
1995-96 to 1999-00	2.3	0.4	2.6	0.4	0.7	5.3	25.8
1980-81 to 1989-90	2.9	0.5	2.7	0.7	0.4	6.1	25.4
1990-91 to 1999-00	2.6	0.4	2.8	0.5	0.7	5.8	25.2

Source : National Accounts Statistics, Government of India.

Response of the private sector to the reform process has not been adequate to offset the declining public investment on account of inadequate institutional reforms, lack of clarity regarding infrastructure development priorities, non-transparency in project outsourcing processes, and numerous time consuming clearances. In the absence of rationalisation of user charges, the infrastructure sectors such as railways, public transport, power continue to suffer from the levy of inadequate user charges, thereby putting off potential private participation. Keeping in view the long gestation period for infrastructure projects, the issue of initial risk sharing by the Government assumes importance, given the inability of the private sector to assess the long-term risks.

Summing Up

The industrial sector in the reform period (1992-93 to 2001-02) reported a slowdown in all its major segments. The manufacturing slowdown noticed since the latter part of 1996 had its origin in the cyclical slowdown of exports and subdued agricultural performance. The slowdown persisted in the subsequent period due to inadequate industrial restructuring and the resultant loss of competitiveness. The lack of institutional and structural reforms, which affected the pace and content of industrial restructuring operates as the major binding constraint on manufacturing growth in a liberalised trade regime. The manufacturing slowdown has possibly been reinforced by the observed decline in productivity growth in the 1990s and the cyclical downturn in demand, both in the domestic and external markets.

Industrial performance continues to be hampered by physical infrastructure bottlenecks with demand-supply imbalances persisting during the reform period. The deteriorating infrastructure services have been a direct fall-out of shrinkage in infrastructure investment in the context of inadequate availability of internal resources of public infrastructure entities and dwindling Plan outlay earmarked for infrastructure. The declining public investment in infrastructure has not been offset by the private investment on account of inadequate institutional reforms. There are, however, signs of improvement in a few sectors, like communication.

The credit flow from the banking system has significantly slowed down for SSIs and medium and large industries in the second phase of the reform period. The deceleration has been more pronounced for the SSIs. Besides, disbursements from the all India financial institutions

(AIFIs) to industry have witnessed a considerable slowdown. Such developments on the credit front need to be assessed in the context of increasing recourse to internal resources and private placement by corporates, high real cost of credit coupled with its downward inflexibility, and prudential requirements such as capital adequacy and provisioning norms for banks and financial institutions, as well as the existing structure of the credit delivery system. The high real interest rate for industrial sector, ruling above industrial growth rate, also seems to have inhibited investment and capacity build-up in industry.

The increase in competition resulting from the reform measures viz., delicensing, opening up of trade has had a mixed impact on the industrial sector. This is evidenced amply in the fact that the manufacturing inflation in the late 1990s was around 3 per cent as against 10 per cent in the early 1990s. The sharp decline in the manufacturing prices has impacted adversely on the profit margins of companies. Further, inadequate industrial restructuring has hampered industrial growth. Adequate flexibility in industrial restructuring involves more rapid bankruptcy procedures, easier reallocation of capital, faster transformation of urban land use and flexibility in labour use.

The reservation for SSI producers has created an anomalous situation where foreign producers irrespective of size are able to bring in reserved products but existing SSI producers are not allowed to expand investment and scale to economically efficient levels to compete with imports. Therefore, there is a need for dereservation in select products with strong export potential.

Increase in competition denotes that any rise in the input costs is difficult to cope with. The dwindling public investment on infrastructure in the latter half of the 1990s, caused by deterioration in Government capital expenditure, has clearly impacted on the availability as well as the quality of infrastructure services. Simultaneously the high cost of infrastructure, particularly power and railways freight, has been loaded on to the industry. Together, the prevailing high real interest rates have adversely impacted the price competitiveness of the industrial sector. Exchange rate appreciation witnessed in the late 1990s increased further pressure on the competitiveness. Generally exchange rate adjustments compensate for the rise in input costs, but the large capital inflows into the Indian economy during the late 1990s have prevented such an adjustment.

APPENDIX

Revision of IIP

The index of industrial Production (IIP) is published as a monthly series since 1950. Revisions of IIP are carried out from time to time by shifting the comparison base to a more recent period by reviewing coverage of items/ industries for reflecting changes in the structure of industry. The last revision was effected in 1980-81. The Department of Statistics set up in June 1995 a Technical Advisory Committee (TAC) to examine all technical issues relating to comparable state level IIPs and make recommendations thereon. Subsequently in November 1996, the TAC was entrusted with the responsibility to examine all issues and provide technical guidance in the matter of shifting the base period of IIP. On the recommendations of the TAC, IIP base has been shifted to a more recent period (1993-94). The new series was released on May 26, 1998. The features of the revised IIP series are captured in Box–1.

BOX 1

REVISION OF IIP SERIES

The Background

- The IIP, a measure of the trends of industrial production, is being published as a monthly series since 1950.
- IIP has been revised from time to time by shifting the base year to a more recent period, by reviewing the coverage of items and by effecting improvements in the technique of construction with a view to appropriately reflect the pattern of industrial growth.
- At the time of commencement of the Index in India, the base year was 1946. The base year was subsequently revised at various points of time to 1951, 1956, 1960, 1970 and 1980-81.
- The number of items covered in the monthly series of IIP increased from 35 in 1946 to 88 in 1951 and further to 201, 312 and 352 respectively in 1956, 1960 and 1970. The 1980-81 base series retained the number of items at 352.
- Based on the recommendations of the Technical Advisory Committee (TAC) set up by the Department of Statistics in June 1995, the base year of IIP has now been shifted to 1993-94.

Salient features of the new IIP series

— Items have been selected on the basis of results of ASI (1993-

94), as has been the practice in the past.

— The new series includes 18 items from the small scale sector which also belonged to the 1980-81 series.

— The new series follows NIC 1987 classification as compared to NIC 1970 followed in 1980-81 series.

— A comparative illustration of the number of items and the weighting diagrams for broad sectors (mining, manufacturing and electricity) of IIP for the 1980-81 and 1993-94 series is provided below:

	No. of Items		Weights	
Broad Sector	1980-81	1993-94	1980-81	1993-94
Manufacturing	290	478	77.11	79.36
Mining	61	64	11.46	10.47
Electricity	1	1	11.43	10.17
Total	**352**	**543***	**100.00**	**100.00**

* Clubbed into 287 groups: Manufacturing-285, Mining-1 and Electricity-1.

— Due to adoption of NIC 1987 classification, erstwhile groups 30 (Rubber, plastic, petroleum and coal products) and 31 (Basic chemical products except products of petroleum and coal) of IIP 1980-81 have interchanged places in the revised series. One new group (24: wool, silk and man-made electrical machinery) and 36 (Electrical machinery, apparatus, appliances and supplies and parts) have been amalgemated under the heading 'Machinery and equipment other than Transport equipment'.

21

Industrial Policy

THE 1991 Industrial Policy States that "the goals and objectives set out for the nation on the eve of Independence, namely, the rapid agricultural and industrial development of our country, rapid expansion of opportunities for gainful employment, progressive reduction of social and economic disparities, removal of poverty and attainment of self-reliance, remain as valid today as at the time when Pandit Jawaharlal Nehru first set them out before the nation. Any industrial policy must contribute to the realisation of these goals and objectives at an accelerated pace."

In 1948, immediately after independence, government introduced the first Industrial Policy Resolution. This outlined the approach to industrial growth and development. It emphasised the importance to the economy of securing a continuous increase in production and ensuring its equitable distribution. After the adoption of the Constitution and the socio-economic goals, the industrial policy was comprehensively revised and adopted in 1956.

Industrial Resolution of 1956

The Industrial Policy Resolution of 1948 was followed by the Industrial Policy Resolution of 1956 which had as its objective the acceleration of the rate of economic growth and the speeding up of industrialisation as a means of achieving a socialist pattern of society. In 1956, capital was scarce and the base of entrepreneurship not strong enough. Hence, the 1956 Industrial Policy Resolution gave primacy to the role of the state to assume a predominant and direct responsibility for industrial development.

Important Provisions of the 1956 Resolution were:–

(i) New Classification of Industries: The resolution laid down three categories which bear a close resemblance to the earlier classification,

but were more sharply defined and were broader in coverages as to the role of the State. These categories were:-

(a) *Schedule A*: Those which were to be an exclusive responsibility of the state;

(b) *Schedule B*: Those which were to be progressively state-owned and in which the state would generally set up new enterprises, but in which private enterprise would be expected only to supplement the effort of the state; and

(c) *Schedule C*: All the remaining industries and their future development would, in general be left to the initiative and enterprise of the private sector.

Under Schedule 'A' were listed seventeen industries: arms and ammunition, atomic energy, iron and steel, heavy castings and forgings of iron and steel; heavy machinery required for iron and steel production, mining, machine tool manufactures; etc. heavy electrical industries, coal; mineral oils, mining; iron ore and other important minerals like copper, lead and zinc; aircraft; air transport, railway transport, ship-building; telephone, telegraph and wireless equipment; generation and distribution of electricity.

Under Schedule 'B', twelve industries were listed: other mining industries, aluminium and other non-ferrous metals not included in Schedule A; machine tools, ferroy-alloys and tool steels, the chemical industry; antibiotics and other essential drugs; fertilizers; synthetic rubber, carbonization of coal; chemical pulp; road transport and sea transport.

The Schedule 'C' category industries consisted of the rest of the industries and had to fit into the framework of social and economic policy of the state and be subject to control in terms of the Industries (Development and Regulation) Act and other relevant legislations.

Inspite of this clear cut grouping of industries under three schedules, categories were not watertight compartments and room for exceptions could be made. In appropriate cases, private units might produce an item in category 'A' for meeting the industry's own requirements or as by-products. Further, heavy industries in the public sector could obtain some of their requirements of higher components from the private sector while private sector in turn would rely for many of its needs on the public sector. Moreover, the State reserved the right to enter category 'C', which would normally be reserved for the private enterprise, when the needs of planning required or for other important reasons. Though the State was now to act as the senior partner unlike under the 1948 policy, the public and the private sector were still expected to work closely together. The basic objective was to create a mixed economy in India.

(ii) Fair and non-discriminatory treatment for the private sector: In order that the private sector may feel confident and function efficiently the State was to facilitate and encourage the development of industries in the private sector by ensuring the development of transport, power and other services, and by appropriate fiscal and other measures. When there exist in the same industry both private and publicly owned units, it would continue to be the policy of the state to give full and non-discriminatory treatment to both of them.

(iii) Encouragement to village and small-scale enterprises: The State would support cottage and village and small-scale enterprises by restricting volume of production in the large-scale sector, by differential taxation, or by direct subsidies. The state would concentrate on measures designed to improve the competitive strength of the small scale producer by constantly improving and modernising the techniaue of production.

(iv) Removing regional disparities: The Resolution stressed the necessity of reducing the regional disparities in levels of development in order that industrialisation may benefit the country as a whole. The resolution fully supported the idea that only by securing a balanced and coordinated development of the industrial and the agricultural economy in each region, can the entire country attain higher standards of living.

(v) The need for the provision of amenities for labour: The Resolution also recognised that in a socialist democracy, labour is a partner in the common task of development and should participate in it with enthusiasm and for this the maintenance of industrial peace is one of the essential conditions. It stressed that the living and working conditions of workers should be improved and their standard of efficiency raised.

(vi) Attitude towards foreign capital: The Resolution, made it amply clear, "that as a rule, the major interest in ownership and effective control, should always be in Indian hands. In all cases, however, the training of suitable Indian personnel for the purpose of eventually replacing foreign experts will be insisted upon." Thus, while recognising the need for foreign capital in the industrialisation of the economy, the government insisted upon the progressive Indianisation of foreign concerns.

To meet new challenges, from time to time, the Industrial Policy of 1956 was modified through statements in 1973, 1977 and 1980.

The Industrial Policy statement of 1973, inter-alia, identified high-priority industries where investment from large industrial houses and foreign companies would be permitted.

The industrial policy statement of 1977 laid emphasis on decentralisation and on the role of small-scale, tiny and cottage industries.

The industrial policy statement of 1980 focussed attention on the need for promoting competition in the domestic market, technological upgradation and modernisation. The policy laid the foundation for an increasingly competitive export base and for encouraging foreign investment in high-technology areas.

These policies created a climate for rapid industrial growth in the country. Thus on the eve of the Seventh Five-Year Plan, a broad-based infrastructure had been built up. Basic industries had been established. A high degree of self-reliance in a large number of items—raw materials, intermediates, finished goods—had been achieved. New growth centres of industrial activity had emerged, as also a new generation of entrepreneurs. A large number of engineers, technicians and skilled workers had also been trained.

The Seventh Plan recognised the need to consolidate on these strengths and to take initiatives to prepare Indian industry to respond effectively to the emerging challenges. A number of policy and procedural changes were introduced in 1985 and 1986 under the leadership of Rajiv Gandhi aimed at increasing productivity, reducing costs and improving quality. The accent was on opening the domestic market to increased competition and to make our industry ready to stand on its own in the face of international competition. The public sector was freed from a number of constraints and given a larger measure of autonomy. The technological and managerial modernisation of industry was pursued as the key instrument for increasing productivity and improving our competitiveness in the world. The net result of all these changes was that Indian industry grew by an impressive average annual growth rate of 8.5 per cent in the Seventh Plan period.

LIBERALISATION OF THE 90's

New Industrial Policy - 1991

The 1991 policy[1] states, "the major objectives of the new industrial policy package will be to build on the gains already made, correct the distortions or weaknesses that may have crept in, maintain a sustained growth in productivity and gainful employment and attain international competitiveness. The pursuit of these objectives will be tempered by the need to preserve the environment and ensure the efficient use of available resources. All sectors of industry whether small, medium or large, belonging to the public, private or cooperative sector will be encouraged to grow and improve on their past performance. Government's policy will be continuity with change."

In pursuit of the above objectives, government has decided to take a series of initiatives in respect of the policies relating to the following areas:

a. Industrial licensing
b. Foreign investment
c. Foreign technology agreements
d. Public sector policy
e. MRTP Act

Industrial Licensing

Industrial Licensing is governed by the Industries (Development and Regulation) Act, 1951. The Industrial Policy Resolution of 1956 identified the following three categories of industries: those that would be reserved for development in the public sector, those that would be permitted for development through private enterprise with or without state participation, and those in which investment initiatives would ordinarily emanate from private entrepreneurs.

Over the years, keeping in view the changing industrial scene in the country, the policy has undergone modifications. Industrial licensing policy and procedures have also been liberalised from time to time. A full realisation of the industrial potential of the country calls for a continuation of this process of change.

---

1. Full text of the Policy in Indian Economy Since Independence (ed) Uma Kapila, Ch. 31, (1999-2000 edition)

In the above context, industrial licensing will henceforth be abolished for all industries, except those specified, irrespective of levels of investment.

These specified industries, will continue to be subject to compulsory licensing for reasons related to security and strategic concerns, social reasons, problems related to safety and over riding environmental issues, manufacture of products of hazardous nature and articles of elitist consumption.

The exemption from licensing will be particularly helpful to the many dynamic small and medium entrepreneurs who have been unnecessarily hampered by the licensing system.

"As a whole, the Indian economy will benefit by becoming more competitive, more efficient and modern and will take its rightful place in the world of industrial progress," states the 1991 Industrial Policy.

Foreign Investment

While freeing Indian industry from official controls, opportunities for promoting foreign investment in India should also be fully exploited.

This is particularly necessary in the changing global scenario of industrial and economic cooperation marked by mobility of capital. The government will, therefore, welcome foreign investment which is in the interest of the country's industrial development.

In order to invite foreign investment in high priority industries requiring large investments and advanced technology, it has been decided to provide approval for direct foreign investment upto 51 per cent foreign equity in such industries. There shall be no bottlenecks of any kind in this process. This group of industries has generally been known as the "appendix industries" and are areas in which FERA companies have already been allowed to invest on a discretionary basis.

This change will go a long way in making Indian policy on foreign investment transparent. Such a framework will make it attractive for companies abroad to invest in India.

Foreign Technology

There is a great need for promoting an industrial environment where the acquisition of technological capability received priority. In the fast changing world of technology the relationship between the suppliers and users of technology must be a continuous one. Such a relationship becomes difficult to achieve when the approval process includes unnecessary governmental interference on a case to case basis involving endemic delays and fostering uncertainty.

With a view to injecting the desired level of technological dynamism in Indian industry, government will provide automatic approval for technology agreements related to high priority industries within specified parameters.

Similar facilities will be available for other industries as well if such agreements do not require the expenditure of free foreign exchange. Indian companies will be free to negotiate the terms of technology transfer with their foreign counterparts according to their own commercial judgement.

Public Sector

The public sector has been central to our philosophy of development. In the pursuit of our development objectives, public ownership and control in critical sectors of the economy has played an important role in preventing the concentration of economic power, reducing regional disparities and ensuring that planned development serves the common good.

The Industrial Policy Resolution of 1956 gave the public sector a strategic role in the economy. Massive investments have been made over the past four decades to build a public sector which has a commanding role in the economy. Today, key sectors of the economy are dominated by mature public enterprises that have successfully expanded production, opened up new areas of technology and built up a reserve of technical competence in a number of areas.

After the initial exuberance of the public sector entering new areas of industrial and technical competence, a number of problems have begun to manifest themselves in many of the public enterprises. Serious problems are observed in the insufficient growth in productivity, poor project management, over manning, lack of continuous technological upgradation, and inadequate attention of R&D and human resource development.

In addition, public enterprises have shown a very low rate of return on the capital invested. This has inhibited their ability to regenerate themselves in terms of new investments as well as in technology development. The result is that many of the public enterprises have become a burden rather than being an asset to the government. The original concept of the public sector has also undergone considerable dilution.

The most striking example is the takeover of sick units from the private sector. This category of public sector units accounts for almost one third of the total losses of central public enterprises. Another category of public enterprises, which does not fit into the original idea of the public sector being at the commanding heights of the economy, is the plethora of public enterprises which are in the consumer goods and services sectors.

It is time, therefore, that the government adopts a new approach to public enterprises. There must be a greater commitment to the support of public enterprises which are essential for the operation of the industrial economy. Measures must be taken to make these enterprises more growth oriented and technically dynamic. Units which may be faltering at present but are potentially viable must be restructured and given a new lease of life.

The priority areas for growth of public enterprises in the future will be the following: Essential infrastructure goods and services; exploration and exploitation of oil and mineral resources; technology development and building of manufacturing capabilities in areas which are crucial in the long term development of the economy and where private sector investment is inadequate; manufacture of products where strategic considerations predominate such as defence equipment.

At the same time, the public sector will not be barred from entering areas not specifically reserved for it. In view of these considerations, government will review the existing portfolio of public investments with greater realism. This review will be in respect of industries based on low technology, small scale and non-strategic areas, inefficient and unproductive areas, areas with low or nil social considerations or public purpose, and areas where the private sector has developed sufficient expertise and resources.

Government will strengthen those public enterprises which fall in the reserved areas of operation or are in high priority areas or are generating good or reasonable profits. Such enterprises will be provided a much greater degree of management autonomy through the system of memoranda of understanding.

Competition will also be induced in these areas for private sector participation. In the case of selected enterprises, part of government holdings in the equity share capital of these enterprises will be disinvested in order to provide further market discipline to the performance of public enterprises.

M R T P

The thrust of policy will be more on controlling unfair or restrictive business practices. The MRTP Act will be restructured by eliminating the legal requirement for prior governmental approval for expansion of present undertakings and establishment of new undertakings. The provisions relating to merger, amalgamation, and takeover will also be repealed. Similarly, the provisions regarding restrictions on acquisition of and transfer of share will be appropriately incorporated in the Companies Act.

Simultaneously, provisions of the MRTP Act will be strengthened in order to enable to MRTP Commission to take appropriate action in respect of the monopolistic, restrictive and unfair trade practices. The newly empowered MRTP Commission will be encouraged to investigate complaints received from industrial consumers or classes of consumers.

Decisions of the Government

In view of the considerations outlined above, government has decided to take a series of measures to unshackle the Indian industrial economy from the cobwebs of unnecessary bureaucratic control. These measures compliment the other series of measures being taken by government in the areas of trade policy, exchange rate management, fiscal policy, financial sector reform and overall macroeconomic management.

(i) Industrial licensing will be abolished for all projects except for a short list of industries related to security and strategic concerns, social reasons, hazardous chemicals, overriding environmental reasons, and items of elitis consumption. Industries reserved for the small scale sector will continue to be so reserved.

(ii) Areas where security and strategic concerns predominate, will continue to be reserved for the public sector.

(iii) In projects where imported capital goods are required, automatic clearance will be given: a) In cases where foreign exchange availability is ensured through foreign equity, or b) if the CIF value of imported capital goods required is less than 25 per cent of total value (net of taxes) of plant and equipment, upto a maximum value of Rs. 2 crore.

In other cases, imports of capital goods will require clearance from the Secretariat for Industrial Approvals (SIA) now renamed as secretariat for Industrial Assistance in the Department of Industrial Development according to availability of foreign exchange resources.

In locations other than cities of more than 1 million population, there will be no requirement of obtaining industrial approvals from the Central government except for industries subject to compulsory licensing. In respect of cities with population greater than 1 million, industries other than those of a non-polluting nature such as electronics, computer software and printing will be located outside 25 kms of the periphery, except in prior designated industrial areas.

A flexible location policy would be adopted in respect of such cities (with population greater than 1 million) which require industrial regeneration. Zoning and land use regulation and environmental legislation will continue to regulate industrial locations.

Appropriate incentives and the design of investments in infrastructure development will be used to promote the dispersal of industry particularly to rural and backward areas and to reduce congestion in cities. The system of phased manufacturing programmes run on an administrative case by case basis will not be applicable to new projects. Existing projects with such programmes will continue to be governed by them.

Existing units will be provided a new broad banding facility to enable them to produce any article without additional investment. The exemption from licensing will apply to all substantial expansions of existing units. The mandatory convertibility clause will no longer be applicable for term loans from the financial institutions for new projects.

Industrial Policy: Recent Policy Initiatives

The Government has been constantly reviewing the policy framework to bring about improvements to suit the emerging situation. Some of the major policy developments which have taken place in recent years are outlined below:

Industrial Licensing

During the year 1998-99, three industries, viz., i) coal and lignite, ii) petroleum (other than crude) and its distillation products and iii) sugar were delicensed. Accordingly, there are only six industries now under compulsory licensing (Box–1). Two industries, viz., coal and lignite and mineral oils were taken out from the list of industries reserved for the public sector. At present there are only four industries reserved for the public sector (Box–2). Nine items (six from 'farm implements and tools' and three from 'leather') were removed from the list of industries reserved for exclusive manufacture by the Small Scale Industry (SSI). Entries on toys now excludes electronic toys from the purview of reservation. During the year 1998-99, the number of items reserved for the SSI sector stood at 812.

BOX 1

LIST OF INDUSTRIES REQUIRING COMPULSORY INDUSTRIAL LICENSING

1. Distillation and brewing of alcoholic drinks
2. Cigars and cigarettes of tobacco and manufactured tobacco substitute
3. Electronic aerospace and defense equipment; all types
4. Industrial explosives including detonating fuses, safety fuses, gun powder, nitrocellulose and matches
5. Hazardous chemicals
6. Drugs* and pharmaceuticals (according to the modified Drug Policy issued in September, 1994 and subsequently amended in February, 1999).

* Bulk drugs industry has been delicensed.

Notes: The compulsory licensing provisions would not apply in respect of the small scale units taking up the manufacture of any of the above items reserved for exclusive manufacture in small-scale sector.

BOX 2

LIST OF INDUSTRIES RESERVED FOR THE PUBLIC SECTOR

1. Arms and ammunition and allied items of defence equipment, defence aircraft and warships
2. Atomic energy
3. Railway transport

Location Policy

At present, there is no requirement of obtaining industrial approvals from the Central Government (except for the industries under compulsory licensing) for locations not falling within 25 kms. of cities having population of more than one million. However, industries of no-polluting nature such as electronics, computer software and printing can be located within 25 kms. of the periphery of cities with more than 1 million population. Other industries are permitted only if they are located in Industrial Areas designated prior to July 25, 1991. Further, zoning and land use regulations as well as environmental legislation continue to regulate industrial locations.

Foreign Direct Investment

Foreign direct investment (FDI) directly impacts on output growth in India by augmenting the available investible capital. However, a far more important impact of FDI is through externalities leading to higher efficiency and productivity. FDI typically serves to increase competition in markets, bring new technology into India, and foster skill acquisition amongst domestic labour. FDI by international corporations is also central to the process of India being utilised as a platform for global production chains, which would pave the way for strong exports growth.

The Government is committed to promoting increased flow of Foreign Direct Investment (FDI) for better technology, modernisation, exports and for providing products and services of international standards. Therefore, the policy of the Government has been aimed at encouraging foreign investment, particularly in core infrastructure sectors so as to supplement national efforts. Towards this, the Government has been striving not only to provide greater transparency in the policy and procedures but also to enable a more dynamic and investor-friendly policy framework. At the same time, to provide a level playing field to the domestic industry and also to protect national interests, on the basis of sectoral sensitivities, simultaneous measures have been introduced in the form of dividend balancing, foreign exchange neutrality, foreign equity capital, etc.

Box 3 summarises the initiatives taken in 2002-03 in fostering FDI, which constitute a part of the ongoing effort from 1991 onwards at steadily opening access to India for FDI flows. A committee headed by N.K. Singh, Member, Planning Commission, has drafted a set of proposals for further augmenting these flows, which are currently under evaluation.

BOX 3

MAJOR INITIATIVES TO ATTRACT FDI DURING 2002-03

- FDI upto 100 per cent permitted under the automatic route in the advertising sector. FDI under the automatic route upto 100 per cent is available for film sector and will not be subject to conditions about debt equity ratio, minimum level of equity investment etc.
- FDI upto 100 per cent allowed in tea sector, including tea plantations, permitted subject to compulsory disinvestment of 26 per cent equity in favour of Indian partner within a period of five years and prior approval of the state government in case of any future land use change.
- Re-issuance of ADR/GDR permitted to the extent of ADRs/GDRs which have been redeemed into underlying shares and sold in the domestic market.
- FDI upto 100 per cent permitted with prior approval of the government for development of integrated township, including housing, commercial premises, hotels, resorts and regional level urban infrastructure facilities such as roads and bridges and mass rapid transit system, subject to the guidelines issued vide press note No. 3 (2002 Series) dated January 4, 2002.
- Automatic route of FDI upto 100 per cent allowed in all manufacturing activities in Special Economic Zones, except some of the activities such as arms and ammunitions, explosives and allied items of defence equipment, defence aircrafts and warships, automatic substances, narcotics, distillation and brewing of alcoholic drinks and cigarettes and cigars.
- FDI in print media sector as allowed upto 26 per cent of paid-up equity capital of Indian entities publishing periodicals and newspapers dealing with news and current affairs.

Image and Attitude

Though economic reforms welcoming foreign capital were introduced in the nineties. It does not seem so far to be really evident in our overall attitude. There is a lingering perception abroad that foreign investors are still looked at with some suspicion. There is also a view that some unhappy episodes in the past have a multiplier effect by adversely affecting the business environment in India. Besides the "Made in India" label is not conceived by the world as synonymous with quality.

When a foreign investor considers making any new investment decision, it goes through four stages in the decision making process and action cycle, namely, (a) screening, (b) planning, (c) implementing and (d) operating and expanding.

The biggest barrier for India is at the first, screening stage itself in the action cycle. "Often India looses out at the screening stage itself" (BCG). This is primarily because we do not get across effectively to the decision-making "board room" levels of corporate entities where a final decision is taken. Our promotional effort is quite often of a general nature and not corporate specific. India is, moreover, a multi-cultural society and a large number of multi-national companies (MNC) do not understand the diversity and the multi-plural nature of the society and the different stakeholders in this country. Though in several cases, the foreign investor is discouraged even before he seriously considers a project, 220 of the Fortune 500 companies have some presence in India and several surveys (JBIC, Japan Exim bank, A T Kearney) show India as the most promising and profitable destination.

On the other hand China is viewed as 'more business oriented,' its decision-making is faster and has more FDI friendly policies (ATK 2001). Despite a very similar historical mistrust of foreigners and foreign investment arising from colonial experience, modern (post 1980 China) differs fundamentally from India. Its official attitude to FDI, reflected from the highest level of government (PM, President) to the lowest level of government bureaucracy (provinces) is one of consciously enticing FDI with a warm welcome. They recognise the multifaceted and mutual benefits arising from FDI.

All investments, foreign and domestic are made under the expectation of future profits. The economy benefits if economic policy fosters competition, creates a well functioning modern regulatory system and discourages 'artificial' monopolies created by the government through entry barriers. A recognition and understanding of these facts can result in a more positive attitude towards FDI.

22

Public Sector in the Indian Economy

THE declared social objective of the Indian development strategy since Independence has been growth with social justice which was sought to be achieved within the democratic political framework and for which India adopted the concept of mixed economy. The expansion of the public sector was considered to be a major instrument with which the state in a mixed economy operating under the democratic framework can influence the pace as well as the composition of economic activity with a view to pursuing the social objective. However a large part of the economic activity will remain market based, decentralised in nature and in the private sector.

The Rationale

In India, the rationale for the public sector has been explicit or implicit in all plan documents as well as policy statements although the emphasis has changed in degrees depending upon the constraints faced and the emerging major issues of the time.

Tracing the chronological developments in this connection, we find that as far back as 1948, the Industrial Policy Resolution declared that "a dynamic national policy must... be directed to a continuous increase in production by all possible means, side by side with measures to secure its equitable distribution". For this purpose, while recognizing that the "State must play a progressively active role in the development of industries", it was conceded that in the conditions then prevailing "the mechanism and the resources of the State may not permit it to function forth within Industry as widely as may be desirable". The First Five Year Plan that followed did not have a clear-cut strategy of development and hence it did not contain any operational statements on the public sector.

It was in the context of the Mahalanobis strategy that the approach to the public sector got further crystallized. The long-term growth orientation in an import-substitution dominated strategy required that the domestic capacity creation be biased in the direction of producing capital goods to produce more capital goods. According to Prof. Tendulkar[1], the distinct preference for the public sector in this strategy can be traced to the following reasons.

First, the concentration of economic power that would result from the uncontrolled operation of the market forces can be reduced through the extension in the public ownership of means of production.

Secondly, private investors may demand a higher risk premium for investment in certain industries than would be socially justified. Off-shore drilling of oil is one example in this connection.

Thirdly, the scale of investment efforts in certain heavy industries may be beyond the capital-raising capacity of the private sector e.g. steel mills, heavy electrical machinery.

Fourthly, the public sector, through the appropriate price policy for its output will generate investible surpluses for further investment in the economy.

Fifthly, by production as well as distribution of certain universal intermediate inputs like coal, steel, electricity etc. the State will be able to control the composition of private economic activity in a socially desirable direction.

Finally, the public sector would assume the role of a model employer and its employment and wage policies would have a moderating influence on the corresponding policies in the private sector.

Analyzing these reasons, one finds that public sector was expected to fulfill varied and sometime conflicting objectives. The generation of investible surplus was bound to conflict with subsidies involved in keeping the prices of certain universal intermediates at low levels as well as the public sectors role as a model employer.

In the sixties and seventies, the public sector policy has been largely guided by the Industrial Policy Resolution of 1956 which gave the public sector a strategic role in the economy. Massive investments have been made over the past four decades to build a public sector which

---

1. S.D. Tendulkar, *Approach to the Public Sector in the Context of an Overall Development Strategy*, in (Ed.), Uma Kapila, Indian Economy Since Independence.

had a commanding role in the economy. Many key sectors of the economy are today dominated by mature public enterprises that have successfully expanded production; opened up new areas of technology and built up a reserve of technical competence in a number of areas.

As a result, the country's ranking in terms of industrialisation with other developing countries is quite high. India's comparative advantages such as a large pool of well-trained work-force, technical skills in manufacturing and chemical industries primarily stem from the public sector.

Growth in Investment in Central Government Enterprises

According to Economic Survey 1999-2000, there were 236 Central Government undertakings, excluding banks, financial institutions and departmental undertakings like the Railways, Ports etc. in 1998. Their number has increased from 5 in 1950-51 to 236 in 1998 with investment increased from Rs. 29 crores in 1957 to Rs. 223047 crores in 1998 (Table-1).

TABLE – 1

GROWTH OF INVESTMENT IN CENTRAL GOVERNMENT ENTERPRISES

As on March 31	*No. of Units*	*Total Investment (Rs. crores)*
1951	5	29
1961	47	950
1980	179	18,150
1990	244	99,330
1998	236	2,23,047

Source: Government of India, Public Enterprise Survey, (1997-98).

Public Enterprises Survey, 1997-98 gives some interesting information regarding the pattern of investment. Bulk of the investment is in those producing and selling goods; at the end of March 1998, 65.5 per cent of investment was in these industries. Even here, bulk of the investment (about 55 per cent) is in basic industries like Steel, Coal, Power, Petroleum etc. Nearly 32 per cent of investment is in enterprises rendering services; of these, the most prominent are financial services

(15.1 per cent)

The giant top 10 enterprises in the Central Public Sector (Table-2) accounted for a total investment of Rs. 98,280 crore on 31st March 1998 (48 per cent of total investment of Rs. 2,04,050 crores in 240 enterprises).

TABLE – 2

TOP 10 ENTERPRISES IN TERMS OF INVESTMENT

Rs. crores

		Investment as on 31-3-1998
1.	National Thermal Power Corporation Ltd.	16,180
2.	SAIL	15,140
3.	ONGC	10,600
4.	Indian Rly. Finance Corporation	9,500
5.	Power Grid Corporation of India	8,630
6.	National Hydro Electric Power Corporation	8,620
7.	Rashtriya Ispat Nigam Ltd.	7,870
8.	Nuclear Power Corporation	7,450
9.	MTNL	7,180
10.	Rural Electricity Corporation	7,110
	Total	98,280

Source: Public Enterprises Survey (1997-98).

In terms of investment, National Thermal Power Corporation Ltd. tops the list of top 10 enterprises in the Central public sector in India, closely followed by SAIL. But in terms of gross turnover in 1997-98, Indian Oil Corporation tops the list with a total turnover of Rs. 59,220 crores followed by Bharat Petroleum Corporation (Rs. 20,700 crores) and Food Corporation of India (Rs. 19,820 crores).

Role of Public Sector

One may look at the role of Public Sector in Indian economy in terms of its share in providing employment, its share in investment, its share in national income generated and its share in savings and capital formation.

Public Sector and Employment

Since employment in the public sector is confined to the organised sector, public sector employs 70 per cent of the workers employed in organised sector of the Indian economy. (Economic Survey 1999-2000).

TABLE – 3

PUBLIC AND PRIVATE SECTOR EMPLOYMENT IN INDIA

(in lakhs)

	Public Sector	*Private Sector*	*Total*	*1 as % of 3*
	(1)	*(2)*	*(3)*	*(4)*
1971	71	121	192	55
1981	155	74	229	68
1991	190	77	267	71
1998	194	87	281	70

From Table 3, it may be noted that 50 per cent of the total employment (i.e., 194 lakhs) in the public sector was in Government administration and community and personal services. The biggest chunk of employment in economic enterprises was in transport, storage and communications was of the order of about 31 lakhs and next in importance was manufacturing (17 lakh). 5.3 lakh persons employed in agriculture and other allied activities reflect employment under Employment Guarantee Scheme rather than any productive activity in the normal sense.

The share of public sector in total employment in the organised sector (public plus private) reveals that in transport and communications, electricity, gas and water and construction, the share of the public sector is in the range of 95-98 per cent, a situation of total dominance. However, in manufacturing, the share of the public sector was about 27 per cent of the total since its entry in this area is of recent origin. With the nationalisation of coal mines and takeover of 20 major commercial banks, there has been a significant improvement in the position of the public sector. In an overall sense, the public sector is a big employer (70 per cent of total) in so far as the organised sector of the Indian economy is concerned (Table-4).

TABLE – 4

EMPLOYMENT IN THE PUBLIC SECTOR IN 1998

		(Lakhs)	Percent of total
1.	Manufacturing	16.1	8.5
2.	Transport, storage and communications	30.8	15.7
3.	Financing, insurance, real estate and business services	12.9	6.6
4.	Government administration, community, social and personal services	97.4	50.0
5.	Other sectors	37.0	19,2
	Total	194.2	100.0

Source: Economic Survey 1999-2000.

Share of the Public Sector in GDP

During the last five decades, the share of the public sector in net domestic product (NDP) has shown a steady improvement. Measured at current prices, public sector accounted for 7.5 per cent NDP in 1950-51, its share in 1995-96 had risen to 26.2 per cent. Public sector, therefore, accounts for about one-fifth of national output. This is largely due to a rapid expansion of the public sector enterprises.

There is a very small increase in the share of public administration and defence from 4.5 per cent to 8.8 per cent between 1950-51 and 1996-97. The share of public sector enterprises, however, rose from 3 per cent in 1950-51 to 14.7 per cent in 1996-97. Despite this fact, the private sector still occupies a dominant position in the economy. There are some sectors such as agriculture and small-scale sector in which the share of the state is almost zero.

Share of the Public Sector in Savings and Capital Formation

Gross domestic capital formation has increased from 10.7 per cent of GNP during the First Plan to 24.6 per cent during the Eighth Plan (Table 5).

TABLE – 5

SHARE OF PUBLIC AND PRIVATE SECTORS IN GROSS DOMESTIC SAVINGS AND GROSS DOMESTIC CAPITAL FORMATION

Averages for Plan Periods		*As % of GNP at market prices*	
	Public sector	*Private sector*	*Total*
Gross Domestic Savings			
First Plan: 1951-56	1.7	8.7	10.4
Second Plan: 1956-61	2.0	10.4	12.4
Third Plan: 1961-66	3.4	10.9	14.3
Fourth Plan: 1969-74	3.0	14.4	17.4
Fifth Plan: 1974-79	4.6	17.0	21.6
Sixth Plan: 1980-85	3.6	16.5	20.1
Seventh Plan: 1985-90	2.3	18.1	20.4
Eighth Plan: 1992-97	1.4	21.9	23.3
1997-98	1.4	23.3	24.7
1998-99	0.0	22.3	22.3
Gross Domestic Capital Formation			
First Plan	3.5	7.2	10.7
Second Plan	6.6	8.8	15.4
Third Plan	8.4	8.3	16.7
Fourth Plan	7.2	10.9	18.1
Fifth Plan	9.5	11.7	21.2
Sixth Plan	11.1	10.5	21.6
Seventh Plan	10.7	12.1	22.8
Eighth Plan	9.2	15.4	24.6
1997-98(P)	6.5	17.5	26.9*
1998-99(Q)	6.7	16.6	25.1*

Source: C.S.O. 1998, National Accounts Statistics, RBI. Compiled from RBI Handbook of Statistics on Indian Economy (1999) and Economic Survey 1999-2000.

* Adjusted for errors and omissions.

P Provisional Estimates

Q Quick Estimates

However, the share of the public sector improved from 3.5 per cent during the First Plan (1951-56) to 9.2 per cent during the Eighth Plan. The share of the public sector which accounted for one-third of capital formation during the First Plan gradually increased to about one-half during the Sixth Plan, and has thereafter declined to 29 per cent.

However, the share of savings by the public sector has not undergone a similar change. The share of the public sector in gross domestic saving rose from 1.7 per cent of GNP during 1951-56 to merely 4.6 per cent during the Fifth Plan but declined thereafter and touched a low of 1.4 per cent during Eighth Plan.

(a) It has been mainly on account of the inefficiency of the government and the public sector enterprises and their consequent failure to generate internal surplus commensurate with the increase in their capital stock.

(b) The self-defeating efforts of the government to make up the shortfall in resources through excessive borrowings from the banking sector (better known as deficit financing).

Performance of Public Enterprises

However, after the initial exuberance of the public sector entering new areas of industrial and technical competence, a number of problems began to manifest themselves in many enterprises. Problems were observed in terms of low productivity, poor project management skills, overmanning, lack of technological upgradation, inadequate attention to R&D and low priority to human resource development.

There has been lot of criticism about the poor performance and in some cases utter failure of government undertakings in the country. Some economists have argued that profit should not be used as a criterion for judging the performance of public enterprises. According to them, public enterprises are guided by a variety of considerations in determining prices and it would not be appropriate to use profit as a criterion of their efficiency. This is particularly so in social utility services, like railways, posts and telegraphs, supply of water, electric energy, etc. The State should not raise the prices of these services, even though costs may have risen. Similarly, the public enterprises have a bulk of their investment in heavy and basic enterprises. Such enterprises have long gestation period and a part of the investment may be under construction. It would, therefore, be appropriate to calculate the rate of return on effective capital employed and thus not include the capital employed in undertakings under construction or in expansion or capital work-in-progress. In other words, "profitability" of the running concerns alone should be the index of their performance (Table 6).

TABLE – 6

PERFORMANCE OF PUBLIC SECTOR
(AT CURRENT PRICES)

(percentage share in total economy)

item	*1980-81*	*1987-88*	*1994-95*	*1995-96*
1. Gross Domestic Product	19.7	27.0	26.7	26.2
1.1 Administrative Departments	7.3	9.4	8.3	8.4
1.2 Departmental enterprises	3.2	4.4	4.0	3.8
1.3 Non-Departmental enterprises	9.2	13.2	14.4	14.0
2. Gross Domestic Capital Formation	41.4	44.1	35.9	29.0
2.1 Administrative Departments	10.6	10.5	8.1	7.1
2.2 Departmental enterprises	11.4	9.4	7.5	6.9
2.3 Non-Departmental enterprises	19.3	24.2	20.3	15.0
3. Gross Domestic Saving	16.2	10.4	7.1	8.9
3.1 Administrative Departments	8.9	-7.7	-10.2	-8.0
3.2 Departmental enterprises	0.9	3.0	4.0	3.7
3.3 Non-Departmental enterprises	6.4	15.1	13.2	13.2

Source: C.S.O. 1998, National Account Statistics.

According to K.S. Krishnaswami[2], in judging the performance of the public sector, it is also necessary to recognize that public sector units are required to secure other objectives besides maximization of the return on capital employed. According to the Bureau of Public Enterprises, they are required not only to give an adequate return to the nation on the investments, but also to (i) capture the commanding heights of the economy; (ii) share the burden of industrialization; (iii) generate additional employment; (iv) promote balanced regional development of the country and (v) develop ancillary industries, small-scale industries etc. As is well known, all of these objectives or intentions have been stressed by policy-makers and advocates of the public sector one time or another. Undoubtedly, each of these is a value

2. K.S. Krishnaswamy, *What Ails the Public Sector*, in (Ed.) Uma Kapila, Indian Economy Since Independence, 1993, (Academic Foundation).

that merits consideration in the special circumstances of our country. Even so, the question remains; can we continue to accept a low rate of return on investments in the public sector indefinitely? In the initial stages of massive investment, when new industries and new capacities are being established, it is natural for yields from investment, however measured, to be low. But can we accept this even after nearly 40 years of growing effort in the public sector?

The shortfalls in the returns from public sector investment have been a matter of concern to planners and others interested in the mobilization of resources for the development programmes, especially in the Central and State Government sectors. Since the early sixties, at any rate, all forecasts of resources for the Five-Year Plans have depended heavily on the availability of sizeable investible resources from public sector enterprises.

The Public Enterprises Survey gives financial performance of all running Central PSUs excluding insurance companies. The following facts can be highlighted -

(i) Gross profit before tax in 1970-71 was about Rs. 150 crores or 4 per cent of the total capital employed amounting to Rs. 3,600 crores. In fact, gross profit before tax ranged between 11 to 13 per cent of the capital employed between 1981-82 to 1993-94. Gross profit before tax rose almost continuously till it touched as high as Rs. 36,090 crores or 16.2 per cent of the capital employed in 1997-98 amounting to Rs. 2,23,050 crores. This appears quite respectable but gross profit before tax includes besides net profit, interest liabilities, and provision for depreciation and corporate tax. Therefore, the more useful concept is net profit after tax.

(ii) In 1970-71, net profit before tax was negative i.e. minus Rs. 3 crores for a total capital employed to Rs. 3,600 crores; this works out to be -0.1 per cent. In fact, for some years around this period, net profit after tax was negative for Central PSUs. Again between 1977-78 and 1980-81, net profit after tax was also negative.

(iii) It was only after 1981-82 that the Central PSUs turned the corner and started yielding positive net profit after tax - from about Rs. 50 crores in 1981-82 to about Rs. 13,720 crores in 1997-98. In percentage terms, the net profit after tax ranged between 2 per cent to 6.2 per cent of total capital employed between 1982 and 1998. In most of the years, however, net profits after tax used to average around 2 to 3 per cent only.

(iv) A very interesting point about the financial performance of the Central PSUs is that the overwhelming bulk of the profits was contributed by the petroleum sector enterprises. For instance, in 1990-91 net profit after tax came to Rs. 2,370 crores of which about Rs. 1,780 crores (or 75 per cent) came from petroleum enterprises alone.

(v) Public Enterprises Survey estimates the net profit by the profit-making enterprises along with the losses suffered by loss-making enterprises. In 1997-98, 134 profit making enterprises earned a total net profit of about Rs. 20,270 crores and 100 loss making units incurred a total loss of 6,540 crores. In recent years, an attempt has been made by the Government of India to study each loss-making enterprise to determine the factors responsible for the persisting situation and initiate remedial action (Table 7).

TABLE – 7

PROFITABILITY OF CENTRAL PUBLIC SECTOR UNDERTAKINGS

(Rs. billion)

	91-92	*92-93*	*93-94*	*94-95*	*95-96*	*96-97*	*97-98*	*98-99*
1. Number of units	237	239	240	241	239	238	236	235
2 Paid-up capital	457.0	519.4	559.7	582.9	595.9	624.3	721.2	770.7
3. Net Worth	603.3	705.3	795.3	899.5	991.8	1138.9	1350.6	1480.2
4. Capital employed	1179.9	1401.1	1598.4	1624.5	1739.6	2311.8	2536.6	2737.0
5. Gross profit	136.7	159.6	185.6	226.3	275.9	309.1	372.1	397.7
6. Pre-tax profits	40.0	50.8	66.6	97.7	136.2	153.8	193.5	197.3
7. Profit after tax (PAT)	23.6	32.7	45.5	71.9	95.7	101.9	137.2	132.3
8. Gross Margin to Capital employed (%)	18.8	18.0	17.3	20.6	23.1	19.2	20.9	20.7
9. Gross profit to Capital employed (%)	11.6	11.4	11.6	13.9	15.9	13.4	14.7	14.5
10. Pre-tax profit to Capital employed (%)	3.4	3.6	4.2	6.0	7.8	6.7	7.6	7.2
11. PAT to Net Worth (%)	3.9	4.6	5.7	8.0	9.6	8.8	10.2	8.9

There have been a variety of factors affecting the working of public sector enterprises; some of these have been economic, while others derive from social and political factors outside the enterprises or industry. It will therefore not be possible to single out any one or two elements as being the sole - or even the principal – causes of under-achievement by public sector enterprises. And it follows that there are no simple or quick remedies.

In the final analysis, the problems of public sector units boil down to two principal categories – *financial and managerial*. However, both these are traceable in one way or another to the multiplicity of responsibilities thrust on these units. Each of the multiple objective confers on the unit extra costs, additional managerial responsibility and very limited scope for price adjustments.

Let us briefly look at the costs side. In respect of many, if not most, of public sector enterprises, it has been the experience that construction periods, were much longer than originally projected. Some of this delay has arisen from such elementary facts as inadequate project preparation or unrealistic assumption about supply lags. More frequently, there have been changes in the size or the design of the project at various stages of its construction. Whatever the cause, the result often is a cost over-run together with loss of production for several months in the initial period. Further, because of the desire to locate large-sized industrial projects in hitherto backward areas, both the cost and execution of the project depend heavily on the creation of adequate infrastructure facilities. There have also been delays because of the inter-linking of projects, steel plants with heavy engineering plants, or with coal mines or with railway facilities, electricity generation with the manufacture of electrical machinery, cables, transmission towers and so on by other public sector units, port development with the production of cranes and other berthing equipment by public sector units. While there is nothing inherently wrong in such practices, it obviously enhances the transmission of delays and high cost in one unit to the other. Over and beyond all these, the construction of various facilities required for a whole township to house the employees have to be provided. Once the units start operating, cost increases have occurred because of inadequate utilisation of capacity, inefficient inventory management, absence of adequate purchase or selling arrangements. These are admittedly defects or weaknesses that may seem to have had a tendency to appear more often and affect more significantly the public sector units. Equally, all of these can be remedied by better project preparation, management and organisational adjustments.

Even more important from the financial angle is the question of price formation in public sector enterprises. For most of the public sector enterprises selling prices are administered rather than market-determined. The approach to pricing of public sector products has been influenced over the years by conflicting considerations. Like most of the industry in the last 40 years, public sector units have also operated in markets effectively insulated from international competition through import control or tariffs or just a lack of foreign exchange. Because of reservation of spheres of activity for the public sector, many, of them also enjoyed monopoly or semi-monopoly status. Given these factors, and given the progressive increase in Plan expenditure, a full-market-oriented approach would have afforded large opportunities for these enterprises to sell at high prices even without any recourse to restriction of output. But the association of public sector enlargement with socialistic or welfare objectives naturally meant that such temptations should be resisted and public sector enterprises treated somewhat like public utilities in the traditional sense. In other words, the urge to follow price policies in public enterprises which resulted in a no-profit no-loss situation over a period of years was very strong. This was further strengthened by the fact that many of the public sector units being in the area of basic industries, unduly high prices of their products could cause cost increases over a large segment of the economy. Thus the pressure to adopt in some sense a minimal price policy was strong and persistent.

However, at the same time there was appreciation of the fact that a large volume of public expenditure had been undertaken to establish these units and if the process of public investment were to maintain an increasing trend, these investments had to yield a sizeable return. In a fundamental sense, apart from maintaining the investments in fact, it was necessary that the operations of these enterprises generated a surplus for further investment in the economy. This meant that the price recovery for the products of the public enterprises had in a real sense to yield a profit that could be, if necessary, transmitted to another industry or another sector of the economy. At any rate, in all of the Plans it was envisaged that apart from the depreciation and interest on capital invested in these enterprises, there would be a net return to Government which would enhance the saving of the public sector.

Public Utility Versus Rate of Return Approach: The conflict between the two approaches which may briefly be called the "public utility approach" and the "rate of return approach" has meant in practice the adoption of a minimal acceptable return on capital, together with subsidisation of consumers in various ways - such as preferential rates for priority consumers of weaker sections, subsidisation of transport costs etc. While such policies of preferential price discrimination for short periods may be warranted in particular cases, its continued application would in logic require the charging of relatively higher prices to the non-priority or stronger sections of society. Or, alternatively, the loss or reduced return to the producing unit should be compensated from the budget. But this is in effect not done, so that the emphasis on subsidised prices for particular classes of consumers frequently reduces the return on capital sometimes to negative magnitudes.

Because of these consequences of price policies, some of the largest of the public sector units have been unable to provide for their own growth either in size or in terms of research and technology. The deficiencies in the system of pricing of public sector products have had the obvious effect of enlarging the burden on the budgets of the Central and State Governments. Progressively, some of these burdens have been transferred to the long-term financing institutions and banks. Even with their support it is becoming increasingly difficult for many units in the public sector to provide adequately for maintenance and enlargement of capacity. Further persistent loss or underachievement tends to have serious effects on the morale of both the management and labour in public enterprises.

Management Problems: The other major problem with public enterprises has been that of management. This is a matter on which much has been said, mostly by observers from outside rather than those who have been in the public sector. Given the fact that public sector units are largely, if not wholly, owned by the Government, it is unrealistic to talk of the autonomy or independence of management from Government control. Government being the shareholder has to have the right to appoint or dispense with the managers of public enterprises. Likewise, since a large part of the funds are provided by Government directly or indirectly, there can be no argument about the public accountability of these enterprises. The points that have to be considered therefore are not whether public enterprises should be completely free to pursue their own ends and objectives, but whether the methods which Government follow to control or regulate these enterprises are conducive to their health and progressive development.

In principle, the desiderata for efficient management of a public enterprise is that in its market-related operations it should be able to decide objectively and act quickly. For this purpose, both the proximate and long-term objective should be clear to the management, and should be within the competence of the micro-system to achieve. This implies that the initiatives and structures for making business decisions within the pattern of objectives should vest with the management of the enterprises.

It would appear from all this that the shortcomings of public enterprises arise from a variety of factors, both internal and external. Overcoming them will require changes in policies, practices as well as attitudes. Attempts have frequently been made to reorganize particular units, or modify particular policies to improve the situation. If, however, no significant improvement has in fact occurred, the question naturally arises: why is this so?

High Management Standards: The public sector cannot effectively contribute to the realization of a variety of social objectives if it is not economically viable. In a rapidly changing and complicated environment, the attainment and maintenance of such viability requires not only efficient current operation but planned development of larger or newer products. All of this will require that management standards in the public sector should be high, and the chief executives should be enabled to experiment and innovate. While requiring the management to operate within a set of consistent policy parameters, there should be a premium put on the adoption of cost-effective methods of operation. This will mean, at a minimum, two things: first, there should be at governmental level, an acceptance of the right of the management to take certain operational decisions without prior reference to or clearance from government. And secondly, it should be recognized that all managements are prone to errors of judgment; and as long as these are not frequent and serious, there should be no penalization of the managers. Observance of these conditions will be possible only when the administrative and legislative wings of Government adopt strict conventions of non-interference in the day-to-day management of public enterprises. Just as the effectiveness of the defence sector is enhanced by the civil authority keeping out of field decisions, the functioning of public enterprises will benefit from the exercise of self-restraint by civil servants, legislators and ministers.

Quick Settlement of Industrial Disputes: A second general change that should help the public sector function better is in respect of settlement of industrial disputes. If productivity standards in public enterprises have deteriorated, it is in part a reflection of the general trend. In all sectors of the economy production and productivity have suffered both from the frequency of industrial disputes and from the lengthy processes of settlement. Conflicts totally outside the questions of wages or conditions of work have led to strikes and go-slow tactics in the public sector, as in other sectors. There is little social pressure to promote a work ethic conducive to better performance. While the growth in labour organization and clearer appreciation of the right of labour to a proper reward are movements in the right direction, the tendency to weaken the link between higher reward and higher productivity is basically inimical to both growth and distributive justice. This tendency affects the public sector particularly badly since a variety of forces in society tend to treat it as an instrument for subsidisation of wages and salaries.

Pricing Policy: Finally while the inflationary effects of unduly high prices for basic goods should be borne in mind, it would be injurious to the general interest to reduce prices to such a level as to inflict the burden of financing cash losses on the budget or the banking system. This would be of no help in fighting inflation, while it would only exacerbate the position of the enterprises. The objective of covering not only the "full costs" but also providing a net return on investments in public enterprises can be realised if the distributive role assigned to them is a modest one, and if frequent mismatches between costs and administered prices are avoided. Both of these will, once again, need changes in attitudes as well as in methods of working.

New Directions of Policy: 1991 Industrial Policy

To improve the performance of the public sector, the Government of India announced in July 1991 the new Industrial Policy which contained the following decisions pertaining to the public sector.

(i) Portfolio of public sector investments will be reviewed with a view to focus the public sector on strategic, hi-tech and essential infrastructure. Whereas some reservation for the public sector is being retained, there would be no bar for area of exclusivity to be opened up to the private sector selectively. Similarly the public sector will be allowed entry in areas not reserved for it.

(ii) Public enterprises which are chronically sick and which are unlikely to be turned around will, for the formulation of revival/rehabilitation schemes, be referred to the Board for Industrial and Financial Reconstruction (BIFR), or other similar high level institutions created for the purpose. A social security mechanism will be created to protect the interests of workers likely to be affected by such rehabilitation packages.

(iii) In order to raise resources and encourage wider public participation, a part of the government's share-holding in the public sector would be offered to mutual funds, financial institutions, general public and workers.

(iv) Boards of public sector companies would be made more professional and given greater powers.

(v) There will be a greater thrust on performance improvement through the Memoranda of Understanding (MOU) system through which managements would be granted greater autonomy and will be held accountable. Technical expertise on the part of the Government would be upgraded to make MOU negotiations and implementation more effective.

Till the end of March 1998, 62 PSUs have been referred to BIFR which has so far approved revival packages in respect of 21 PSUs.

Disinvestment of Public Sector Share-holding

The Government has gone in for a programme of disinvestment of public sector enterprises. The 1991 Industrial Policy Statement envisaged the disinvestment of a part of the Government shareholding in selected PSUs to provide financial discipline and improve their performance. In the 1991-92 budget, the Government announced the intention of partial disinvestment in selected PSUs in order to raise resources, encourage wider public participation and promote greater accountability. Upto 20 per cent of the Government equity in 31 selected enterprises was offered to Mutual Funds, Financial/Investment Institutions, workers and general public.

As a consequence of the sharp criticism of the Government regarding the process of disinvestment by the PAC and in view of the Report of the Rangarajan Committee, the Government set up the Disinvestment Commission in August 1996 to advise on the extent, strategy, methodology and timing for disinvestment in each PSU.

Issue of Privatisation

Privatisation is a term that is employed to convey a variety of ideas such as part or full transfer of public assets to the private sector; providing autonomy in management with respect to investment decisions or liberalising administrative pricing or other controls without change in ownership of assets; dismantling and regulating monopolies owned by the public sector hitherto. The variety of ideas reflect diversity in perceptions regarding privatisation. They have resulted partly from political circumstances, partly from country specific attitudes to growth and equity and partly from ethnic preferences for foreign capital.

Although it began as a necessity in a situation of widening fiscal deficits, privatisation as an ideology has come to stay in many countries primarily on account of the consequential benefits reaped by consumers in terms of greater choice and lower costs of goods. According to a World Bank study, the number of privatisation transactions have increased significantly as illustrated in the table below:

TABLE – 8

DISINVESTMENT TRANSACTIONS WORLD WIDE

(US$ Billions)

	1980-87	*1988-93*		
Region	*No.*	*No.*	*Value*	*%*
Africa	210	254	3.2	3
Asia	108	367	19.7	21
Latin America	136	561	55.1	57
Eastern Europe & Central Asia	2	1097	17.9	19
Total for Developing Countries	456	2279	95.9	100
Total for Developed Countries	240	376	174.9	
Total World-Wide	696	2655	270.8	

Source: Disinvestment Commission, Dec. 1996, Disinvestment Strategy & Issues.

It is clear from the above table that privatisation is common to both developing as well as developed countries and the number of transactions is more significant in developing countries in the second period. But importantly, Argentina, Brazil, Hungary, Mexico, and Poland alone accounted for about 30 per cent of developing-country transactions and 60 per cent of the value of the enterprises sold in 1988-93. Though the number of transactions are low, the value of privatisation transactions in developed countries is much higher as disinvestment transactions have included large state owned enterprises in public utilities such as electricity, water and telecommunications sectors.

The increasing trend of partial or full transfer of state owned enterprises coupled with the declining share of investments in this sector may suggest a diminishing role for state owned enterprises over the past decade in developing countries.

Considering the financial magnitudes involved in the disinvestment process, and the resultant impact on the country's macroeconomic balance, many countries have set up high-powered committees to draw out a comprehensive long term disinvestment programme. India is a late comer in this respect.

The process of disinvestment of state owned commercial assets needs to balance several considerations. If shares are relatively underpriced in the short run as strategy to attract investor participation, there is a lower realisation to the exchequer, while relative overpricing may drive away investors and jeopardise the future disinvestment process. In particular, the reserve price for disinvestment has to be fixed in uncertain and volatile capital markets.

The process of disinvestment also needs to balance Government's needs along with the need for equity requirements of the PSU. Given the limited availability of investible resources in the capital market, there is a need to balance disinvestment with the capital requirements of the private sector.

Disinvestment has been attempted in the past primarily for meeting budgetary targets as well as subjecting PSUs to market discipline such as emphasis on profits and shareholder returns. In addition, disinvestment can cut down on the budgetary support to some profit making PSUs as they can access capital markets after listing. Government withdrawal on specific loss making PSUs can cut down on the non-plan budgetary support. Taken together, this can help contain fiscal deficit. This can happen if the PSUs are disinvested through the most appropriate method after restructuring, if required, to enhance share value.

Issues in Disinvestment in India

In India, a distinction needs to be made between privatisation and disinvestment. In the Indian context, privatisation has meant opening up certain sectors for private sector participation rather than outright privatisation of state owned enterprises. Unlike other countries, the public sector will continue to play an important role even in a privatised economy.

According to Rangarajan[3], broadly speaking, there are two major reasons adduced for disinvestment. One is to provide fiscal support and the other is to improve the efficiency of the enterprise. The fiscal support argument has to be given due weightage. The demands on the governments, both at the centre and the states are increasing. There is a compelling need to expand the activities of the state in areas such as education, health and medicine. It is therefore legitimate that a part of the additional resources needed for supporting these activities comes out of the sale of shares built up earlier by the government out of its resources. It is sometimes argued that the resources raised through disinvestment must be utilised for retiring past debts and thereby bringing down the interest burden of the government. So long as government is a net borrower of a fairly large magnitude year after year, it does not make any material difference whether the resources are utilised to retire past debts or simply utilised as part of the receipts. In the latter case, it only results in a lower borrowing requirement.

The second important argument in favour of disinvestment is the contribution that it can make to improving the efficiency of the working of the enterprise. Leaving aside the extreme case where the dilution results in the transfer of ownership, even in the case of disinvestment where the dilution is of lesser order and where the government control is still retained, the induction of public ownership can have a salutory effect on the functioning of an enterprise. It increases the accountability of those in charge of the enterprise. The shareholders would require to be compensated and this will in turn compel the enterprise to run more efficiently and earn more profits. This must be regarded as part of the reform and restructuring of public enterprise. Flexibility in ownership can in effect impart efficiency. In fact, the induction of the public into the ownership structure can also create conditions in which there could be greater autonomy for the functioning of the public sector enterprise. Disinvestment can therefore be regarded as a tool for enhancing economic efficiency.

The issue of disinvestment has raised wider questions such as the need for restructuring PSUs, the extent of disinvestment of Government shareholding in operating sectors and the partial/total withdrawal of Government from certain industries.

---

3. C. Rangarajan, *Disinvestment: Strategies and Issues*, Ch. 26, in Uma Kapila, (ed.) Indian Economy Since Independence, 2000-01 edition.

The main dimensions of the disinvestment process are: preparation of the PSU, valuation and finally choosing appropriate disinvestment and sale modalities so as to meet overall goals.

The studies of global experiences indicate that it may often be useful to restructure the PSU before privatisation as it can maximise sale proceeds. In particular, restructuring with a clear view to disinvest in a time bound fashion has been found to enhance share value. On the other hand, if restructuring requires considerable effort, or is laced with uncertainties, it has been found prudent to disinvest on an as-is-where-is-basis.

In India, views expressed with regard to restructuring of PSUs focus on three areas: Corporate Governance, Financial Restructuring, Business and Technological Restructuring. Restructuring in one or more of the above ways will enhance future profitability and investor perception. Where restructuring involves administrative action without significant outlays and enhances share value, it could precede disinvestment. However, in cases which requires considerable restructuring, a cost-benefit analysis may have to precede the actual exercise.

The prioritisation and timing of disinvestment will be driven to a large degree by the extent of restructuring required in PSUs. Views have been expressed that while it may not be feasible to restructure the PSUs in one go before disinvestment, it may be helpful to map out the entire process so that the results are known to a potential investor.

The Disinvestment Commission in its last report submitted in August 1999 has made the following observations:

The Disinvestment Commission had, since its very first report submitted to Government in February 1997, given recommendations in respect of a number of important issues basic to the process of disinvestment which needed to be addressed by Government. These covered creation of a Disinvestment Fund, Restructuring, Corporate Governance, Grant of Autonomy, Setting up of Pre Investigation Board, Selection and Remuneration of Top Management, Professionalising the Boards of the PSUs, addressing labour issues through VRS, ESOPs etc. It had also suggested procedural measures for speeding up the disinvestment process through setting up of a full-time implementation machinery, selection of global financial advisers and modalities of disinvestment that could be adopted by the Government in individual cases.

The Commission had observed that Disinvestment should be a part of a well thought out strategy of public sector reform and not made to serve merely as a means of raising revenues for the Budget.

The Commission had, in its very First Report (February, 1997), laid out the strategy for disinvestment and recommended, inter alia, the setting up of a Disinvestment Fund in which all receipts from disinvestment should be deposited. It was recommended that this fund be used for temporarily meeting the losses of some PSUs where required, for strengthening marginally loss making PSUs in preparation for disinvestment, meeting expenses on VRS for surplus work force and funding specific social sector projects.

In order to give thrust to the process of disinvestment in PSUs, a new Department of Disinvestment has been set up. The Department is responsible for all matters related to disinvestment of Central Government equity in Central Public Sector Undertakings, implementation of disinvestment decisions and recommendations of the erstwhile Disinvestment Commission.

Disinvestment: Policy and Practice[4]

The policy of the government on disinvestment has evolved over the last decade. It started with the sale of minority shares in 1991-92, which continued with some modifications till 1999-2000. During this period Rs. 18,638 crore were realised through this method of market sale of shares. The policy changed around March 31, 2000 and was announced by the finance minister in the Budget speech of 2000-2001: "Government have recently established a new department for disinvestment to establish a systematic policy approach to disinvestment and privatisation and to give a fresh impetus to this programme which will emphasise increasingly on strategic sales of identified PSUs."

In accordance with this decision all the disinvestments since 2000 have been strategic sales. Strategic sale is defined as a sale of equity by government where the management control of the entity is handed over to the strategic partner. Typically the strategic partner is required to purchase an equity stake which is large enough to ensure a workable majority. This policy has been implemented vigorously. Table 9 lists the strategic sales over the period April 1, 2000 to August 2002.

The central government's equity stake, both direct and through holding companies was of the order of about Rs. 80,000 crore on March

---

4. Baijal, Pradip (2002), *Privatisation: Compulsions and Options for Economic Reform* in EPW, October, 12.

TABLE – 9

STRATEGIC SALES OF PSEs

Sr. No.	*Name of PSE*	*Date*	*Ratio of Paid Up 'Equity Sold (Per cent)*	*Face Value of Equity Sold (Rs. Crore)*	*Realisation (Rs. Crore)*
1.	Modern Foods	January 2000	74(i) 26(ii)	9.63(i) 3.38(ii)	105(i) 44(ii)
2.	LJMC	July 2000	74	0.7	2.53
3.	BALCO	March 2001	51	112.52	826.5
4.	CMC	October 2001	51	7.73	152
5.	HTL	October 2001	74	11.1	55
6.	VSNL	February 2002	25	71.2	3,689
7.	IBP	February 2002	33.6	7.4	1,153.7
8.	PPL	February 2002	74	320.1	151.7
9.	Jessop	February 2002	74	68.1	18.2
10.	HZL	April 2002	26	109.8	445
11.	IPCL	May 2002	26	64.5	1,490.8
12.	Maruti Udyog	May 2002	23	66	2,424(iii)
13-14.	HCL (3 hotels)	2001-02 (various dates)	100	14.7	242.5
15-32	ITDC (18 Hotels)	2001-02 (various dates)	100	23.9	414.9
	Total			891	11,214.8

Notes: (i) Realisation in the case of Jessop is on accrual basis. (ii) Realisation of Rs. 153 crore from the sale of three ITDC hotels yet to be received (iii) in the case of Maruti Udyog the realisation is anticipated and could be higher.

31, 2000. The increase in the levels of available PSE stock in the market has resulted in an upsurge in the share prices of disinvesting companies and also in the overall market capitalisation of PSE shares. The market capitalisation of listed PSEs increased by 73.5 per cent, i.e., from Rs. 96,063 crore to Rs. 1,66,672 crore as compared to a 14 per cent increase in total market capitalisation of all BSE listed companies, between January and May 16, 2002. The market capitalisation in 32 listed public sector companies tracked by BSE has increased in value by about Rs. 70,000 crore in four months. Government share holding has thus gained about Rs. 50,000 crore. If this performance can be improved by initiation of more privatisations, significant benefits would accrue to the economy, government and financial institutions. This will also catalyse improvement in the performance of our stock markets, which are vital for economic development. The performance of our stock markets is less than satisfactory, with markets growing only by 0.5 per cent against an overall GDP growth of about 6 per cent last year. This is in sharp contrast to Indonesia and Thailand, where the local stock market indices have registered over 30 per cent increase in the last year, even though economic growth has been much lower than in the case of India.

Disinvestment Strategies

Before the year 2000, the government had primarily sold minority shares in public sector companies. From 1991 to 1999 through this method of market sale of shares Rs. 18,638 crores were realised, an average of Rs. 2,071 crore per year. The price earning ratio on the basis of the sales value realised by the government, even in blue chip companies like IOC, BPCL, HPCL, GAIL and VSNL was 4 to 6. In comparison over a two-year period 2000-01 to 2002-03 (till August 2002), more than Rs. 11,315 crore has been realised through strategic sale of Thirty Three PSEs or an average of Rs. 4,526 per year. The price earnings (PE) ratio for sales through the strategic disinvestment route has been far higher, from 11 to 89. The experience gained so far seems to justify the assumption that the strategic sale 'discovers' the fundamental, long-term value of the company as opposed to the sale of small lots of shares in the market which get valued on short-term considerations linked to the current expectations of the market. The higher sales realisations through strategic sale reflect the control premium, which the investor is willing to pay for managing the company. Three examples will illustrate this proposition:

- A profitable monopoly like VSNL was sold at a PE ratio of 6 earlier, while the subsequent strategic sale of VSNL in February 2002, despite substantial deregulation of the Telcom industry and erosion of its monopoly status, has yielded a PE ratio of 11.

  One half of the equity of Maruti Udyog was given to Suzuki of Japan in 1994. Shares were sold at a price of Rs. 269 per share. While foregoing the Rights Issue and transferring management control to Suzuki, the government realised a price of Rs. 3,280 per share in May 2002. No control premium was charged in 1994. Possibly at that time there was insufficient recognition that the transfer of management control to a strategic investor extracts fundamental value far beyond the current market levels. The government has now received Rs. 1,000 crore as control premium in the case of Maruti. The market sale of the residual stock of the government of India in Maruti of 66 lakh shares will fetch additional gains for government.

During the last two years the government has sold about 1 per cent of its total equity yielding more than Rs. 11,000 crore. While a simple extrapolation may be misleading and inexact, it indicates that offloading the entire stock of PSE equity held by government could result in incremental capital resources of about Rs. 10,00,000 crore. In addition to the potential for receipt of such capital gains are the benefits related to reduction in the revenue expenditure of government. The government has received around Rs. 11,335 crore from strategic sales. The government of India's long-term interest rate for market borrowing fell from 12 per cent in January 1999 to 8 per cent in January 2002. The average rate over this period being 10 per cent. Using this average rate for market borrowing, the avoided interest cost of borrowing Rs. 11,335 crore is Rs. 1,133 crore every year, in perpetuity. As against this benefit, the dividends received by government on its equity, which has now been sold, averaged Rs. 52.41 crore during the last eight years.

Welfare Gains from Privatisation of Profitable PSEs

It is often argued that the government should not sell profit-making companies. Three examples will suffice to illustrate that profitability, by itself, is an insufficient indicator of the efficiency of public investment.

- BALCO was a profit making company, which paid the government an average dividend (over eight years) of Rs. 5.69 crore every year on the portion of equity subsequently sold to a strategic investor. The avoided interest cost on Rs. 826.5 crore received from strategic disinvestment is Rs. 82.65 crore every year. The net gains for government are nearly Rs. 75 crore per year in avoided interest cost.
- CMC was a very well managed and profitable company, yet the average dividend was only 0.80 crore per year. The avoided interest cost for Government on the Rs. 152 crore realised from its sale is Rs. 15.2 crore annually.
- Maruti Udyog gave average returns to the tune of Rs. 13 crore

annually through dividends for government. In comparison the avoided interest cost on the realisations received through the strategic sale of shares is Rs. 242 crore per year.

– IPCL gave dividends on average of Rs. 16.24 crore per year. In comparison the avoided interest cost on the realisations received through the strategic sale of shares is Rs. 149 crore per year.

During the period 1991-2000, the sale of minority shares of public sector undertakings has led to realisation of about Rs. 19,000 crore for government. Most of these shares were bought by financial institutions. Unit Trust of India was one such institution, which had picked up substantial quantities of such stock. However the prices of these shares fell in a number of cases, with the result that UTI lost Rs. 5,056 crore on an investment of Rs. 6,403 crore made by them. With the commencement of the policy of strategic sale there has been a dramatic reversal. The PSE index has increased steadily since then. The market looks favourably on the transfer of management control of PSEs to a private investor as a means of unlocking the inherent business value of such PSEs. The loss to UTI on its PSU portfolio decreased to Rs. 3,673 crore by March 1, 2002. By May 16, 2002 the BSE-PSU index had increased from its level of 932.32 on January 8, 2002 to 1,662.82. This should allow UTI to recover its loss even further.

A fear is often expressed that the employees would lose if companies were privatised. Recent privatisations have shown that these fears are totally unfounded. Privatised companies have not retrenched a single person. Some of the companies are now in the process of restructuring and would accept some voluntary retirement applications. These companies are giving VRS to the employees, at terms, which are normally better than the government VRS shareholders agreement with private companies normally have a provision that if there is a need for rationalising the employee strength, the interests of employees would be protected by ensuring VRS, which is better or equal to the government VRS. In any case linking rationalisation of the employee strength with disinvestment is not appropriate. This is a measure of business restructuring which is needed and has been implemented extensively over the last decade, even in PSEs when employment declined from 2.18 million in 1991-92 to 1.74 million in 2001-01. Some examples will illustrate that fears of unemployment post privatisation or deterioration in the terms of employment are exaggerated.

- Wages have increased by an average of Rs. 1,600 per month per employee in Modern Food Industries post privatisation. Within a month after privatisation, the company had been referred to BIFR. At the time of privatisation everyone knew that based on its past performance, Modern Food was fast approaching BIFR. Hindustan Lever is now taking measures to financially restructure the company and bring it out of BIFR, at their own expense. Had Modern Foods remained a PSE, the taxpayer would have paid for financial restructuring of the company without any assurance of improvement in the long-term financial viability of the company.
- In BALCO, under public sector management, wages had stagnated and had not been increased since April 1, 1999, even though a revision was due. In spite of a loss of about Rs. 200 crore due to the strike after disinvestment, an ex-gratia payment of Rs. 5,000 was paid to all employees and a long term wage agreement for a period of five years entered into by the privatised management with the employees on October 7, 2001, which guaranteed a benefit of 20 per cent of basic pay to each employee, besides increase in a number of allowances.

These are not isolated incidents and upward wage revisions and rationalisations have been made in the other privatised companies as well.

Conclusion

Through the decade of the 1990s, there has been an increasing consensus on the merits of privatisation. The aggregate balance sheet assets of all public sector companies amounts to roughly Rs. 22 lakh crore. This suggests that relatively modest improvements in the efficiency of their functioning would have a significant impact upon GDP growth. Hence, policies on privatisation are an important component of policies for efficiency and productivity.

The privatisation process began in 1991-92 with sale of minority stakes in some PSUs. From 1999-2000 onwards, the focus shifted to strategic sales. Table 10 highlights the actual disinvestment proceeds as compared with targets for the year.

TABLE – 10

DISINVESTMENT IN PUBLIC SECTOR UNDERTAKINGS

Year	*Target (Rs. crore)*	*Proceeds (Rs. crore)*
1991-92	2,500	3,038
1992-93	2,500	1,913
1993-94	3,500	-
1994-95	4,000	4,843
1995-96	7,000	362
1996-97	5,000	380
1997-98	4,800	902
1998-99	5,000	5,371
1999-00	10,000	1,860
2000-01	10,000	1,871
2001-02	12,000	5,632#
2002-03	12,000	3,348
2003-04	14,500	15,547

\# Figures inclusive of amount realized by way of control premium, dividend/ dividend tax and transfer of surplus cash reserves prior to disinvestment etc.

Source: Ministry of Disinvestment.

Table 11 summarises the transactions which have taken place in 2003-04, which have given proceeds of Rs.15547 crore.

TABLE – 11

DISINVESTMENT PROCEEDS DURING 2003-04

(Rs. crore)

Sl. No.	*Name*	*Type of Sale*	*Percentage of equity disinvested*	*Proceeds realisation to be realized*
1.	Maruti Udyog Ltd.	Offer for sale	27.5	993.34
2.	Jessop & Co. Ltd.*	Strategic Sale	72.0	18.18
3.	HZL**	Call option	18.9	323.88
4.	ICIL	Limited Auction	9.2	77.10
5.	IBP	Offer for Sale	26.0	350.66
6.	IPCL	Offer for Sale	28.9	1202.85
7.	CMC	Offer for Sale	26.3	190.44
8.	DCIL	Offer for Sale	20.0	221.20
9.	GAIL	Offer for Sale	10.0	1627.36
10.	ONGC	Offer for Sale	9.9	10542.40
	Total			**15547.42**

* Amount has been received by Bharat Bhari Udyog Ltd., the holding company of Jessop & Co. Ltd.

** Excise of Call Option by the Strategic Partner.

Source : Ministry of Disinvestment.

It is interesting to note that while much is made of the likely adverse impact of disinvestments on employment, in fact, over the last 10 years, as reported by the PSE Survey 2000-01, public sector undertakings have seen a net reduction in employment from a level of 2,179 million employees in 1991-92 to a level of 1,742 million in 2000-01, or a reduction of 20 percent over this period. Till March 31, 2001, 3.69 lakh employees had opted for VRS. In comparison, the retrenchment of employees after disinvestment has been marginal.

In eight disinvested PSUs and five disinvested ITDC Hotels, against an initial employee strength of 27,967 at the time of disinvestments, only 2,119 employees were retrenched through VRS, and another 910 for other reasons. As against a total of 3,029 post disinvestment separations, 855 fresh appointments have been made resulting in a net reduction of 2,174 employees or about 7.8 percent employees, compared to the employment level at the time of disinvestments.

As per the Common Minimum Programme (CMP), the United Progressive Alliance (UPA) Government is committed to a strong and effective public sector whose social objectives are met by its commercial functioning. But for this, there is need for selectivity and a strategic focus. The UPA is pledged to devolve full managerial and commercial autonomy to successful, profit-making companies operating in a competitive environment. Generally profit-making companies will not be privatized.

All privatizations will be considered on a transparent and consultative case-by-case basis. The UPA will retain existing "navaratna" companies in the public sector while these companies raise resources from the capital market. While every effort will be made to modernize and restructure sick public sector companies and revive sick industry, chronically loss-making companies will either be sold-off, or closed, after all workers have got their legitimate dues and compensation. The UPA will induct private industry to turn-around companies that have potential for revival.

The Government has enacted a new law, the Competition Act, 2002, for upholding competition in the Indian market. The main objectives of the Act are to provide for the establishment of a Commission to prevent practices having adverse effect on competition, to promote and sustain competition in markets in India, to protect the interests of consumers, and to ensure freedom of trade carried on by participants in market in India and for related matters. The Competition Act provides for the establishment of a Competition Commission of India, which was established on October 14, 2003.

23

Small Scale Industrialisation

Small Industry [1]

Rationale for Supporting Small Scale Enterprises

THE arguments advanced in the literature for promotion of small scale enterprises involve both certain desirable characteristics of such enterprises and also a common belief that under normal market conditions many such enterprises would not be able to survive in the economy. A list of desirable characteristics of such enterprises include, inter alia, higher labour intensity and related positive income distribution effects, their potential for balanced regional development through greater decentralisation, their contribution to the promotion of entrepreneurship, their flexibility in operation, and their ability to export. If these positive characteristics are seen to be important and if there is reason to believe that market failures inhibit the growth of small scale enterprises then it would be appropriate to frame policies that attack these market imperfections.

It is believed that small scale enterprises are hampered in their growth because of imperfections in factor markets, in labour, capital and land. Typically, the factor market most focussed on is the capital market, distortions in which are seen to especially discriminate against small scale enterprises. Similarly, imperfections in the labour market lead to factor price distortions causing larger than justifiable wage differences between large and small enterprises. It can be argued,

1. This section draws from Rakesh Mohan's paper *"Small Scale Industry Policy in India: A Critical Evaluation"*, Conference on "Indian Economic Prospects: Advancing Policy Reforms" Centre for Research on Economic Development and Policy Reform, Stanford University, May 31-June 1, 2000.

however, that the higher wages facing large firms can generally be compensated by higher efficiency of the work force so that the wage cost difference per efficiency unit of labour is much less than the observed difference in the prices of capital. Thus it can be argued that distortions in the capital market are much more important than those in the labour market. Large firms are able to compensate the higher wages through higher efficiency, but small firms are not able to compensate for the high cost of capital through higher efficiency of the capital used. Similarly in the land market small enterprises could face greater regulatory hurdles in achieving appropriate access to land.

The economic argument would then be that in the face of factor market distortions special support policies for small scale industries would tackle the problems at their source. The best solution would be to enact policies that remove the various factor market distortions that are observed at their source. In practice, it is found that it is difficult to remove such factor market distortions through direct interventions. The result is that a whole plethora of other supportive policies for small scale enterprises are observed. India has been no different from other countries in its concern for supporting small scale enterprises. In fact, amongst developing countries, India was the first to display special concern for small scale enterprises, before it became fashionable to do so. A basic focus of Indian government thinking has been that employment generation is of paramount importance in a labour surplus economy. Small enterprises manufacturing labour intensive products make economical use of capital and absorb abundant labour supply which characterises an under developed economy. The belief has been that large enterprises are capital intensive and reward only a small minority of labour which is skilled and urban. Indian concern and support for small scale enterprises has focussed excessively on small scale industries as distinguished from small scale enterprises in general.

All Industrial Policy Statements since independence have provided some special attention to the problem of small scale industries.

The basic structure of institutional promotion of small scale industries was put in place in the 1950s. This institutional structure had aimed to provide for a development programme for small scale industries through the establishment of organisations for providing technical assistance and industrial extension.

The basic idea then was promotion of small scale enterprises through positive technical and marketing support.

A policy of reserving items for the exclusive manufacture in the small scale sector was begun in 1967 when 47 items were reserved. This number rose gradually to 180 by 1976. With the 1977 Industrial Policy Statement a major expansion took place in the number of items reserved for small scale sector. A major shift in small scale industry policy took place with the promulgation of the Industrial Policy Statement of 1977. It was then decided that the sole criterion for reservation of products in the small scale sector would be merely its ability to physically manufacture them. It was stated in the policy that "whatever can be produced on a small scale must be so produced". The regime for small scale industry developed has remained virtually unchanged after that.

The key elements of India's policy for the support of small scale industries have been small scale industry reservations, fiscal concessions by way of lower excise duties, preferential allocation of and subsidisation of bank credit, extension of business services by the government, and preferential procurement by the government. *Thus small scale industry has been sought to be protected from the competition of large companies both through reservations as well as fiscal concessions.* Extension of business services by the government was considered necessary in the absence of equivalent services being available in the private sector.

In his study Rakesh Mohan has argued that this support structure may have reflected well the needs of the 1950s, 1960s and 1970s. The argument is that these policies have now become obsolete and are now likely to be harmful to the development of small scale industries and of industrial development in general. There has been vast growth of small units over the years. Thus the governmental structure for technical support of small scale industries has become both obsolete and inadequate. There is now much greater availability of private sector business and technological support service which should be fostered. Second with the opening of the economy the reservation policy has become counter productive. Third, the fiscal concessions can also be operating so as to discourage growth into large units. Thus it is argued that a whole new approach for supporting small scale industries has to be adopted in India to serve the changing needs of the new open economy.

Definition of Small Scale Industries

Most countries define small scale industries or enterprises in terms of employment levels. Usually small scale industries are taken to be those units which employ more than 5 but less than 50 or 100 workers. India is among the few countries that has used investment ceilings to define small scale industries. Further, in India itself, different definitions are used for different purposes. The Factories Act defines a factory as one which employs 10 workers or more if the unit uses power, or 20 workers or more if it does not use power. All such units have to be registered under the Factories Act and are subject to various labour laws including the provision of medical insurance and some social security. This is known as the registered sector. Within this definition, those units which employ more than 50 workers (if using power) or more than 100 (if not using power) have to compulsorily register themselves with the state governments in order to operate. The main source of data for manufacturing is the Annual Survey of Industries (ASI). The coverage of this survey is limited to those factories which are registered under the Factories Act. The third definition is that used for giving fiscal concessions. At present units which have less than Rs. 3 million turn over are fully exempted from the excise taxes and there is a sliding scale of concessions available for small scale enterprises which have turn over of upto Rs. 30 million.

In 1950, the investment limits was upto Rs. 0.5 million in fixed assets employing less than 50/100 persons with or without power. From 1960 onwards, there are no conditions regarding employment but investment limit has been raised to keep up with inflation and hence to preserve the real value of investment limits. In 1966 Investment limit was raised to 0.75 million in plant and machinery then 1 million in 1975, 2 million in 1980, 3.5 million in 1985, upto 6 million in 1991 and upto 30 million in 1997. A curious development took place in 1999 when, for the first time, a reversal in investment limit was put in to effect by lowering the investment limit to 10 million. The current definition is therefore more restrictive in real terms relative to 1991.

The current status of the investment ceilings for small scale industries is provided in the following Statement.

STATEMENT

INVESTMENT CEILINGS FOR SMALL SCALE INDUSTRY (DECEMBER 1999)

Type of Small Scale Industry	*Investment Limit*	*Remarks*
Small Scale Industry	Rs. 10 million	Historical cost of plant and machinery
Ancillary	Rs. 10 million	At least 50 per cent of its output should go to other industrial undertakings
Export Oriented	Rs. 2.5 million	Obligation to export 30 per cent of production
Tiny Enterprise	Rs. 0.5 million	No location limits
Service and business enterprise	Rs. 10 million	No location limit
Women Enterprise	Rs. 10 million	51 per cent equity holding by women

Small Scale Reservation Policy

The policy of small scale reservations was initiated in 1967 as a promotional and protective measure for the small scale sector vis-a-vis the large scale sector. Under this policy selected products are identified for exclusive production in the small scale sector. The overwhelming consideration for reservation is whether it is technically feasible to produce that item in the small scale sector, the manufacturing process is of a simple nature i.e. is essentially labour intensive, and whether the small scale units can meet the requirements of consumers both in terms of quantity and quality. The rationale for reservation was based on the advantages of the small scale sector like labour intensity and adaptability to a semi-urban and rural environment. Another objective was to make SSI products competitive with those of the large scale by offsetting the disadvantage of mass scale production, economies of scale, wider marketing network, better credit availability and publicity through mass media and advertisements.

In April 1967 there were only 47 items in the reserved category which increased to 504 by April 1978. In 1978 it was decided to recast the reserved list by following codes adopted in the NIC and in this process, the list of reserved items expanded from 504 to 804. The number had increased to 873 in October 1984 and in 1989 after some dereservation it came down to 836.

Throughout this whole period of reservation there has been little analysis of the effects of this policy. The government has conducted two small scale industries censuses so far; one in 1972 and the other in 1987-88. The share of production in the reserved categories was 25 per cent in total small scale industry production in 1972 and 28 per cent in 1997-98. This small increase in the share was surprising given the large scale expansion of products under reservation that took place in 1977. In both cases capacity utilisation in units producing reserved items was 47 to 48 per cent on average, whereas the average level of capacity utilisation was over 50 per cent in units producing unreserved items. It was also found in 1987-88 that a large number of reserved items were not produced at all in any unit.

The second census of small scale industries provides persuasive evidence of the misplaced importance given the policy of reservation. Out of a total of 200 products leading in value of output produced by the small scale sector, it was found that reserved products accounted for only 21 percent. Only 210,000 small scale units, less than half out of a total of 5,82,000 units, manufactured the reserved products at all. No less than 233 reserved items out of a total of 1,076 (when expanded at a lower level of aggregation in the NIC code) were found not be manufactured at all according to the census. Although further inquiries have revealed that many of these products are found to be manufactured by some units, the fact remains that their production is in negligible quantities.

Conversely, very few of the reserved products attracted significant levels of participation from small scale units. As many as 90 products were found to be manufactured by just one company each. The sum total of the value of production of all small scale companies in as many as 692 items was a low of Rs. 100 million or less. Just 68 reserved items accounted for 81 per cent of the total value of production of reserved products and 83 per cent of the units.

In recent years, with the opening of Indian trade almost 75 per cent of all reserved items are now already importable with the removal of quantitative restrictions (QRs) in the last few years. India is also committed to remove the remaining QRs by April 2001. We therefore now have a curious situation that the reserved items can be produced by large foreign enterprises and imported into India whereas Indian large enterprises are not allowed to produce the same items! Even this change in the external environment has so far not persuaded the authorities to change this policy of small scale industry reservation.

Reviewing the framework of Indian policies protecting and supporting small scale industries, Rakesh Mohan remarks, "that these policies and programmes are thinly spread thereby leading to relative ineffectiveness. Many of the policies are such that discourage growth of small scale units into larger ones and thereby are likely to have a stunting effect on manufacturing employment and output growth. Some of these policies may have been useful in the earlier stage of Indian industrialisation and in the context of a highly controlled and closed economy. With all the changes in economic environment that have taken place in the 1990s the indication is that future policies for the promotion of small scale industries must be more growth oriented and more general rather than being sector oriented. It would be more useful if such policies are designed to promote entrepreneurial entry, growth of enterprises technology upgradation and labour productivity in a pervasive manner regardless of specific sectors."

Spatial Distribution of SSEs

One of the aims of India's SSI policy was the dispersed development of units in rural areas and in less developed "backward" areas. There has been only limited success in attaining this objective.

The SIDO figures suggest that 85 districts with more than 2,000 units in each account for 51 per cent of the total. More than 81 per cent of SSEs are concentrated in 204 districts, and more than 50 per cent of the districts do not have any significant number of small enterprises (NCAER, 1993 3.7.6, p.81).

Rakesh Mohan argues, the objective of dispersal might be in conflict with the dynamic growth of modern and efficient growth. There has been important spatial concentration of SSEs in "clusters" in particular product lines. The external economies which these clusters generate in terms of easy availability of raw materials, skilled labour, markets etc. have been known to have been instrumental in the growth of SSEs in many countries, including Italy and Germany. India is proving no exception to this basic economic impulse. It is appropriate that these trends might be more emphatically encouraged in official policies and objectives. A closer look needs to be taken at the methods for fostering development in "backward areas" through such methods as tax concessions and special allotment of scarce materials.

Impact of SSI Reservation on Exports

According to Rakesh Mohan, the policy of small scale industry reservations has had a very deleterious effect on the growth of both manufacturing employment and exports. An important feature of industrialisation of the fast growing East Asian countries during the last three decades or so has been high growth in manufactured exports accompanied by high growth in manufacturing employment. The Indian experience has been different. Our record of growth in manufacturing employment has been poor and so has our export growth. The share of exports in Indian GDP has barely reached 10 per cent now. Although this is a significant improvement over the 3 per cent share of 1970 and 5 per cent in 1980, the Indian economy remains the least open among major countries in Asia, including China. The volume of Indian exports in 1970 was the third highest among the 10 Asian countries. Today it is the second lowest. While Chinese exports grew from about US $ 18 billion in 1980 to about US $ 120 billion in 1994 Indian exports during that period grew from US $ 8.6 billion to US $ 25 billion. Given that the composition of exports of industrialising countries is largely labour intensive, one of the reasons behind slow employment growth in manufacturing in India is clearly related to the slow growth in exports.

It is possible that the damage caused by such policies was not very high in the 1970s, when competition in exports of low technology products was not as high as it is now. Furthermore, changing industry structure and demand patterns in the developed world now place a much higher premium on both product quality and service quality with the inexorably rising incomes there. The average quality demanded for products such as clothing, footwear, toys and sports equipment and the like is getting higher and higher. Furthermore, the integration of information technology in even these industries also requires greater investment and greater labour sophistication. Such products are no longer seen as free standing products but are increasingly becoming parts of long value chains with the share of value added in plain manufacturing perhaps falling. Higher quality requires high level designing upstream even for simple products. Downstream marketing involves linkages with large organisations which buy such products in bulk. Small enterprises sandwiched between such high level organisations find it increasingly difficult to operate and be competitive. Thus, apart from the loss that India has suffered over the last 2-3 decades it is likely that the future scenario will become even more difficult for Indian small enterprises to survive, particularly in the reserved sector. Another issue of note is the prospective dismantling of the Multi Fibres Agreement. Paradoxically, although it may have seemed that textile quotas were inhibiting Indian exports, it is likely that we were actually protected through the MFA mechanism. This is shown in Somnath Chatterjee and Rakesh Mohan (1993) who documented the fact that Indian clothing exports went primarily to quota countries and were almost absent in the markets of non quota countries. Thus the removal of small scale reservation is especially necessary in the items affected by the removal of MFA.

Looking at the record of Indian exports in comparison with East Asian countries, it is difficult to avoid the conclusion that Indian exports have been heavily constrained by the policy of SSI product reservation.

Conclusions

The major conclusions of Rakesh Mohan's study are as below:

- We may distinguish the 'small scale modern' sector - consisting of units employing 6 or more workers and the 'tiny' sector including household enterprises. In terms of employment around 1990, the former accounted for roughly 20 per cent of all manufacturing employment, but nearly a half of employment in the modern manufacturing sector. The tiny and household sector is 2.5 to 3 times as large, depending on whether or not we include secondary workers in the labour force. The contribution of SSI in terms of value added is, of course, much smaller - only a third as far as the modern manufacturing sub-sector is concerned and no more than 40 per cent of all manufacturing value added. The last point emphasises the enormous difference in labour productivity between the different sub-sectors of manufacturing.
- As in other countries, the household sub-sector has declined slowly over the last two or three decades. A more surprising finding is that in spite of the vigorous policy of protecting the small scale, this decline has not been fully compensated for by the growth of non-household production in the small scale sector. The SIDO figures of high growth rates of SSI's under their purview seem to be grossly exaggerated.
- Inspite of the vast increase in the number of reserved items, much of the growth in the SSI sector seems to have been in product lines outside the reserved list. It is possible that the policy of reservation might be merely protecting inefficient units in stagnant industries.

- A finding of some concern is the unequal distribution of units of small and large sizes within the SSI sector. There seems to be an increase in the concentration of output in larger units over the last two decades. A comparison of the data from the two SIDO censuses of 1972 and 1987-88 show a sharp fall in the mean employment size but an increase in capital-intensity of the SIDO units – which is consistent with a more skewed distribution of enterprises, and increased contribution of the more productive units.
- The claim that there has been substantial dispersal of units to backward and rural areas under the SSI policy might be exaggerated. As far as the modern SSI's are concerned there is considerable evidence of spatial concentration of SSE's in 'clusters' in specific product groups. We have already emphasised in earlier chapters that there is a need for policies of de-centralization to come to terms with the economic logic of external economies which 'clusters' provide.
- All the evidence suggests that the Indian manufacturing sector is likely to have been constrained by the various, anti-growth policies promoting the small scale sector, particularly that of product reservation. Indian manufacturing employment growth has been the lowest among large Asian countries over the past three or four decades.
- A particular casualty of SSI product reservations has been growth in Indian manufacturing exports. A large number of categories in which India exhibits comparative advantage have been reserved for SSI. Consequently, Indian industry is unable to upgrade quality on a continuous basis and is also not able to diversify to higher technology and higher value added item, thereby stunting export growth.

New Small Enterprise Policy

The document on the new small enterprise policy (NSEP) titled 'Policy Measures for Promoting and Strengthening Small, Tiny and Village Enterprises' was tabled in parliament on August 6, 1991. The NSEP is presented under the major heads of (a) small and tiny enterprises, and (b) village industries. Since the emphasis on objectives in the NSEP of these two groups is not the same, as also because the measures proposed for them are substantially different, it is best to examine the NSEP separately under these heads.

Small and Tiny Enterprises

The primary objective of the NSEP as mentioned under the above head, is to impart "more vitality and growth impetus". In as-much-as vitality is founded basically on cost-efficiency, and is prone to promote growth, the NSEP may be said to have for this sub-sector, the objective of increase in efficiency, and through it to promote growth "of output, employment and exports". In this context, a number of changes are proposed, but four, according to Sandesara, are path-breaking.[2] They are discussed in detail below.

First, the definition of a tiny unit is changed, and this change is two-fold. It may be recalled that the Industrial Policy of May 1990 had announced an increase in the investment limit of tiny units from Rs.2 lakh to Rs.5 lakh. However, it had retained the location requirement to villages and smaller towns (limit of 50,000 population). The NSEP has done away with this requirement. The population of tiny units will, thus, increase, as all units within the investment limit of Rs.5 lakh and located in bigger towns (population of 50,000 plus) will now become a part of the tiny group.

The other definitional change is more basic. Earlier, 'industry' meant, by and large, manufacturing industry. The NSEP has widened the scope to include industry-related services and business enterprises also. All such enterprises, irrespective of their location are now recognised as small scale industries, but their investment ceiling corresponds to those of tiny enterprises. What we really have now, is, thus, a tiny enterprise/business policy instead of a tiny industry (manufacturing) policy as earlier. Thus, this change also increases the number of enterprises in the small sector, more than in the tiny group.

This is to be welcomed for three reasons. First, service and business activities are more labour-intensive than manufacturing activities. Thus, state assistance to these activities will subserve the employment objective. Second, of late, a number of large, high wage/salary paying companies in the manufacturing sector have been getting considerable auxiliary, servicing work done from outside — from smaller, low wage/salary enterprises to reduce the costs of such services. Among such activities are: cleaning, security, typing, transportation and distribution, catering, etc. Partly because of this as also because of other developments, over the years the tertiary sector has grown greatly in

2. J.C. Sandesara, "*Small Enterprise Policy : Implications and Prospects*", in Uma Kapila (ed) 2000-01 edition.

relative terms, following the growth of the secondary sector. To illustrate, the former's share in gross domestic product increased from 28 per cent in 1950-51 to 39 per cent in 1989-90 and the latter's from 15 per cent to 27 per cent, with a corresponding decline in the share of the primary sector from 56 to 24 per cent over the same period. With its share of nearly two-fifths, the tertiary sector has now become the largest, and cannot be neglected by the state. Third, in the US, in the UK and in a number of other countries, for the small sector, it has been really a small business policy and not a small industry policy. It is, thus, in the fitness of things that the NSEP includes non-manufacturing service enterprises.

The third major change relates to equity participation. The NSEP provides for equity participation by other industrial units in the small industrial units not exceeding 24 per cent of the total shareholding. This provision should prove mutually beneficial both to large units and the small units, especially ancillary units, and cement further the economic bonds between the two sectors. Marketing is one of the most difficult problem of small industry, and ancillarisation takes care of this problem in varying measures. Large units are also known to take care of the working capital and quality problems of small units, by giving them advances and by making available their testing facilities. The provision of equity participation not only relieves the small units of the burden of full equity funding, but it also builds up the stakes of large units in the survival and growth of small units.

The fourth special feature of the NSEP is the introduction of a new legal form of organisation of business, namely, restricted or limited partnership. In this form, the liability of at least one partner is unlimited, whereas other partners have their liability limited to invested capital. Following the example of the US and Japan, the A.R. Bhatt Committee had recommended the introduction of this form of organisation in the 70s, but no follow-up action seems to have been initiated until the NSEP. This is a welcome provision. It will attract equity capital especially from friends and relatives of the entrepreneurs of small units, who may like to help their kith and kin, but who fight shy because of unlimited liability in the partnership firm (under which a large number of small units are organised). On the other hand, small units short of funds but wishing to avoid sharing of decision-making will welcome augmentation of risk capital from such sleeping partners.

Village Industries

Although the objectives and policy measures for village industries are presented separately for handlooms, handicrafts and other village industries, there is a lot that is common for them in the NSEP as regards both objectives and measures. To avoid repetition, it may therefore be best to examine first the proposals of the NSEP for these industries together and then draw attention to their special features individually.

A major objective for the group of village industries seems to be, as the word village suggests, to promote rural industrialisation. The other major objective is to promote employment, with a view especially to help the weaker sections of society. Thus, here, employment is more welfare-oriented than efficiency-oriented.

A number of measures are proposed to serve these objectives. Almost all the measures are of routine type, and relate to supply of raw materials, sale of products, upgradation of production methods and improvement in the quality of products, expansion of training facilities, strengthening of the existing support organisations, etc.

The NSEP has broadened the definition of 'tiny' and 'women' enterprises. It has also introduced a new form of legal organisation — restricted partnership — to enable small units to raise equity from private sources. It also permits limited equity participation by other industrial enterprises. It also envisages greater role of non-government agencies like co-operatives, industry associations, voluntary agencies and the like in administering some assistance programme. It also speaks of simplifying rules and procedures.

Performance of Small Scale Industries

The performance of small scale industries sector in terms of critical parameters like number of units (both registered and unregistered), production, employment and export is given in the Table 1. During 1999-2000, the SSI sector recorded production growth of 8.23 per cent over the previous year, higher growth rate than the industrial sector as a whole. Details of comprehensive package on SSI sector announced by Prime Minister on August 30, 2000 are given in Box 1. Other steps taken to promote the sector have been detailed in Box 2 and Box 3.

Sickness in SSI Sector

As on March 31, 2001, there were 2,49,630 sick SSI units which had obtained loans from banks. An amount of Rs. 4,506 crore of bank credit was blocked in these units. Of these only 13,076 units were considered potentially viable by the banks with outstanding credit of

Rs. 399 crore. Further, banks had identified 2,25,488 units with outstanding bank credit amounting to Rs. 3,943 crore as unviable. Rehabilitation of sick units is a costly proposition as it involves rescheduling of past overdues with concessions on interest amount due, additional credit for modernisation and technology upgradation and provision for fresh working capital. Presently, the State Level Inter-Institutional Committee (SLIIC) of banks and financial institutions is the only forum looking into rehabilitation of potentially viable sick SSI units. However, in the absence of statutory backing, SLIICs has no power to enforce its decisions.

There are two main issues in respect of sick SSIs. One is the existence of large number of sick units which are non-viable and the other is the rehabilitation of potentially viable units.

TABLE – 1

OVERALL PERFORMANCE OF SMALL SCALE INDUSTRY

Year	*No. of units (in lakhs)*	*Production (Rs. crore)*		*Employment Nos. in lakh*	*Exports (Rs. crore)*
		(at current prices)	*(at constant prices) (1993-94)*		*(at current prices)*
1994-95	25.71 (7.66)	2,98,886 (23.69)	2,66,054 (10.10)	146.56 (5.15)	29,068 (14.86)
1995-96	26.58 (3.88)	2,62,656 (21.34)	2,96,385 (11.40)	152.61 (4.13)	36,470 (25.46)
1996-97	28.03 (5.46)	4,11,858 (13.57)	3,29,935 (11.32)	160.00 (4.84)	39,248 (7.61)
1997-98	29.44 (5.03)	4,62,641 (12.33)	3,57,749 (8.43)	167.20 (4.50)	44,442 (13.23)
1998-99	30.80 (4.62)	5,20,650 (12.54)	3,85,296 (7.70)	171.58 (2.62)	48,979 (10.21)
1999-00	32.12 (4.29)	5,72,887 (10.03)	4,16,736 (8.16)	178.50 (4.03)	54,200 (10.66)
2000-01	33.12 (3.11)	6,39,024 (11.54)	4,51,033 (8.23)	185.64 (4.00)	69,797 (28.78)
2001-02	34.42 (3.91)	6,90.316 (8.03)	4,78,456 (6.08)	192.23 (3.55)	NA (10.66)
2002-03 (Projected)	35.72 (3.8)	742021 (7.5)	514292 (7.5)	199.65 (3.9)	NA

Notes : Figures in the brackets show percentage growth over previous year.
Source: Economic Survey, 2002-03.

BOX 1

DETAILS OF COMPREHENSIVE POLICY PACKAGE ON SSI & TINY SECTOR ANNOUNCED BY THE PRIME MINISTER ON 30TH AUGUST 2000

(i) Raising the exemption for excise duty limit from Rs. 50 lakh to Rs. One crore to improve the competitiveness of small scale sector.

(ii) Providing Credit Linked capital subsidy of 12 per cent against loans for technology upgradation in specified industries.

(iii) Conducting of the third census of small scale industries by the Ministry of SSI & ARI after a gap of 12 years. This census would also cover sickness and its causes.

(iv) Raising the limit of investment in Industry related service and business enterprise from the present level of Rs. 5.00 lakh to Rs. 10 lakh.

(v) Continuation of the ongoing scheme of granting Rs. 75,000 to each small scale enterprise for obtaining ISO 9000 certification till the end of the X Plan.

(vi) SSI associations encouraged to develop and operate testing laboratories. One time capital grant of 50 per cent will be given on reimbursement basis to such associations after detailed examination of each case.

(vii) Raising of the limit for composite loans from Rs. 10 lakh to Rs. 25 lakh.

(viii) Constitution of group under the Cabinet Secretary to suggest/ recommend streamlining of inspection and repeal of redundant laws and regulations applicable to the sector.

(ix) Increasing the coverage of ongoing Integrated Infrastructure Development (IID) scheme to progressively cover all areas in the country with 50 per cent reservation for rural areas and 50 per cent of plots will be earmarked for tiny sector.

(x) Raising the family income eligibility limit of Rs. 24,000 to Rs. 40,000 per annum. Under the Prime Minister's Rozgar Yojana (PMRY) which finances setting up of micro enterprises and generates employment for the educated unemployed.

BOX 2

OTHER MEASURES TAKEN TO PROMOTE THE SSI SECTOR

1. Two new schemes aimed at addressing to the problem of collaterals faced by the SSI units and to encourage technology upgradation are:

   (i) Credit Guarantee Fund (Scheme) for SSI - The Credit Guarantee Scheme has been launched to provide guarantee for loans upto Rs. 25 lakh extended by Commercial Banks, selected well performing Regional Rural Banks and other Financial institutions without any collateral including third party guarantee.

   (ii) Credit Linked Capital Subsidy Scheme for Technology Upgradation - Government has approved this scheme on 20th September, 2000, wherein 12 per cent back ended capital subsidy would be admissible on loans advanced to SSI by the Scheduled Commercial Banks designated SFCs for technology upgradation in certain sub sectors.

2. Enhancing the excise exemption limit for SSIs - The limit has been enhanced from Rs. 50 lakh to Rs. 1 crore with effect from 1st September, 2000.

3. Improving Credit to SSIs - Steps taken to improve credit flow to SSIs are

   (i) Composite Loan Scheme Limit enhanced to Rs. 25 lakh.

   (ii) For loans upto Rs. 5 lakh, the collateral security requirement has been dispensed with.

   (iii) RBI has constituted a committee to monitor the flow of credit to SSI under the Chairmanship of its Deputy Governor.

4. Dereservation of Readymade Garments - The dereservation is expected to help the sector by technology upgradation, enhancement of productivity, quality consciousness, product diversification, increase in exports and innovative marketing strategies and maximising employment opportunities.

5. Enhancement of investment ceiling for Small Scale Service and Business (industry related) Enterprises - The limit has been enhanced from Rs. 5 lakh to Rs. 10 lakh.

BOX 3

DEVELOPMENTS THAT HAVE TAKEN PLACE DURING THE YEAR 2001-02 FOR THE SSI SECTOR

1. The investment limit for units in hosiery and hand tool sub sectors was enhanced from Rs. 1 crore to Rs. 5 crore.
2. The corpus fund set up under the Credit Guarantee Fund Scheme has been raised to Rs. 200 crore from Rs. 125 crore.
3. Credit Guarantee cover against an aggregate credit of Rs. 22.88 crore was provided till the end of December, 2001.
4. 14 items were dereserved on June 29, 2001 related to leather goods, shoes and toys.
5. A new scheme named Market Development Assistance Scheme was launched exclusively for the SSI sector.
6. Under the Cluster Development Programme, 4 UNIDO assisted projects have been commissioned during the year.

Source : Economic Survey, 2001-02.

The Working Group submitted its report in May, 2001. All the major recommendations of the working group have been accepted by the RBI, including a change in the definition of Sick SSI units, norms for deciding on the viability of sick units, etc. The revised definition would enable banks to take action at an early stage for revival of the units. Based on the accepted recommendations of the Working Group, the RBI has drawn up the revised guidelines for Rehabilitation of Sick SSI units, which have been circulated on January 16, 2002 to all the Banks for implementation.

Box 4 summarises policy initiatives on the SSI sector in 2003-04.

BOX 4

POLICY INITIATIVES ON SMALL-SCALE INDUSTRIES IN 2003-04

- 75 items reserved for exclusive manufacture in the SSI Sector consisting of chemicals and their products, leather and leather products, laboratory reagents etc. were dereserved in June, 2003.
- Selective enhancement of investment in plant and machinery from Rs. 1 crore to Rs. 5 crore carried out in respect of 13 items in stationery sector and 10 items of drugs and pharmaceutical sector from June 5, 2003.
- The Union Budget 2003-04 announced that banks would provide credit to SSI sector within an interest rate band of 2 per cent above and below their Prime Lending Rates (PLR). All public sector banks have adopted this norm.
- The composite loan limit for SSI units was enhanced from Rs. 25 lakhs to Rs. 50 lakhs.
- In its Mid-term Review of Monetary and Credit Policy 2003-04, the RBI announced that banks may enhance the limit of dispensation of collateral requirement for loans from the existing Rs. 15 lakh to Rs. 25 lakh on the basis of good track record and financial position of the units.
- The lower limit of Rs. 5 lakh on loans covered under the Credit Guarantee Scheme has been removed. All loans up to Rs. 25 lakh made eligible for guarantee cover under the Credit Guarantee Scheme.
- 417 SSI specialised bank branches made operational throughout the country.
- The Final Results of Third All India Census of Small Scale Industries were released on January 17, 2004.
- 60 clusters identified in the First Phase (July, 2003) for focused development, by including their credit requirements in the respective State Credit Plans.
- Setting up of a Small and Medium Enterprise (SME) Fund of Rs. 10,000 crore under SIDBI, to *inter alia*, address the problem of inadequacy of financial resources at highly competitve rates for small scale sector.
- Laghu Udyami Credit Card scheme liberalized with enhanced credit limit of Rs. 10 lakh (up from 2 lakh) for borrowers with satisfactory track records.

Source: Economic Survey, 2003-04.

24

Foreign Trade

Constraints arising from Foreign Trade and Import Substitution based Policies

INDIAN economic development strategy, particularly relating to industrialization has been driven by perceived foreign exchange scarcities and the desire to ensure that scarce foreign exchange is used only for purposes deemed "essential" from the perspective of development. Industrialization and self-sufficiency in essential commodities have been important objectives of policy because of the fear that dependence on other, more powerful countries, for imports of essential commodities would lead to political dependence on them as well. Nearly a decade before independence, in 1938, the National Planning Committee was set up by the Indian National Congress (the political party that led the struggle for independence) under the chairmanship of the future prime minister Jawaharlal Nehru. This committee viewed, "... the objective for the country as a whole was the attainment, as far as possible, of national self-sufficiency, International trade was certainly not excluded, but we were anxious to avoid being drawn into the whirl pool of economic imperialism."

Later the First-Year Plan went further :

Control and regulation of exports and imports, and in the case of certain select commodities state trading, are necessary not only from the point of view of utilising to the best advantage the limited foreign exchange resources available but also for securing an allocation of the productive resources of the country in line with the targets defined in the Plan.[1]

1. Planning Commission, First Five Year Plan, (1950) P. 42.

Inward Looking Strategy

India adopted an 'inward looking' strategy of industrialisation. This strategy relied on encouraging domestic production for the domestic market behind high tariffs and high degree of effective protection to the domestic industry. This resulted in an uncompetitive domestic industrial structure. T.N. Srinivasan has argued that the development strategy based on import substituting industrialisation and the system of controls that were implemented failed to produce rapid growth, self-reliance, and eradication of poverty, but instead led to lackluster growth, an internationally uncompetitive industrial structure, a perpetually precarious balance of payments, and, above all, rampant rent seeking and the corruption of social, economic, and political systems.[2]

Far from viewing foreign trade as an engine of growth, Indian planners sought to minimize import demand and viewed exports more or less as a necessary evil mainly to generate the foreign exchange earnings to meet that part of the import bill not covered by external assistance. They created an elaborate administrative regulatory machinery in an attempt to control investment and resource allocation in the economy and ensure their consistency with five-year plan targets. Controls over imports and exports were also part of this regulatory system.

Changing Structure of India's Foreign Trade

In order to study the structure of India's foreign trade we have to analyse the changing pattern of imports and exports.

Since the purpose of the import control regime was to confine imports to essential consumer goods, raw materials, and investment goods needed for domestic production and exports, it is not surprising that changes in the commodity composition of India's imports reflected this. For example, foodgrains and edible oils accounted for about 16 per cent of total imports in 1960/61, and about 1 per cent in 1990/91. Imports of gems, which were negligible in 1960/61, accounted for US $2.079 million or nearly 8 per cent of imports in 1990/91, reflected the fact that gems and jewellery exports at $1.667 million comprised nearly a sixth of total exports. The share of crude petroleum, oils, and lubricants in total imports rose from about 6 per cent in 1960/61 to a high of roughly 40 per cent in 1980/81. However, it fall to about 23 per

2. T.N. Srinivasan, *Foreign Trade Policies and India's Development* in Uma Kapila (ed.) Indian Economy Since Independence, Ch. 25 (2003-04 edition)

cent partly on account of fall of crude petroleum prices and partly also to rapid growth of domestic crude output from the Bombay High Field.

Turning to exports, India's share of world exports has fallen steadily from about 2 per cent in 1950 to less than 0.5 per cent in 1990. Since world export grew rapidly between 1950 and 1973 and somewhat more slowly thereafter, India's exports grew in absolute terms inspite of a declining share. But the dramatic fall in share reflects the fact that other countries were able to take greater advantage of growing world trade.

TABLE – 1

VALUE OF EXPORTS AND IMPORTS IN THE PLANNING PERIOD

(US $ million)

Year	*Exports*	*Imports*	*Trade Balance*	*Rate of Change*	
				Exports	*Imports*
(1)	*(2)*	*(3)*	*(4)*	*(5)*	*(6)*
1950-51	1269	1273	-4	24.9	-1.5
1960-61	1346	2353	-1007	0.3	16.7
1970-71	2031	2162	-131	8.8	3.5
1980-81	8486	15869	-7383	6.8	40.2
1990-91	18143	24075	-5932	9.2	13.5
1993-94	22238	23306	-1068	20.0	6.5
1994-95	26330	28654	-2324	18.4	22.9
1995-96	31797	36678	-4881	20.8	28.0
1996-97	33470	39133	5663	5.3	6.7
1997-98	35006	41484	6478	4.6	6.0
1998-99	33218	42389	-9171	-5.1	2.2
1999-2000	36822	49671	-12849	10.8	17.2
2000-01	44560	50536	-5976	21.0	1.7
2001-02	43827	81413	-7586	-1.6	1.7
2001-02 (Apr.-Dec.)	**32572**	**38362**	**-5790**	**0.6**	**0.3**
2002-03(P)	**38115**	**43882**	**-6767**	**20.4**	**14.5**

Source: Government of India, Economic Survey, 1998-99, Statement 7.1 (B) p. S-81 and Economic Survey 2002-03, p. (S-79).

In recent years, however, primary exports have been virtually stagnant, and manufactured products have accounted for almost the entire growth in total exports. Among manufactured products, just four items leather, gems, garments, and textiles – account for most of the growth in recent years. In contrast, the export of engineering goods, which rose by over 20 per cent per year in value terms between 1950/51 and 1975/76 and between 1970/71 and 1978/79, declined between 1980/81 and 1985/86. The value of engineering goods exports grew at an average annual rate of 20.5 per cent during the period 1985/1990. Chemical exports show a similar pattern.

TABLE – 2

COMPOSITION OF INDIAN IMPORTS

Commodities	*1960-61*	*1970-71*	*1980-81*	*1996-97*	*1997-98*	*1999-00*	*2000-01*	*2001-02*
	% of total	*% of total*	*% of total*	*% of total*	*% of total*	*% of total*	*% of total*	*% of total*
1. Food and live animals for food	**19.1**	**14.8**	**3.0**	**N.A.**	**N.A.**			
of which :								
Cereal and cereal preparations	16.1	13.0	0.8	0.4	0.7	0.4	-	-
2. Raw materials and intermediate manufactures	**47.0**	**54.4**	**77.8**	**N.A.**	**N.A.**			
of which								
(a) Edible oils	0.4	1.4	5.4	2.1	1.8	3.7	2.6	2.8
(b) Petroleum oil and lubricants	6.1	8.3	41.9	25.6	20.2	25.4	31.0	29.3
(c) Fertilisers	1.1	5.3	6.5	2.3	2.5	2.8	1.5	1.5
(d) Iron and Steel	11.0	9.0	6.8	4.9	3.7	1.6	1.4	1.5
(e) Chemicals elements and compounds	3.5	4.2	2.8	7.5	8.0	7.9	6.7	7.5
(f) Pearls and precious stones	0.1	1.5	3.3	7.5	7.7	10.9	9.6	8.3
3. Capital goods	**31.7**	**24.7**	**15.2**	**21.5**	**17.5**			
of which :								
(a) Non-electrical machinery*	18.1	15.8	8.7	10.7	9.7	5.5	5.4	5.4
(b) Electrical machinery*	5.1	4.3	2.1	0.8	0.9	0.9	1.0	1.2
(c) Transport equipment	6.4	4.3	2.1	0.8	0.9	2.3	1.9	1.1
4. Others (unclassified)	**2.2**	**6.1**	**4.0**	**N.A.**	**N.A.**			
Total	100.0	100.0	100.0	100.0	100.0			

* From the year 1991-92 onwards, non-electrical machinery and electrical machinery exclude electronic goods.

Source: Government of India, Economic Survey, 1998-99, Statement 7.2 (A), pp. S-83 to S-85 and Economic Survey, 2001-02.

The composition of India's exports has, as expected, shifted moderately away from primary products to manufactured goods, whose share rose from about 45 per cent in 1950-51 to 79 per cent in 1990-91. In recent years, however, primary exports have been virtually stagnant, and manufactured products have accounted for almost the entire growth in total exports (Table 3). Among manufactured products, just four items leather, gems, garments, and textiles — accounted for most of the growth in recent years. In contrast, the export of engineering goods, which rose by over 20 per cent per year in value terms between 1950-51 and 1975-76 and between 1970-71 and 1978-79, declined between 1980-81 and 1985-86. From the low point of US $780 million in 1985-86, the value of engineering goods exports grew at an average annual rate of 20.5 per cent during the period 1985-1990. Chemical exports show a similar pattern.

The export of gems has grown rapidly since the early 1970s. This export is heavily dependent, however, on the import of uncut small gems, the cost of which is determined in large part by the South African monopoly De Beers. The exports of garments and textiles are governed by India's quotas under the multifibre arrangement (MFA). Bhalla (1989) points out that until the 1980s, India did not fully use quotas, and India's competitors did better in quota, as well as, non-quota countries. It is possible that the recent spurt in India's garment and textile exports reflects better use of quotas and higher prices realized on the average. Whether India will be able to compete in the textile and apparel market in the absence of the MFA is debatable, particularly in view of the fact that the Indian textile industry has fallen behind technologically in the past four decades primarily because of the government's textile policy.

During the recent high-growth phase of India's exports, that is, between 1993-94 and 1995-96, major export items which had contributed significantly to the growth process included engineering goods, cotton yarn, fabrics, chemicals and allied products, rice, coffee, processed fruits, juices and miscellaneous processed items and marine products. The growth rates of export of all these items have dropped considerably during the last two years. Among the manufactured exports, the deceleration of growth rate has been most marked for engineering goods. Within the agricultural and allied products group, export levels of both rice and coffee declined between 1995-96 and 1997-98.[3]

---

3. Reserve Bank of India, Report on Currency and Finance, 1997-98, Vol.1.

TABLE – 3

COMPOSITION OF INDIAN EXPORTS

Commodities	*1960-61*	*1970-71*	*1980-81*	*1996-97*	*1997-98*	*1999-00*	*2000-01*	*2001-02*
	% of total	*% of total*	*% of total*	*% of total*	*% of total*	*% of total*	*% of total*	*% of total*
1. Agriculture and allied products	**44.2**	**31.7**	**30.6**	**20.4**	**18.8**	**15.2**	**13.5**	**13.3**
of which :								
(a) Tea and mate	19.3	9.6	6.3	1.2	1.3	1.1	1.0	1.0
(b) Cashew kernels	3.0	3.7	2.1	1.1	1.1	1.5	0.9	0.8
(c) Raw cotton	1.9	0.9	2.5	1.3	0.7	–	0.1	–
(d) Fish and fish preparations	0.8	2.0	3.2	3.4	3.4	3.2	3.1	3.1
2. Ores and Minerals (excluding coal)	**8.1**	**10.7**	**6.2**	**2.7**	**2.4**	**2.5**	**2.6**	**2.6**
of which								
Iron Ore	2.6	7.6	4.5	1.4	1.4	0.7	0.8	0.7
3. Manufactured goods	**45.3**	**50.3**	**55.8**	**74.5**	**76.6**	**80.7**	**78.0**	**76.1**
of which :								
(a) Readymade garments	0.1	1.9	8.2	11.2	11.1	12.9	12.5	11.3
(b) Jute manufactures	21.0	12.4	4.9	0.5	0.3	8.4	7.9	7.4
(c) Leather and Leather manufactures	4.4	5.2	5.8	4.7	4.3	2.6	2.9	3.1
(d) Handicrafts	1.7	4.7	14.2	16.9	17.8	3.6	3.1	2.6
of which								
Gems and Jewellery	0.1	2.9	9.2	14.2	15.1	20.4	16.6	16.0
(e) Chemicals and allied products	1.1	1.9	3.3	9.6	10.7	4.5	4.3	4.5
(f) Engineering goods	3.4	12.9	12.3	14.7	14.8	3.2	3.7	4.0
4. Others	**2.4**	**7.3**	**7.4**	**2.4**	**2.2**	**1.5**	**1.7**	**2.7**
Total	100.0	100.0	100.0	100.0	100.0	100.0	100.0	100.0

Source: Compiled from Economic Survey, 1998-99, Statement 7.2 (A), pp. S-83 to S-85 and Economic Survey 2001-02.

TABLE – 4

COMPOSITION OF RECENT EXPORT GROWTH IN INDIA, 1980-81-1990-91

	Average annual value (US $ millions at current prices)			
	1980/81-1985/86	*1986/87-1990/91*	*Increase*	*Contribution to growth (%)*
Manufactured exports	5,296	10,83	5,542	97
Consumption goods	3,408	6,514	3,106	55
Leather	502	1,046	544	10
Gems (gross)	1,097	2,551	1,454	26
Garments	757	1,612	855	15
Textiles	1,052	1,305	253	4
Investment goods[a]	860	1,518	658	12
Intermediate goods	1,028	2,805	1,777	31
Chemicals	382	1,138	756	13
Petroleum products	238	421	183	3
Other[b]	407	1,247	839	15
Primary exports	3144	3,287	143	3
Fish	340	442	102	2
Rice	210	227	17	0
Cashews	165	231	66	1
Coffee	185	195	9	0
Tea	497	493	-4	0
Spices	145	181	37	1
Iron ore	408	490	83	1
Other primary exports	1,195	1,028	-167	-3
Total exports (Customs)[c]	8,440	14,124	5,685	100
Discrepancy	641	416	-226	
Total exports (BOP)[d]	9,081	14,540	5,459	
Memo				
Gems(net)	290	688	398	

a Refers to engineering goods.

b Including unclassified exports.

c Total exports, f.o.b., net of crude oil.

d Exports less imports of gems and jewellery.

Source : Ministry of Commerce. Directorate General of Commercial Intelligence and Statistics: Reserve Bank of India.

India's Foreign Trade: Policy, Performance and Structural Change During Nineties

Liberalisation of external trade formed an important aspect of the economic reforms programme launched in July, 1991. Although policy efforts directed towards external liberalisation can be traced back to late-'seventies and mid-'eighties, it is only during the 'nineties that such measures received a momentum as well as definitive direction. Responding to such policy changes, India's foreign trade exhibited considerable buoyancy during the period 1993-94 to 1995-96 with both exports and imports recording, on an average, an increase of around 20 per cent per annum. The growth in India's foreign trade, however, decelerated during the next three years i.e., during 1996-97 to 1998-99.

A review of India's trade performance over the years reveals the influence of a variety of factors – both external and internal. While exact quantification of the relative impact of policy measures vis-a-vis other factors on India's trade performance may not be possible, it would be worthwhile to explore whether the major structural indicators of India's foreign trade have undergone noticeable changes during the 'nineties as compared with the 'eighties.

Comparison between 90's and 80's

For the purpose of analysis at the aggregate level, India's trade performance during 1992-93 to 1998-99 (referred to here as the 'nineties) has been compared with that during 1980-81 to 1990-91 (the 'eighties). The year 1991-92 witnessed considerable strain on the balance-of-payments. To meet the crisis, severe restrictions were placed on imports and the Rupee was adjusted downward in July 1991. Being an exceptional year, 1991-92 should be excluded in any time series based analysis of trade developments. The periodisation of the analysis captures the structural shifts in the growth of exports and imports during the sub-periods. For instance, on an average annual basis, export growth during 1992-93 to 1998-99 at 9.8 per cent was higher than that of 8.2 per cent registered during 1980-81 to 1990-91. Similarly, the average import growth observed during the 'nineties at 12.0 per cent remained substantially higher than that of 7.8 per cent recorded during the 'eighties (1980-81 to 1990-91).

The world trade has undergone significant changes since 1996 due to a host of developments including a sharp fall in international prices for manufactured products and the emergence of economic crises in certain parts of the world. In addition, protectionist policies and practices adopted by various industrialised countries during the recent years and perhaps most importantly anti-dumping and countervailing measures seriously affected the export efforts of the developing countries (Stiglitz, 1999). These unfavourable factors have had their impact on the developing countries including India's trade performance.

In the light of the above factors, it would be appropriate to examine the trade performance of India during the two sub-periods of the 'nineties; the first sub-period covering the first four years following the introduction of reforms (i.e., 1992-93 to 1995-96) and the second sub-period consisting of the subsequent three years (i.e., 1996-97 to 1998-99). During the first sub-period, on an average basis, India's exports and imports increased by 15.7 and 17.5 per cent, respectively, which were significantly higher than the growth rates during the 'eighties. Broadly in line with the unfavourable external developments, between 1996-97 and 1998-99, growth in India's exports and imports, on an average basis, decelerated to 2.0 per cent and 4.5 per cent, respectively. India's share in world exports, which had declined from 0.52 per cent to 0.47 per cent between 1984 and 1987, improved to 0.53 per cent in 1992. Notwithstanding the slowdown in India's export growth since 1996, reflecting the relatively better performance by India vis-a-vis rest-of-the-world, its share in global exports reached 0.62 per cent during 1997 (IMF, 1998).

Trade GDP Ratio

India's trade-GDP ratio showed substantial improvements during the 'nineties as compared with the 'eighties. The export-GDP ratio declined from 4.9 per cent in 1980-81 to 4.2 per cent in 1985-86 and thereafter it gradually improved and reached 6.1 per cent in 1990-91. During the 'nineties, the ratio reached its highest level at 8.7 per cent in 1995-96. The ratio declined, marginally, during the next three years and was at 8.1 per cent in 1998-99. On an average basis, export-GDP ratio increased from 5.0 per cent to 8.2 per cent between the 'eighties and the 'nineties. Between these two periods, on an average basis, India's import-GDP ratio increased from 7.7 per cent to 9.4 per cent. The noticeable improvements in the export-GDP and import-GDP ratios point to the increasing openness of India's foreign trade regime to global trade.

Trade Deficit-GDP Ratio

Along with the increase in trade-GDP ratio, there has been a decline in India's trade deficit-GDP ratio between the two periods. This is borne out by the fact that the difference between export and import-GDP ratio on an average basis, declined from 2.7 per cent in the 'eighties to 1.2 per cent in the 'nineties. This indicates that the divergence between export and import performance was more pronounced during the 'eighties than in the 'nineties. Similarly, the export-import ratio (on an average basis) increased substantially from 65.1 per cent during the 'eighties to 87.0 per cent during the 'nineties reflecting thereby the increasing alignment between India's export and import performance during the 'nineties as compared with the 'eighties.

TABLE – 5

INDIA'S FOREIGN TRADE RATIOS

(Per cent)

Period Average	*X/GDP*	*M/GDP*	*T/GDP*	*X/M*
	1	*2*	*3*	*4*
1980-81 to 1989-90	4.6	7.2	11.8	64.0
1990-91 to 1999-00*	8.0	9.5	17.4	84.1
1990-91 to 1994-95*	7.3	8.4	15.7	86.9
1995-96 to 1999-00	8.5	10.4	18.9	81.8
2000-01 to 2001-02	9.4	10.8	20.2	86.7

* Excluding 1991-92.

Note : X=Exports, M-Imports, T=Exports+Imports, GDP=Gross Domestic Product at current market prices in rupees.

Sources : 1. Directorate General of Commercial Intelligence & Statistics.
2. Economic Survey, Government of India.

Structural Change in Exports

Changes in terms of Broad Categories

Reflecting the development of a large and diversified industrial sector, during the post-independence period, India has gradually transformed from a predominantly primary product exporting country into an exporter of manufactured products. In the mid-'eighties, manufactured exports accounted for about two-thirds of India's total exports while the rest comprised of primary products. During the years preceding the introduction of economic reforms, i.e., between 1987-88 and 1991-92, while the share of manufactured goods increased from 67.8 per cent to 73.8 per cent, that of primary products declined from

26.1 per cent to 23.1 per cent. These trends were reinforced during the subsequent period (i.e., 1992-93 to 1998-99). On an average basis, the share of manufactured products increased by 4 percentage points while that of primary commodities declined by 2 percentage points between the 'eighties and the 'nineties. The share of residual exports including petroleum products declined almost continuously between 1987-88 and 1998-99.

An analysis of the commodity composition of India's exports shows that the combined share of the top six export categories, namely, gems and jewellery, readymade garments, engineering goods, textile yarn, fabrics, made-ups, etc., leather and manufactures and chemicals and allied products increased steadily from 59.4 per cent in 1987-88 to 65.7 per cent in 1991-92. On an average basis, the combined share of these exports at 66.8 per cent during the period 1992-93 to 1998-99 was 3 percentage points higher than that during the 'eighties.

The increase in the share of the top six categories of exports in the total exports by 9 per cent between 1987-88 and 1998-99 reflects a rise in the concentration of India's exports in terms of broad export categories. It may, however, be mentioned that each of these top export categories consists of a large number of individual items. Even if the export shares of traditional items within a broad category decline, the share of the whole product category in total exports can increase due to appearance of newer products within that group. The emergence of newer export items, however, indicate export diversification and in order to get a clear picture about the change in the concentration of exports, it is essential to examine the issue at a more disaggregated level.

Commodity Composition: Exports

The changes in the structure of India's exports is more noticeable at the disaggregated level. Items that registered considerable improvements in relative export performance between the 'eighties and the 'nineties include coffee, processed fruits, juices and miscellaneous processed items, rice, spices, works of art excluding floor coverings and other items like sugar and mollases and raw cotton (not elsewhere included). On an average basis, the total export earning from these six items taken together declined by 2.9 per cent in the 'eighties, while they registered an impressive 20.5 per cent growth rate in the 'nineties. Items, which have exhibited steady relative export performance through the two periods include drugs, pharmaceuticals and fine chemicals, other agricultural and allied items, cotton year, fabrics, made-ups, etc. On an average basis, the total export earning from these three items taken together increased by 16.1 per cent and 12.8 per cent during the 'eighties and the 'nineties, respectively. The relative export performance of items such as oil meal, hand-made carpets excluding silk carpets, other ores and minerals and rubber, glass, paints, enamels and products worsened considerably during the 'nineties as compared to the 'eighties. As against an average growth of 18.1 per cent during the first period, the average growth rate of export earnings by these four items taken together decelerated sharply to 6.5 per cent during the 'nineties. Items which registered relatively low growth rates during the both periods include cashew, gems and jewellery, iron ore, leather and manufactures, natural silk yarn, fabrics, made-ups, etc., petroleum products and tea. The combined export earnings of these seven items taken together, on an average basis, increased by 6.3 per cent and 6.7 per cent, during the pre-1992 and post-1992 periods, respectively.

The change in the relative performance of individual export items between the two periods indicates that the change in the structure of agriculture and allied exports has been more marked than manufactured exports. Items such as coffee, rice, processed fruits, juices and miscellaneous processed items remained relatively less important export items during the 'eighties. These items, however, can be identified as crucial emerging exports during the 'nineties. In terms of average growth rate, these exports had declined by 3.2 per cent in the 'eighties, while they increased by an impressive 29.7 per cent in the 'nineties. The combined share of these three exports in India's total agricultural and allied exports had declined from 23.3 per cent in 1987-88 to 15.4 per cent in 1990-91. Their share more than doubled to reach 34.2 per cent in 1998-99. Alongside the emergence of newer products, the relative importance of some of India's traditional agricultural and allied export items such as cashew, oil meal, tea and tobacco declined considerably as between the two periods. On an average, the growth rate of these exports decelerated from 7.9 per cent in the 'eighties to 4.2 per cent in the 'nineties. More importantly, their combined share in total agricultural and allied exports, which increased from 38.1 per cent in 1987-88 to 43.6 per cent in 1989-90, declined sharply to 26.2 per cent in 1998-99.

Move Towards Value-addition

There are indications that during the 'nineties, some of the Indian exports have moved upwards in the value-addition chain whereby instead of exporting raw materials, the country has switched over to the export of processed items. For example, while the value of iron ore exports declined, that of primary and semi-finished iron and steel increased many fold between the two periods. Reflecting this trend, the share of ores and minerals in total exports declined, on an average basis, from 5.5 per cent to 3.5 per cent between the 'eighties and the 'nineties.

There were also significant compositional shifts within the major manufactured product groups such as engineering goods, chemicals and allied products, etc. as between the two periods. On an average basis, the share of basic chemicals, pharmaceuticals and cosmetics within the chemicals and allied group, declined from 71.4 per cent to 62.4 per cent between the 'eighties and the 'nineties. In particular, the average export share of cosmetics, toiletries, etc. within this group declined sharply from 12.4 per cent to 4.7 per cent between these two periods. Within the same group, the average export share of plastic and linoleum increased from 6.4 per cent during the 'eighties to 13.2 per cent in the 'nineties. Among the components of engineering goods, the average share of machinery and equipment in total engineering exports declined from 30.6 per cent to 21.7 per cent while that of primary and semi-finished iron and steel increased from 2.9 per cent to 11.9 per cent as between the two periods. Among the textile products, while the importance of man-made yarn, fabrics, made-ups increased as between two periods, that of jute manufactures declined sharply. The internal export composition of leather and leather manufactures and readymade garments remained stable before and after the initiation of economic reforms.

Moving away from Traditional Exports towards New Manufactured Products

India's manufacturing exports are showing tendencies of shifting away from traditional exports towards relatively new manufactured products. Another interesting point about the compositional change in the manufactured exports is that, by and large, major export items within the category for which internal composition remained unchanged between the 'eighties and the 'nineties (e.g., leather and leather products, ready-made garments) recorded relatively poor export performance as compared with groups which recorded changes in their internal composition (e.g., chemicals and allied products, engineering goods). This indicates the existence of a close link between export performance and structural change in the case of India's manufactured exports.

As mentioned earlier, since 1996-97 there has been a marked deceleration in the growth of India's manufactured exports. Apart from its negative impact on the overall export growth, a fall in the growth of manufactured exports also likely to have constrained structural transformation within the category of manufactured exports. A number of external as well as domestic factors contributed to the process of slowdown in India's exports in general and manufactured exports in particular. These included: decline in international manufactured prices, increased protectionism by the industrialised countries coupled with non-implementation of the transitional agreements on integration of trade in textiles and clothing with the WTO by the industrialised countries. While these factors had adverse implications for Indian manufacturing exports, particularly exports of engineering goods, chemicals and allied products and textiles and clothing, the sharp price fluctuation in the international market for raw diamonds and gold between 1996 and 1998, had contributed to the decline in gems and jewellery exports, the single largest export item of India.

India's Share in Global Exports: Compositional Change

The foregoing discussion focuses solely on the internal change in the commodity composition of India's exports. It is also important to study whether there has been any change in India's share in global trade. It may be noted that commodities for which India's share in global exports have increased considerably as between the two periods include rice, coffee and substitutes, feeding stuff for animals, textile yarn (in particular, cotton yarn), pearls, precious and semi-precious stones and gold and silver jewellery. Items for which India's global export share declined as between the two periods include shellfish, tea and mate, spices, iron ore concentrate, leather, leather manufactures and certain categories of textile and garment articles.

It is interesting to note that during the 'eighties, there were many export items for which India's global market shares were high while growth in world trade for those products was low. It is argued that lack of alignment between the composition of India's export basket and the demand structure in foreign markets has been a major constraint for expansion of India's exports. Reversing such trends, during the 'nineties, by and large, India's global shares have improved for those commodities for which world trade showed relatively high growth potential and India's global shares declined for those commodities for which growth in world trade decelerated. In other words, the alignment between the structure of world demand and the composition of India's exports has improved during the 'nineties as compared to the 'eighties. This is likely to have major impact on the future behaviour of India's exports.

India's export share in world trade has increased perceptibly during the recent period. India's exports as a percentage of world exports improved to 0.56 per cent during 1991-96 and further to 0.65 per cent during 1996-2002 from 0.48 per cent in the 1980s. The ratio was 0.71 per cent in 2000-01, the highest achieved so far since the 1970s. Nonetheless, India's share in world exports is still very low and appears unimpressive when compared with the other major trading Asian countries, such as, China and other East Asian economies like Malaysia, Thailand, Singapore, Korea and Indonesia (Table 6). China demonstrated the most dramatic change as its share in world exports more than doubled in a decade from 2.0 per cent in 1991 to 4.4 per cent in 2001. Group-wise, India's share in the imports of industrialised countries in the 1990s declined as compared to that in 1986. In respect of the developing countries as a group, however, it has increased from 0.5 per cent in 1986 to 1.1 per cent during 1996-2000.

TABLE – 6

SHARE OF SELECT EAST ASIAN COUNTRIES IN WORLD EXPORTS

(Per cent)

Country	*Annual*					*Average*	
	1991	*1995*	*1999*	*2000*	*2001*	*1991-1995*	*1996-2000*
	1	*2*	*3*	*4*	*5*	*6*	*7*
India	0.5	0.6	0.6	0.7	0.7	0.6	0.6
China	2.0	2.9	3.5	4.0	4.4	2.5	3.4
Indonesia	0.8	0.9	0.9	1.0	0.9	0.9	0.9
Korea	2.0	2.4	2.6	2.7	2.5	3.0	2.5
Malaysia	1.0	1.4	1.5	1.6	1.4	1.2	1.5
Singapore	1.7	2.3	2.0	2.8	2.0	2.0	2.3
Thailand	0.8	1.1	1.0	1.0	2.0	1.0	1.0

Source : International Financial Statistics, February 2003.

The Ministry of Commerce and Industry, Government of India has set an export target of 1 per cent share of world exports by 2006-07 for the medium-term which would be co-terminus with the Tenth Five Year Plan. This target is based on historical trends, current prospects and the requirement of a compound annual growth rate of about 12 per cent for exports till the year 2006-07 (Government of India, 2002a). The export performance is known to depend on price competitiveness, as well as non-price factors. As regards the price competitiveness, a number of earlier studies have emphasised that real exchange rate may be an important variable influencing the price competitiveness of India's exports. In India, large exchange rate misalignment has not occured in the last one decade as the market itself has corrected the misalignment gradually over different episodes.

India's export performance is affected by domestic as well as external impediments. The domestic factors inhibiting India's export growth are infrastructure constraints, high transactions cost, small-scale industry reservations, inflexibilities in labour laws, lack of quality consciousness and constraints in attracting FDI in the export sector. High levels of protection in relation to other countries also explain why FDI in India has been much more oriented to the protected domestic market, rather than as a base for exports. The exports of developing countries like India are facing increasing difficulties by emerging protectionist sentiments in some sectors in the form of technical standards, environmental and social concerns besides non-trade barriers like anti-dumping duties, countervailing duties, safeguard measures and sanitary and phyto-sanitary measures. Indian products which have been affected by such barriers include floriculture products, textiles, pharmaceuticals, marine products and basmati rice exports to the European Union and mushroom and steel exports to USA and also grapes, egg products, gherkins, honey, meat products, milk products, tea, and spices. Differential tariffs against developing countries have also adversely affected market access into these countries (Government of India, 2002b; WTO, 2002). According to the WTO, exports from India are currently subject to 40 anti-dumping and 13 countervailing measures mainly for agricultural products, textiles and clothing products and chemicals and related products. This brings into focus the importance of non-price factors like quality, packaging and the like mentioned earlier, where India still seems to be lacking as compared to the international standards. This has adversely affected India's export performance vis-a-vis other developing countries which may have an improved standing in these non-price factors.

Commodity Composition of Imports

In the discussion on the structural change in India's imports in this sub-section, the relative shares of the major commodities/groups in total imports should generally be exclusive of gold and silver imports. This has been done keeping in view the sharp increase in gold and silver imports in the recent years, which obscures the changes in the relative shares of other items. The import of gold and silver rose from US $ 4 million in 1990-91 to US $ 4,876 million in 1998-99 and formed as much as 11.6 per cent of India's total imports during that year.

The relative share of capital goods in India's total imports net of gold and silver improved, marginally, from 25.6 per cent during 1987-91 to 26.0 per cent during 1992-99. Within the capital goods group, the rise in import was more pronounced in the case of manufacture of metals, machine tools, and electrical machinery (including electronic and computer goods), while that of non-electrical machinery and transport equipment recorded a relatively low order of increase. While the overall increase in the import of industrial raw materials and intermediate goods was less pronounced, certain individual items mainly catering to export activities such as cashew nuts, textile yarn, fabrics, made-ups etc., and chemicals (organic and inorganic), however, recorded sharper rise.

Among other items, the imports of petroleum (crude and products) showed wide fluctuations, reflecting *inter alia*, the movements in international prices. There was a sharp increase in its import during 1989-90 (25.2 per cent) and 1990-91 (60.0 per cent) and the average annual growth rate during 1988-91 was considerably higher at 27.2 per cent as compared with the 12.0 per cent growth in total imports. After attaining a high base in 1990-91, the oil imports declined during 1991-92 by 11.7 per cent. During the period 1992-93 to 1998-99, the growth rate in oil imports ranged between 33.4 per cent in 1996-97 and a negative of 21.2 per cent in 1998-99. Although the average annual growth rate of this item during 1992-99 was low (4.6 per cent), the average value at US $ 7,134 million stood 79.2 per cent higher than US $ 3,981 million during 1987-91. Consequently, the relative share of oil imports moved up to 22.5 per cent during 1992-99 from 19.4 per cent during 1987-91.

Similarly, the average level of import of manufactured fertilizers during 1992-99 also stood 77.7 per cent higher than that during 1987-91, although the average annual growth rate remained considerably lower at 9.5 per cent during 1992-99 than that of 79.5 per cent during 1988-91. The increase in the imports of consumption goods was relatively less pronounced (27.3 per cent), with its share dropping from 4.3 per cent during 1987-91 to 3.6 per cent during 1992-99. Within this category, the import of edible oils, however, increased by 55.9 per cent and that of sugar increased by 269.3 per cent.

The changes in the structure of India's imports are reflective of the influence of three factors:

(1) movements in international prices;

(2) changes in trade policy; and

(3) pattern of domestic demand.

The role of international prices in shaping the trends in the import of petroleum, crude and products has already been discussed earlier. This apart, it may be indicated that the international prices of manufactured goods have declined considerably during the recent years, keeping their import value depressed.

The surge in the imports of gold and silver, edible oils and manufactured fertilizers were to some extent policy driven. Similarly, reflecting the impact of further easing of the restrictions on the import of capital goods, these items recorded higher import growth during 1992-99. Since a sizable part of India's imports cater to the needs of the industrial sector, the trends in the demand for imports may be judged from the overall growth in industrial production.

Direction of Foreign Trade

Prior to Independence, a large part of India's trade was either directly with Great Britain or its colonies or allies. This pattern continued for some years after Independence as well since India had not till then explored the possibilities of developing trade relations with other countries of the world. For example, the combined share of U.K. and U.S.A. in India's export earnings was 42 per cent in 1950-51. Their share in India's import expenditure was as much as 39.1 per cent in the same year. With other capitalist countries like France, Germany, Italy, Japan, etc. India either did not have trade relations at all or they were very insignificant. As political and diplomatic contacts developed with other countries, economic relations also made a headway. Thus new vistas for developing trade relations with other countries opened up. The situation has changed very much since, and now after four and a half decades of planning, the trading relations exhibit marked changes. The diversification in trade relations has reduced the vulnerability of the economy to outside political pressures.

In the year 1950-51, the share of U.K. in India's imports was 20.8 per cent and that of U.S.A. was 18.3 per cent. Thus the combined share of these two countries was 39.1 per cent. This reflected the colonial heritage of the country. Within a decade, the picture started showing some changes. New trading partners like West Germany, Canada and U.S.S.R. emerged. There was a change in the relative position of U.K. and U.S.A. as well, with the latter pushing down the former to the second place. Excepting a year or two, U.S.A. has continuously maintained the first position thereafter. During the planning period as a whole, India has obtained maximum imports from U.S.A., the reason

TABLE – 7 : DIRECTION OF INDIA'S FOREIGN TRADE

(percentage share)

	Imports					Exports					
	1960-61	*1970-71*	*1980-81*	*1990-91*	*1999-00*	*1960-61*	*1970-71*	*1980-81*	*1990-91*	*1999-00*	*2001-02*
1. OECD	**78.0**	**63.8**	**45.7**	**54.0**	**44.8**	**66.1**	**50.1**	**46.6**	**53.5**	**57.6**	**49.3**
of which											
(a) EU	37.1	19.6	21.0	29.4	21.9	36.2	18.4	21.6	27.5	25.1	22.5
of which											
(i) Belgium	1.4	0.7	2.4	6.3	7.4	0.8	1.3	2.2	3.9	3.7	
(ii) France	1.9	1.3	2.2	3.0	1.6	1.4	1.2	2.2	2.4	2.4	
(iii) Germany	10.9	6.6	5.5	8.0@	4.0@	3.1	2.1	5.7	7.8@	4.8@	
(iv) U.K.	19.4	7.8	5.8	6.7	5.8	26.9	11.1	5.9	6.5	6.0	
(b) U.S.A.	29.2	27.7	12.9	12.1	7.7	16.0	13.5	11.1	14.7	22.7	19.4
(c) Japan	5.4	5.1	6.0	7.5	5.0	5.0	13.3	8.9	9.3	4.5	
2. OPEC	**4.6**	**7.7**	**27.8**	**16.3**	**4.1**	**6.4**	**11.1**	**9.7**	**5.6**	**10.6**	**11.9**
of which											
(i) Iran	2.6	5.6	10.7	2.4	2.1	0.8	1.7	1.8	0.4	0.4	
(ii) Iraq	0.2	0.2	6.0	1.1	0.4	0.5	0.6	0.8	0.1	0.1	
(iii) Kuwait	0.0	0.3	2.7	0.8	3.3	0.5	1.0	1.4	0.2	0.4	
(iv) Saudi Arabia	1.3	1.5	4.3	6.7	4.8	0.5	0.9	2.5	1.3	2.0	
3. Eastern Europe	**3.4**	**13.5**	**10.3**	**7.8**	**1.7**	**7.0**	**21.0**	**22.1**	**17.9**	**3.0**	**2.9**
of which											
(i) Russia@@	1.4	6.5	8.1	5.9	1.3	4.5	13.7	18.3	16.1	2.5	
4. Developing Nations*	**11.8**	**14.6**	**15.7**	**18.4**	**22.6**	**14.8**	**19.8**	**19.2**	**16.8**	**25.1**	**30.9**
of which											
(i) Africa	5.6	10.4	1.6	2.2	3.2	6.3	8.4	5.2	2.1	3.0	5.2
(ii) Asia	5.7	3.3	11.4	14.0	17.5	6.9	10.8	13.4	14.3	20.4	23.6
(iii) Latin America and Carribean	0.4	1.0	2.5	2.3	1.9	1.6	0.7	0.5	0.4	1.7	
5. Others	**2.2**	**0.5**	**0.5**	**3.5**	**7.2**	**8.0**	**2.6**	**1.0**	**6.2**	**3.6**	**2.1**
Total	**100.0**	**100.0**	**100.0**	**100.0**	**100.0**	**100.0**	**100.0**	**100.0**	**100.0**	**100.0**	**100.0**

@ Figures for unified Germany. @@ Refers to former USSR before 1992-93

* Excluding members of OPEC.

Source: Government of India, Economic Survey, 2000-01, Statement 7.4(A), p. S-91 and 7.4(B), p. S-92. Economic Survey 2000-01 and 2002-03

being that India has imported large scale quantities of capital goods, intermediate products and foodgrains (under P.L.480 agreement) from that country. With the expansion of trading relations with Japan, West Germany and U.S.S.R., the dependence on the U.K. declined considerably. Thus the share of U.K. in Indian imports declined from 19.4 per cent in 1960-61 to 5.7 per cent in 1997-98. On the other hand, the share of Japan increased from 1.5 per cent in 1950-51 to 5.4 per cent in 1960-61 and further to 7.5 per cent in 1990-91. However, thereafter, it decreased in percentage terms to 6.5 per cent in 1995-96 and 5.2 per cent in 1997-98.

Another significant development was the expansion in trading relations with the socialist countries especially the erstwhile U.S.S.R. Imports from U.S.S.R. were negligible in 1950-51. In 1960-61 they amounted to a meagre Rs. 16 crore. However, thereafter, they increased rapidly increasing the share of U.S.S.R. in India's imports from 1.4 per cent in 1960-61 to 6.5 per cent in 1970-71. For a number of years it occupied the second place after U.S.A. For instance, during 1980-81 to 1983-84, U.S.A. occupied the first place in India's imports and U.S.S.R. was second. In 1984-85, the share of U.S.S.R. was 10.4 per cent and it displaced U.S.A. from the first place. The picture changed thereafter. In 1985-86, U.S.A. was first, Japan second and U.S.S.R. third. In 1990-91, with a share of 12.1 per cent, U.S.A. occupied the first place. It was followed by Germany with a share of 8.0 per cent (the figure is for unified Germany). Japan had the third position (share 7.5 per cent). U.K. and Saudi Arabia shared the fourth position with a share of 6.7 per cent each, Belgium had the fifth position (share 6.3 per cent) while U.S.S.R. had the sixth position (share 5.9 per cent). With the disintegration of U.S.S.R. the direction of imports has now changed markedly. For instance, in 1997-98, U.S.A. occupied the first position in India's imports (share 8.9 per cent), followed by Saudi Arabia (Share 6.2 per cent), Germany (share 6.1 per cent), Belgium (share 6.0 per cent), Kuwait and U.K. (share 5.7 per cent each) in that order.

Direction of Exports

As is clear from Table 7, OECD group accounts for a major portion of India's exports. The share of this group in 1960-61 was 66.1 per cent and in 1997-98 was 55.7 per cent. Almost 46 per cent of these exports were accounted for by the EU countries in 1997-98. The OPEC group accounted for 4.1 per cent of exports in 1960-61 and its share in 1997-98 rose to 10.0 per cent. Most significant was the rapid increase in exports to the countries of Eastern Europe particularly U.S.S.R. For instance, Eastern Europe accounted for 7.0 per cent of export earnings in 1960-61 and its share shot up to 22.1 per cent in 1980-81. During recent years, exports to this group have suffered a setback due to marked political upheavels in these countries and the disintegration of the U.S.S.R. In 1997-98 the share of Eastern Europe in total exports had slumped to a mere 3.1 per cent. Developing nations of Africa, Asia and Latin America accounted for more than one-fourth of India's export earnings in 1997-98. Most important in this group have been the countries of Asia. In fact, exports to Asian countries accounted for 21.3 per cent of India's total export earnings in 1997-98. Thus, countries of Asia now account for more than one-fourth of India's export earnings.

Direction of exports in 1999-00 show significant increases in India's exports to its major destinations like OECD, Asia and OPEC regions. Exports in US Dollar value, grew by 12.8 per cent to OECD, 20.1 per cent to Asia (other than OPEC countries) and 12.3 per cent to OPEC in 1999-00 as compared with declines of 1.5 per cent, 14.4 per cent and low growth of 0.8 per cent respectively in 1998-99. Other regions recording robust growth in exports included Eastern Europe (due mainly to turnaround in exports to Russia) and Latin America & Carribean region with Mexico, Peru, Chile, Barbados and Panama accounting for major increases. Exports to developing countries in Africa, however, declined by 5.4 per cent in 1999-00 as against a rise of 9.9 per cent in the previous year. In terms of region-wise share in total exports, while the share of OECD, OPEC and developing countries from Africa declined in 1999-00, those of Eastern Europe and Asian developing countries from Africa declined in 1999-00, those of Eastern Europe and Asian developing countries increased during this period. The share of developing countries from the Latin America & Carribean region was, however, maintained at 1.7 per cent. Although the share in total exports to OECD countries, as a group, registered a marginal decline from 57.8 per cent in 1998-99 to 57.6 per cent in 1999-00, exports to many developed countries like Canada (25.8 per cent), U.K. (21.1 per cent), U.S.A. (18.5 per cent), Netherlands (16.1 per cent), France (10.9 per cent) and Belgium (7.2 per cent), in this region recorded significant increases during the year. The share rise in share of exports to developing countries of Asia was largely on account of the recovery from the crisis by East Asian countries as a result of which the share of our exports to selected East Asian countries rebounded from 11.6 per cent in 1998-99 to 13.7 per cent in 1999-00

Direction of Imports

Sources of imports reveal a sharp decline in share of imports in total imports from OECD countries from 51.6 per cent in 1998-99 to 44.8 per cent in 1999-00 as imports from these countries declined by 3.2 per cent in 1999-00. Bulk of this decline in share was appropriated by imports from the OPEC region whose share rose to 23.8 per cent in 1999-00 (as compared to 18.3 per cent in 1998-99) mainly because of increase in international petroleum crude oil prices. Similarly, the share of imports sourced from non-OPEC developing countries (of Africa, Asia and Latin America & Carribean) improved from 21.1 per cent in 1998-99 to 22.6 per cent in 1999-00. The share of imports from Eastern Europe was broadly maintained in 1999-00 due mainly to recovery in imports from Russia. Imports from developing countries of Africa and Latin America & Carribean regions grew by 21.9 per cent and 20.3 per cent respectively in 1999-00 and was contributed among others, by countries like Egypt, Ghana, Brazil, Chile and South Africa. Imports from developing countries from Asia also recorded a high increase of 18.5 per cent with robust growth from countries like China, Hong Kong, Malaysia and Thailand. The share of selected East Asian countries in total imports increased from 14.9 per cent in 1998-99 to 15.5 per cent in 1999-00 due partly to the share depreciation of currencies of these countries during the Asian crisis.

A sharp increase in imports from other residual destinations, coupled with decline in share of OPEC region, may suggest a change in sourcing of oil imports away from the OPEC region during the current financial year.

Structural changes are also discernible from the data on sources of India's imports. While there has been a sharp increase in the relative share of the developing countries, that of the industrialised countries declined. Between 1987-91 and 1992-99, the relative share of the developing countries as a group moved up from 18.0 per cent to 23.0 per cent. This was largely on account of the increase in the imports from the newly industrialised countries in South East Asia. Among the commodities that contributed to the import growth, petroleum (crude and products) from Malaysia and Singapore, vegetable oils from Malaysia, chemicals from Republic of Korea and Singapore, and electronic goods from Hong Kong, Republic of Korea, Malaysia and Thailand were prominent. Between the two periods, the relative shares of the countries belonging to the OPEC group also increased from 14.5 per cent to 21.9 per cent. This is mainly reflective of the surge in the oil import bill on account of higher prices.

The share of the OECD as a group in India's imports dropped considerably from 59.4 per cent during 1987-91 to 52.1 per cent during 1992-99. Within this group, the relative share of the EU countries fell from 31.8 per cent during 1987-91 to 26.9 per cent during 1992-99. The import shares of some of the individual EU countries such as Denmark, Greece, Ireland and Italy, however, recorded relatively high growth, while those from traditionally important countries such as Germany, Netherlands, Sweden and UK showed lower rise. The relative share of the UK fell to 5.8 per cent during 1992-99 from 7.9 per cent during 1987-91. Among other OECD countries, the imports from Australia, New Zealand and Switzerland recorded relatively large growth. The relative share of Switzerland moved up from 1.1 per cent during 1987-91 to 4.0 per cent during 1992-99. This was largely on account of the import of gold and silver and non-electrical machinery. It may be indicated that during 1992-99, the import of gold and silver formed as much as 69.2 per cent of India's total import from Switzerland, while Switzerland along accounted for 58.1 per cent of India's total import of gold and silver during this period. The relative share of the East European countries declined from 8.1 per cent during 1987-91 to just 2.9 per cent during 1992-99 with absolute decline in the imports from most of the countries belonging to this group.

Summing Up

Notwithstanding the earlier policy initiatives aimed at liberalisation of India's foreign trade, the outward-looking trade policy measures announced in 1991 marks the initiation of a new era in India's foreign trade. India's foreign trade performance improved significantly during the recent years and there has been a perceptible change in the structure of India's foreign trade between the 'eighties and the 'nineties.

The share of manufactured products has increased in India's total exports. At the same time, since the introduction of reforms, the proportions of high-value and differentiated products have increased in India's export basket.

Along with the increase in India's aggregate share in world trade, the alignment between the country's export basket and world demand has increased during the 'nineties.

The relative share of certain capital goods in India's total imports has also increased in this period. Imports of manufactured fertilizers and edible oils also recorded higher growth during the post-1991 period.

In line with the policy changes, imports of gold and silver have increased sharply during the 'nineties.

Reflecting the increased link between exports and imports, the shares of certain export-related imports have also increased during the recent years.

The most remarkable change in the country-wise composition of India's exports and imports since 1991 has been the increase in the share of developing countries in India's overall trade.

While the share of the East European countries has declined in India's total trade, that of the OECD countries has declined in the case of imports.

India's foreign trade has, however, been adversely affected by certain unfavourable external developments since 1996.

Notwithstanding these negative developments, India's trade performance during the 'nineties as a whole has been better than that during the 'eighties.

APPENDIX TABLE

SELECTED INDICATORS FOR THE EXTERNAL SECTOR

(In US$ million)

	1990-91	1996-97	1997-98	1998-99	1999-00	2000-01	2001-02	2002-03	2003-04*
1. Growth of Exports - BOP (%)	9.0	5.6	4.5	-3.9	9.5	19.6	0.0	16.9	12.5
2. Growth of Imports - BOP (%)	14.4	12.1	4.6	-7.1	16.5	7.0	-2.8	13.5	20.8
3. Exports/Imports - BOP (%)	66.2	69.7	69.7	72.1	67.8	75.8	78.0	80.3	74.2
4. Import cover of FER (No. of months)	2.5	6.5	6.9	8.2	8.2	8.6	11.3	13.8	16.2
5. External assistance (net)/TC (%)	26.3	10.6	9.7	10.4	8.3	4.3	10.2	-19.1	-10.3
6. ECB (net)/TC (%)	26.8	27.3	42.6	55.4	2.9	39.7	-14.3	-18.2	-21.2
7. NR deposits/TC (%)	18.3	32.1	12.0	12.2	14.2	24.6	25.1	23.2	19.9
8. Short-term debt / FER (%)	146.5	25.5	17.2	13.2	10.3	8.6	5.1	6.0	5.7
9. Debt service payments as % of current receipts	35.3	23.0	19.5	18.8	17.1	16.2	13.4	15.8	18.1
As per cent of GDPmp									
10. Exports	5.8	8.9	8.7	8.3	8.4	9.8	9.4	10.3	
11. Imports	8.8	12.7	12.5	11.5	12.4	13.0	12.0	12.8	
12. Trade balance	-3.0	-3.8	-3.8	-3.2	-4.0	-3.2	-2.6	-2.5	
13. Invisibles balance	-0.1	2.7	2.4	2.2	2.9	2.3	2.8	3.3	
14. Current account balance	-3.1	-1.2	-1.4	-1.0	-1.1	-0.8	0.2	0.8	
15. External Debt	28.7	24.6	24.3	23.6	22.1	22.6	21.1	20.2	
16. Debt Service Payments	2.8	3.2	2.7	2.6	2.5	2.8	2.3	2.9	

* Calculated on the basis of figures upto Apr.-Dec. 2003-04.

Notes : (i) TC: Total capital flows (net).

(ii) ECB: External Commercial Borrowing.

(iii) FER: Foreign Exchange Reserves, including gold and SDRs.

(iv) GDPmp: Gross domestic product at current market prices.

(v) As total capital flows are netted after taking into account some capital outflows, the ratios against item no. 5, 6 and 7 may, in some years, add up to more than 100 per cent.

(vi) Rupee equivalents of BOP components are used to arrive at GDP ratios. All other percentages shown in the upper panel of the table are based on US dollar values.

25

Balance of Payments and Trade Policy

Concepts

BALANCE of payments (BOP) is a systematic record of all economic transactions between the residents of a country and the rest of the world. Like all double-entry book keeping accounts it always balances i.e., Sum of credit entries = Sum of debt entries.

There are two types of accounts in BOP, namely, (i) Current Account and (ii) Capital Account.

Current Account records transfers of goods and services i.e., merchandise trade and net invisibles which includes services like travel, transportation, insurance etc. and transfer payments.

Capital Account shows transfers of claims to money or titles to investment between a country and the rest of the world. It includes foreign investment inflow minus the foreign investment outflow, loans including external assistance and external commercial borrowings (inflow – outflow) and other capital which includes rupee debt service, IMF transactions and SDR allocation.

A current account deficit is financed through net inflow of capital on the capital account and the change in the Government's foreign exchange reserve position.

Trade Policy: An Overview[1]

AS we embarked on a period of planning, during the fifties, import

1. This section draws from C. Rangarajan's paper, *India's Balance of Payments: The Emerging Dimensions*, in Uma Kapila (ed) op. cit.

substitution came to constitute a major element of India's trade and industrial policies. Planners more or less chose to ignore the option of foreign trade as an engine of India's economic growth. This was primarily due to the highly pessimistic view taken on the potential for export earnings. A further impetus to the inward orientation was provided by the existence of a vast domestic market. In retrospect, it is now abundantly clear that the policy makers not only under-estimated the export possibilities but also the import intensity of the import substitution process itself. It has been as a consequence that India's share of total world exports declined from 1.91 per cent in 1950 to about 0.53 per cent in 1992.

The inward looking industrialisation process did result in high rates of industrial growth between 1956 and 1966. However, several weaknesses of such a process of industrialisation soon became evident, as inefficiencies crept into the system and the economy turned into an increasingly 'high-cost' one. Over a period of time this led to a 'technological lag' and also resulted in poor export performance.

In the meantime, some change in the attitude towards exports became perceptible. Several export promotion measures were put in place from the early 1960s. The 1966 devaluation, while not resulting in the expected improvement in trade deficit due to a combination of circumstances, brought out the problems stemming from an overvalued exchange rate. Nevertheless, it will be correct to say that until the end of the 1970s, exports were primarily regarded as a source of foreign exchange rather than as an efficient means of allocating resources. Import substitution over a wide area remained the basic premise of the development strategy.

The Political Economy of the Foreign Exchange Regimes

The political economy of India's foreign trade and exchange control regimes before reforms were initiated in 1991 can be understood from the implications of its selective, discretionary, and non-market-oriented character. First, macroeconomic instruments, including most importantly the exchange rate of the rupee, were never used to address balance of payments problems except for the rupee devaluation of 1966. Given that QRs on imports were substantially below market demand, the domestic price of an imported commodity far exceeded its landed cost inclusive of tariff duties and other taxes. As such there were rents associated with a license to import. It hardly requires much imagination to realize that if rents could be created and allocated, individuals and groups would spend resources in influencing their creation and allocation in their favour.

It should be evident even to a casual observer of the Indian scene that a significant amount of scarce talents and material resources that could have been used for producing goods and services were spent instead on seeking and dispensing rents. Senior bureaucrats who wielded power spent much of their time in meetings that decided individual cases rather than set broad policies. Of course, if adoption of favourable decisions and the prevention of unfavourable decisions had to be bought, so to speak, only those who could afford to pay the price would enter the market. Clearly entrepreneurs with relatively few material resources and contacts at crucial decision-making agencies were unlikely to enter the market.

Foreign trade policy issues became the subject of intensive discussion in early eighties. It came to be realised that a scheme of import licensing under which imports were permitted only to the extent that domestic production fell short of domestic demand irrespective of difference in cost and prices, could only lead to inefficiency. The view gained ground that a more liberal policy of imports of capital goods and technology would enable India to reap the benefits of international division of labour. *The attempt therefore was to move away from import substitution per se towards efficient import substitution,* so that considerations relating to cost and efficiency were incorporated in the overall policy framework. It also became increasingly clear that production for export could not be isolated from production for the home market and that trade policy had to be integrated with the policy for domestic industrialisation.

While the signs of liberalised trade policy became visible in the latter half of eighties, it was only in 1991 that the country embarked on a truly liberalised trade policy with a short negative list of exports and imports and with quantitative controls over imports withdrawn for all, except consumer goods. It was recognised that trade, exchange rate and industrial policies must form part of an integrated policy framework if the aim was to improve the productivity and efficiency of the economic system.

Trade Policy Since 1991

The trade policy changes in the post 1991 period sought to minimise the role of quantitative restrictions and substantially reduce the tariff rates on the lines suggested by the Tax Reforms Committee (Chairman:

Raja J. Chelliah). The developments in India's trade policy during this period needs to be viewed in conjunction with policy reforms initiated in other spheres of the economy. The devaluation of the Rupee in July 1991 and the transition to the market-based exchange rate regime deserve mention in this regard. These measures were aimed at enhancing the price competitiveness of exports. The policies governing foreign investment and foreign collaboration also have undergone significant change, which have a bearing on trade performance. Apart from unilateral measures, the liberalisation of India's trade policies also reflects the multilateral commitments of the country to the World Trade Organisation (WTO).

The focus of these reforms has been on liberalization, openness, transparency and globalization with a basic thrust on outward orientation focusing on export promotion activity and improving competitiveness of Indian industry to meet global market requirements. In early 2002, the Government presented a Medium Term Export Strategy (MTES) for 2002-07 providing a vision for creating a stable policy environment with indicative sector-wise targets, with a mission to achieve one percent of global trade by 2007. The new Export and Import (EXIM) Policy framed for the period 2002-07 and unveiled on 31 March, 2002 also seeks to usher in an environment free of restrictions and controls (Box 1). Synergy between these policies/ strategies is expected to realize India's strong export potential and enhance the overall competitiveness of its exports.

BOX 1

EXPORT IMPORT (EXIM) POLICY 2002-07

The Special Economic Zone (SEZ) scheme has been strengthened by permitting the setting up of offshore Banking Units, hedging of commodity price risks and sourcing of short term External Commercial Borrowings. Supplies by domestic units to SEZs would entitle the former to avail of Duty Entitlement Passbook Scheme benefit. The policy has also ensured procedural simplification in the process of subcontracting carried out by the SEZ units. To ease the power situation in and around the SEZs, units for generation and distribution of power have been permitted to be set up in the SEZs.

The Policy gives a major thrust to agricultural exports by removing export restrictions on designated items. The efforts to promote exports of agro and agro-based products in the floriculture and horticulture sector have been sustained with the notification of 32 Agri-Export Zones across the country. Non-actionable subsidies such as transport subsidy have been provided for the export of fruits, vegetables, floriculture, poultry and dairy products. All Quantitative restrictions on exports (except a few sensitive items) have been removed with only a few items being retained for export through State Trading Enterprises. To improve the productivity and export competitiveness of small scale, cottage and handicrafts sector, the Policy provides a package of incentives, including exemption from maintaining the average export obligation under the Export Promotion Capital Goods (EPCG) scheme, permission to achieve a lower threshold level for achieving the Export House status, preferential access to Market Access Initiative funds and duty free access to trimming and embellishment for achieving value added exports. The towns of export excellence (such as Tirupur for hosiery, Panipat for woolen blanket and Ludhiana for woolen knitwear) are intended to be regional rural motors of economic development for the small scale sector, focusing on plugging critical infrastructural bottlenecks and enhancing quality of support services for industrial development.

To provide the necessary impetus to star achievers, EXIM Policy provides a strategic package for status holders comprising of new/special facilities like issuance of Licence on self-declaration basis, fixation of input-output norms on priority, exemption from compulsory negotiation of documents through banks, cent per cent retention of foreign exchange in Exchange Earners' Foreign Currency account, enhancement in normal repatriation period from 180 days to 360 days and not mandating exports in each of the three licensing years for achieving the status. The Policy has operationalised the procedure for duty free import of fuel under the Advance Licensing Scheme, provided the license holder has a captive power plant.

In view of phasing out of all restrictions on textile products by 2005 under the Agreement on Textile and Clothing (ATC), the EXIM Policy has focused on measures to encourage value added exports in the garment sector. Electronic Hardware Technology Park (EHTP) scheme has been modified to enable hardware sector to face the zero duty regime under Information Technology Agreement (ITA-1), mandating only a positive net foreign exchange as a percentage of exports criteria and obviating any other export obligation for units in Electronic Hardware Technology Parks. The changes carried out in the gems & jewelry scheme include abolition of the licensing regime for the import of rough diamonds, reduction in the value addition norms for export of jewelry and permitting personal carriage of jewelry.

The medium term Policy continues with all the duty exemption/remission schemes, along with existing dispensation of not having any value caps. Procedural simplifications introduced in the policy include abolition of DEEC Book and withdrawal of Annual Advance License under the Advance License scheme, dispensation with technical characteristics for audit purposes under the Duty Free Replenishment Certificate scheme, 12 years export obligation period with 5 years moratorium for Export Promotion Capital Goods licenses of Rs.100 crore or more and supplies under deemed exports to be eligible for export obligation fulfillment along with deemed export benefits.

Procedural simplifications have been made in the EXIM policy to further reduce transaction costs covering Directorate General of Foreign Trade, customs and banks. These include adoption of 8 digit commodity classification for imports which would eliminate the classification disputes, reduction of maximum fee limit for electronic filing from Rs.1.5 lakhs to Rs.1 lakh, introduction of same day licensing, new norms for reduction in percentage of physical examination of export cargo, introduction of the simplified brand rate of drawback scheme and permitting direct negotiation of export documents. Other salient features of the EXIM Policy 2002-07 include widening of the scope of the Market Access Initiative scheme to include activities considered necessary for a focused market promotion of exports, setting up of "Business Centre" in India missions abroad for visiting Indian exporters/businessmen for ensuring a facilitatory environment for exporters, transport subsidy for exports to units located in North East, Sikkim and J&K and introduction of Focus Africa with Focus CIS to follow, to diversify markets.

Policy measures announced in the Union Budget 2002-03 included a comprehensive package for development of Special Economic Zones (SEZ) including entitlement by these Zones to procure duty free equipment, raw materials, components, etc. whether imported or purchased locally, further decontrol and deregulation of agriculture sector to encourage higher exports of farm products (with measures like decanalisation of export of agricultural commodities, phasing out of remaining export controls, setting up of more Agri-Export Zones in various states and enhanced incentives for export of food grains), de-reservation from small scale industry (SSI) provisions for over 50 items (of knitwear, selected agricultural implements, chemical & drugs and others) to facilitate higher investment, technology upgradation and exports from these sectors and fiscal measures for strengthening certain key industries (including textiles, steel, non ferrous metals and IT industry) for improving their competitiveness and exports. The Budget announced a reduction in peak customs duty from 35 per cent to 30 per cent and also provided an indication of further reductions/ rationalization in these duties into only two slabs of 10 per cent (for raw material, intermediate and components) and 20 per cent (for final products) by 2004-05. A detailed roadmap has been recommended by the Finance Ministry Task Force on Indirect taxation for, inter alia, further reforms in areas related to customs tariffs, rationalization of export promotion schemes, trade facilitation and other changes in tax administration.

India's Balance of Payment Trends 1950-2000

The Decades of Fifties and Sixties

Prior to 1956-57, for most years in the fifties, India had a current account surplus. But the position changed in 1956-57 when India faced BOP crisis. The trade deficit increased from 3.8 per cent of GDP at market prices to 4.5 per cent. The BOP crisis of 1956-57 precipitated the imposition of exchange controls which then became endemic to the import substitution regime.

The BOP position deteriorated once again in 1966-67. In 1965, the United States suspended its aid in response to the Indo-Pakistan war and later refused to renew the PL 480 agreement on a long-term basis. There was a concerted effort by the United States, the World Bank, and the IMF to use external assistance as an instrument to induce India (a) to adopt a new agricultural strategy and (b) to devalue the rupee. The rupee was devalued by 36.5 per cent in June 1966, and tariffs and export subsidies were simultaneously rationalized, on the understanding that the inflow of aid would be substantially increased.

The BOP improved after 1966-67 but largely because of the decline in imports. Exports performed indifferently despite the devaluation.

Balance of Payments in the Seventies

A Decade of Comfort

India's balance of payments remained comfortable during the Seventies. The adjustment to the first oil shock of 1973-74 was rendered smooth by a happy combination of buoyant exports, spurt in private transfer receipts and increased inflow of aid. Exports, benefited by the expansion in global trade, rose at an annual rate of 6.8 per cent in volume terms and by 15.6 per cent in US dollar terms during the decade. An effective depreciation of the rupee occurred due to the link with Pound Sterling until 1973 and later, because of the lower growth in prices in India relative to other countries. Private transfers rose sevenfold from $296 million in 1974-75 to $2175 million in 1979-80 and in fact, in the post first oil shock period, financed roughly 80 per cent of the trade deficit. Within two years of the shock, the current account balance turned into surplus and it was only in 1978-79 that a deficit of about 0.2 per cent of GDP appeared. The utilisation of aid was significant and was substantially higher than the financing requirement for the decade, allowing for a build up of reserves. At the close of the decade the foreign exchange reserves stood at $7361 million providing cover for over 7 months of imports.

Balance of Payments upto 1981-82

The Period of Difficulties

During the eighties, issues relating to the balance of payments came to occupy the centre stage in terms of India's macroeconomic management. The impact of the second oil shock of 1979, the full effects of which spilled over into the eighties, was more severe than of the 1973-74. Between 1978-79 and 1981-82, imports almost doubled. The increase in POL imports accounted for a little over half the increase in the overall imports. This was followed by the second-round effects on non-POL imports. Export performance was depressed by the severe international recession of 1980-83 and recorded a volume growth of just a little over 3 per cent. Net invisible receipts continued to provide support to the balance of payments, largely in the form of earnings from tourism and the sustained buoyancy of private transfers. However, the sharp widening in the merchandise trade deficit resulted in a turnaround in the current account balance from a surplus in 1977-78 to a deficit in 1981-82 of the order of US $3,166 million or 1.8 per cent of GDP. Adjustment efforts consisted essentially of an Extended Fund Facility (EFF) negotiated with the IMF, although there were also intensified efforts to improve domestic production of crude petroleum.

Balance of Payments during 1982-83 to 1984-85

Easing of Pressure

A reprieve came during the period 1982-83 to 1984-85, with the easing of pressure on the balance of payments mainly due to a decline in the volume growth of imports from an average rate of 11.0 per cent during 1978-82 to a little over 2 per cent. Net oil imports (net of crude oil exports which commenced in 1981-82 after the discovery of crude oil in Bombay High), declined substantially as domestic production spurted to 29.0 million tonnes by 1984-85. This indeed was the main cause of the easing of the balance of payments. Non-POL imports rose at an average rate of 3.6 per cent in dollar terms. Exports however, grew only at an average rate of 3.2 per cent, in volume terms, due to a combination of adverse internal and external conditions. The invisibles account deteriorated as the interest payments to service external borrowing acquired a steady rising trend. Private transfers stagnated with the arrest in the labour migration boom. As a result, invisibles including private transfers and other surpluses, which had financed 89 per cent of the trade deficit in 1978-79 could meet only 57 per cent of the trade deficit in 1984-85. The current account deficit fell to US $ 2,416 million or 1.2 per cent of GDP in 1984-85 and reserves, which were US $5,952 million at the end of the year, stood to cover a little over 4 months of imports. 29 per cent of the financing requirement of the first half of the eighties was met by the EFF. Commercial borrowings and non-resident deposits emerged as important sources of finance, meeting 21 per cent and 15 per cent respectively of the financing need. However, external assistance remained the major source of foreign capital inflows, accounting for 39 per cent of the financing requirement.

Balance of Payments During 1985-90

The Build up to the Crisis

The second half of the eighties witnessed the building up of strains on the balance of payments. Current account deficits acquired a structural character, remaining at high levels throughout. Large trade deficits occurred year after year despite a robust growth in exports. Recovering from the stagnation in 1985-86, the volume growth of exports in the succeeding four years ranged between 10 to 12 per cent per annum on an average. The share of manufactured exports rose from 56 per cent in 1980-81 to 75 per cent in 1989-90. Imports in US dollar terms rose in every year of the period. The volume of net POL imports increased from 12.4 million tonnes in 1984-85 to 23.5 million tonnes in 1989-90. However, the fall in crude oil prices during the period helped to contain the oil import bill. On the other hand, non-oil imports rose sharply by an average of 13.4 per cent in US dollar terms partly due to large imports of foodgrains in 1988-89. Imports of capital goods rose by an average of 16.2 per cent during the period. Export-related imports as well as other miscellaneous imports also rose significantly. The category of non-DGCIS imports, comprising defence imports and imports of ships and aircrafts etc., also rose significantly from about US $1.2 billion in 1985-86 to US $ 3.1 billion by 1989-90. The support from invisible receipts fell in the face of steadily growing interest payments and the outgo on account of profits, dividends, royalty, technical fees and professional fees. The current account deficit averaged $ 5.8 billion or 2.4 per cent of GDP during the period as against the Planning Commission's estimate of 1.6 per cent. The period also marked a deterioration in fiscal imbalances as the ratio of gross fiscal deficit to GDP rose from 6.3 per cent in the first half of the eighties to 8.2 per cent during 1985-90. Repurchases from the IMF under the EFF exacerbated the deterioration in the balance of payments. External assistance, commercial borrowing and non-resident deposits shared equiproportionally in the financing need. The result was a doubling of external debt and a rise in the debt service ratio from 13.6 per cent in 1984-85 to 30.9 per cent in 1989-90.

The Crisis: 1990-92

In 1991, India found itself in its worst balance of payments crisis since 1947. That there was a crisis in the making during the second half of 1980s had been evident for a long time. The inflow of foreign borrowing had increased at a rapid rate during the late 1980s. This was due to the excess domestic expenditure over income – the fiscal deficit of the Centre and the States soared to over 11 per cent in 1991. During this period total public debt as a proportion of GNP doubled reaching the level of 60 per cent and foreign currency reserves were depleted rapidly.

Matters were made worse by an accompanying double-digit inflation in 1990-91. The oil price increase resulting from Iraq's invasion of Kuwait in August 1990 reinforced the crisis-like situation in India.

India's credit rating got downgraded as, for the first time in its history, India was on the verge of defaulting on its international commitments and was denied access to external commercial credit markets. A net outflow of Non-Resident Indian (NRI) deposits commenced in October 1990 and continued during 1991. The only way left for India was to borrow against the security of its gold reserves transported abroad.

But something good emerged out of the BoP crisis of 1991 – the long overdue economic reforms. Apart from an immediate programme of macroeconomic stabilisation, structural reforms were also introduced in the industrial and trade policy regimes with a view to improving the efficiency, productivity and international competitiveness of India's economy.

The overvalued exchange rate was corrected by devaluation in 1991, followed by partial convertibility of rupee in 1992-93 and then making the rupee fully convertible on trade account in 1993-94. Tariffs were also cut steeply to open Indian industry to foreign competition. The focus of import liberalisation has primarily been on intermediate and captial goods industries with the imports of consumer goods remaining, by and large, regulated.

The initial response of the economy, especially exports, was very good. The years 1993-94 to 1995-96 were years of excellent economic performance with GDP having grown at 6.2 per cent in 1993-94 and by more than 7.5 per cent during 1994-95 and 1996-97. Exports grew by 19.7 per cent during 1993-94 to 1995-96.

The major reasons for such a high growth rate in exports were[2]:

- World GDP grew by an average rate of 4.1 per cent per annum during 1994-97 compared with 2.4 per cent during 1990-1993.
- World trade (dollar terms) grew by an average rate of 9.8 per cent per annum during 1994-1997 compared with 6.0 per cent during 1990-1993.
- Imports of advanced countries (dollar terms) grew by an average rate of 11.5 per cent during 1994-1997 compared with 2.1 per cent during 1990-1993.
- Increase in India's share in world exports of its three major commodity groups, viz. Textiles, yarn and fabrics; pearls, precious and semi-precious stones; and clothing and accessories during 1994-96.
- Increase in the Index of comparative Advantage (ICA) of the above.
- Other export commodity groups in which India gained in terms of ICA during 1994-96 include fish and fish preparations; rice;

2. Rajesh Chadha, *Balance of Payments and Trade Policy*, paper presented at ADB - NCAER Seminar on Economic and Policy Reforms in India (Dec. 9, 1999) India International Centre, New Delhi.

coffee and substitutes; organic chemicals; footwear; and gold and silver jewellery.

However the boom was short-lived. Since 1996, India's export performance has been poor.

There could be several explanations for this. Firstly, there has been a major downturn in world trade since 1996, which has affected India's trade as well. Export growth has been further hampered by an appreciation of the real effective exchange rate in 1996-97 and 1997-98. This trend has, however, been reversed since 1998-99. There has also been an adverse movement in terms of trade, which appears to have affected exports. Finally, there are the host of domestic factors – both policy related and administrative – which continue to hamper imports. These include infrastructure constraints, high transaction costs, SSI reservations, labour inflexibility, quality problems and quantitative restrictions on export of agricultural commodities.

However the surplus on invisibles has helped to reduce the deficit on the current account. Earnings from invisibles have helped particularly during the critical years of 1996-97 and 1997-98 when the deficit on the trade account touched alarming levels close to $ 1.5 to 1.6 billion.

Capital Account, External Debt and Exchange Rate

Approach, Developments and Issues

Reflecting the inward oriented economic policies in pursuit of self-reliance through export bias and import substitution, the role of the capital account during the 1980s was basically that of financing the current account deficits (RBI, 1999). The widening of the current account deficit during the 1980s coupled with the drying up of traditional source of official concessional flows necessitated a recourse to additional sources of financing in the form of debt creating commercial borrowings, non-resident deposits and exceptional financing in the form of IMF loans.

The external payment crisis of 1991 brought to the fore the weaknesses of the debt-dominated capital account financing. Recognising this, structural reforms and external financial liberalisation measures were introduced during the 1990s. The policy shift underscored the need for gradually liberalising capital account recognising that this is a process rather than a single event (Jalan, 1999). Throughout the 1990s the role assigned to foreign capital in India has been guided by the consideration of financing a level of current account deficit that is sustainable and consistent with absorptive capacities of the economy (Rangarajan, 1993; Tarapore, 1995; Reddy, 2000). In India, the move towards full capital account liberalisation has been approached with extreme caution. Taking lessons from the international experience, the Committee on Capital Account Convertibility, 1997 (Chairman: S. S. Tarapore) suggested a number of pre-conditions, attainment of which was considered necessary for the success of the capital account liberalisation programme in India (Box 2). The High Level Committee on BoP had recommended the need for achieving this compositional shift. Keeping in line with the policy thrust, capital flows have undergone a major compositional change in the 1990s in favour of non-debt flows.

BOX 2

COMMITTEE ON CAPITAL ACCOUNT LIBERALISATION
(CHAIRMAN: S.S. TARAPORE)

With the growing role of private capital flows and the possibility of occasional sharp reversals, the issue of capital account liberalisation and convertibility has spurred extensive debate since 1992 - the period which witnessed a series of currency crises; in Europe (1992-93), Mexico (1994-95), East Asia (1997-98), Russia (1998), Brazil (1999), Turkey (2000) and Argentina (2001-02). These crises have raised the question of desirability of liberalisation and whether it is advisable to vest the IMF with the responsibility for promoting the orderly liberalisation of capital flows. The IMF in its study (1998) stated that "as liberalised systems afford opportunities for individuals, enterprises and financial institutions to undertake greater and sometimes imprudent risks, they create the potential for systematic disturbances. There is no way to completely suppress these dangers other than through draconian financial repression, which is more damaging." The view of IMF itself has changed over time (RBI, 2001). While opening up of the capital account may be conducive to economic growth as it could make available larger stocks of capital at a lower cost for a capital-deficient country, the actual performance of the economy, however, typically depends on a host of other factors. For a successful liberalised capital account, emerging market countries could: (i) pursue sound macroeconomic policies; (ii) strengthen the domestic financial system; (iii) phase capital account liberalisation appropriately and (iv) provide information to the market. At the international level, there is also the role of surveillance to consider, including the provision of information and the potential need for financing (Fischer, 1997).

In India, the move towards full capital account liberalisation has been approached with extreme caution. The Report of the Committee on Capital Account Convertibility, 1997 (Chairman: S.S.Tarapore) taking into account lessons from international experience suggested a number of signposts, the attainment of which are a necessary concomitant in the move towards capital account convertibility. *Fiscal consolidation, lower inflation and a stronger financial system were seen as crucial signposts for India.*

India followed a gradualist approach to liberalisation of its capital account. India did not experience reversal of its policies towards the capital account as was the case with some emerging market economies that had followed a relatively rapid liberalisation without entrenching the necessary preconditions. This is particularly important since cross-country studies do not provide clear evidence of increase in capital flows resulting from capital account openness across all developing countries, with only 14 developing countries accounting for about 95 per cent of net private flows to developing countries in the 1990s. Besides, empirical evidence on the positive effects of financial capital flows on economic growth is not yet conclusive (Edison et al, 2002).

Foreign Investment

During the first three decades after independence, foreign investment in India was highly regulated. In the 1980s, there was some easing in foreign investment policy in line with the industrial policy regime of the time. The major policy thrust towards attracting foreign direct investment (FDI) was outlined in the New Industrial Policy Statement of 1991. Since then, continuous efforts have been made to liberalise and simplify the norms and procedures pertaining to FDI. At present, FDI is permitted under automatic route subject to specific guidelines except for a small negative list. In the recent period, a number of measures have been taken to further promote FDI. These include: raising the foreign ownership cap to 100 per cent in most of the sectors, ending state monopoly in insurance and telecommunications, opening up of banking and manufacturing to competition and disinvestment of state ownership in Public Sector Undertakings (PSUs). Though the FDI companies have generally performed better than the domestic companies, FDI to India has been attracted mainly by the lure of the large market.

Magnitude

Responding to the policy efforts, foreign investment inflows to India (direct and portfolio investments taken together) picked up sharply in 1993-94 and have been sustained at a higher level with an aberration in 1998-99, when global capital flows were affected by contagion from the East Asian crisis. Total foreign investment has averaged at US $ 5.4 billion during the three year period 1999-2000 to 2001-02 as against negligible levels of the 1980s. Foreign portfolio investment (FPI) on the other hand, has shown larger year-to-year variations, moving in the range of a net inflow of US $ 3.8 billion in 1994-95 to a net outflow of US $ 61 million in 1998-99.[3]

FPI

Like FDI, the environment for FPI was also made more congenial through procedural changes for investment and by offering more facilities for investment in equity securities as well as in debt securities to a select category of portfolio investors, viz., the Foreign Institutional Investors (FIIs). Furthermore, the sectoral limits for FIIs in the Indian companies were progressively increased over time; these limits have been done away with altogether, except in select specified sectors. The NRIs, Overseas Corporate Bodies (OCBs) and Persons of Indian Origin (PIOs) are also permitted to invest in shares and debentures of Indian companies, government securities, commercial papers, company deposits and mutual funds floated by public sector banks and financial institutions.

NRI Deposits

NRI deposits in the form of Non-Resident (External) Rupee Account (NR(E)RA) and Foreign Currency Non-Resident Account (FCNR(A)) emerged as a steady flow of foreign capital in India from the 1970s, following the labour migration boom in West Asia in the wake of the first oil shock. The onset of the 1990s saw the introduction of as many as five NRI deposit schemes [Foreign Currency Bank and Ordinary (FC(B&O)), Foreign Currency Ordinary Non-Resident (FC(ON)), Non-Resident Non-Repatriable Rupee Deposit (NR(NR)RD), Non-Resident Special Rupee Account (NR(S)RA) and Foreign Currency Non-Resident Bank (FCNR(B))] between 1990 and 1993 designed to attract foreign exchange in the face of external payments crisis of 1991. The policies with regard to NRI deposits during the 1990s have been aimed at

3. For more details see Ch.26.

attracting stable deposits. This has been achieved through: (i) a policy induced shift in favour of local currency denominated deposits; (ii) rationalisation of interest rates on rupee denominated NRI deposits; (iii) linking of the interest rates to LIBOR for foreign currency denominated deposits; (iv) de-emphasising short-term deposits (up to 12 months) in case of foreign currency denominated deposits; and (v) withdrawal of exchange rate guarantees on various deposits. The Reserve Bank has also made an active use of reserve requirements on these deposits as an instrument to influence monetary and exchange rate management and to regulate the size of the inflows depending on the country's requirements.

The NRI deposits have emerged as a major source of capital inflows during the 1990s. Apart from the size, the success of the policy towards NRI deposits is also reflected in an increase in the proportion of local currency denominated deposits (from around one-fourth in 1991 to almost two-third by 2002) and a substantial decline in short-term NRI deposits.

External Commercial Borrowings

Commercial debt capital includes a whole range of sources of foreign capital where the overriding consideration is commercial. External commercial loans include bank loans, buyers' credit, suppliers' credit, securitised instruments such as Floating Rate Notes and Fixed Rate Bonds, commercial borrowings and the private sector window of multilateral financial institutions.

The policies towards External Commercial Borrowings (ECBs) since the reform programme have been guided by the overall consideration of prudent external debt management by keeping the maturities long and cost low. ECBs are approved within an overall annual ceiling. Over time, the policy has been guided by a priority for projects in the infrastructure and core sectors such as power, oil exploration, telecom, railways, roads and bridges, ports, industrial parks, urban infrastructure and for 100 per cent Export Oriented Units (EOUs). To allow further flexibility to borrowers, end-use and maturity prescriptions have been substantially liberalised. Moreover, corporates have been allowed to borrow upto a certain limit under the 'automatic route'. Apart from these, special bonds (India Development Bonds (IDBs), Resurgent India Bonds (RIBs) and India Millennium Deposits (IMDs)) were issued by the State Bank of India aimed at NRIs. The success in mobilising foreign exchange resources through such exceptional schemes reflected the confidence of the global investor community in the Indian economy and imparted an element of stability to the external sector and the overall balance of payments position.

At times, the rationale behind raising such high cost debt capital has been questioned. Experience, however, would suggest that each time this option was resorted to, it helped in strengthening the confidence in the Rupee and the ability of the country to honour its obligations. The costs of an exchange rate crisis are too severe in relation to cost of debt capital. In a situation of moderate debt-service ratio, such debt capital makes more sense than allowing the exchange rate to fall under pressure.

Decline in Foreign Aid

Over the same period, official aid has waned in importance. This reflected mainly growing amortisation payments in the face of sluggish disbursements of external assistance as also availability of alternative private capital flows. Unlike aid, the share of ECBs in total capital flows have increased from around 31 per cent in 1990-91 to around 40 per cent in 1997-98. This has been mainly on account of the higher appetite for ECBs in view of the strong import demand and industrial growth.

Impact of Reforms on BOP

The impact of the continuum of reforms initiated in the aftermath of the balance of payments crisis of 1991 on India's current account and capital account resulted in an accumulation of foreign exchange reserves of over US $ 70 billion as at end-February 2003. Capital account surplus increased from US $ 3.9 billion during the 1980s to US $ 8.6 billion during 1992-2002 with a steadily rising foreign investment. As a proportion of GDP, capital flows increased from 1.6 per cent during 1980s to 2.3 per cent during 1992-2002. The significant increase in capital flows during the 1990s raises the issue of their determinants as well as their impact on growth.

The sustained increase in capital inflows as discussed above, coupled with the moderate current account deficit, resulted in a surplus from 1993-94 onwards (excepting 1995-96) in the overall balance of payments (Table 1). The surplus amounted to US $ 11.8 billion in 2001-02 as against a deficit of US $ 0.6 billion in 1992-93.

The evolution of capital flows over the 1990s reveals a shift in emphasis from debt to non-debt flows with the declining importance of external assistance and ECBs and the increased share of foreign investment - both direct and portfolio. Apart from financing the current account gap, capital flows have played a significant role in India's growth performance.

TABLE – 1

BALANCE OF PAYMENTS – KEY INDICATORS

(Per cent)

Item	*1990-91*	*1995-96*	*1999-00*	*2000-01*	*2001-02*
	1	*2*	*3*	*4*	*5*
1. Trade					
i) Exports/GDP	5.8	9.1	8.4	9.8	9.3
ii) Imports/GDP	8.8	12.3	12.4	12.9	12.0
iii) Trade Balance/GDP	-3.0	-3.2	-4.0	-3.1	-2.7
2. Invisibles Account					
i) Invisible Receipts/GDP	2.4	5.0	6.8	7.5	7.4
ii) Invisible Payments/GDP	2.4	3.5	3.8	4.9	4.5
iii) Invisibles (Net)/GDP	-0.1	1.6	3.0	2.6	2.9
3. Current Account					
i) Current Receipts@/ GDP	8.0	14.0	15.1	17.2	16.7
ii) Current Receipts Growth@	6.6	18.2	12.9	17.1	1.4
iii) Current Receipts@/ Current Payments	71.5	88.8	93.0	96.4	101.2
iv) CAD/GDP	-3.1	-1.7	-1.0	-0.5	0.3
4. Capital Account					
i) Foreign Investment/GDP	–	1.4	1.2	1.1	1.2
ii) Foreign Investment/ Exports	0.6	14.9	13.8	11.4	13.2
5. Others					
i) Debt-GDP Ratio	28.7	27.0	22.2	22.3	20.8
ii) Debt Service Ratio	35.3	24.3	16.2	17.3	14.1
iii) Liability Service Ratio	35.6	24.7	17.0	18.3	15.3
iv) Import Cover of Reserves (in months)	2.5	6.0	8.2	8.6	11.3

@ Excluding official transfers. – Negligible.

Evidence of strong complementarity with domestic investment suggests that capital flows brighten the overall investment climate and stimulate domestic investment even when a part of the capital flows actually gets absorbed in the form of accretion to reserves. The growth-augmenting role of foreign capital, particularly FDI, however, seems to have been constrained by the low levels of actual and planned absorption of foreign capital in India (RBI, 2001). The key indicators of balance of payments as explained in Table 1 show considerable improvement in India's balance of payments since 1991.

External Debt Management

Key indicators of debt sustainability point to the continuing consolidation and improved solvency in the 1990s. Although, in nominal terms, India's total outstanding external debt increased from US $ 83.8 billion at end-March 1991 to US $ 98.5 billion at end-March 2002, external debt to GDP ratio declined sharply from 28.7 per cent at end-March 1991 to 20.9 per cent at end-March 2002. Prudent external debt management is also reflected in the proportion of short-term debt to total debt declining from 10.2 per cent in 1991 to 2.8 per cent in 2002 and in the ratio of short-term debt to foreign exchange reserves from a high of 146.5 per cent in the crisis period of 1991 to only 5.1 per cent in 2001-02. Debt service ratio declined from 35.3 per cent in 1990-91 to 14.1 per cent in 2001-02 (Table 2). Interest payments to current receipts ratio declined from 15.5 per cent in 1990-91 to 5.4 per cent in 2001-02.

TABLE – 2

MAJOR INDICATORS OF EXTERNAL DEBT
(AS AT END-MARCH)

(Per cent)

Items	*1991*	*1996*	*2000*	*2001*	*2002*
	1	*2*	*3*	*4*	*5*
I. Total Debt to GDP	28.7	27.0	22.1	22.4	20.9
II. Short-term Debt (original maturity) to GDP	2.9	1.4	0.9	0.8	0.6
III. Concessional Debt to Total Debt	45.9	44.7	38.9	35.5	36.0
IV. Short-term Debt (original maturity) to Foreign Exchange Reserves	146.5	23.2	10.3	8.6	5.1
V. Short-term Debt (original maturity) to Foreign Currency Assets	382.1	29.5	11.2	9.2	5.4
VI. Non-Debt Liabilities and Short-term Debt to Reserves	148.2	92.3	99.9	100.8	88.4
VII. Short-term Debt and Non-debt Reversible Liabilities to Reserves	146.6	71.1	59.0	58.5	48.1
VIII. Debt Service Ratio	35.3	24.3	16.2	17.5	14.1
IX. Debt to Current Receipts	328.9	188.9	145.6	126.2	122.5
X. Liability Service Ratio	35.6	24.7	17.0	18.3	15.3

The decade of 1990s witnessed a steady move towards consolidation of India's external debt statistics in terms of size, composition and indicators of solvency and liquidity. Containing the increase in the size of external debt to a modest level in the face of a tremendous growth in foreign exchange reserves during the decade definitely points towards the success of India's debt management strategy. Reflecting this, in terms of indebtedness classification, the World Bank has categorised India as a less indebted country since 1999. Among the top 15 debtor countries of the world, India improved its rank from third debtor after Brazil and Mexico in 1991 to ninth in 2000 after Brazil, Russian Federation, Mexico, China, Argentina, Indonesia, Korean Republic and Turkey. Moreover, among them, key external debt indicators such as short-term debt to total debt and short-term debt to forex reserve ratios are the lowest for India; the concessional to total debt ratio is the highest, while debt to GNP ratio is the second lowest after China.

Exchange Rate Management

In the context of globalisation and currency crises, recent years, particularly, have seen a renewed interest on the issues relating to exchange rate regime, which is evident in the large and growing body of theoretical and empirical literature on the subject. Nevertheless, both in theory as well as in practice, the state of the debate is unsettled. A worldwide consensus is still evolving in search of an appropriate and credible exchange rate regime. In India also, discussion and debate on issues relating to the appropriate exchange rate system, policies on intervention, capital control and foreign exchange reserves figure very prominently. This is especially relevant with the introduction of a market-based exchange rate system in March 1993 and in the context of global currency crises, particularly the East Asian Crisis.

In India the exchange rate system has undergone a paradigm shift from a system of fixed exchange rate (until March 1992) to a market determined regime in March 1993. Since the switchover to a market determined exchange rate regime in March 1993, the behaviour of the exchange rate has remained largely orderly, interspersed by occasional episodes of pressures, which were relieved through appropriate intervention operations consistent with the stated policy of avoiding undue volatility in the exchange rate without reference to any target, whether explicit or implicit. The financial crises encountered by the emerging markets in the last decade have brought to the fore the importance of an appropriate exchange rate policy. The present Indian regime of managed flexibility that focuses on managing volatility without reference to any target has gained increasing international acceptance and well served the requirements of the country in the face of significant liberalisation of external sector transactions. This is particularly so in the context of the series of exchange rate crises experienced by several emerging economies undertaking similar macroeconomic reforms.

In the post-Bretton Woods period, the Rupee was effectively pegged to a basket of currencies of India's major trading partners from September 1975. This system continued through the 1980s, though the exchange rate was allowed to fluctuate in a wider margin and to depreciate modestly with a view to maintain competitiveness. However, the need for adjusting exchange rate became precipitous in the face of the external payments crisis of 1991.

Transition to Market Determined Exchange Rate System

As a part of the overall macroeconomic stabilisation programme, the exchange rate of the Rupee was devalued in two stages by 18 per cent in terms of the US dollar in July 1991. The transition to market determined exchange rate system took place in two stages and the sequencing was based on the Report of the High Level Committee on Balance of Payments, 1993 (Chairman: C. Rangarajan). The Liberalised Exchange Rate Management System (LERMS) instituted in March 1992 was a dual exchange rate arrangement under which 40 per cent of the current receipts were required to be surrendered to the Reserve Bank at the official exchange rate while the rest 60 per cent could be converted at the market rate. The 40 per cent portion surrendered at the official rate was for meeting the essential imports at a lower cost. Although the experience with the dual exchange rate system in terms of volatility in the market determined segment of the forex market was satisfactory, it involved an implicit tax on exports and other invisibles receipts and thereby emerged as a source of distortion. As a system in transition, the LERMS performed well in terms of creating the conditions for transferring an augmented volume of foreign exchange transactions on to the market.

The unified market determined exchange rate regime replaced the dual regime on March 1, 1993 and since then "*the objective of exchange rate management has been to ensure that the external value of the Rupee is realistic and credible as evidenced by a sustainable current account deficit and manageable foreign exchange situation. Subject to this predominant objective, the exchange rate policy is guided by the need to reduce excess volatility, prevent the emergence of destabilising speculative activities, help maintain adequate level of reserves, and develop an orderly foreign exchange market"* (Jalan, 1999). In order to reduce the excess volatility in the foreign exchange market, the Reserve Bank has undertaken market clearing sale and purchase operations in the foreign exchange market to moderate the impact on exchange rate arising from lumpy demand and supply as well as leads and lags in merchant transactions. Such interventions, however, are not governed by any predetermined target or band around the exchange rate.

The experience with the market determined exchange rate regime has been satisfactory, although the exchange rate management had to occasionally contend with a few episodes of volatility. The period from March 1993 till August 1995 was a phase of significant stability. Capital inflows coupled with robust export growth exerted upward pressure on the exchange rate. However, the Reserve Bank absorbed the excess supplies of foreign exchange. In the process, the nominal exchange rate of the Rupee vis-a-vis the US Dollar remained virtually unchanged at around Rs.31.37 per US Dollar over the extended period from March 1993 to August 1995. The real appreciation that resulted from the positive inflation differentials prevailing during this period triggered off market expectations and resulted in a market led correction of the exchange rate of the Rupee during September 1995 - February 1996. In response to the upheavals, the Reserve Bank intervened in the market and also resorted to monetary tightening so as to restore orderly conditions in the market after a phase of orderly correction for the perceived misalignment.

The period since 1997 has witnessed a number of adverse internal as well as external developments. The important internal developments include the economic sanctions imposed in the aftermath of nuclear tests conducted during May 1998 and the border conflict during May-June 1999. The external developments included, inter alia, the contagion from the Asian crisis, the Russian crisis during 1997-98, sharp increases in international crude oil prices in the period beginning with 1999, especially May 2000 onwards, and the post-September 11, 2001 developments in the US. These developments created a large degree of uncertainty in the foreign exchange market at various points of time, leading to excess demand conditions in the market. The Reserve Bank responded through appropriate intervention supported by monetary and other administrative measures like variations in the bank rate, repo rate, cash reserve requirements, refinance to banks, surcharge on import finance and minimum interest rates on overdue export bills. These measures helped in curbing destabilising speculation, while at the same time allowing an orderly correction in the value of the Rupee.

NEER or REER

A related issue that has figured in the literature is whether the exchange rate should be managed by monitoring Nominal Effective Exchange Rate (NEER) or Real Effective Exchange Rate (REER). "From a competitive point of view and also in the medium term perspective, it is the REER, which should be monitored as it reflects changes in the external value of a currency in relation to its trading partners in real terms. However, it is no good for monitoring short term and day-to-day movements as 'nominal' rates are the ones which are most sensitive of capital flows... Thus, in the short run, there is no option but to monitor the nominal rate" (Jalan, 2002).

Since the introduction of the market determined regime in March 1993, the Rupee has depreciated by 35 per cent upto February 2003 against the US dollar, i.e., from Rs.31.52 to Rs.48.73 per US dollar. In terms of effective exchange rates, the NEER depreciated by 31.1 per cent, while the REER (5 country trade based index) recorded a depreciation of 2.2 per cent during the period 1993-94 to 2002-03 (up to February 2003) (Table 3). A notable feature of the exchange rate in the recent years has been the two-way movement that has increased the risk profile of such market players who maintain open positions guided by the perception that the exchange rate can move only one way in India.

The Indian Rupee depreciated against all the other major currencies during the 10-year period 1993-94 to 2002-03 (up to February 2003). The Rupee depreciated against the Pound Sterling and the Japanese Yen by 37 per cent and 27 per cent, respectively, during this period. It depreciated against the Euro by 6 per cent between 1999-2000 and 2002-03 (up to February 2003).

According to RBI Report on Currency and Finance (2001-02) as a whole, India's current exchange rate policy seems to have stood the test of time. It has focused on the management of volatility without fixed rate target, while underlying demand and supply conditions are allowed to determine the exchange rate movements in an orderly way. The Reserve Bank will continue to follow the approach of watchfulness, caution and flexibility by closely monitoring the developments in the domestic and financial markets in home and abroad. It will co-ordinate its market operations carefully, particularly in regard to forex market with appropriate monetary, regulatory and other measures as considered necessary from time to time.

TABLE – 3

EXCHANGE RATE AND THE REER AND NEER OF THE INDIAN RUPEE

Year	*Rupees per US Dollar*	*REER*	*NEER*
		(5 country trade weights with 1993-94=100)	
	1	*2*	*3*
1990-91	17.94	141.69	175.04
1991-92	24.47	116.48	131.54
1992-93	30.65	112.31	117.81
1993-94	31.37	100.00	100.00
1994-95	31.40	105.81	96.09
1995-96	33.45	102.29	87.69
1996-97	35.50	103.43	86.38
1997-98	37.16	105.84	86.43
1998-99	42.07	97.79	76.45
1999-00	43.33	96.74	74.22
2000-01	45.68	100.76	73.77
2001-02	47.69	102.09	73.18
2002-03 (up to Feb '03)	48.46	97.77	68.88

FOREIGN EXCHANGE RESERVES: APPROACH, DEVELOPMENTS AND ISSUES

Approach

The subject of foreign exchange reserves has received renewed interest in recent times in the context of increasing globalisation, acceleration of capital flows and integration of financial markets. The debt-banking-financial crises in several countries have also necessitated the need for an international financial architecture in which the management of foreign exchange reserves has emerged as one of the critical issues.

Contextually, the subject of foreign exchange reserves may be broadly classified into two inter-linked areas, viz., the theory of reserves and the management of reserves. The theory of reserves encompasses issues relating to institutional and legal arrangements for holding reserve assets, conceptual and definitional aspects, objectives for holding reserve assets, exchange rate regimes and conceptualisation of the appropriate level of foreign reserves. In essence, a theoretical framework for reserves provides the rationale for holding foreign exchange reserves. Reserve management is mainly guided by the portfolio management consideration, i.e., how best to deploy foreign reserve assets subject to statutory stipulations? The portfolio considerations take into account inter alia, safety, liquidity and yield on reserves as the principal objectives of reserve management. The institutional and legal arrangements are largely country specific and these differences should be recognised in approaching the critical issues relating to both reserve management practices and policy-making (Reddy, 2002).

The motives for holding reserves may be broadly classified under three categories, viz., transaction, speculative and precautionary. International trade gives rise to currency flows, which are assumed to be handled by banks driven by the transaction motive. Similarly, speculative motive is left to individuals or corporates. Central bank reserves, however, are characterised primarily as a last resort stock of foreign currency for unpredictable flows, which is consistent with precautionary motive for holding foreign assets. Precautionary motive for holding foreign currency, like the demand for money, can be positively related to wealth and the cost of covering unplanned deficit, and negatively related to the return from alternative assets. Furthermore, foreign exchange reserves are instruments to maintain or manage the exchange rate, while enabling orderly absorption of international capital flows. Official reserves are mainly held for precautionary and transaction motives keeping in view the aggregate of national interests, to achieve balance between demand for and supply of foreign currencies, for intervention, and to preserve confidence in the country's ability to carry out external transactions.

The objectives for maintaining reserves are:

(i) maintaining confidence in monetary and exchange rate policies;

(ii) enhancing capacity to intervene in foreign exchange markets;

(iii) limiting external vulnerability by maintaining foreign currency liquidity to absorb shocks during times of crisis including national disasters or emergencies;

(iv) providing confidence to the markets, including credit rating agencies, that external obligations can always be met (thus reducing the overall costs at which foreign exchange resources are available to all the market participants); and

(v) adding to the comfort of the market participants, by demonstrating the backing of domestic currency by external assets.

India's approach to reserve management, until the balance of payments crisis of 1991 was essentially based on the traditional approach, i.e., to maintain an appropriate level of import cover defined in terms of number of months of imports equivalent to reserves. For example, the import cover of reserves shrank to three weeks of imports by the end of December 1990, and the emphasis on import cover constituted the primary concern say, till 1993-94. The approach to reserve management, as part of exchange rate management, and indeed the overall external sector policy underwent a paradigm shift with the adoption of the recommendations of the High Level Committee on Balance of Payments, 1993 (Chairman: C. Rangarajan). The Committee had recommended that the foreign exchange reserve targets be fixed in such a way that they are generally in a position to accommodate imports of three months. In the view of the Committee, the factors that are to be taken into consideration in determining the desirable level of reserves are:

(i) the need to ensure a reasonable level of confidence in the international financial and trading communities about the capacity of the country to honour its obligations and maintain trade and financial flows;

(ii) the need to take care of the seasonal factors in any balance of payments transaction with reference to the possible uncertainties in the monsoon conditions of India;

(iii) the amount of foreign currency reserves required to counter speculative tendencies or anticipatory actions amongst players in the foreign exchange market; and,

(iv) the capacity to maintain the reserves so that the cost of carrying liquidity is minimal.

With the introduction of market determined exchange rate, a change in the approach to reserve management was warranted and the emphasis on import cover had to be supplemented with the objective of smoothening out the volatility in the exchange rate, which has been reflective of the underlying market condition. Against the backdrop of currency crises in East-Asian countries and in the light of country experiences of volatile cross-border capital flows, there emerged a need to take into consideration a host of factors. The shift in the pattern of leads and lags in payments/receipts during exchange market uncertainties brought to the fore the fact that besides the size of reserves, the quality of reserves also assumes importance. Unencumbered reserve assets (defined as reserve assets net of encumbrances such as forward commitments, lines of credit to domestic entities, guarantees and other contingent liabilities) must be available at any point of time to the authorities for fulfilling various objectives assigned to reserves. As a part of prudent management of external liabilities, the policy is to keep forward liabilities at a relatively low level as a proportion of gross reserves.

An important issue which has figured prominently in the current debate on foreign exchange management is the question of appropriate policy for management of foreign exchange reserves. In a regime of free float, it can be argued that there is no need for reserves. In the light of volatility induced by capital flows and self-fulfilling expectations that this can generate, there is now a growing consensus among emerging market economies to maintain 'adequate' reserves (Jalan, 2002). Therefore, while focusing on prudent management of foreign exchange reserves in recent years, the 'liquidity at risk' associated with different types of flows has come to the fore. With the changing profile of capital flows, the traditional approach to assessing reserve adequacy in terms of import cover has been broadened to include a number of parameters which take into account the size, composition, and risk profiles of various types of capital flows as well as the types of external shocks to which the economy is vulnerable. A sufficiently high level of reserves is necessary to ensure that even if there is prolonged uncertainty, reserves can cover the liquidity at risk on all accounts over a fairly long period. Taking these considerations into account, India's foreign exchange reserves have reached a very comfortable level. The current thinking in this regard has been clearly articulated: "The prevalent national security environment further underscores the need for strong reserves. We must continue to ensure that, leaving aside short-term variations in reserves level, the quantum of reserves in the long-run is in line with the growth of the economy, the size of risk-adjusted capital flows and national security requirements. This will provide us with greater security against unfavourable or unanticipated developments, which can occur quite suddenly" (RBI, 2002c). In the context of the uncertain ramifications of the current developments in Iraq, the relevance of a comfortable reserve level appears particularly important. Unlike 1990-91, implications of such developments in the Gulf region for the external sector appears modest and manageable, mainly due to the comfortable reserve level.

The foregoing discussion points to the *evolving considerations and a paradigm shift in India's approach to reserve management. The shift has occurred from a single indicator to a menu or multiple indicators approach.* Furthermore, the policy of reserve management is built upon a host of factors, some of which are not quantifiable, and in any case, weights attached to each of them do change from time to time.

Developments: In India, reserves have been steadily built up by encouraging non-debt creating flows and de-emphasising debt creating flows, particularly short-term debt. This strategy, coupled with the maintenance of an acceptable level of current account deficit and market determined exchange rate regime was the cornerstone of the policy of external sector management. In the context of the changing interface with the external sector and the importance of the capital account, reserve adequacy is now evaluated by the Reserve Bank in terms of several indicators and not merely through conventional norms, such as, the import cover. As a matter of policy, as far as possible, foreign exchange reserves are kept at a level which is adequate to withstand both cyclical and unanticipated shocks.

India is amongst the top ten reserve holding emerging market nations. India's foreign exchange reserves increased from US $ 4.7 billion in June 1991 to US $ 73.9 billion as on March 13, 2003. The predominant component of foreign exchange reserves is in the form of foreign currency assets that increased from US $ 1.1 billion to US $ 71.7 billion during the same period. The gold holdings of the Reserve Bank remained broadly stable at around US $ 3-4 billion during the same period. SDR holdings of the Government came down from US $ 63 million in June 1991 to US $ 4 million as on March 13, 2003. The movement in India's foreign exchange reserves since 1993-94 can be divided into three phases: (i) the period March 1993 to March 1995, when reserves increased sharply from US $ 9.8 billion to US $ 25.2 billion, (ii) the period March 1995 to March 1999, when reserves increased moderately to US $ 32.5 billion, and (iii) finally since 1999-2000, when there was a phenomenal increase in reserves - as much as US $ 41.3 billion cumulatively (by US $ 5.5 billion in 1999-2000, US $ 4.2 billion in 2000-01, US $ 11.8 billion in 2001-02, and US $ 19.8 billion during 2002-03 (up to March 13, 2003)).*

While the significant accretion to foreign exchange reserves has provided comfort on external sector management, two contentious issues

* During the week ended July 26, 2003, Foreign Exchange Reserves reached a record level close to $85 billion ($84.9 billion).

have come to the fore. These are the trade-off between costs and benefits accruing from the reserves accretion and the associated monetary impact that emanates from it.

Capital Inflows, Foreign Exchange Reserves and Growth

The coexistence of slowdown in the growth rate of the Indian economy in the recent period and the sharp build-up of foreign exchange reserves, has fuelled the debate on their possible inter-relationship and has called into question, in some quarters, the extant policy of reserve accretion. A recent study by Lal Bery and Pant (NCAER) for example, has contended that India could have attained a higher growth trajectory had capital inflows been allowed to be absorbed by the economy (instead of accumulating them as foreign exchange reserves of the central bank) and had fiscal deficits not been incurred.

The need for raising domestic absorption is well recognised and the Tenth Plan document already envisages a current account deficit of 2.8 per cent of GDP to attain a growth target of about 8 per cent. In the context of the Tenth Plan requirements, current levels of reserves and capital flows appear to be inadequate. Even if large capital flows materialise in future to meet the financing gap of 2.8 per cent of GDP as envisaged in the Tenth Plan document, the flows need to be regulated so that the CAD does not expand beyond the sustainable level. Hence, even though expanding absorption of foreign capital is a major policy challenge in the short-run, the overall medium to long-run policy strategy demands that the CAD be necessarily maintained within the sustainable level. This has been the most important lesson from the balance of payments crisis in 1991. Rather than engendering real appreciation, other counter-cyclical policies can be applied to revive aggregate demand, which in turn can improve absorption of foreign capital.

Summing Up

The external sector reform programme initiated in the wake of the balance of payments crisis of 1991 was all encompassing. Even though the reforms were largely crisis led, the policy initiatives were unique in terms of their gradual, cautious and country specific approach. As against balance of payments problems of varying intensities experienced during 1956-1991, India's balance of payments position strengthened over the 1990s even as the period coincided with the liberalisation of external account, external currency crises and domestic political uncertainties.

Prudent exchange rate management, low current account deficit, steady flow of non-debt creating capital flows, particularly in the form of FDI, a significant reduction in the external debt to GDP ratio and containment of short-term debt to manageable and prudent limits have been some of the positive outcomes of policy reform in the external sector. Resilience of the external sector has helped India successfully avert the contagion effects of the East Asian crisis.

There are, however, a few areas, which require further efforts. India's competitiveness in exports would require to be strengthened to achieve a sustained export growth of at least 12 per cent per annum in order to achieve the medium-term goal of increasing India's share in world exports to 1 per cent by 2006-07. India also needs to make the transition from exports of labour-intensive low technology goods to a wider variety of goods, including technology intensive goods. India's tariff levels continue to be high; accelerated pace of reduction of tariffs and removing the constraints on the small-scale industries would be conducive to industrial growth and exports. Rapid growth in exports would also require addressing the domestic constraints of supply bottlenecks and inadequate infrastructure.

A sustained surge in capital flows in the recent past has implications for monetary and inflation management although, the Reserve Bank has so far been able to sterilise the monetary impact of foreign exchange reserves through large open market sales of government securities. The financial cost of additional reserve accretion in the recent period is low.

There has been a debate that high accretion to forex reserves has resulted in a substantial output loss in the 1990s. It needs to be recognised, however, that the steady growth path is functionally related more to macroeconomic constraints of saving and investment than to the reserve management policy *per se.* The reserve management policy, coupled with the exchange rate management and monetary policy pursued by the Reserve Bank has created an atmosphere of softer interest rate regime, which is conducive to higher economic growth. In addition, the recent policy initiatives have created an investment atmosphere where foreign investment supplements domestic investment, which in a medium-term perspective would ensure a higher growth trajectory.

APPENDIX TABLE – 1

VARIOUS RECOMMENDATIONS FOR CAPITAL ACCOUNT CONVERTIBILITY (TARAPORE COMMITTEE)

Recommendations	Developments
Fiscal Consolidation	
1. Reduction in gross fiscal deficit as percentage of gross domestic product from budgeted 4.5 in 1997-98 to 4.0 in 1998-99 and further to 3.5 in 1999-2000.	1. Gross fiscal deficit as a percentage of gross domestic product stood at 5.9 during 2002-03.
Mandated Inflation Rate	
1. The mandated rate of inflation for the three-year period 1997-98 to 1999-2000 should be an average of 3 to 5 per cent.	1. Annual inflation rate based on WPI (base 1993-94=100) averaged at 4.7 per cent during the three years period 1999-2000 to 2001-02.
2. The Reserve Bank should be given freedom to attain mandated rate of inflation approved by the Parliament.	2. Although inflation is an important determinant of monetary policy, in India there is no target/mandated rate of inflation approved by Parliament.
Strengthening of Financial System	
1. Interest rates to be fully deregulated in 1997-98 and any formal or informal interest rate controls to be abolished.	1. All interest rates (except savings bank deposit rate) have been deregulated.
2. CRR to be reduced in phases to 8 per cent in 1997-98, 6 per cent in 1998-99 and to 3 per cent in 1999-2000.	2. CRR was reduced to 4.75 per cent in 2002-03.
3. Gross Non-Performing Assets (NPA) as percentage to total advances to be brought down in phases to 12 per cent in 1997-98, 9 per cent in 1998-99 and to 5 per cent in 1999-2000.	3. Gross NPA of the public sector banks as a percentage to total advances has come down from 16 per cent in end-March 1998 to 11.1 per cent in end-March 2002.

(Contd...)

(...contd...)

Recommendations	Developments
Fiscal Consolidation	
4. 100 per cent marked to market valuation of investments for banks.	4. The concept of 100 per cent marked to market valuation has been done away with. The modern concept works on the basis of banks classifying their entire portfolio into three categories 'Held to Maturity', 'Available for Sale' and 'Held for Trading'. While in the first category, the investment should not exceed 25 per cent, in the other two categories the banks have a freedom to decide the proportion that would be marked to market.
5. Best practices for forex risk management by banks.	5. Risk management guidelines were issued in October 1999, broadly covering areas of credit risk and market risk.
6. Banks to follow international accounting disclosure norms.	6. The range of disclosures as 'Notes to Accounts' in bank's balance sheet in 'Schedule 17' has been gradually expanded over the years.
7. Capital prescription be stipulated for market risks.	7. In March 2000, standard assets were given a risk weight of 0.25 per cent.
Important Macroeconomic Indicators	
1. A monitoring band of +/-5 per cent around the neutral Real Effective Exchange Rate (REER) to be introduced and intervened by the Reserve Bank when REER is outside the band.	1. No such band is maintained in India.
2. Debt service ratio to be reduced to 20 per cent from 25 per cent.	2. Debt Service ratio has steadily declined from 19.5 per cent in 1997-98 to 14.1 per cent in 2001-02.
3. The foreign exchange reserves should not be less than 6 months imports.	3. As of end-February 2003. foreign exchange reserves covers more than a year's imports.

26

Foreign Direct Investment in India

Policy, Trends and Impact

FDI Policy: A Historical Perspective

OVER the last five decades, there have been significant changes in approaches and policies relating to FDI in India in tune with the developments in the industrial policies and also foreign exchange situation, from time to time. There is a view in the literature that the attitude and approach to FDI reflected the under current of balance of payments crisis in the respective periods. Depending upon the thrust and direction of the policies at different time period, one can identify four distinct phases in the evolution of the policies :

i) first phase from 1950 to 1967-characterised by receptive attitude or cautious welcome;

ii) second phase from 1967 to 1980- marked by restrictive and selective policies;

iii) third phase from 1980 to 1990-gradual liberalisation; and

iv) fourth phase from 1991 till date-paradigm shift to open door policy (Jain, 1994, Subrahmanian, et al. 1996, and Kumar, 1998). Major features of FDI policies during the above four phases are reviewed below. Exhibit 1 provides the major features of FDI policies during the four phases.

Excerpted from P.D. Jeromi (2003), *Foreign Direct Investment in India: Policy, Trends and Impact*, in Economic Developments in India, Vol.62, Academic Foundation, Delhi.

First Phase 1950-1967

After independence, especially with the second Five-Year Plan, India's development strategy focused on import substituting industrialisation. At that point of time, the availability of capital, technology, skills, entrepreneurship, etc., was very limited. Hence, the attitude towards FDI was increasingly receptive (Kumar, 1998). During this period, FDI was sought on mutually advantageous terms, though the majority local ownership was preferred. As foreign investment was considered necessary, foreign investors were assured of non-discriminatory treatment on par with domestic enterprises. There were no restrictions on the remittances of profits and dividends. Foreign investors were assured of fair compensation in the event of acquisition. However, it was provided that, as a rule, the major interest in ownership and effective control would always be in Indian hands. With the foreign exchange crisis in 1957-58, FDI policies were further liberalised and offered a host of incentives and concessions. During this phase, market seeking FDIs have been specially encouraged by the locational advantage in production as there was protection to local manufacture in the domestic market. Thus, during this phase, the country had given cautious welcome to the foreign capital.

Second Phase 1968-1980

By the middle of sixties, there was considerable investment in various industries. Besides, India's scientific and technological knowledge and infrastructure were developing and manpower was getting more skilled and constraints on local supply of capital and entrepreneurship have begun to ease somewhat. On the other hand, outflow on account of servicing of FDI and technology imports from the earlier period has begun to rise in the form of dividends, profits, royalties, and technical fees, etc. These factors forced the government to adopt a more restrictive attitude towards FDI (Kumar, 1998). Major features of the policies followed during the phase are:

i) restrictions were imposed on proposals of FDIs without technology transfer and those seeking more than 40 per cent foreign ownership;

ii) the government listed industries in which FDI was not considered desirable in view of local capabilities;

iii) foreign collaborations required exclusive use of Indian consultancy services wherever available;

iv) the renewals of foreign collaboration agreements were restricted;

v) from 1973 onwards the further activities of foreign companies along with those of local large industrial houses were restricted to a select group of core or high priority industries. The enactment of Foreign Exchange Regulation Act (FERA), 1973 became the key to guiding and controlling FDI inflows. The phase of tight regulation and selective policy was implemented by an administrative system based on discretionary power.

EXHIBIT – 1

MAJOR FEATURES OF FDI POLICIES DURING THE FOUR PHASES

Phase I 1950-67	*Phase II 1968-80*	*Phase III 1980-90*	*Phase IV 1991 Onwards*
Receptive Attitude or Cautious Welcome.	*Restrictive Attitude*	*Gradual Liberalisation.*	*Open Door Policy.*
• Non-discriminatory treatment to FDI.	• Restriction on FDI without technology	• Higher foreign equity in export-oriented units allowed.	• Liberal policies relating to technology collaboration, foreign trade and foreign exchange.
• No restrictions on remittance of profits and dividends.	• Above 40% stake not allowed.	• Procedure for remittance of royalty and technical fees liberalised	• Encouraging FDI in core and infrastructure industries.
	• Allowed only in priority area.		• FERA replaced with FEMA
• Ownership and control with Indians.	• FDI controlled by FERA	• Fast channel for FDI clearance.	• Procedures transparent
			• Liberal approach for NRI investments
	• Discretionary power in sanctioning the projects.		• FDI need not be accompanied by technology
			• FDI through Mergers and Acquistions.
			• FDI in services and financial sector-banks, NBFCs, insurance.

Third Phase 1980-90

There was a gradual liberalisation of FDI policies in the eighties due to the deterioration of foreign exchange position in the wake of second oil crisis and India's failure to boost her manufactured exports. Hence, eighties witnessed a gradual but discernible sign of easing of restrictions on foreign investment inflows with the liberalisation of industrial and trade policies. Policies were framed to attract more FDIs and foreign licensing collaborations. During this phase policies were specially designed to encourage higher foreign equity holding in export-oriented units and investments from Oil Exporting Developing countries. Approval systems were streamlined. A degree of flexibility was introduced in the policy concerning foreign ownership, and exceptions from the general ceiling of 40 per cent on foreign equity were allowed on the merit of individual investment proposals. The rules and procedures concerning payments of royalties and lump sum technical fees were relaxed and withholding taxes were reduced. The approvals for opening liaison offices by foreign companies in India were liberalised. New procedures were introduced enabling direct application by a foreign investor even before choosing an Indian partner. A fast channel was set up in 1988 for expediting clearances of FDI proposals from major investing countries, viz. Japan, Germany, the US and the UK. Thus, the third phase witnessed a concrete move towards liberalisation of FDI policies.

Fourth Phase-1991 Onwards

There has been a paradigm shift in the policies on FDI right from the early nineties with the adoption of the Industrial Policy Statement of July 1991. One of the objectives of Industrial Policy Statement was that "foreign investment and technology collaboration will be welcomed to obtain higher technology, to increase exports and to expand the production base". The Industrial Policy Statement of 1991 has followed an 'open-door' policy on foreign investment and technology transfer. The policy since then has been aimed at encouraging foreign investment particularly in the core and infrastructure sectors. During the fourth phase, favourable policy environment consisting of the liberalisation policies on foreign investment, foreign technology collaboration, foreign trade and foreign exchange, have been exerting positive influence on foreign firms' decisions on investment and business operations in the country.

During this period, the FERA, 1973 has been amended and restrictions placed on foreign companies by the FERA have been lifted.

In 1999, FERA has been replaced with Foreign Exchange Management Act. Government has permitted, except for a small negative list, access to the automatic route for FDI. Hence, foreign investors only need to inform the RBI within 30 days of bringing in their investment. Companies with more than 40 per cent of foreign equity are now treated on par with fully Indian owned companies. New sectors such as mining, banking, telecommunications, highways, construction, airports, hotel and tourism, courier service and management have been thrown open for FDI. Even the defence industry sector is opened upto 100 per cent for Indian private sector participation with 26 per cent FDI, subject to licensing. (FDI is not permitted in the following industrial sectors: i) arms and ammunition, ii) atomic energy, iii) railway transport, iv) coal and lignite and v) mining of iron, manganese, chrome, gypsum, sulphur, gold, diamonds, copper and zinc). The liberal policies have been accompanied by active courting of foreign investors at the highest level. The international trade policy regime has been considerably liberalised too with removal of quantitative restrictions lowering of peak tariffs to 30 per cent and sharp pruning of negative list for imports. The rupee was made convertible on current account and gradually to capital account.

Now FDI is permitted under the following four forms of investments: i) through financial collaboration, ii) through joint ventures and technical collaborations, iii) through capital markets via Global Depository Receipts (GDRs) (Euro issues), and iv) through private placements or preferential allotments.

Transparency and openness have been the most significant features of FDI policies in the fourth phase. The degree of openness is reflected in (i) the sectors open to FDI, (ii) higher level of foreign equity participation, and (iii) transparency in approval procedures. One striking aspect of the present liberalisation policy is that unlike the previous phases, it is not necessary that FDI is accompanied by foreign technology agreements. There is a liberal approach towards investment by non-resident Indian (NRIs): NRIs and overseas corporate bodies can invest up to 100 per cent in high priority industries. Another distinctive feature of the policy is the simplification of procedures.

Thus, the ongoing measures taken since 1991 are focused towards a virtual elimination of the both direct and indirect barriers to foreign direct investment [indirect barriers in the form of investor protection, differences in accounting standards, legal and regulatory structure]. In short, the evolution of FDI policies in India are characterised by receptive attitude till the mid-sixties to a policy of restrictions and controls till 1980 and then to gradual liberalisation till 1990 and finally to a policy of full-fledged liberalisation since 1991.

Trends in FDI – An Aggregative Picture

The net result of the nature of FDI policies followed during the four phases described in the preceding section can be found in terms of number of foreign collaboration approvals. A summary of the data presented in Table 1 shows that during the second phase of restrictive policies, the number of collaborations has declined from the average number of collaborations in the first phase. However, during the 'eighties, the third phase, there was a notable rise in the average number of collaborations. What is more striking is the substantial rise (2.5 times of the eighties) in the average number of approvals during the 'nineties till October 2001. Along with the rise in the number of approvals, the share of financial collaborations has risen steadily from 16.7 per cent in the second phase to 65.7 per cent in the fourth phase. The decline in the number of technical collaborations from 982 in 1995 to 418 in 2000 is a matter of concern, especially when the country needed advanced technology (Table 1).

TABLE – 1

AVERAGE NUMBER OF FOREIGN COLLABORATION APPROVALS

(Yearly Average no. of approvals during the period)

Phase	*Period*	*All Collaborations*	*Financial Collaborations*	*Share of Financial Collaborations*
I	1956-65	244	n.a.	n.a.
II	1966-79	239	40	16.7
III	1980-90	724	174	24.0
IV	1991-01*	1887	1240	65.7

* At the end of October 2001

Source:

1. Reserve Bank of India Bulletin, various issues, compiled and reported in Subrahmanian, et al, (1996).
2. Annual Report 1999-2000, Ministry of Commerce and Industry, Government of India
3. Economic Survey 2001-02, Government of India.

During the 'seventies and 'eighties, the amount of approval of FDI was very low- Rs. 63 crore and Rs. 1,273 crore, respectively. However, during the 'nineties, till October 2001, the total amount of approval was

Rs. 270,063 crore, which is 212 fold higher than the amount approved in the 'eighties. In case of FDI, actual inflow is more important than the number of projects and amount approved. During the nineties, the actual inflow was Rs.1,05,414 crore, which formed only 39.0 cent of total amount approved during this period. Actual inflows as a per cent of gross capital formation rose from 0.2 per cent in 1991 to 4.7 per cent in 1997, subsequently it declined and formed only 3.8 per cent in 1999 (Table 2).

TABLE – 2

FDI-AMOUNT APPROVED, ACTUAL INFLOWS AND PER CENT OF CAPITAL FORMATION

(Rs. Crore)

Year	*Amount Approval*	*Actual Inflow*	*Inflow % of Approval*	*Inflow % of GCF*
1991	534	351	65.8	0.2
1992	3888	675	17.4	0.4
1993	8859	1787	20.2	1.0
1994	14187	3289	23.2	1.4
1995	32072	6820	21.3	2.2
1996	36147	10389	28.7	3.4
1997	54891	16425	29.9	4.7
1998	30814	13340	43.3	3.6
1999	28367	16868	59.5	3.8
2000	37039	19342	52.2	-
2000*	32631	13810	42.3	-
2001*	23266	16127	69.3	-

* : January-October, GCF: Gross capital formation.
Source : Economic Survey 2001-02, Government of India.

From a closer look at the data, one can identify two distinct phases in the growth of FDI during the 'nineties. The four year period from 1994 to 1997 is characterised by high growth of approvals and lower inflows and realisation rate. During this period, there was a significant rise in the number of projects and amount approved for FDI – the average annual growth of FDI amount approved was 63 per cent. However, inflows as a per cent of amount approved was lower: 26 per cent during 1994-97

Phase I: 1994 to 1997 – High growth of approval and low growth of inflow and realisation rate.

Phase II: 1998 to 2001 – Low growth of approvals and high growth of inflow and realisation rate.

On the other hand, during the next four year period from 1998 to 2001 (till October) there was a slow down in both number and amount of approvals but growth of inflows and realization rate was higher. During this low growth phase, the yearly average number of approvals declined to 1,998 from 2,205 during the high growth phase. Further, the average annual growth of amount approved during this period was lower at 12 per cent as against 63 per cent during the previous phase. Though there was a lower growth of approvals during this period, the actual inflow has been higher in terms of absolute amount and realisation rate. Average amount of inflow during this period was Rs.16,419 crore as against Rs. 9,231 crore during 1994 to 1997. Actual inflows as a per cent of amount approved rose from 26 per cent to 56 per cent.

Since inflows in a particular year need not be entirely related to the approvals given in that year, it is possible to infer that higher inflows during the second phase may be on account of lag involved in the realization of projects for which approvals were given in the earlier phase. If that is the case, it can also be inferred that lower approvals during the second phase may lead to lower inflows in the coming years. The reasons for the reduction in the number of approvals can be traced to i) the effect of restrictions on India following nuclear tests, ii) political uncertainty and iii) very slow progress in second generation reforms, particularly relating to real sector and privatisation of public enterprise.

Changes in Sectoral Composition

In tune with the government's priorities with respect to FDI, sectoral composition of FDI has undergone significant changes during the last two decades. Till 1990, the government policy was to channel FDI inflow in technology-intensive branches of manufacturing. Thus, more than four-fifth of FDI stock in 1990 was in the manufacturing industries. The share of petroleum and power and service sectors were only marginal. However, with the changes in the FDI policies in the 'nineties, the share of manufacturing has been more than halved to 40.1 per cent. Within the manufacturing industries, FDI is shifting away from heavy capital goods industries to light industries. With the opening up of the infrastructure industries, on the other hand, the share of petroleum and power sector rose substantially to 30.6 per cent in 1999 from just 0.1 per cent of FDI stock in 1990. Similarly, the share of service sector rose to 27.8 per cent from just 5.2 per cent, respectively, during the above period.

Three high priority industries, namely, power, telecommunication and oil refinery accounted for nearly half of the total amount of FDI approvals during 1991 to 1999. Among the different industries, power and telecommunication accounted for the highest share (17.5 per cent each) of FDI approvals during the 'nineties. They are closely followed by oil refinery, which accounted for 13.1 per cent of FDI approvals. Transportation industry and financial sector were the other two prominent sectors accounting for larger share of FDI approvals. Thus, what is noticeable in the 'nineties is the rise of FDI inflows in the priority infrastructure sectors like power, telecommunication, oil refinery, transportation, finance and banking. Perhaps, this is on account of the opening up of these industries for FDI in recent times.

Changes in the Sources of FDI

Over the years, there has been diversification of sources of FDI. Until 1990, European countries have been the major sources of FDI inflows in India. They accounted for nearly two-third of total stock of FDI in 1990. However, their share drastically declined to around one-fifth during the 'nineties. Among the European countries, the decline was significantly high in case of the U.K. from 48.8 per cent in 1990 to just 7.6 per cent during the 'nineties. The share of European countries, America and Japan taken together accounted for nearly 90 per cent of total stock of FDI in 1990, however, it has declined to 46.6 per cent during the 'nineties. The decline in the share of the above group is essentially due to the rise in the inflows from other countries. What is more striking is the fact that after USA, Mauritius is the second largest source of FDI in India. Because of lower taxes in Mauritius, they are able to attract foreign capital from different parts of the world, which is in turn invested in countries like India.

Country-wise, the number of approvals of FDI during the nineties shows that USA accounts for nearly one-fifth of total approvals. Four countries, namely, USA, Germany, United Kingdom and Japan, together share around half of the approvals. Around 95 per cent of foreign collaboration approvals from Mauritius and NRIs are financial in nature. However, in case of Japan and Italy, technical collaborations are more than financial collaborations.

Pattern of FDI by Type of Approvals

There are two major routes, namely, Government - through Foreign Investment Promotion Board (FIPB) and Secretariat for Industrial Assistance (SIA) – and the Reserve Bank, through which FDI approvals are given. An analysis of institution-wise approval of the amount of inflows reveals that the share of Government through FIPB/SIA has been on the decline and it formed around three-fifth of the approvals in 2001-02. The share of RBI's automatic approval, on the other hand, has increased to 19.4 per cent in 2000-01 from 13.3 per cent in 1992-93. NRI direct investments constituted around one-third of total FDI inflows in 1995-96. However, of late, their share has declined and it formed only to 2.9 per cent in 2000-01 as NRI investments are increasingly taking place in the form of acquisitions of shares of domestic companies. The share of acquisition of shares by Non-residents rose significantly from 0.5 per cent in 1995-96 to 15.5 per cent in 2000-01 (Table 3).

TABLE – 3

SHARE OF DIFFERENT APPROVAL SOURCES IN ACTUAL FLOW OF FDI

(per cent)

Sources of Approval	*1992-93*	*1995-96*	*1998-99*	*2000-01*
1. Government (FIPB/SIA)	70.5	58.3	74.0	62.2
2. Reserve Bank (automatic route)	13.3	7.9	7.3	19.4
3. NRIs (40% and 100% scheme)	16.2	33.3	2.5	2.9
4. Acquisition of Shares by Non-Residents*	0.0	0.5	16.2	15.5
Total	100.0	100.0	100.0	100.00

Note: * : Acquisition of shares of Indian companies by non-residents under Section 5 of FEMA, 1999.

Source : Economic Survey 2001-02, Ministry of Finance, Government of India, New Delhi.

Comparative Performance of India and China

While discussing about FDI in India, often a comparison is made with China, as it is the major recipient of FDI among the developing countries. According to the World Investment Report 2001, India's inward FDI in 2000 stood at US$ 2.3 billion as against US$ 40.8 billion in China, nearly 18 fold higher than India. Further, the accumulated stock of FDI in India was US$ 19.0 billion in 2000 as against US$ 346.7 billion in China, nearly 18 fold higher than India. India compares very poorly with China in terms of inflow of FDI during the last two decades.

During the 'nineties from 1991 to 2000, China accounted for 27.0 per cent of total flow of FDI to developing countries as against India's share at 1.0 per cent.

As a result of higher FDI inflows, in China the number of foreign-invested firms constituted 16 per cent of all companies in 1998, which contributed 24.7 per cent of total industrial output, 17.6 per cent of total assets and 18.8 per cent of total revenue. Further, FDI inflows in India as per cent of her gross fixed capital formation and GDP was very much lower than that of China. In 1999, FDI inflows in India as per cent of gross fixed capital formation was just 2.4 per cent as against 11.3 per cent in case of China (Table 4). Similarly, FDI inflows in India as per cent of GDP was as low as 3.6 per cent as against 30.9 per cent in case of China (Table 5). These facts indicate that India is relatively slow in restructuring growth and orienting policies to encourage FDI The comparison shows that there is considerable scope for attracting more FDI in India as the country has the potential to absorb it.

TABLE – 4

INWARD FDI FLOWS AS PER CENT OF GROSS FIXED CAPITAL FORMATION IN INDIA AND CHINA

(per cent)

Country	*1986-95*	*1997*	*1998*	*1999*
India	0.6	3.80	2.9	2.4
China	6.4	14.6	12.9	11.3
Developing Countries minus China	4.7	10.9	11.7	13.8
World	4.0	7.5	10.9	16.3

Source: UNCTAD, 2001.

TABLE – 5

INWARD FDI FLOWS AS PER CENT OF GROSS DOMESTIC PRODUCT IN INDIA AND CHINA

(per cent)

Country	*1985*	*1990*	*1995*	*1999*
India	0.5	0.6	1.7	3.6
China	3.4	7.0	19.6	30.9
Developing Countries minus China	14.1	13.4	15.6	28.0
World	7.8	9.2	10.3	17.3

Source: UNCTAD, 2001.

Here it is worthwhile to examine why China is able to get more FDI than India despite her many relative advantages like prevalent English fluency, top-notch engineers, a well developed IT industry and low wages. One significant factor cited for the difference is the contrasting discretion in adopting policies of openness by the respective governments. Chinese governments pragmatic reform and policy of openness is exemplified through their Prime Ministers famous remark, "...it doesn't matter if a cat is black or white, so long as it catches mice". However, India's openness policy is applied to relatively restricted sectors, mainly social overhead projects such as roads, ports, telecommunication, electricity, etc., where capital requirement is very large with low profitability.

Another factor is the differences in the structure of local governments and their authority. In China, local governments play an important role in attracting FDI because they have a great deal of autonomy in issuing permits as well as offering various administrative services. Since China is still a highly planned economy, the Central governments openness policy tends to be executed easily and efficiently throughout the economy. In contrast, in India under democratic setup, the sovereignty of the local governments is well guaranteed, and hence, some of the local governments are still passive with regard to attracting FDI.

Another inhibiting factor in India is the uncertainty of policy decisions which obscures predictable future profits and establishment of well-guided management plans. Factors like lack of well-established investment procedures, unpredictable costs for factory construction and operation and corrupt bureaucracy aggravates the level of uncertainty in the eyes of potential foreign investors. The India-China comparison shows that a government's firm determination to pursue a policy of openness and capability to ensure efficient coordinated implementation systems can outweigh the inherent advantages of another government (Kim, 2002).

Another major reasons for China's success is that they are able to attract more investment from their own people who are doing business in America, Hong Kong, Macao and in other countries. Further, the level of infrastructure in China is better than India. On the policy front, in case of India, the initial reform measures were mostly in the area of financial sector. Only recently reform measure were contemplated for the real sector. In fact, for attracting FDI, real sector reforms are essential as the investment essentially takes place in sectors like manufacturing, infrastructure and services.

Impact of FDI

Impact of FDI can be felt on a number of areas and it varies depending upon the nature of the projects and the degree of integration with the rest of the economy.

Impact of FDI from the Performance of FDI-Companies in India

The Reserve Bank's regular surveys on "Foreign Collaboration in Indian Industry", provide valuable information on the status of industries which are having foreign collaboration. The latest survey (the sixth in the series) pertains to the period 1986-87 to 1993-94 and it covered 1,108 companies in the private sector (132 subsidiaries, 572 minority capital participation companies and 404 purely technical collaboration companies). Major relevant findings of the survey are:

(i) There was significant concentration of foreign capital in the manufacturing sectors like chemicals and chemical products, machinery and machine tools, electrical machinery and apparatus and transport equipment.

(ii) As compared with the previous survey period (1981-86), there has been an improvement in the profitability of the companies during 1986-87 to 1993-94, especially in case of companies with minority capital participation and pure technical collaborations.

(iii) Production of the surveyed companies rose at an average annual rate of 20.3 per cent; the leading contributors to production were chemicals and chemical products, transport equipment, machinery and machine tools and the diversified groups.

(iv) During the survey period (1986-87 to 1993-94), on an average, exports accounted for 63.3 per cent of imports by the companies; trade deficit was more pronounced in the case of pure technical collaboration companies.

(v) Import intensity of production increased during the survey period; value of imports formed 11.6 per cent of total production of technical collaboration companies, 11.5 per cent of minority capital participation companies and 8.6 per cent in case of subsidiaries.

(vi) Dividend remittances were high in case of chemicals and chemical products, followed by machinery and machine tools (Reserve Bank, 1999).

Comparative Performance:
FDI versus Non-FDI Companies

Another source of information on the performance of FDI companies is their balance sheet data. Periodically, the Reserve Bank compiles the balance sheet data of about 300 companies to assess their financial performance. A comparison of performance of FDI companies with that of non-FDI companies will give an understanding on their relative efficiency. During the eight-year period from 1992-93 to 1999-2000, sales growth of public limited FDI companies was lower than non-FDI companies in four years. However, in case of private limited FDI companies, the sales growth was higher in all the years, except in 1999-2000 (Table 6).

TABLE – 6

COMPARATIVE RATES OF SALES GROWTH OF FDI COMPANIES AND OTHER COMPANIES

(Per cent)

Type of Company	*1992-93*	*1993-94*	*1994-95*	*1995-96*	*1996-97*	*1997-98*	*1998-99*	*1999-00**
1. Public Limited Companies	12.2	15.4	20.5	23.7	12.2	7.5	6.1	11.9
i) Selected FDI Companies	10.9	16.4	16.3	22.6	15.2	5.9	8.1	9.9
ii) Others	12.6	15.2	21.5	24.0	11.0	5.8	5.8	11.9
2. Private Limited Companies	14.6	17.3	22.0	20.9	10.9	10.3	7.3	11.9
i) Selected FDI Companies	26.1	27.0	36.5	25.9	11.7	20.8	17.3	9.4
ii) Others	14.2	17.0	21.6	20.6	10.8	9.3	6.7	11.11
3. FDI Companies [1(i)+2(ii)]	11.0	16.5	16.4	22.6	15.1	5.9	7.0	9.9

Note : The number of companies considered to arrive at the sales growth rate is different for different years. In 1998-99, 1848 public limited companies were selected for the analysis; of which, 257 were FDI companies and 1591 were non-FDI companies. In case of private limited companies, 890 companies were considered; of which, 64 were FDI companies and 826 were non-FDI Companies.

* Relate to 274 public limited FDI companies and 60 private limited FDI companies.

Source : Reserve Bank of India Bulletin, Various Issues, Reserve Bank of India, Mumbai.

Rate of return on equity, which essentially decides the investment, was higher in case of FDI companies than the non-FDI companies, irrespective of whether they are public limited or private limited companies (Table 7). From the above, it is reasonable to conclude that, in general, performance of FDI companies, in terms of sales growth and return on equity was better than non-FDI companies.

TABLE – 7

COMPARATIVE RATE OF RETURN ON EQUITY OF FDI COMPANIES AND OTHER COMPANIES

(Per cent)

Type of Company	*1992-93*	*1993-94*	*1994-95*	*1995-96*	*1996-97*	*1997-98*	*1998-99*	*1999-00*
1. Public Limited Companies	9.4	12.0	14.0	14.4	9.8	7.6	56	n.a
i) Selected FDI Companies	12.3	14.4	17.2	18.1	15.7	11.7	12.5	13.2
ii) Others	8.6	11.6	13.5	13.9	8.3	6.9	5.0	n.a
2. Private Limited Companies	13.1	16.1	17.4	13.5	8.7	9.2	8.4	n.a
i) Selected FDI Companies	28.7	19.6	24.5	23.7	11.4	11.3	15.1	11.4
ii) Others	12.0	15.9	17.1	12.9	8.3	8.9	8.3	n.a
3. FDI Companies [1(i)+2(ii)]	12.4	14.5	17.2	18.1	15.6	11.7	12.5	13.2

Note and Source: Same as Table 6. n.a : Not available.

In case of FDI companies, their export performance vis-a-vis total sales and import intensity of exports is closely watched to understand their interest in exports and foreign exchange inflows or outflows. Table 8 shows that during the early 'nineties (till 1993-94) there was some increase in export intensity of sales but it came down during the subsequent years, except in 1997-98. In 1999-2000, export intensity of sales remained at 9.3 per cent, the same level as in 1990-91. In this context on the other hand, import intensity of exports has been increasing during the nineties, till 1996-97. However, it declined subsequently and stood at 112.4 per cent in 1990-2000 (Table 8).

TABLE – 8

EXPORT INTENSITY OF SALES AND IMPORT INTENSITY OF EXPORTS OF FDI COMPANIES

(Per cent)

Item	*1990-91*	*1991-92*	*1992-93*	*1993-94*	*1994-95*	*1995-96*	*1996-97*	*1997-98*	*1998-99*	*1999-2000*
i) Export Intensity of Sales	9.3	9.9	10.6	10.4	9.9	9.2	9.7	10.6	9.4	9.3
ii) Import Intensity of Exports	84.1	66.1	77.6	80.6	107.6	139.1	179.2	120.6	122.9	112.4

Note and *Source*: Same as Table 6.

The insights derived from the theoretical understanding, empirical literature and performance of FDI companies in India give a mixed picture. A comparative analysis of performance of FDI companies with that of non-FDI companies, however, revealed that the former is doing well, in terms of sales growth and return on equity than the latter. However, the trends in export-intensity of sales and import-intensity of exports of FDI companies are not very encouraging. It implies that FDI companies are concentrating more on the domestic market for sales and their import requirements are relatively high.

Prospects of FDI

The concerted move for attracting FDI, without many restrictions, was initiated in the beginning of the 'nineties, as part of a wide-ranging reform process implemented in the country. The inflow of FDI during the nineties looks impressive when compared with the position in the earlier periods of restrictive policy regime. However, FDI inflows as a per cent of capital formation and GDP in India is very low, which indicates the potential and requirement of India. The slow down in FDI approvals since 1997, especially technical collaborations, is a matter of concern when the country is aiming for faster growth. India's record in attracting FDI is relatively poor when compared with that of China. Though FDI companies could not contribute much for exports and technological advancement of the country, their overall performance is better than non-FDI companies. Given the subdued trend in the domestic savings rate, it is imperative for the country to channelise higher amounts of foreign capital to achieve the goal. Though there are divergent views on the impact of FDI, it is relatively more desirable than other forms of foreign capital. Hence, measures should be in place for its inflows in the desired directions in the coming years.

In case of India, three major pre-requisites for the larger flow of FDI are real sector reforms, development of infrastructure and privatisation of public enterprises. In India, real sector reforms, the major component of the second generation reforms, is underway now. Real sector reforms are needed for removing controls or restrictions on economic activities so as to improve productivity and competitiveness of the sectors. Privatisation is an important component of real sector reforms and it has implication for the inflow of FDI. FDI can be encouraged to speed up the privatisation of public sector enterprise. The experience of emerging countries like Brazil, Chile, Indonesia, Malaysia and Philippines shows that privatisation can provide strong impetus for FDI (OECD, 1999). Once measures are taken for equal treatment of domestic and foreign players in sectors like manufacturing, infrastructure and services, FDI is likely to rise in the future. Infrastructure constraints are another inhibiting factor of FDI, which need to be addressed with very high priority. In fact, in recent times, several measures were taken for improving the infrastructure, especially in sectors like power, telecommunication, civil aviation, ports, etc. by private sector participation. Once, an atmosphere is created for the economic principles to guide investment activity, the FDI will naturally flow to the country.

On the policy front, given the deficiencies in markets and existing institutions, there is a need for careful design of FDI policies. Ideally, policies should be designed to attract sufficient FDI, extract all the benefits offered and to ensure that they operate within a framework similar to international best-practices. Efforts are needed to counter two sets of market failures relating to FDI (UNCTAD, 1999). First, there can be coordination failures in the investment process, which can result in insufficient FDI in certain sectors or inflow of wrong quality of FDI. Second, there can be a conflict of interests of the host country with that of the investor. Hence, in a liberalised environment, market signals and its direction need to made more explicit so as to direct FDI inflows in the desired direction.

27

Globalisation and Indian Economy

Introduction

THE term "globalisation" is used to describe a wide range of things and, in the process, there is no consensus on what it actually means. It has, over time, become an expression of common usage. Any analysis of globalisation raises several questions — starting from its definition to the inequitous implication and the obvious concern of where India stands.

As we begin analysing the implications of globalisation, several questions arise. What is globalisation? Is it purely an economic concept? Is this a new phenomenon? What are the benefits of globalisation? Who gets hurt in the process of globalisation? Is globalisation intrinsically inequitous? Is it possible for individual countries to isolate themselves from globalisation? What are the complementary institutions and policies that countries can build to protect themselves or to gain maximum benefits? Where does India stand in this race for globalisation? Is she a potential gainer or loser?

Broadly speaking, the term 'globalisation' means integration of economies and societies through cross country flows of information, ideas, technologies, goods, services, capital, finance and people. The essence of globalisation is connectivity. Cross border integration can have several dimensions — cultural, social, political and economic. In fact, some people fear cultural and social integration even more than economic integration. However, we use the term globalisation in this

---

Excerpts from C. Rangarajan (2003), *Globalisation and Its Impact*, in Economic Developments in India, Vol.58, Academic Foundation, Delhi.

chapter in the more limited sense of economic integration which can happen through the three channels of (a) trade in goods and services, (b) movement of capital and (c) flow of finance (d) through movement of people.

Historically, globalisation has been a process with highs and lows and during 1870 to 1914, there was a rapid integration of the economies in terms of trade flows, movement of capital and migration of people. Empirical evidence shows that capital markets are no more globalised today than they were at the end of the nineteenth century.

Today, the concerns are more on the nature and speed of transformation and the enormous impact of new information technologies on market integration, efficiency and industrial organisation. These go together with two major concerns: one, that globalisation leads to a more inequitous distribution of income among countries and within countries; and two, that globalisation leads to loss of national sovereignty and imposes constraints on the pursuit of independent domestic policies.

Empirical evidence on the impact of globalisation on inequality is not clear. In aggregate world exports, the share of developing countries increased from 20.6 per cent in 1988-90 to 29.9 per cent in 2000. Similarly, the share of developing countries in aggregate world output has increased from 17.9 per cent in 1988-90 to 40.4 per cent in 2000. However, what is essentially required is a balancing mechanism to ensure that the handicaps of the developing countries are overcome. And, while globalisation may accelerate the process of technology substitution in developing economies, these countries, even without globalisation will face the problem associated with moving from lower to higher technology. If the growth rate of the economy accelerates sufficiently, part of the resources can be directed by the State to re-equip people who may have been affected adversely by the process of technology upgradation.

On the second concern, as nations come together whether it be in the political, social or economic arena, some sacrifice of sovereignity is inevitable, but it need not necessarily result in the abdication of domestic objectives.

India's Attitude

What should be India's attitude in this ambience of growing globalisation? Opting out of the process of globalisation is not a viable choice. What is needed is to evolve a framework to get maximum benefits out of international trade and investment. This should include making a list of explicit demands that India would like to make on the multilateral trade system; measures that the developed countries should undertake to enable developing countries gain more from international trade; and steps that India should take to realise the full potential from globalisation.

Gains and Losses from Globalisation

The gains and losses from globalisation can be analysed in the context of the channels of economic globalisation identified earlier.

Trade in Goods and Services

According to the standard theory, international trade leads to allocation of resources that is consistent with comparative advantage. This results in specialisation which enhances productivity. While the classical theory of comparative advantage was based on assumptions of perfect competition, constant returns to scale and fixed technology, the "new trade theory" which takes into account imperfect competition, increasing returns to scale and changing technology also comes to the conclusion that openness leads to improved rates of growth (Frankel, 2000). The new trade theory talks of dynamic gains from international trade. It is accepted that international trade, in general, is beneficial and that restrictive trade practices impede growth. That is the reason why many of the emerging economies which originally depended on a growth model of import substitution have moved over to a policy of outward orientation. Obviously, even in relation to trade in goods and services, there is one concern. Emerging economies will reap the benefits of international trade only if they reach the full potential of their resource availability. This will probably require time. That is why international trade agreements make exceptions by allowing longer time to developing economies in terms of reduction in tariff and non-tariff barriers. Special and differential treatment has become an accepted principle.

Movement of Capital

Capital flows across countries have played an important role in enhancing the production base. This was very much true in 19th and 20th centuries. Capital mobility enables the total savings of the world to be distributed among countries which have the highest investment potential. Under these circumstances, one country's growth is not constrained by its own domestic savings. The inflow of foreign capital has played a significant role in the development in the recent period of the East Asian countries. The current account deficit of some of these countries had exceeded 5 per cent of the GDP in most of the period when growth was rapid. In fact, at the peak, the foreign capital inflow into Malaysia in 1993 was 17.4 per cent of its GDP, while in Thailand in 1995 it was 12.7 per cent of the GDP.

Capital flows can take either the form of foreign direct investment or portfolio investment. For developing countries the preferred alternative is foreign direct investment. Portfolio investment does not directly lead to expansion of productive capacity. It may do so, however, at one step removed. Recent events have shown that portfolio investment can be volatile particularly in times of loss of confidence. That is why countries want to put restrictions on portfolio investment. However, in an open system such restrictions cannot work easily.

Even in relation to foreign direct investment, two aspects have raised concerns. First, there is always the fear that some part of the domestic economy will be controlled by external factors. In India, it is very often referred to as the "East India Company Syndrome". However, there is an increasing realisation on the part of transnational companies also not to act in a manner inconsistent with the policies of countries in which investment is made. Even in recent East Asian crisis it was found that foreign direct investment was a stable element. While to some extent fresh capital inflow was moderated, there was no outflow of foreign direct investment.

The second aspect of concern in relation to foreign direct investment has been the fact that a significant part of foreign direct investment has been in the form of cross border mergers and acquisitions[1]. It is felt that FDI entry through the take over of domestic firms is less beneficial because such foreign acquisitions do not add to the productive capacity but simply transfer ownership and control from domestic to foreign hands. While this is correct, it overlooks the fact that the funds released to the domestic entrepreneurs because of the acquisition can be utilised for expanding capacity by the domestic entrepreneurs. Whether or not mergers and acquisitions lead to technological upgradation in the short-term is not clear. However, it is reported that over the longer term, effects could be different. Cross

1. The ratio of the value of cross border M&As to FDI inflows in developing countries has risen from one-tenth in 1987-89 to more than one-third in 1997-99. Among developing regions, the ratio is the highest in Latin America and the Caribbean: it increased from 18 per cent to 61 per cent between these two periods, while in developing Asia it increased from 8 per cent to 21 per cent between the same periods (United Nations, 2000).

border mergers and acquisitions can be followed by transfer of new or better technology, when acquired firms are restructured to increase the efficiency of their operations. As recent events in India have shown while foreign direct investment is beneficial, public policy will have to be extremely careful in setting the conditions under which private capital is invited. Seeking guarantees and providing guarantees are inconsistent with an open system. Risk taking is the basic element of entrepreneurial spirit.

Financial Flows

The rapid development of the capital market has been one of the important features of the current process of globalisation. While the growth in capital and foreign exchange markets have facilitated the transfer of resources across borders, the gross turnover in foreign exchange markets has been extremely large. It is estimated that the gross turnover is around $ 1.5 trillion per day worldwide (Frankel, 2000). This is of the order of hundred times greater than the volume of trade in goods and services. Currency trade has become an end in itself. The expansion in foreign exchange markets and capital markets is a necessary pre-requisite for international transfer of capital. However, the volatility in the foreign exchange market and the ease with which funds can be withdrawn from countries have often created panic situations. The most recent example of this was the East Asian crisis. Contagion of financial crisis is a worrying phenomenon. When one country faces a crisis, it affects others. It is not as if financial crisis are solely caused by foreign exchange traders. What the financial markets tend to do is to exaggerate weaknesses. Herd instinct is not uncommon in financial markets. When an economy becomes more open to capital and financial flows, there is even greater compulsion to ensure that factors relating to macroeconomic stability are not ignored. This is a lesson all developing countries have to learn from East Asian crisis. As one commentator aptly said "The trigger was sentiment, but vulnerability was due to fundamentals" (Reddy, 2000). In this context, it has been emphasised that opening of the capital account need not preclude moderate controls, either price based or regulatory, on capital flows. Controls should be selective, designed to achieve the specific objective of containing speculative capital. While there is, no doubt, that countries benefit by capital flows, the need to keep a watchful eye on foreign exchange markets becomes essential. What applies to trade may not necessarily apply to finance in full measure. However, while stringent capital controls may be adopted as a temporary shield as part of crisis management, they cannot be a permanent solution.

Concerns and Fears

On the impact of globalisation, there are two major concerns. These may be described as even fears. Under each major concern there are many related anxieties. The first major concern is that globalisation leads to a more inequitous distribution of income among countries and within countries. The second fear is that globalisation leads to loss of national sovereignity and that countries are finding it increasingly difficult to follow independent domestic policies. These two issues have to be addressed both theoretically and empirically.

Effects on Distribution of Income

The argument that globalisation leads to inequality is based on the premise that since globalisation emphasises efficiency, gains will accrue to countries which are favourably endowed with natural and human resources. Advanced countries have had a head start over the other countries by at least three centuries. The technological base of these countries is not only wide but highly sophisticated. While trade benefits all countries, greater gains accrue to the industrially advanced countries. This is the reason why even in the present trade agreements, a case has been built up for special and differential treatment in relation to developing countries. By and large, this treatment provides for longer transition periods in relation to adjustment. However, there are two changes with respect to international trade which may work to the advantage of the developing countries. First, for a variety of reasons, the industrially advanced countries are vacating certain areas of production. These can be filled in by developing countries. Second, international trade is no longer determined by the distribution of natural resources. With the advent of information technology, the role of human resources has emerged as more important. Specialised human skills will become the determining factor in the coming decades. Productive activities are becoming "knowledge intensive" rather than "resource intensive". While there is a divide between developing and the advanced countries even in this area — some people call it the digital divide — it is a gap which can be bridged. A globalised economy with increased specialisation can lead to improved productivity and faster growth. What will be required is a balancing mechanism to ensure that the handicaps of the developing countries are overcome.

Apart from the possible inequitous distribution of income among countries, it has also been argued that globalisation leads to widening income gaps within the countries as well. This can happen both in the developed and developing economies. The argument is the same as was advanced in relation to inequitous distribution among countries. Globalisation may benefit even within a country those who have the skills and the technology. The higher growth rate achieved by an economy can be at the expense of declining incomes of people who may be rendered redundant. In this context, it has to be noted that while globalisation may accelerate the process of technology substitution in developing economies, these countries even without globalisation will face the problem associated with moving from lower to higher technology. If the growth rate of the economy accelerates sufficiently, then part of the resources can be diverted by the state to modernise and re-equip people who may be affected by the process of technology upgradation.

Autonomy

The second concern relates to the loss of autonomy in the pursuit of economic policies. In a highly integrated world economy, it is true that one country cannot pursue policies which are not in consonance with the world wide trends. Capital and technology are fluid and they will move where the benefits are greater. However, this is not a new phenomenon. For example, in the days of gold standard, maintenance of the external value of the currency in terms of gold content became paramount. Domestic monetary policy actions were subordinated to this overriding consideration. In fact, the fixed exchange rate system under the Bretton Woods arrangement also imposed similar constraints. In a more or less fixed exchange rate regime, no country can allow its inflation rate to be out of alignment with the inflation rate in the rest of the world. Of course, the flexible exchange rate regime which is now prevalent, gives a little more autonomy in the pursuit of domestic monetary policy. It is, however, impossible for any country to have domestic autonomy, fixed exchange rate and free capital flows. This is the famous impossible trinity. Similar to the limitations of monetary policy in an open economy, the process of globalisation imposes some constraints on fiscal policies of countries as well. Multilateral commitments have led many developing countries to reduce import duties which traditionally have been a major source of revenue. Free capital mobility results in tax competition among countries. At any rate, no country wants its tax regime to be less attractive for investment. While fiscal autonomy in this sense is reduced, the overall fiscal impact will depend on the elasticity of revenues to GDP and the impact of globalisation on growth of GDP and the tax base. As the nations come together whether it be in the political, social or economic arena, some sacrifice of sovereignty is inevitable. The constraints of a globalised economic system on the pursuit of domestic policies have to be recognised. However, it need not result in the abdication of domestic objectives.

Insecurity and Volatility

Another fear associated with globalisation is insecurity and volatility. When countries are inter-related strongly, a small spark can start a large conflagration. Panic and fear spread fast. The only hope here is that despite integration, different parts of the world economy can be at different phases of the business cycle. In fact, until recently there had been a lag between the time the US reached the peak of the cycle and the European Union reached it. Such non-synchronised movements have had a beneficial effect. However, we are now facing for the first time since the 1980s the first synchronised downturn. There is greater insecurity because of the constant drive towards efficiency and competition. The downside to globalisation essentially emphasises the need to create countervailing forces in the form of institutions and policies at the international level. Global governance cannot be pushed to the periphery, as integration gathers speed.

Empirical evidence on the impact of globalisation on inequality is not very clear. The share in aggregate world exports and in world output of the developing countries has been increasing. In aggregate world exports, the share of developing countries increased from 20.6 per cent in 1988-90 to 29.9 per cent 2000 (IMF, 2001 and Table 1A). In fact, in comparing the share of the developing countries over time, care has to be taken to compare the share of the same set of countries over the entire time frame. In fact, four of the countries which are now classified as newly industrialised Asian economies, are excluded from developing countries when data on developing countries are presented in the various documents. We have included these four countries in the category of developing countries while computing the share and comparing the trend. Similarly the share in aggregate world output of developing countries has increased from 17.9 per cent in 1988-90 to 40.4 per cent in 2000 (IMF, 2001 and Table 1B). The growth rates of the developing countries both in terms of GDP and per capita GDP have been higher than those of the industrial countries. These growth rates have been in fact higher in the 1990s than in the 1980s. All these data do not indicate that the developing countries as a group have suffered in the process of globalisation. In fact, there have been substantial gains. But within developing countries, Africa has not done well and some of the South Asian countries have done better only in the 1990s.

TABLE – 1A

SHARE IN AGGREGATE WORLD EXPORTS

per cent

Year	*Major Industrial Countries**	*Developing Countries***	*Asia*	*Africa*
1988-90	55.5	20.6	10.8	2.0
1995	50.0	26.9	17.5	1.8
2000	47.7	29.9@	19.1	2.1

Note : * Major Industrial Countries include US, Japan, Germany, France, Italy, UK and Canada.

** Developing Countries also includes Newly Industrialised Asian Economies.

@ Excluding share of Israel which is shifted to Industrial Countries group.

Source: Various Issues of World Economic Outlook, IMF.

TABLE – 1B

SHARE IN AGGREGATE WORLD OUTPUT

per cent

Year	*Major Industrial Countries**	*Developing Countries***	*Asia*	*Africa*
1988-90	62.7	17.9	7.2	1.7
1995	46.2	41.2	24.4	3.3
2000	45.4	40.4@	25.0	3.2

Note : * Major Industrial Countries include US, Japan, Germany, France, Italy, UK and Canada.

** Developing Countries also includes Newly Industrialised Asian Economies.

@ Excluding share of Israel which is shifted to Industrial Countries group.

Source : Various Issues of World Economic Outlook, IMF.

India and the External Sector

India's economic policy towards foreign trade and foreign investment in the first four decades after India's Independence was restrictive. Import substitution constituted a major element of country's foreign trade and industrial policies. The approach to foreign investment was equally constrained. The deficit on the current account was met mainly by borrowing and particularly from official sources. India's share in world exports which stood at 1.85 per cent in 1950 fell to 0.58 per cent in 1992.[2] In the wake of the economic crisis that overtook the country in 1991, the approach to and content of economic policy underwent a far reaching change. This change was reflected in trade and investment policies. An outward orientation began to emerge. Tariff rates have been steadily brought down while quantitative controls have been dismantled. Foreign investment policy has become proactive. Majority ownership by foreign investors is allowed over a wide spectrum of industries. Authorised foreign institutions are allowed to invest in Indian stock markets. The exchange rate of the rupee is by and large determined by the forces of supply and demand, although the central bank does intervene to avoid instability and volatility.

How has the Indian economy fared as a result of the steady opening up? India's growth rate has definitely been higher in the period following 1992-93, even though there are concerns about falling growth rate in the last two years. In relation to the external sector, the situation has been comfortable. The current account deficit which peaked to 3.2 per cent of GDP in 1990 has been declining and is remaining around only one per cent of GDP in the last few years. The foreign exchange reserves of the country has been increasing and stands today at $ 55.6 billion. The import growth rate has not shown any alarming rise. The increasing integration has not resulted in a jolt to the economy. On the contrary, the broad macroeconomic indicators have shown an improvement. However, many concerns have been raised in relation to the impact of globalisation on Indian industries, agriculture in general and food security in particular and on the stability of the financial sector.

While recognising the fact that the Indian economy in the last decade has become more open, it is also necessary to note that the Indian economy is much less open than many other economies. Taking the most commonly used indicator of openness which is the proportion of import and export of goods and services to GDP, it is seen that this ratio has increased from 15 per cent in 1980 to 25 per cent in 1998[3]. However, this ratio of 25 per cent is much smaller than many other countries. For small countries like Malaysia and Singapore with a high outward

2. India's share in world exports experienced a declining trend since 1950 up to 1980. Afterwards, the share started increasing slowly from 0.4 per cent in 1980 to reaching 0.67 per cent in 2000-01 (Table 8). It can also be noted that, India's share in the world trade was as high as close to 4 per cent during 1860-1889 (Kuznets, 1972). During the first four decades since Independence, India's exports share in the GDP remained almost constant, where as India's share in world exports witnessed a declining trend (Table 8). This phenomenon is due to the fact that, the world exports were increasing at a faster rate than the growth rate of India's GDP.
3. Compared to this, the ratio of sum of merchandise exports and imports to NDP in India was 18.83 per cent and 19.57 per cent in the year 1894 and 1899, respectively (Brahmananda, 2001).

TABLE – 2

FOREIGN TRADE AS PERCENTAGE OF GDP

Country	*1970*	*1999*
US	11	24
Canada	43	84
Japan	20	19
UK	44	53
France	30	50
Germany	**	57
Italy	32	49
EU	3.6	2.7
HongKong	181.0	261.0
Singapore	232	**
Korea	37	77
India	8	27

Note : Foreign Trade refers to exports and imports of goods and services.
Source : World Development Indicators, 2001, World Bank.

TABLE – 3

TARIFF BARRIERS IN DIFFERENT COUNTRIES

Country	*Weighted Mean Tariff (All)*		*Standard Deviation*		*Weighted Mean Tariff (Primary)*		*Weighted Mean Tariff (Manfd.)*	
	1988/89/90	*1999*	*1988/89/90*	*1999*	*1988/89/90*	*1999*	*1988/89/90*	*1999*
US	4.1	2.8	6.7	11.4	2.1	2.0	4.5	2.9
Canada	6.5	3.2	7.0	22.3	2.4	5.9	7.2	2.9
Japan	3.3	2.3	8.0	7.3	3.7	4.0	2.9	1.4
EU	3.6	2.7	5.6	5.0	2.8	1.8	4.1	3
HongKong	0.0	0.0	0.0	0.0	0.0	0.0	0.0	0.0
Singapore	0.5	0.0	2.2	0.0	0.0	0.0	0.6	0.0
Korea	13.8	5.9	8.1	5.9	8.1	5.5	16.9	6.1
India	49.8	29.5	43.8	12.4	26.0	24.9	69.9	32.3

Source: World Development Indicators, 2001, World Bank.

orientation, this ratio exceeds 200 per cent. Among the industrially advanced countries, the United States is the only country which has a ratio similar to that of India (Table 2). Tariff levels are another indicator of openness. Here again, while India's weighted mean tariff rate has come down from 49.8 per cent in 1989-90 to 29.5 per cent in 1999, it is still high compared with many other countries (Table 3). While the weighted average tariff rate is nil for Hong Kong and Singapore, it is as low as 2.7 per cent in European Union countries and 2.8 per cent in the US. However, it is of significance to note that the standard deviation of the tariff rates in US is high at 11.4 per cent which means that the rates on certain products are very high (World Bank, 2001).

Framework of Policy

What should be India's attitude in this environment of growing globalisation?

At the outset it must be mentioned that opting out of globalisation is not a viable choice. There are at present 142 members in the World Trade Organisation (WTO). Some 30 countries are waiting to join the WTO. China has recently been admitted as a member. What is needed is to evolve an appropriate framework to wrest maximum benefits out of international trade and investment. This framework should include

(a) making explicit the list of demands that India would like to make on the multilateral trade system,

(b) measures that rich countries should be required to undertake to enable developing countries to gain more from international trade and

(c) steps that India should take to realise the full potential from globalisation.

Demands on the Trading System

There is considerable concern about the next round of negotiations in the WTO. Developing countries including India should project strongly their viewpoint. Without being exhaustive, the demands on the multilateral trading system should include (1) establishing symmetry as between the movement of capital and natural persons, (2) delinking environmental standards and labour related considerations from trade negotiations, (3) zero tariffs in industrialised countries on labour intensive exports of developing countries, (4) adequate protection to genetic or biological material and traditional knowledge of developing countries, (5) prohibition of unilateral trade action and extra territorial application of national laws and regulations, and (6) effective restraint on industrialised countries in initiating anti-dumping and countervailing action against exports from developing countries (Ganesan, 1999).

Concerns have been expressed about the impact of present WTO arrangements on Indian agriculture. However, under the present provisions, the degree of protection enjoyed by Indian agriculture is below what is permissible. In fact, in relation to some agricultural products, very recently the import duty was increased considerably. On the contrary, Indian agricultural products can gain greater market access in the advanced countries, as the tariff barriers come down in those countries. This expectation has not been fulfilled so far. The developed countries have played a clever game by taking recourse to 'Green Box' and 'Blue Box' provisions. But possibilities do exist for expanding the market for Indian agricultural products.

Negotiations are not that easy. We have to give in some areas to gain in others. The manoeuvring abilities of developed countries to steer the international trading system in the direction of meeting their own needs and concerns cannot be underestimated. They have shown themselves to be crafty in this area. However what is important is the approach. We must stay and fight whether they be intellectual property rights or public policy considerations. Doha showed some success in this direction. But the benefits of being part of the larger system should not be lost sight of.

Rich Country Initiatives

The purpose of the new trading system must be to ensure "free and fair" trade among countries. The emphasis so far has been on "free" rather than "fair" trade. It is in this context that the rich industrially advanced countries have a role to play. They have often indulged in "double speak". While requiring developing countries to dismantle barriers and join the main stream of international trade, they have been raising significant tariff and non-tariff barriers on trade from developing countries. Very often, this has been the consequence of heavy lobbying in the advanced countries to protect 'labour'. Although average tariffs in the United States, Canada, European Union and Japan — the so called Quad countries — range from only 4.3 per cent in Japan to 8.3 per cent in Canada, their tariff and trade barriers remain much higher on many products exported by developing countries. Major agricultural food products such as meat, sugar and dairy products attract tariff rates exceeding 100 per cent. Fruits and vegetables such as bananas are hit with a 180 per cent tariff by the European Union, once they exceed quota. Even in the case of dismantling the Multi-Fibre Agreement (MFA), it is stretched up to 2005 and has been back loaded so that much of the benefits will accrue to countries like India only towards the end (Stern, 2001). In fact, these trade barriers impose a serious burden on the developing countries. It is important that if the rich countries want a trading system that is truly fair, they should on their own lift the trade barriers and subsidies that prevent the products of developing countries from reaching their markets. It is important that these issues are brought to the forefront of the discussions at all international fora.

Actions by India

The third set of measures that should form part of the action plan must relate to strengthening India's position in international trade. India has many strengths, which several developing countries lack. In that sense, India is different and is in a stronger position to gain from international trade and investment. India's rise to the top of the IT industry in the world is a reflection of the abundance of skilled manpower in our country. It is, therefore, in India's interest to ensure that there is a greater freedom of movement of skilled manpower. At the same time, we should attempt to take all efforts to ensure that we continue to remain a frontline country in the area of skilled manpower. India can attract greater foreign investment, if we can accelerate our growth with stability. Stability, in this context, means reasonable balance on the fiscal and external accounts. We must maintain a competitive environment domestically so that we can take full advantage of wider market access. We must make good use of the extended time given to developing countries to dismantle trade barriers. Wherever legislations are required to protect sectors like agriculture, they need to be enacted quickly. Infact, we had taken a long time to pass the Protection of Plant Varieties and Farmers' Rights Bill. We must also be active in ensuring that our firms make effective use of the new patent rights. South Korea has been able to file in recent years as many as 5000 patent applications in the United States whereas in 1986, the country filed only 162 (Bergsten, 1999). China has also been very active in this area. We need a truly active agency in India to encourage Indian firms to file patent applications. In effect, we must build the complementary institutions necessary for maximising the benefits from international trade and investment.

Conclusion

Nothing is an unmixed blessing. Globalisation in its present form though spurred by far reaching technological changes is not a pure technological phenomenon. It has many dimensions including ideological. To deal with this phenomenon, we must understand the gains and losses, the benefits as well as dangers. To be forewarned, as the saying goes, is to be forearmed. But we should not throw the baby with bath water. We should also resist the temptation to blame globalisation for all our failures. Most often, as the poet said, the fault is in ourselves.

Risks of an open economy are well known. We must not, nevertheless, miss the opportunities that the global system can offer. As an eminent critic put it, the world cannot marginalise India. But India, if it chooses, can marginalise itself. We must guard ourselves against this danger. More than many other developing countries, India is in a position to wrest significant gains from globalisation. However, we must voice our concerns and in cooperation with other developing countries modify the international trading arrangements to take care of the special needs of such countries. At the same time, we must identify and strengthen our comparative advantages. It is this two fold approach which will enable us to meet the challenges of globalisation which may be the defining characteristic of the new millennium.

28

WTO and India

WTO Issues*

INDIA is one of the founding members of the World Trade Organisation (WTO) and participation in the WTO rule based system implies greater stability, transparency and predictability in the governance of international trade. The importance of WTO in promoting multilateral trade is being increasingly acknowledged. The WTO rules envisage non-discrimination in the form of national treatment and most favoured nation (MFN) treatment to our exports in the markets of other WTO members. National treatment ensures that our exports to other member countries would not be discriminated vis-a-vis their domestic products. MFN treatment likewise ensures non-discrimination among various members in their tariff regimes and also other rules and regulations.

Emerging from continued discussions in various multilateral fora, developmental issues along with trade related issues are being increasingly focused at the international level. Poverty concerns of developing countries along with development and trade policies are also being given cognisance. Need has been felt for integration of trade policies with development strategies, increasing support to areas of finance and debt relief, recognising the importance of technology for development, improvement in market access for developing countries in sectors like textiles, clothing and agriculture, and providing better access to the dispute settlement mechanisms for these countries. The issue of abuse of the anti-dumping procedure, the problems of rules of origin criteria, technical barriers to trade, regional trading blocs, etc., are also being considered at various levels in the WTO.

The Government of India has taken several steps to implement the policy commitments made under some of the agreements, particularly

---

* Planning Commission, Tenth Five Year Plan (2002-07) Ch.4, pp. 120-122.

under the Agreement on Tariffs and Quantitative Restrictions, Agreement on Agriculture (AoA), Trade Related Intellectual Property Rights (TRIPs), Trade Related Investment Measures (TRIMs), General Agreement on Trade in Services (GATS), apart from others. A strategy for tariff negotiations is, however, required. The additional 'non-trade' issues relating to transparency in government procurement practices, trade and competition policy, trade and environment, and trade and labour standards proposed in the Singapore and the Geneva Ministerial need to be addressed for negotiations. The commitments regarding the technical barriers to trade, social agenda covering labour standards and environmental and phyto-sanitary issues also require establishment of certain national standards and technical regulations in a standardised and transparent system.

At the same time, there are some issues on which India has expressed certain reservations. These are:

- During the implementation of WTO agreements in the last six years, India has experienced certain imbalances and inequities in the WTO agreements. It is found that some developed countries have not fulfilled their obligations in letter and spirit of the WTO agreements, and many of the Special and Differential Treatment clauses. in favour of developing countries, added in various WTO agreements have remained inoperational.
- Taking advantage of the exception clauses provided in the WTO, most industrialised countries are still enforcing various regulations on foreign producers and suppliers.
- Extending the scope of the investment regime in WTO beyond Trade Related Investment Measures and General Agreements on Trade in Services, is not appropriate.
- A multilateral framework cannot guarantee an increase in FDI inflows although it threatens to adversely affect the quality of the inflows.
- There are also other asymmetries present, as the WTO does not address the responsibilities of corporations which often impose trade restrictive clauses on their subsidiaries.
- WTO has not been able to ensure abolition of non-trade barriers being imposed on labour and environmental considerations, including the linkage in certain Generalised System of Preferences (GSP) schemes to these issues.

The present negotiations strategy is based on the decisions taken at the Doha Ministerial in November 2001. The Doha Declaration focused mainly on TRIPs agreement, public health, trade and environment and the implementation related issues and concerns. Elaborate timetables on work programme for current negotiations in agriculture and services and other issues have been worked out.

The Doha Conference presented mixed results for India. India's main concern was to speed up implementation of various agreements and to undo the imbalances and inequities present in some WTO agreements. From India's point of view, faster removal of the textile quotas maintained by developed countries like the USA was the most important implementation issue, which was, however, met with limited success. As far as environmental issues are concerned, the Doha declaration has mandated negotiations to clarify WTO rules in the light of multilateral environmental agreements. These negotiations could lead to developed countries raising barriers against goods from developing countries on the pretext of environmental protection. India had also reservations on starting negotiations on four new 'non-trade' areas, namely, multilateral investment, global rules on competition, transparency in government procurement and trade facilitation, i.e., framing of uniform custom's procedures for clearance of goods. India could secure only a two-year respite and the study process would continue for two more years, i.e. up to the Fifth Ministerial Conference, when a decision about negotiations will be taken on the basis of an explicit consensus.

Apart from mandated negotiations in agriculture and services where the process has already started, negotiations on market access for non-agricultural products is quite important for India, as reduction or elimination of tariffs, tariff peaks and tariff escalation as well as removal of non-tariff barriers will be quite helpful in exports. India would, of course, have to make offers even though the negotiations will be carried out under less than full reciprocity as far as developing countries are concerned.

The other area where action is required is in regard to extension of protection of geographical indications to products other than wines and spirits under Article 23 of TRIPs and the relationship between TRIPs and the Convention on Biological Diversity (CBD), and Traditional Knowledge (TK) under Article 71.1. The process of legislation in regard to geographical indications needs to be completed. In the area of TRIPs and access to medicine, where additional flexibility is provided in separate ministerial declarations in terms of compulsory licensing and parallel imports, India can benefit in terms of lower prices of crucial life saving drugs and even promoting exports of pharmaceutical products.

India and other developing countries should now ensure an average balance of reciprocity in these negotiations. There is need for a continued effort to handle some of the complex issues, as per international requirements as well as our domestic resources and other constraints, during the Tenth Five Year Plan.

For details of text of agreements already accepted and proposed for negotiations refer to Tenth Plan Documents Vol.1, Ch.4, pp. 122-133 and Indian Economy Since Independence 16th Edition (2004-05) Ch.24, pp. 658-666.

Bibliography

Acharya, Shankar (2003), *India's Economy: Some Issues and Answers*, (Academic Foundation), New Delhi.

——— (2002), 'Macroeconomic Management in the Nineties', *Economic and Political Weekly* (hereafter EPW), (April 20).

——— (1999), 'Managing External Economic Challenges in the Nineties: Lessons for the Future', in *Economic Developments in India,* Kapila, Raj & Uma (ed), Vol. 21 (Academic Foundation).

Ahluwalia, I.J. (1985), *Industrial Growth in India: Stagnation since the Mid-Sixties,* (Oxford University Press), New Delhi.

——— (1991), *Productivity and Growth in Indian Manufacturing* (Oxford University Press), New Delhi.

Ahluwalia, Montek S. (2000), 'Economic Reforms: A Policy Agenda for the Future', in *Economic Developments in India*, Vol. 25 (Academic Foundation).

Baijal, Pradip (2002), *Privatisation: Compulsions and Options for Economic Reform*, EPW, (Oct 12.)

Bagchi, Amaresh (1986), 'Fiscal Policy for Financing Development: The Indian Experience', in Kapila, Uma (ed.) *Indian Economy Since Independence*, (Academic Foundation), New Delhi.

Bhaduri, A. and Nayyar, D. (1996), *The Intelligent Person's Guide to Liberalisation*, (Penguin Books), New Delhi.

Bhagwati, Jagdish (1998), 'The Design of Indian Development', in Ahluwalia I.J. and Little I.M.D (ed.) *India's Economic Reforms and Development.* Essays for Manmohan Singh, (Oxford), Delhi.

Bhagwati, J. and Desai, P. (1970), *India Planning for Industrialisation*, (Oxford University Press) London.

Bhagwati, Jagdish and Srinivasan, T.N. (1993), 'India's Economic Reforms', Ministry of Finance, GOI, New Delhi. Reproduced in Kapila, Uma (ed.) *Indian Economy Since Independence* (2001 edition) (Academic Foundation).

Bhattacharya, B.B. (2002), Report of the Committee on Capital Formation in Indian Agriculture.

Bhattacharya, B.B. and Lodh Madhumita (1990), 'Inflation in India: An Analytical Survey', Artha Vijnana (March), Vol. 32 No.1, pp 25-68, reproduced in Kapila, Uma (ed.) *Indian Economy Since Independence.*

Brahmananda, P.R and Panchmukhi, V.R. (eds) (1987), *Development Process of the Indian Economy* (Himalaya Publishing House), Mumbai.

Byres, Terence J. (ed) (1993), *The State and Development Planning in India*, (Oxford University Press), SOAS.

——— (1998), *The Indian Economy, Major Debates Since Independence*, (Oxford University Press).

Cassen, R.H., *India: Population, Economy, Society*. Ch. 4.

Cassen, Robert and Joshi, Vijay (eds) (1995), *India: The Future of Economic Reform*, (Oxford University Press), Delhi.

Chakravarthy, Sukhamoy (1987a), *Development Planning: The Indian Experience*, (Oxford University Press).

Chaudhuri, Pramit (1979), *Indian Economy: Poverty and Development*, (Vikas) 4th reprint.

Dantwala, M.L. (1967), 'Incentives and Disincentives in Indian Agriculture', *Indian Journal of Agricultural Economics*, (April-June), Vol. 22, No.2.

——— (1981), *Understanding Poverty and Unemployment*, Artha Jignasa, (April-June), Indian Merchants Chamber, Bombay.

Das, T. (1999), 'East Asian Economic Crisis and Lessons for Debt Management', in *External Debt Management-Issues, Lessons and Preventive Measures*, Reserve Bank of India, Mumbai.

Desai, A.V. (2001), 'A Decade of Reforms', in *Economic Developments in India*, Vol. 47, (Academic Foundation), New Delhi.

Dhar, P.N. (1991), 'Constraints on Growth: Reflections on the Indian Experience', *Journal of Indian School of Political Economy,* (July-Sept. 1991), Vol. 3, No.3.

——— (1992), 'Economic Reforms – Why We Need Them'? Occasional Papers 1992, Observer Research Foundation. Reproduced in Kapila, Raj & Uma (ed.) *Understanding India's Economic Reforms*, Vol. II (Academic Foundation), New Delhi.

Dhawan, B.D. (1996), 'Relationship between Public and Private Investments in Indian Agriculture with Special Reference to Public Canals', *Indian Journal of Agricultural Economics*, (Jan.-June), Vol. 51, Nos. 1&2.

Dreze, Jean and Sen Amartya (2002), *India: Development and Participation*, (Oxford University Press).

Government of India (2004), Report of the Task Force on Implementation of Fiscal Responsibility and Budget Management Act, 2003, (Chairman: Vijay Kelkar), (Ministry of Finance), (July), New Delhi.

——— (2004), *Economic Survey, 2003-04* and Various Issues, (Ministry of Finance) New Delhi.

——— (2001), 'Report of the Task Force on Employment Opportunities' (Chairman: M.S. Ahluwalia), Reproduced in Planning Commission *Reports on Labour and Employment*, Academic Foundation, (2002), New Delhi.

——— Tenth Five Year Plan 2002-07, Planning Commission, Vol.1, (2003), India's Five Year Plans, 1st Plan to 10th Plan, (Academic Foundation), New Delhi (2003)

——— (2003), Report on FDI, (Chairman: N.K. Singh), (Academic Foundation).

——— (2001a), *Report of The Advisory Group on Tax Policy and Tax Administration for the Tenth Plan* (Chairman: Parthasarathi Shome), Planning Commission, (May).

——— (2002a), 'Medium Term Export Strategy', (Ministry of Commerce and Industry), New Delhi. Reproduced in *Economic Developments in India*, Vol.50, (Academic Foundation).

——— (2002b), *Export Import Policy 2002-07*, (Ministry of Commerce and Industry), New Delhi.

——— (2002c), *India's External Debt: A Status Report*, New Delhi.

——— (2002a), *Task Force on Direct Taxes – Consultation Paper* (Chairman: Vijay Kelkar), (Ministry of Finance and Company Affairs), (October), New Delhi.

——— (2002b), *Task Force on Indirect Taxes – Consultation Paper* (Chairman: Vijay Kelkar), (Ministry of Finance and Company Affairs), (October), New Delhi.

——— (2001), Recommendations of Prime Minister's Economic Advisory Council on Economic Reforms, *A Medium-term Perspective*, New Delhi. Reproduced in Kapila, Uma (ed.) *Indian Economy Since Independence* (2003).

Gulati, Ashok and Chadha, Rajesh (1995), 'India Poised for Take-off? Reforms in Trade, Industry, Agriculture, Stock-taking and Future Challenges', in Kapila, Uma (ed) *Indian Economy Since Independence* (2000-01 edition), (Academic Foundation).

Hayami, Yujiro (1998), *Development Economics: From the Poverty to the Wealth of Nations*, Ch. 7. pp 183-195, (Oxford).

Hirschman, A.O. (1958), *Strategies of Economic Development*, New Haven, Connecticut, (Yale University Press).

Hussain, Abid (1997), *Report of the Expert Committee on Small Enterprises*, Ministry of Industry.

Jalan, Bimal (ed) (1992), *The Indian Economy: Problems and Prospects*, (Viking Penguin), New Delhi, India.

——— (1996), *India's Economic Policy – Preparing for the 20th Century*, (Viking Penguin), India.

Joshi, Vijay and Little I.M.D. (1997), *India's Economic Reforms: 1991-2001*, (Oxford University Press).

Kelkar, Vijay (2001), 'Economic Reforms Agenda: Micro, Meso and Macro Economic Reforms', in *Economic Developments in India*, Vol. 44 (Academic Foundation).

Krishna, K.L., 'Industrial Growth and Diversification', in Kapila, Uma (ed) *Indian Economy Since Independence*.

Kindleberger Charles P. & Herrik, Bruce (1977), *Economic Development*, 3rd (ed) International Students Edition.

Krishnaji (1990), 'Agricultural Price Policy: A Survey with Reference to Indian Foodgrains Economy', in Kapila, Uma (ed), *Indian Economy Since Independence* (2001-02 edition).

Krishnaswamy, K.S. (1980), *What Ails the Public Sector?* The 4th Ajit Bhagat Memorial Lecture, Ahmedabad, (Dec. 21), (RBI Bulletin).

Kumar, Nagesh (1998), 'Liberalisation and Changing Patterns of Foreign Direct Investment : Has India's Relative Attractiveness as a Host to FDI Improved'? EPW, Vol. 33, No.22, (May 30-June 5). Reproduced in Kapila, Uma (ed) *Indian Economy Since Independence.*

——— (2000), *Economic Reforms and the Macro Economic Impact*, EPW (March 4).

Kapila, Uma, *Indian Economy Since Independence*, (Academic Foundation), New Delhi, (Various editions 1989 to 2003 edition).

Kapila, Raj & Uma (ed) (2004), *Economic Developments in India*, (Various volumes) latest volume 76 (Monthly update), (Academic Foundation).

Kurien, C.T (1978), *Small Sector in New Industrial Policy*, EPW, (March 4).

Meier, G. *Leading Issues in Economic Development*, 6th Ed. Ch. I-A pp, 7-9.

Minhas, B.S., Jain, L.R. and Tendulkar, S.D. (1991), *Declining Incidence of Poverty in India in 1980's*, EPW (July 6-13).

Mohan, Rakesh (1992), 'Industrial Policy and Controls', in Bimal Jalan (ed) *The Indian Economy: Problems and Prospects*. (Viking Penguin), India.

——— (2000), 'Fiscal Correction for Economic Growth', EPW (June 10-16), No. 24. Reproduced in Kapila, Uma (ed) *Indian Economy Since Independence*, (2003).

Nagaraj, R. (2004), "Fall in Organised Manufacturing Employment: A Brief Note", *Economic and Political Weekly*, Vol. 39, No. 30, (July 24-30).

Nagaraj, R. (1990), *Industrial Growth: Further Evidence and Towards an Explanation and Issues*, EPW Vol. XXV No.41, (Oct. 13), pp 2313-32.

——— (2000), 'Indian Economy Since 1980: Virtuous Growth of Polarisation', EPW, (August 5), Reproduced in Kapila, Uma (ed) *Indian Economy Since Independence*, (2003).

National Council of Applied Economic Research (1996), *The Indian Infrastructure Report*, Vol. I, New Delhi.

Nayyar, Deepak (1993b), 'The Foreign Trade Sector, Planning and Industrialisation in India' in Terence J Byres (ed), *The State & Development Planning in India.*

———(ed) (1994), *Industrial Growth and Stagnation: The Debate in India*, (Oxford University Press), Published for Sameeksha Trust.

Nurkse, Ragnar (1953), *Problems of Capital Formation in Underdeveloped Countries*. (Oxford – Basil Blackwell).

Pandit, V.N. (1978), 'An Analysis of Inflation in India', 1950-1975, *Indian Economic Review*, (Oct.) pp.89-99.

——— (1993), *Controlling Inflation: Some Analytical and Empirical Issues*, EPW (Jan. 2-9), pp 39-41.

Pant, K.C. (2003), *India's Development Scenario: Next Decade and Beyond*, (Academic Foundation).

Papola, T.S. (1992), 'The Question of Unemployment', in Bimal Jalan (ed) *Indian Economy Problems and Prospects.*

Parikh, Kirit S., (ed) (2001 & 02), *India Development Report*, Indira Gandhi

Institute of Development Research, (Oxford University Press),

Parthasarthy, G. (2003), *Economic Reforms and Rural Development*, (Academic Foundation), New Delhi.

——— (1979), 'Land Reforms and Changing Agrarian Structure', in C.H. Shah (ed) *Agricultural Development of India: Policies and Problems.*

Pursell, Garry and Gulati, Ashok (1993), 'Liberalising Indian Agriculture: An Agenda for Reform', Working Paper, Policy Research Department, The World Bank (September), WPS 1172, reproduced in (ed) Kapila, Uma, *Indian Economy Since Independence.*

Rangarajan, C. (2003), *Select Essays on Indian Economy*, (Academic Foundation), New Delhi.

——— (2000), *Perspectives on Indian Economy*, (UBSPD).

——— (2002), 'Globalisation and its Impact on Economic Development in India', in *Economic Developments in India*, Vol. 58.

——— 'India's Balance of Payments: The Emerging Dimensions', in (ed) Kapila, Uma, *Indian Economy Since Independence* (2003 edition).

——— (1995), *Impact of Liberalisation on Foreign Direct Investment*, RBI Bulletin, (Jan.)

——— (1998b), 'Development, Inflation, and Monetary Policy' in Ahluwalia I.J. and Little I.M.D (ed) *India's Economic Reforms and Development:* Essays for Manmohan Singh, (Oxford University Press), Ch. 3.

Rangarajan, C. and Prasad, A. (1999), 'Capital Account Liberalisation and Controls: Lessons from the East Asian Crisis', ICRA Bulletin, Money and Finance, (April-June). Reproduced in *Economic Developments in India*, Vol.19.

Rao, C.H.H (2003), *Reform Agenda for Agriculture*, EPW, Feb 15.

——— (1994a), *Agricultural Growth, Rural Poverty and Environmental Degradation in India*, (Oxford University Press).

——— (1989), 'Technological Change in Indian Agriculture: Emerging Trends and Perspectives', *Indian Journal of Agricultural Economics*, (Oct-Dec).

Rao, C.H.H and Gulati, Ashok (1994c), 'Indian Agriculture Emerging Perspectives and Policy Issues', EPW Dec. 31. Reproduced in (ed) Kapila, Uma, *Indian Economy Since Independence.*

Rao, V.K.R.V. (1983), *Changing Structure of the Economy: India's National Income 1950-80*, (Sage) New Delhi.

Rao, V.M. and Jeromi, P.D. (2000), 'Modernising Indian Agriculture, Priority Tasks and Critical Policy', Study No. 21, DRG, DEAP, Reserve Bank of India, reproduced in Kapila, Uma, *Indian Economy Since Independence.*

Ray, S.K. (1996), 'Reforms in Land System in Post-Independent India', *Indian Journal of Agricultural Economics*, Vol. 51, (June), reproduced in Kapila, Uma (ed), *Indian Economy Since Independence* (2003).

Reserve Bank of India (2003), Report on Currency and Finance 2002-03 and Various Issues.

Reserve Bank of India, RBI Bulletins, various issues.

Radhakrishna, R. and Subbarao, K. (1997), *India's Public Distribution System*, Discussion Paper No. 380, Washington D.C., World Bank.

Sandesara, J.C. (1991), *New Small Enterprise Policy: Implications and Prospects*, EPW, Oct 19, Vol. XXVI, No. 42, pp 2423-2426.

——— (1993), 'Modern Small Industry: Aspects of Growth and Structural Change', EPW, Feb. 6, reproduced in Kapila, Uma, *Indian Economy Since Independence*.

Sawant, S.D. and Achuta, C.V. (1995), 'Agricultural Growth Across Crops and Regions, Emerging Trends and Patterns', EPW, (March 25), reproduced in Kapila, Uma, *Indian Economy Since Independence*.

Sen, Amartya (2000), Development as Freedom, (Oxford University Press), New Delhi.

Sivaraman (1973), 'Scientific Agriculture in Neutral to Scale, The Fallacy and the Remedy', *Journal of Indian Society of Agricultural Statistics*, Vol. XXV, No.1 (June), pp. 75-90, reproduced in Kapila, Uma, *Indian Economy Since Independence*.

Srinivasan, T.N. (2000), *Eight Lectures on India's Economic Reforms*, (Oxford University Press).

——— 'Foreign Trade Policies and India's Development', reproduced in Kapila, Uma (ed), *Indian Economy Since Independence* (2003 edition).

——— (1991), *Reform of Industrial and Trade Policies*, EPW (Sept. 14), Vol. XXVI, No. 37.

Sundaram, K. (1984), *Demography and Development*, Presented at the Institute of Economic Growth Silver Jubilee National Seminar, (April, 27-30), reproduced in Kapila, Uma, *Indian Economy Since Independence*.

——— (2001a), *Employment-Unemployment Situation in Nineties: Some Results, from NSS 55th Round Survey*, EPW (17 March), Vol. XXXVI, No. 11.

——— (2001b), *Employment and Poverty in India in the Nineteen Nineties: Further Results from NSS 55th Round Employment-Unemployment Survey, 1999-2000*, Working paper 95, Centre for Development Economics at the Delhi School of Economics.

Sundaram, K. and Tendulkar, S.D. (2000a), 'Reducing Poverty: A Framework for Banks and Country Operational Strategy', Part I *Poverty in India: an Assessment and Analysis*, Ch. III (III 1 to III 2.3.1) and IV.

Tendulkar, S.D. (1979), *Approach to Public Sector in the Context of An Overall Development Strategy*, Revised version of text presented on (Oct. 27, 28) at Kamla Nehru College, University of Delhi, reproduced in Kapila, Uma (ed), *Indian Economy Since Independence* (2001 edition).

——— (1981), *Indian Development Strategy: Compulsions and Constraints*, Working Paper No. 23, (1 June), Delhi School of Economics, reproduced in Kapila, Uma, *Indian Economy Since Independence* (2001 edition).

——— (1987), 'Economic Inequalities and Poverty in India – An Interpretative Overview', in Brahmananda P.R. and Panchmukhi, V.R (eds): *The*

Development Process of the Indian Economy, Ch. 5, (Himalaya Publishing House).

Tendulkar and Jain (1995), *Poverty and Economic Reforms*, EPW, (June 10).

Tendulkar, S.D. and Minhas and Jain (1991), *Declining Incidence of Poverty in 1980s*, EPW, (July 6-13).

Thamarajakshi, R. (1994), *Intersectoral Relationships in a Developing Economy, The Indian Experience*, (Academic Foundation).

Thirwall, A.P., *Growth and Development*, 5th ed. p 9, pp 181-7.

Todaro, M., *Economic Development*, 6th ed. pp 13-18, pp 38-56.

UNDP (1992), *Human Development Report.*

——— (1995), *Human Development Report*, (Oxford University Press).

——— (2003), *Human Development Report,* (Oxford University Press).

UNDP & Planning Commission (2002), *Successful Governance Initiatives and Best Practices*, (2003 edition), (Academic Foundation), New Delhi.

Vaidyanathan, A. (2003), *Economic Reforms and Development*, (Academic Foundation), New Delhi.

——— (2001), 'Poverty and Development Policy', EPW, (May 26), reproduced in Kapila, Uma, *Indian Economy Since Independence.*

——— (2000), *India's Agricultural Development Policy*, EPW, (May 13), reproduced in Kapila, Uma, *Indian Economy Since Independence.*

——— (1994), *Employment Some Emerging Perspectives*, EPW, (Dec. 10).

Virmani, Arvind (2004), *Accelerating Growth and Poverty Reduction: A Policy Framework for India's Development*, (Academic Foundation), New Delhi.

Visaria, Pravin (1993), 'Demographic Aspects of Indian Experience', *Indian Journal of Social Sciences*, Vol. 6, No.3., reproduced in Kapila, Uma, *Indian Economy Since Independence.*

Visaria and Minhas (1991), *Evolving an Employment Policy for 1990's*, EPW, (April 13).

Vyas, V.S. (2003), *Agrarian Structure, Economic Policies and Sustainable Development*, (Academic Foundation), New Delhi.

Vyas, V.S. (1994), 'Agricultural Policies for the 90s: Issues and Policy Options', EPW, Vol. XXIX, No. 26, (June 25), pp A54-A63, reproduced in Kapila, Uma, *Indian Economy Since Independence*.

Vyas, V.S. and Bhargava, P (1995), 'Public Intervention for Poverty Alleviation: An Overview', EPW, Vols. 41 & 42, (Oct. 14-21), reproduced in Kapila, Uma, *Indian Economy Since Independence* (2001 edition).

Wadhva Charan, D. (ed) (1973, 1977), *Some Problems of India's Economic Policy: Selected Readings on Planning Agriculture and Foreign Trade*, (Tata McGraw Hill Publishing Co. Ltd.)

World Bank (1993), *World Development Report*, (Oxford University Press), New York.

World Development Report (1997), (OUP).

World Development Report (2002), (OUP).